Media Culture

Media Culture develops methods and analyses of contemporary film, television, music, and other artifacts to discern their nature and effects. The book argues that media culture is now the dominant form of culture which socializes us and provides materials for identity in terms of both social reproduction and change. Through studies of Reagan and *Rambo*, horror films and youth films, rap music and African-American culture, Madonna, fashion, television news and entertainment, MTV, *Beavis and Butt-Head*, the Gulf War as cultural text, cyberpunk fiction and postmodern theory, Kellner provides a series of lively studies that both illuminate contemporary culture and provide methods of analysis and critique.

Many people today talk about cultural studies, but Kellner actually does it, carrying through a unique mixture of theoretical analysis and concrete discussions of some of the most popular and influential forms of contemporary media culture. Criticizing social context, political struggle, and the system of cultural production, Kellner develops a multidimensional approach to cultural studies that broadens the field and opens it to a variety of disciplines. He also provides new approaches to the vexed question of the effects of culture and offers new perspectives for cultural studies.

Anyone interested in the nature and effects of contemporary society and culture should read this book. Kellner argues that we are in a state of transition between the modern era and a new postmodern era and that media culture offers a privileged field of study and one that is vital if we are to grasp the full import of the changes currently shaking us.

Douglas Kellner is Professor of Philosophy at the University of Texas at Austin and author (with Michael Ryan) of *Camera Politica: The politics and ideology of Hollywood films* and (with Steven Best) of *Postmodern Theory: Critical Interrogations*. Kellner has also published *Herbert Marcuse and the Crisis of Marxism*; *Critical Theory, Marxism, and Modernity*; *Jean Baudrillard: From Marxism to Postmodernism and Beyond*; *Television and the Crisis of Democracy*; *The Persian Gulf TV War*. He has edited *Jameson/Marxism/Critique* and *Baudrillard: A Critical Reader* and co-edited (with Stephen Bronner) *Critical Theory and Society: A Reader*.

P9-DDY-820

Media Culture

Cultural studies, identity
and politics between the modern
and the postmodern

Douglas Kellner

London and New York

First published 1995
by Routledge
11 New Fetter Lane, London EC4P 4EE

Simultaneously published in the USA and Canada
by Routledge
29 West 35th Street, New York, NY 10001

Reprinted 1995

© 1995 Douglas Kellner

Typeset in Times by Michael Mepham, Frome, Somerset
Printed and bound in Great Britain by
Biddles Ltd, Guildford and King's Lynn

British Library Cataloguing in Publication Data
A catalogue record for this book is available from the British Library

Library of Congress Cataloguing in Publication Data
A catalogue record for this book is available from the Library of Congress

ISBN 0–415–10569–2 (hbk)
ISBN 0–415–10570–6 (pbk)

FOR THE VELVET HAMMER

Contents

Introduction

A media culture has emerged in which images, sounds, and spectacles help produce the fabric of everyday life, dominating leisure time, shaping political views and social behavior, and providing the materials out of which people forge their very identities. Radio, television, film, and the other products of the culture industries provide the models of what it means to be male or female, successful or a failure, powerful or powerless. Media culture also provides the materials out of which many people construct their sense of class, of ethnicity and race, of nationality, of sexuality, of "us" and "them." Media culture helps shape the prevalent view of the world and deepest values: it defines what is considered good or bad, positive or negative, moral or evil. Media stories and images provide the symbols, myths, and resources which help constitute a common culture for the majority of individuals in many parts of the world today. Media culture provides the materials to create identities whereby individuals insert themselves into contemporary techno-capitalist socieities and which is producing a new form of global culture.

Media culture consists of systems of radio and the reproduction of sound (albums, cassettes, CDs, and their instruments of dissemination such as radios, cassette recorders, and so on); of film and its modes of distribution (theatrical playing, video-cassette rental, TV showings); of print media ranging from news-papers to magazines; and to the system of television which stands at the center of media culture. Media culture is a culture of the image and often deploys sight and sound. The various media – radio, film, television, music, and print media such as magazines, newspapers, and comic books – privilege either sight or sound, or mix the two senses, playing as well on a broad range of emotions, feelings, and ideas. Media culture is industrial culture, organized on the model of mass production and is produced for a mass audience according to types (genres), following conventional formulas, codes, and rules. It is thus a form of commercial culture and its products are commodities that attempt to attract private profit produced by giant corporations interested in the accumulation of capital. Media culture aims at a large audience, thus it must resonate to current themes and concerns, and is highly topical, providing hieroglyphics of contemporary social life.

But media culture is also a high-tech culture, deploying the most advanced technologies. It is a vibrant sector of the economy, one of the most profitable sectors and one that is attaining global prominence. Media culture is thus a form of techno-culture that merges culture and technology in new forms and configurations, producing new types of societies in which media and technology become organizing principles.

Media culture spectacles demonstrate who has power and who is powerless, who is allowed to exercise force and violence, and who is not. They dramatize and legitimate the power of the forces that be and demonstrate to the powerless that if they fail to conform, they risk incarceration or death. For those immersed from cradle to grave in a media and consumer society, it is therefore important to learn how to understand, interpret, and criticize its meanings and messages. In a contemporary media culture, the dominant media of information and entertainment are a profound and often misperceived source of cultural pedagogy: they contribute to educating us how to behave and what to think, feel, believe, fear, and desire – and what not to. Consequently, the gaining of critical media literacy is an important resource for individuals and citizens in learning how to cope with this seductive cultural environment. Learning how to read, criticize, and resist media manipulation can help individuals empower themselves in relation to dominant media and culture. It can enhance individual sovereignty vis-à-vis media culture and give individuals more power over their cultural environment and the necessary literacy to produce new forms of culture.

MEDIA CULTURE AND SOCIETY

The following studies help provide an understanding of media culture and suggest ways that it can be understood, used, and appreciated. I want to provide each reader with resources to learn to study, analyze, interpret, and criticize the texts of media culture and to appraise their effects. I examine some of the ways that media culture intersects with political and social struggles and helps shape everyday life, influencing how people think and behave, how they see themselves and other people, and how they construct their identities. Accordingly, the following studies will explore some of the ways that contemporary media culture provides forms of ideological domination that help to reproduce the current relations of power, while also providing resources for the construction of identities and for empowerment, resistance, and struggle. I argue that media culture is a contested terrain across which key social groups and competing political ideologies struggle for dominance and that individuals live these struggles through the images, discourses, myths, and spectacles of media culture.

Culture in the broadest sense is a form of highly participatory activity, in which people create their societies and identities. Culture shapes individuals, drawing out and cultivating their potentialities and capacities for speech, action, and creativity. Media culture is also involved in these processes, yet it is something new in the human adventure. Individuals spend tremendous amounts of time listening to the radio, watching television, going to see films, experiencing music, going shopping, reading magazines and newspapers, and participating in these and other forms of media culture. Thus, media culture has come to dominate everyday life, serving as the ubiquitous background and often the highly seductive foreground of our attention and activity, which many argue is undermining human potentiality and creativity.

This book will explore some of the consequences for a society and culture colonized by media culture. It will probe the nature and effects of the way in which this form of culture is deeply influencing many aspects of our everyday life. A major theme of this book concerns how the forms of media culture induce individuals to identify with dominant social and political ideologies, positions, and representations. In general, it is not a system of rigid ideological indoctrination that induces consent to existing capitalist societies, but the pleasures of the media and consumer culture. Media entertainment is often highly pleasurable and uses sight, sound, and spectacle to seduce audiences into identifying with certain views, attitudes, feelings, and positions. Consumer culture offers a dazzling array of goods and services that induce individuals to participate in a system of commercial gratification. Media and consumer culture work hand in hand to generate thought and behavior that conform to existing values, institutions, beliefs, and practices.

Yet, audiences may resist the dominant meanings and messages, create their own readings and appropriations of mass-produced culture, and use their culture as resources to empower themselves and to invent their own meanings, identities, and forms of life. Moreover, media culture itself provides resources which individuals can appropriate, or reject, in forming their own identities against dominant models. Media culture thus induces individuals to conform to the established organization of society, but it also provides resources that can empower individuals against that society. Exploring these contradictory functions and effects will be one of the goals of this book.

Media culture is highly complex and so far has resisted any adequate general theorizations (although there have been many attempts). Most general theories, as I'll indicate in this book, appear one-sided and blind to important aspects of media culture. Most theories of media manipulation and domination that were highly popular in the 1960s and part of the 1970s assumed that the media were all-powerful forces of social control and that they imposed a monolithic dominant ideology on their victims. Reacting against this model, many theories in recent years emphasized the power of audiences to resist media manipulation, to create their own meanings and uses, and to empower themselves with materials from their culture. As we shall see in the following studies, these and other current theories of the media are also one-sided, limited, and should give way to more comprehensive and multidimensional critical approaches which theorize the contradictory effects of media culture.

Theories of the media and culture are, I believe, best developed through specific studies of concrete phenomena contextualized within the vicissitudes of contemporary society and history. Thus, to interrogate contemporary media culture critically involves carrying out studies of how the culture industries produce specific artifacts that reproduce the social discourses which are embedded in the key conflicts and struggles of the day. This involves seeing how popular texts like the *Rocky* or *Rambo* films, rap music or Madonna, TV cop shows, or advertising and media news and discussion, all articulate specific ideological positions and help reproduce dominant forms of social power, serving the interests of societal domination, or of resistance to the dominant forms of culture and society – or have contradictory effects.

Accordingly, in the studies that follow I attempt to demonstrate how some of the most popular cultural texts of the day are involved in current political and cultural struggles. The study of popular and mass-mediated culture has widely been labelled "cultural studies" and in this book I'll provide some models of a media cultural studies that is critical, multicultural, and multiperspectival. A critical cultural studies conceptualizes society as a terrain of domination and resistance and engages in a critique of domination and of the ways that media culture engages in reproducing relationships of domination and oppression. A critical cultural studies is concerned with advancing the democratic project, conceptualizing both how media culture can be a tremendous impediment for democratizing society, but can also be an ally, advancing the cause of freedom and democracy. Media culture can be an impediment to democracy to the extent that it reproduces reactionary discourses, promoting racism, sexism, ageism, classism, and other forms of prejudice. But media culture can also advance the interests of oppressed groups if it attacks such things as racism or sexism, or at least undermines them with more positive representations of race and gender.

I am therefore interested in the politics of culture and will develop a specific model of media cultural studies and engage in the debates concerning how best to study culture and society in order to fully grasp the production, nature, and effects of media culture. My approach also employs social theory to properly contextualize, interpret, and analyze the nature and effects of media culture. It is my conviction that cultural studies cannot be done without social theory, that we need to understand the structures and dynamics of a given society to understand and interpret its culture. I am also assuming that media cultural texts are neither merely vehicles of a dominant ideology, nor pure and innocent entertainment. Rather they are complex artifacts that embody social and political discourses whose analysis and interpretation require methods of reading and critique that articulate their embeddedness in the political economy, social relations, and the political environment within which they are produced, circulated, and received.

The following studies take this comprehensive approach to the study of media culture and use the resources of history, social theory, communications research, and cultural studies to elucidate some of the meanings and effects of popular cultural forms. Examples range from films that reproduce or contest conservative ideologies during the Age of Reagan, to African-American culture from the films of Spike Lee to rap music, to the images and sounds called Madonna. I also discuss popular television series, such as *Miami Vice*, MTV, advertising, the media spectacle known as "the Gulf War," the frightening futuristic worlds of cyberpunk fiction, and Baudrillard's postmodern theory.

I assume that society and culture are contested terrains and that cultural artifacts are produced and have their effects within determinate contexts. It is my conviction that the analysis of media culture within its matrix of production and reception helps illuminate its artifacts and their possible effects and uses, as well as the contours and trends within the broader socio-political context. Since the forms of culture produced by giant media and entertainment conglomerates are an immediate and pervasive aspect of contemporary life, and since media culture is both constituted by and constitutive of larger social and political dynamics, it is an excellent optic to illuminate the nature of contemporary society, politics, and everyday life. Indeed, I will argue that understanding popular Hollywood films, Madonna and MTV (Music Television), rap music and contemporary black films, and television news and entertainment can help us to understand our contemporary society. That is, understanding why certain artifacts are popular can illuminate the social environment in which they arise and are circulated, and can thus provide insight into what is going on in contemporary societies and cultures.

My focus is on media culture in the United States, but since U.S. culture is increasingly exported to the entire world, this study should illuminate dominant forms of globalized consumer and media culture elsewhere as well. U.S. media culture is invading cultures all over the world, producing new forms of the *global popular*. Such phenomena of U.S. media culture as the *Rambo* and *Rocky* films, Madonna and Michael Jackson, MTV and rap, CNN and U.S. TV news footage, American advertising and commodities, and the forms of American television, music, film, and other aspects of media culture are popular throughout the world, thus the studies collected here should be of global and not merely regional interest.

My studies were conceived and begun during a specific historical moment, that of the triumph of conservatism in the United States and most Western capitalist democracies. Accordingly, after setting out my concept of the sort of cultural studies and social theory needed to understand our contemporary media culture in an opening chapter on the theory and culture wars of recent years, I examine in Chapter 2 the politics and ideology of Hollywood film in the Age of Reagan and demonstrate how popular film reproduced the hegemonic conservative discourses of the era. This study applies and expands the method of reading film politically developed by Michael Ryan and myself in our 1988 book *Camera Politica* and carries out some concrete studies of contemporary Hollywood films, while delineating a model of a critical and multicultural media cultural studies. I argue that one needs a cultural studies that criticizes the intersection of class, gender, sex, race, and other key determinants of culture and identity in order to more fully conceptualize the ideological dimensions of cultural texts and to appraise the full range of their effects.

Next, in Chapter 3, I indicate the need to read media culture against its ideological grain, to ferret out critical and subversive moments, and to analyze how the ideological projects of media texts often fail. I also explicate a concept of diagnostic critique that uses media culture to diagnose social trends and tendencies, reading through the texts to the fantasies, fears, hopes, and desires that they articulate. A diagnostic critique also analyzes how media culture provides the resources for producing identities and advances either reactionary or progressive politics – or provides ambiguous texts and effects that can be appropriated in various ways.

In Part II, I carry through some concrete studies of diagnostic critiques that interrogate dominant representations of class, race, gender, sexuality, youth, and contemporary politics. In Chapter 4, I illustrate the concept of diagnostic critique through a reading of the *Poltergeist* films which I argue articulate middle-class fears of downward mobility, homelessness, dissolution of the family, and threats from other classes and races in cinematic form. I then develop readings of the film *Slacker* and the MTV series *Beavis and Butt-Head* to provide a diagnosis of the plight of disaffected youth in the current moment.

Thus, whereas Chapter 2 showed how Hollywood films transcoded the dominant political discourses during the era of conservative hegemony from 1980 into the 1990s, Chapter 4 shows how the desires, anxieties, and insecurities of ordinary people also find expression in media culture, allowing the depiction of crisis tendencies beneath the ideological facade of a happy, secure consumer society. Appraising the politics of media culture thus ranges from ideological critique of the way that popular texts embody dominant political discourses concerning the major political issues and conflicts of the day to analyzing texts that encode the politics of everyday life and the anxieties and tensions concerning class, race, gender, youth, and the dreams and anxieties of ordinary people.

In Chapter 5, I delineate a model of a multiperspectival cultural studies and illustrate this concept with a detailed study of the films of Spike Lee, which provide an exemplary instance of the cinematic exploration of key issues of race, gender, and class in the contemporary moment. Drawing on black feminist and political criticism of his films, I examine Lee's work and the contributions and limitations of his style, texts, and politics. Contrasting Lee's films with the contemporary rap music of Public Enemy, Ice-T, Ice Cube, Sister Souljah, and others suggests some of the range of socially critical cultural texts being produced today and the ways that radical blacks are pushing beyond the previously established limits of mainstream culture to articulate their experiences of oppression, rage, and rebellion.

During the Reagan–Bush era, television grew in cultural and political importance, through the political spectacles and daily photo opportunities produced by the Reagan Administration and the spectacle of the "Gulf War" which I analyze in Chapter 6. After Reagan, there followed the Bush regime and his effort during the "Gulf War" to establish a "New World Order." In Chapter 2, I indicate how certain Hollywood films produced images that could be mobilized to produce consent to the U.S. war against Iraq in the early 1990s. In Chapter 6, I show how the tools of cultural studies can be utilized to critique the production of "Gulf War," to provide a critical reading of the text, and to help explain its effect on the audience and why the public so massively supported the war.

Over the past decade, media culture has thus been playing an increasingly important role in political elections, in the daily political battles, and in legitimating the political system. Global media events like the Gulf War demonstrated the efficacy of U.S. weapons systems and the hegemony of U.S. military power, while events like the spectacular 1994 TV funeral of Richard Nixon demonstrated the power of the presidency. Nixon's state funeral also conveyed the myth that anyone could rise to the presidency as the camera cut frequently during the ceremony to Nixon's modest birth house.

Moreover, new forms of television entertainment appeared during the era and in Chapter 7, I analyze some key moments of television culture in the 1980s, including *Miami Vice* and other "new look" TV, often labelled "postmodern." The rise of Music Television (MTV) revolutionized the music industry, giving rise to new multimedia stars like Madonna and Michael Jackson. I also explore some ways that advertising provides models of gender and identification, as well as inducements to buy specific products.

Just as image came to play a key role in the politics of the era, so too did it come to play a central role in the media culture of the period and in everyday life, in which one's image, look, and style, became increasingly important in the constitution of individual identity. Within this context, I provide readings in Part III of *Miami Vice*, MTV, advertising, and Madonna in relationship to the claim that they were exemplary in producing shifts to what has been identified as a new postmodern culture and new postmodern identities. I attempt to clarify the faddish discourses of postmodernism, indicating its uses and abuses. Focusing on the politics of representation in contemporary culture, I analyze the construction, rhetorical strategies, and effects of some key artifacts of contemporary media culture, arguing that many texts of our media culture share both modernist and postmodernist aesthetic strategies and thus are best read as residing between the modern and postmodern.

This topic leads into reflections on the role of image and fashion in constructing identity, as well as on the role of popular music, stars, and promotion in our contemporary culture. I argue in Chapter 8 that Madonna's shifts in image and identity articulate transformations in values and politics of the epoch. I claim that her contradictions capture conflicting aspects of her cultural moment and that the "Madonna phenomenon" is symptomatic of key trends of the era, so that interpreting her texts, and Madonna as a text herself, can illuminate features of the present moment. Yet I argue that Madonna is a phenomenon of her own production, promotion, and marketing strategies, and that one needs therefore to focus on the political economy of culture to properly interpret "the Madonna phenomenon."

In "Mapping the present from the future: from Baudrillard to cyberpunk" (Chapter 9), I explore cyberpunk fiction and postmodern theory as artifacts of media culture which in turn provide fictional-theoretical visions of a society increasingly dominated by media and information. Focusing on the similarities between the social analysis of Baudrillard and the novels of William Gibson, I interpret both as attempts to map our present moment which is constantly slipping into the future. Through a close reading of *Neuromancer*, I argue that both Baudrillard and Gibson are providing visions of the future which serve to illuminate the present. This analysis suggests that Baudrillard is best read as dystopic science fiction, although cyberpunk can also be read as a new form of social theory that maps the consequences of a rapidly developing information and media society in the era of techno-capitalism.

In a conclusion, I indicate some remaining tasks for cultural studies and some of the issues that cultural studies should address in the future. My studies ultimately propose developing syntheses of social theory, cultural criticism, and media pedagogy to illuminate our contemporary society, culture, and politics. Combining philosophy, social theory, cultural critique, and political analysis, I present some perspectives on society and culture, methods of cultural criticism, and make some proposals for the reconstruction of cultural studies and critical social theory. Yet the following texts were not only written for an academic audience. Although they respond to academic debates over the proper method and terrain of social theory and cultural criticism, I also address urgent political and cultural issues of the day and thus attempt to write for a popular audience. I aspire to clearly explain complex theoretical terms when they emerge in my arguments and to amply illustrate my key methodological and theoretical positions.

CULTURAL STUDIES AND SOCIAL THEORY

As noted, I believe that cultural studies is best carried out in the context of critical social theory, and in Chapter 1 and succeeding sections, I indicate how the critical theory of the Frankfurt School provides useful perspectives on contemporary society and helpful weapons of critique for cultural studies. But I also indicate the limitations of the Frankfurt School and how the perspectives on culture and society of British cultural studies often provide a corrective to the positions of the Frankfurt School (though I also believe that aspects of the Frankfurt School approach provide correctives to the limitations of British cultural studies). Moreover, I engage the contributions of feminism and the multiculturalist projects which undertake the explorations of gender, sexuality, race, ethnicity, otherness, and marginality that began proliferating in the 1960s. In addition, I explore the relevance for cultural studies of the theoretical innovations in the postmodern theories of Foucault, Baudrillard, Jameson, and others, and attempt to analyze some of the salient aspects of the present moment, such as the consumer and media society; new computer, communications, and information technologies; new forms of fashion and culture; new forms of power and knowledge; and new modes of subjectivity and identity.

In fact, the present moment is marked by heated debates concerning whether we are still living in the modern era or have moved into a new postmodern era. Some of those who argue for the postmodern turn claim that we are living in an entirely new and original moment that requires new theories and politics. French theorist Jean Baudrillard is one of the most influential proponents of a radical break and rupture with the previous forms of society, culture, politics, and theory. Throughout the book, I explore the claim that we are living in a new historical era of "postmodernity" and discuss the relevance of postmodern theory for the study of society and culture.

I argue that although some postmodern theory illuminates some conspicuous new features of our culture and society, the claim concerning a new postmodern rupture in society and history is exaggerated. In several studies, I examine the use and abuse of postmodern theory and the claims that forms of media culture like Madonna, *Miami Vice*, rap, MTV, and various other forms of media culture are "postmodern." I also take on those who claim that we need a new postmodern form of theory and cultural studies to adequately engage our contemporary moment. I argue that we are now living in a transitional era between the modern and the postmodern which requires us to draw on both modern and postmodern strategies and theories, thus resisting claims for a postmodern break in history and the need for entirely new postmodern theories and cultural studies.

Instead I argue that a combination of the best resources of modern theories, along with some new postmodern perspectives, provide the most useful tools with which to do social theory and cultural criticism today. My enterprise intersects throughout with the project of cultural studies which was developed by the Birmingham Centre for Contemporary Cultural Studies in the U.K. from the early 1960s to the present. This project involved reading culture from the perspective of the production and reception of cultural texts within concrete historical contexts. I build on the tradition of British cultural studies, but argue that the project needs to be rethought and reworked in response to contemporary conditions and challenges. I argue that while British cultural studies was on the cutting edge of the study of culture and society for some decades, recent developments in cultural studies, that have de-centered the earlier focus on class, and a failure throughout its history to adequately engage the production and political economy of culture, mean that a different kind of cultural studies is now required. Such a cultural studies, developed in this book, is itself based on revised, updated, and reconstructed readings of British cultural studies, of the Frankfurt School, of some positions of postmodern theory, and of feminism and multicultural theory.

In their best work, proponents of British cultural studies always contextualized their inquiries within current socio-political struggles and events. Throughout my own studies, I accordingly attempt to situate the cultural artifacts under inquiry within the environment in which they were produced and received, and to address the key political issues articulated in cultural texts. The scope of my studies is approximately the last decade of media culture from the early 1980s through the early 1990s. I accordingly situate my studies within the cultural wars between liberals, conservatives, and radicals, resulting in the conservative hegemony of the Reagan and Bush Administrations, its constant contestation by liberals and radicals, and the election of the more liberal Clinton administration in 1992. I show how the political events of the day, such as the triumph of Reaganism and the Gulf War, influenced the media culture of the period and how some popular forms of media culture influenced the social and political ambience of the epoch.

Throughout, I engage in critical media pedagogy that will enable readers and citizens to make sense of their culture and society, that will provide tools of criticism to help individuals to avoid media manipulation and to produce their own identities and resistance, and that will inspire media activism to produce alternative forms of culture and social transformation. A critical media pedagogy develops concepts and analyses that will enable readers to critically dissect the artifacts of contemporary media and consumer culture, help them to unfold the meanings and effects on their culture, and thus give individuals power over their cultural environment.

I assume that cultural criticism and media pedagogy require social theory and that critical social theory in turn should draw upon media and cultural studies and the methods of cultural criticism to gain key insights into the texture of contemporary social life. This project thus combines methodological strategies, theories, and concepts from both modern and postmodern theory in the attempt to provide critical perspectives on salient cultural and social phenomena of the contemporary era. I draw upon and elaborate key ideas set out in my other works of the past years and continue to delineate the trajectories of theory, culture, and politics in the contemporary era. Inspired by the Frankfurt School project that attempts to provide theoretical articulations of the present moment, these studies should be read as examples of cultural critique which provide fragments of a critical theory of society and, hopefully, some inspiration for a new future politics of liberation.

Moreover, the following studies should be read in conjunction with some of my earlier works such as *Camera Politica* (co-authored with Michael Ryan, 1988), which attempted to chart the vicissitudes of Hollywood film from the mid-1960s to the mid-1980s and to develop critical methodologies for the interpretation of cultural texts which would determine how various texts either advanced or inhibited the aims of progressive political movements. The studies in this volume are also congruent with my books *Television and the Crisis of Democracy* (Kellner 1990) and *The Persian Gulf TV War* (Kellner 1992) which map some of the ways that the media have become the terrain for contemporary politics and social struggles. In these texts, I am interested in how the media either inhibit and impede the project of the democratization of society or could promote it. These earlier texts attempt to theorize the role of the media in a democratic society, and I continue this project in this book. But whereas the preceding two books tended to focus on news and information, the following studies interrogate a wide range of phenomena of media culture and analyze how various forms of media culture produce pleasures, positions, and identities, that either inhibit or advance the aims of producing more democratic, egalitarian, and truly multicultural societies.

ACKNOWLEDGEMENTS

For helpful comments on many of the texts and discussion of their thematics, I am grateful to my friend and collaborator Steve Best. Useful comments, insights, and material were also provided by Robert Antonio, David Armstrong, Ann Cvetkovich, Jon Epstein, Henry Giroux, Darrell Hamamoto, Kelly Oliver, Danny Postal, Valerie Scatamburlo, and editors and readers of the journals where some of these articles first appeared, though in different forms. I am extremely grateful to Jon and Margarete Epstein for producing the computer generated illustrations in the book.[1] The images of media culture are circulating through new spaces and require new technologies for their analysis and dissection. I also want to thank Chris Rojek who was highly supportive of the project and very helpful in focusing the text and in starting it through the production process. Thanks also to Diane Stafford who did an excellent job of editing further developments and in putting up with my constant editing and email. But I am especially indebted to Rhonda Hammer for providing constant criticism, materials, detailed editing, and ideas which helped greatly in the development of these studies.

1   Computer images and cover art created by Jon S. Epstein and Margaret J. Epstein for The Web.

Part 1

Theory/context/methods

Chapter 1

Theory wars and cultural studies

We live in a time of dramatic change and upheaval. Since the 1960s, there has been a series of spectacular changes in culture and society throughout the world. The 1960s was an era of protracted social tumult with new social movements mushrooming to challenge established forms of society and culture and to produce new countercultures and alternative forms of everyday life. The 1960s generated an era of intense "cultural wars" between liberals, conservatives, and radicals to reconstruct culture and society according to their own agendas, wars that still rage in the present moment. During the 1970s, worldwide economic recession burst the bubble of post-World-War-II affluence and talk of a "post-scarcity society" was replaced by discourses calling for scaling down of expectations, limits to growth, and the need for reorganization of the economy and state. Such reorganization took place in most parts of the capitalist world during the 1980s under the rule of conservative governments which cut back on social welfare programs, while expanding the military sector and increasing federal deficits, with massive debts that are still unpaid.

The past five years have also seen the collapse of Soviet communism and the end of the Cold War. After World War II, capitalist and communist countries began competing for economic, political, and cultural power. Forces in both blocs promoted cold and hot wars, resulting in heavy militarization and covert and overt wars between the surrogates of the superpowers. Monstrous military establishments on both sides and weapons of total destruction created a tense, fearful epoch, where demagogues and cynical bureaucrats could frighten populations into accepting social policies that mainly benefited the greedy and powerful, while postponing much needed social reform and the creation of a more just and equitable social order.

The tearing down of the Berlin Wall, the collapse of the Soviet Communist empire, and the eventual dissolution of the Soviet Union itself seemed to bring this nightmarish epoch to an end. The result, however, has not been the creation of a new era of peace and stability. Instead, nationalist and religious wars have exploded, bringing about a new era of fear and instability, with no political forces able to offer an attractive way out of the current morass of economic recession, political instability, and cultural confusion. Within the United States, culture wars have also intensified with rightist assaults on "political correctness" functioning as a weapon for attacks on progressive forces and ideas.

New technologies have also emerged in the past decade which have changed the patterns of everyday life and powerfully restructured work and leisure. New computer technologies have replaced many jobs and created new ones, providing new forms of accessing information, communicating with other people, and plugging into the joys of a new computer-mediated public sphere. The new media and computer technologies, however, are ambiguous and can have contradictory effects. On one hand, novel media technologies provide more diversity of choice, more possibility of autonomy over culture, and more openings for the interventions of alternative culture and ideas. Yet the new computer technologies also provide new forms of surveillance and control, with electronic eyes and systems in the workplace providing a contemporary incarnation of Big Brother. The new media technologies also provide powerful forms of social control through more efficient, subtly concealed techniques of indoctrination and manipulation. Indeed, their very existence might sap political energies and keep people safely ensconced within the confines of their home entertainment centers, far from the madding crowds and sites of mass political action.

As a historical phenomenon, media culture is relatively recent. While the new forms of culture industries described by Horkheimer and Adorno (1972) in the 1940s of film, radio, magazines, comics, advertising, and the press began to colonize leisure and stand at the center of the system of culture and communication in the United States and other capitalist democracies, it was not until the advent of television in the post-World War II period that media culture became a dominant force within culture, socialization, politics, and social life (Kellner 1990a). Since then, cable and satellite television, video recorders and other multimedia home entertainment technologies, and more recently home computers have all accelerated the dissemination and increased the power of media culture.

Media culture in the United States and most capitalist countries is a largely commercial form of culture, produced for profit, and disseminated in the form of commodities. The commercialization and commodification of culture has many important consequences. First of all, production for profit means that the executives of the culture industries attempt to produce artifacts that will be popular, that will sell or, in the case of radio and television, that will attract mass audiences. In many cases, this means production of lowest common denominator artifacts that will not offend mass audiences and that will attract a maximum of customers. But precisely the need to sell their artifacts means that the products of the culture industries must resonate to social experience, must attract large audiences, and must thus offer attractive products, which may shock, break with conventions, contain social critique, or articulate current ideas that may be the product of progressive social movements.

Thus, while media culture largely advances the interests of the class that owns and controls the large media conglomerates, its products are also involved in social conflict between competing groups and articulate conflicting positions, sometimes advancing forces of resistance and progress. Consequently, media culture cannot be simply dismissed as a banal instrument of the dominant ideology but must be differentially interpreted and contextualized within the matrix of the competing social discourses and forces which constitute it – as I attempt to do in this book.

Yet, in a certain sense, media culture *is* the dominant culture today; it has replaced the forms of high culture as the center of cultural attention and impact for large numbers of people. Furthermore, visual and oral forms of media culture are supplanting forms of book culture, requiring new types of media literacy to decode these new cultural forms. Moreover, media culture has become a dominant force of socialization, with media images and celebrities replacing families, schools, and churches as arbitors of taste, value, and thought, producing new models of identification and resonant images of style, fashion, and behaviour.

With the advent of media culture, individuals are subjected to an unprecedented flow of sights and sounds into one's own home, and new virtual worlds of entertainment, information, sex, and politics are reordering perceptions of space and time, erasing distinctions between reality and media image, while producing new modes of experience and subjectivity. These far-reaching political, social, and cultural changes have been accompanied by a spectacular proliferation of new theories and methods to help make sense of contemporary culture and society. Already in the 1950s, social theorists were proclaiming the advent of new postindustrial societies in which knowledge and information would be the "axial principle" around which society was organized (Bell 1960, 1973 and 1976). During the 1970s, arguments began appearing that modernity was over and that we were now in a new postmodern era (Baudrillard 1976 and Lyotard 1984) – arguments that generated an explosion of discourses of the postmodern in the 1970s and 1980s (surveyed in Best and Kellner 1991).

Some postmodern theorists argue that contemporary societies with their new technologies, new forms of culture, and new experiences of the present era constitute a decisive rupture with modern forms of life.[1] For these theorists, the couch potato channel-surfing through endless waves of TV programs and the computer jockey jacking into cyberspace and new worlds of information and entertainment constitute a startling evolutionary development, a decisive novelty in the human adventure. The media junkies and technofreaks of the present age are seen as the hunters and gathers of information and entertainment, challenged to survive an "infotainment" overload and to process a stunning array of images and ideas. Like the mutant portrayed by David Bowie in *The Man Who Fell to Earth*, the new postmodern subjects, so it is claimed, will have to learn to live with and process an immense fragmentation and proliferation of new images, information, and technologies.

During the same era, political economists began arguing that we are entering a new "post-Fordist" society in which the regime of accumulation marked by mass production and consumption, state regulation of the economy, and a homogeneous mass culture is being replaced by "more flexible" regimes of accumulation (Harvey 1989). These are marked by transnational corporations replacing the nation-state as arbitrators of production in a new era of global production that erases previous boundaries of space and time. Other social theorists speak of "disorganized capitalism," or new forms of organization, and new legitimation crises, risks, ecological problems, the breakdown of community, growing rifts between rich and poor, deadly new diseases such as AIDS, and a myriad of other new phenomena and problems.[2]

These dramatic changes require new theortical and political responses to interpret our current social situation and to illuminate our contemporary problems, conflicts, challenges, and possibilities. In the conjuncture in which we find ourselves, cultural studies can play an important role in elucidating the significant changes which have taken place in our culture and society. We are indeed surrounded by new technologies, new modes of cultural production, and new forms of social and political life. Moreover, culture is playing an ever more significant role in every realm of contemporary society, with multifarious functions in arenas from the economic to the social. In the economy, seductive cultural forms shape consumer demand, produce needs, and mold a commodity self with consumerist values. In the political sphere, media images have produced a new sort of sound-bite politics which places the media at the center of political life. In our social interactions, mass-produced images guide our presentation of the self in everyday life, our ways of relating to others, and the creation of our social values and goals. As work declines in importance, leisure and culture become more and more the focus of everyday life and the locus of value. Of course, one must work to earn the benefits of the consumer society (or inherit sufficient wealth), but work is supposedly declining in importance in an era in which individuals allegedly gain primary gratification from consuming goods and leisure activities, rather than from their labor activity.[3]

Thus, contemporary society and culture is in a state of ferment and change as competing theories strive to make sense of these new developments. The contested terrain of theory is accompanied by culture wars between conservatives, liberals, and progressives, with conservatives attempting to roll back the advances of the 1960s and impose more traditional values and forms of culture. Throughout the Western world, conservatives have been attempting to gain hegemony by seizing political power and using it to carry through their economic, political, social, and cultural agendas. They have been using their political and economic power to carry through an agenda of cultural transformation, attempting to turn back the clock to an earlier era of conservative rule.

In the United States, intense culture wars have been raging ever since movements of the 1960s launched the first direct assaults on conservative values and institutions. Richard Nixon temporarily established a shaky conservative hegemony in the early 1970s, but his demise in the Watergate scandal triggered a new round of culture wars. The conservative counterrevolution became hegemonic in the U.S. with the election of Ronald Reagan in 1980 and ascent of the New Right which supported his triumph over the Democrats, liberals, and those radicals who preserved their 1960s politics and values. The previous ascendancy of rightists like

Margaret Thatcher in the U.K., Brian Mulrooney in Canada, and the Kohl government in Germany spawned a period of conservative hegemony throughout the Western capitalist world. During this era, conservatives attacked the welfare state, abortion rights, civil liberties, freedom in the arts, the liberalization of education, and attempted to impose a rightist and traditionalist agenda on the public. Yet this offensive of the right never really triumphed in the realm of culture, and culture itself has been a fiercely contested terrain for the past decades.[4]

As we move into the 1990s, conservatives in the United States continue fiercely to contest the liberals who now hold state power after the election of Bill Clinton in 1992. When Clinton attempts to push through a partially liberal agenda, his proposals are fought tooth and nail by conservatives, unlike those of Reagan, who was able to readily implement his economic agenda (probably because it was supported by the big media and business, which exert tremendous control over politicians of both major parties). On the other hand, Clinton has been increasingly pushing a conservative agenda himself and, in a sense, "Reaganism" retains its position as "political common sense" and the dominant discourse of the era. Moreover, both television and radio in the United States continue to be dominated by conservative voices, with the same old right-wing think tanks and publications providing the pundits who pontificate on the state of the nation, while new reactionary brutes like Rush Limbaugh also gain media and cultural power.[5] Hollywood films regularly attack women and feminism and celebrate the most grotesque forms of unrestrained male power and machismo.[6] "White male paranoia" is evident in all cultural milieu from stand-up comics to radio talk shows, and the conservative cultural offensive rages on unabated.

Similar cultural wars rage throughout Europe. In the U.K., the conservative hegemony of the Thatcher and Major regimes has been under attack and conservative power has been eroded, yet the media and culture still evidence strong conservative trends. In France, the socialist government of Mitterand was decisively defeated in 1993 by conservative forces, and social democratic governments in Holland, Denmark, and Sweden have also suffered rare defeats in recent years. Attempts to unify Europe politically and economically are countered by new nationalist surges from Scandinavia to Eastern Europe and the pro- and anti-Europe forces appear evenly divided. In the Arab world, militant fundamentalism is on the march against secular and Westernized regimes, while in the former communist world, struggles between national, ethnic, religious, and political forces have exploded into ugly wars. Misery and oppression continue to grow apace in the more underdeveloped regions of the world and the wretched of the earth appear more wretched than ever.

Yet there are also countervailing trends. The progressive social movements of the 1960s and 1970s are still alive and well and struggles for human rights, the civil liberties of oppressed people, peace and justice, ecology, and a more humane organization of society are everywhere visible. Indeed, the very instability, flux, and uncertainty of the present moment creates openings for more positive futures and possibilities for the creation of a better world out of current nightmares. On the other hand, the penchant for micropolitics and/or identity politics fragments the progressive movements and renders many blind to the necessary linkages and interconnections with others in opposition or in counterhegemonic struggles.

Within this context, it is therefore of vital importance to understand the role of culture in a wide range of current social struggles, trends, and developments. It is the conviction of the studies in this book that our current local, national, and global situations are articulated through the texts of media culture, which is itself a contested terrain, one which competing social groups attempt to use to promote their agendas and ideologies, and which itself reproduces conflicting political discourses, often in a contradictory manner. Not just news and information, but entertainment and fiction articulate the conflicts, fears, hopes, and dreams of individuals and groups confronting a turbulent and uncertain world. The concrete struggles of each society are played out in the texts of media culture, especially in the commercial media of the culture industries which produce texts that must resonate with people's concerns if they are to be popular and profitable. Culture has never been more important and never before have we had such a need for serious scrutiny of contemporary culture.

Consequently, to understand what is going on in our society and our everyday life, we need theoretical perspectives on media culture and social theories that will help us make sense of the changes and conflicts of the present age. Throughout this book, I will thus delineate theoretical perspectives that I find useful in grasping the vicissitudes of contemporary society and culture.[7] But the fortunes of theory are related to the historical matrices which shape and structure them and which they in turn attempt to illuminate. Therefore, in the following study, I will sketch the emergence and effects of some contemporary theories which I will make use of in this work.

THEORY WARS

The past decades of intense cultural, social, and political struggle since the 1960s also saw the rise of many new theories and approaches to culture and society. It is as if the tumultuous struggles of the era sought expression and replication in the realm of theory. The political passions and energies seemed to be sublimated into the discourse of theory and new theories were appropriated with the intensity that marked the assimilation and dissemination of radical political ideas and practices in the 1960s. The proliferation of new theoretical discourses first took the form of theory fever, in which each new, or newly discovered, theoretical discourse produced feverish excitement, as if a new theory virus totally took over and possessed its host. Then the proliferating theory fever took on the form of theory wars between the competing theoretical discourses, often reducing theory to the domain of fashion.

Theory fever emerged in the 1960s in France with the proliferation of new discourses emanating from the post-structuralist turn in theory. Rejecting the totalizing, universalizing, and scientistic theories of structuralism, semiotics,

psychoanalysis, Marxism, and other "master discourses" which produced the theory fevers and wars of an earlier era, the post-structuralist revolution saw the proliferation of new theories of language, the subject, politics, and culture. Yet, drawing on the very theories whose more extravagant claims they rejected, the post-structuralist movement provided new syntheses of Marxism, psychoanalysis, semiotics, and feminism, exploding in a wealth of theoretical discourses, which circulated throughout the world.

In the United States, where forms of what Herbert Marcuse called "one-dimensional thought" reigned in the 1950s and early 1960s, Marxism and feminism were the first forms of theory fever to circulate. Experiences of the Vietnam war in the 1960s drove many in the New Left and antiwar movement to Marxist theory, tabooed during the Cold War and driven underground.[8] Marxist discourse proliferated and a stunning variety of neo-Marxist theories from Europe and the Third World were imported to the United States, producing a wide range of new radical theories.

Feminism quickly became part of the new theoretical discourses throughout the world. In the late 1960s, women began to revolt against what they considered oppressive practices of both contemporary patriarchal societies and their male comrades in the radical movements. First-wave 1960s feminism discovered classics like Simone de Beauvoir's *The Second Sex*, a rich woman's history, and the importance of women's experience and culture for the radical project.[9] Many, often unhappy, marriages between Marxism and feminism took place, while other varieties of feminist theory found important tools in psychoanalysis to analyze women's oppression and experiences, and to provide for the reconstruction of more nurturing, feeling, and loving subjects. Thus, as with Marxism, a tremendous range of feminist theories emerged, which often warred with each other, as well as with male discourses.

Previously marginalized groups sought their own voices and in the United States new African-American, Native American, Mexican-American, Asian-American, and other minority discourses and studies emerged. Gay and lesbian studies problematized sexuality and provided new perspectives on gender, sexuality, culture, and society. Theorists whose national origin was frequently colonized countries generated new subaltern studies, attacking Western colonization, while studies of the "postcolonial subject" and voices from newly emerged nations produced some exciting theoretical innovations and greatly expanded the terrain of critical discourses. Cumulatively, these discourses have contributed to some of the most exciting social theory and cultural criticism of recent years and in the following studies I draw on these new oppositional discourses.

Although the tumult of the 1960s passed into the more quiescent 1970s, the explosion of theories continued and theory wars intensified.[10] A new globalization of theory erupted with the new theoretical discourses being rapidly disseminated across borders and national cultures. Theorists in the Third World and the United States appropriated European discourses, and the resulting new critical theories were circulated in turn throughout Europe. Discourses of race, class, ethnicity, sexual preference, and nationality challenged theoretical discourses to take account of phenomena previously ignored or underplayed. Wars broke out (and persist) between those that privileged class and those that privileged such things as race and gender. Finally, a truce prevailed which agreed that all of these determinants of social identity and structuring social categories were of fundamental importance to social life, cultural analysis, and individual subjectivity.

By the 1980s, the new global discourses of theory provided languages for communication across borders, but they also disseminated the globalization of theory fever and wars. Theory fevers continued to proliferate and from Berkeley to Bombay, from Austin to London, new syntheses of Marxism, feminism, psychoanalysis, post-structuralism, and postmodern theories emerged, while claims were being made for a new discourse of theory which drew on the new critical theories, producing ever-spiralling and complexified theoretical discourses and syntheses. Theory wars intensified between discourses seeking hegemony and dominance. Each new theory was proclaimed by its advocates as the supertheory, as the key to culture, society and the subject. Discoveries of thinkers like Roland Barthes, Jacques Lacan, Michel Foucault, Louis Althusser, Jean Baudrillard, Jean-François Lyotard, Jacques Derrida, and the other stars of "new French Theory" were enthusiastically taken up by followers who took each new theory as the finally discovered oeuvre that would lead the way to theoretical and political salvation.

During the 1980s, various strains of French post-structuralist theory mutated into postmodern theory (see the genealogy in Best and Kellner 1991 and the discussion on p. 40). In a sense, postmodern theory exhibits the passions of the 1960s sublimated into theoretical discourse. The break or rupture desired in the 1960s, a break then described in the discourse of revolution, is projected onto history itself, or more limited domains of society and culture. Yet, the apocalyptic breaks and ruptures postulated in the 1960s as the goal of political struggle are now being described in some postmodern theory as breaks occurring as the result of new technologies, without the effort of revolutionary struggle, thus replicating, in effect, the old discourses of technological determinism.

Moreover, some of the discourses of the postmodern also bear the marks of defeat in the aftermath of the 1960s. Postmodern claims concerning the fragmentation of the subject and doubts concerning the efficacy of political practice are in part effects of the experience of the fragmentation of the political "movement" of the era and disintegration of revolutionary politics and subjects. Postmodern nihilism enunciates the experience of defeat, of disappointment, of despair, over the failures of the 1960s movements to more radically transform social and cultural life. Yet there is a more positive version of postmodern theory that translates some of the progressive tendencies and gains of the 1960s into theoretical discourse and cultural practice. What Hal Foster (1983) has termed the "postmodernism of resistance" attempts to develop oppositional theoretical and cultural practices within the present moment, against the more oppressive features and practices of contemporary culture and society.

By the 1990s, many of the new theoretical discourses positioned themselves under the rubric of "multiculturalism." This way of seeing affirmed otherness and difference, and the importance of attending to marginalized, minority, and oppositional groups and voices previously excluded from the cultural dialogue. Multiculturalism elicited new cultural wars as conservatives defended Western culture, with its canons of great (mostly) European males against the multicultural offensive. Against multiculturalism, conservatives thus (re)affirmed monoculturalism leading to a new round of intense theory and culture wars that are still raging.

As noted, each new product of the theory fever was presented as the solution to the current dilemmas of theory and politics and extravagant claims for the revolutionary nature of each theoretical discourse were endlessly recycled. At this juncture, however, it seems highly questionable to seek a new theoretical Holy Grail that will yield the secrets of Being, culture, or society. Rather, with Foucault, it is perhaps better to conceive of theories as instruments, as providing tools in a toolkit, or, to use an earlier metaphor, as weapons used to attack specific targets.[11] "Theories" are, among other things, ways of seeing, optics; they are perspectives which illuminate specific phenomena and that also have certain blindspots and limitations which restrict their focus. The term "theory" derives from the Greek root *theoria* that privileges seeing, and thus one function of theory is to help individuals see and interpret phenomena and events. Theories are thus ways of seeing that provide understanding and modes of interpretation which focus attention on specific phenomena, linkages, or the social system as a whole.

Post-structuralist theory has made us aware that theories are constructs, products of specific social discourses, practices, and institutions, and thus do not transcend their social fields. Traditional theories that claim to provide a foundation of truth, or universal knowledge transcendent of social conditions, or a metatheory that provides truth which transcends the interests of particular theories, have been widely rejected, as have positivist theories which claim that science provides a privileged mode of truth to which all theory should aspire. Against positivism, it is generally agreed that there is no such thing as an immaculate perception, that seeing, interpreting, explaining, and so on are all mediated by theoretical discourses and embedded in theoretical assumptions.

Thus, on this more modest conception of theory, theories are seen as tools that help us see, operate, and get around specific social fields, pointing to salient phenomena, making connections, interpreting and criticizing, and perhaps explaining and predicting specific states of affairs. Theories provide resources to talk about common experiences, discourses, practices, institutions, and social relations. They also point to conflicts and problems and provide resources to discuss them and to search for solutions.

Theories thus illuminate social realities and help individuals to make sense of their world. Theories use concepts, images, symbols, arguments, and narratives to do their work. Contemporary metatheory (i.e. theory about theory) frequently notes that theories have literary components; they tell stories, utilize rhetoric and symbols, and like literary texts help make sense of our life.[12] Yet theories also have cognitive components that abstract in theoretical concepts common features of their domain, as when critical social theories analyze the structures of capitalism, patriarchy, or social class. Social theories provide maps of societal fields that orient individuals to perceive how their societies are constructed. The categories of social theory conceptualize the structures, relations, and institutions that provide the terrain for social and everyday life.

Social theories are thus heuristic devices to interpret and make sense of social life. They illuminate the context of social action and guide people in their everyday social interactions. Social theories often provide the big picture that allows individuals to contextualize their experience within the broader field of social relations and institutions. Social theories can also illuminate specific events and artifacts by analyzing their constituents, relations, and effects. Dialectical social theory makes connections between isolated parts of society, showing, for instance, how the economy enters into the processes of media culture and structures what kind of texts are produced in the culture industries. Or it shows how listening to music is mediated by specific technologies, cultural spaces, and institutions (Berland in Grossberg, *et al.* 1992). Dialectics is the art of making connections and relating parts to each other and to the system as a whole. Thus, a critical theory of society contains mappings of how society as a whole is organized, delineating its fundamental structures, institutions, practices, and discourses, and how they fit together into a social system.

Critical social theory can utilize the concept of articulation to denote how various societal components are organized into the production of, say, conservative hegemony, or in the popularity of a Madonna. The concept of articulation was introduced by British cultural studies and has become central to its practice (see Hall, 1986b; Grossberg, 1992; and the fast genealogy of the concept in Jameson 1994). Cultural studies delineates how cultural artifacts articulate social ideologies, values, and representations of gender, race, and class, and how these phenomena are related to each other. Situating cultural texts in their social context thus involves tracing the articulations through which societies produce culture and how culture in turn shapes society through its influence on individuals and groups.

Critical social theories conceptualize the structures of domination and resistance. They point to forms of oppression and domination contrasted to forces of resistance that can serve as instruments of change. They illuminate the possibilities of social transformation and progress, as well as the dangers of intensified social domination. Critical social theory thus devolves around social practice and can aid in the construction of better societies by showing what needs to be transformed, what agencies might carry out the transformation, and what strategies and tactics might be successful in promoting progressive social change.

Thus, critical social theories are weapons of critique and instruments of practice, as well as cognitive maps. Critical theory points to aspects of society and culture that should be challenged and changed, and thus attempts to inform and inspire political practice. Practice-oriented theory also posits certain goals and values that are to be realized and sketches ways to transform society to make it better, to increase human freedom and happiness. They provide vocabularies that help mobilize responses to social problems and issues, and thus aim at intervention in the public sphere.

As I have noted, the present situation is characterized by a bewildering multiplicity of competing theoretical paradigms. Different theories can be used for varying purposes in disparate situations. The usefulness or uselessness of specific theories depends on the task at hand and whether the theory in question is appropriate for that task. Theory, as the following studies hope to demonstrate, can be useful, but it is a grave mistake to believe that there is a supertheory or master narrative that will provide the interpretive or explanatory keys to all of our intellectual and political problems. Consequently, instead or arguing for a new supertheory, or privileging a grand synthesis of previous theories, I will draw upon a number of critical theories, offering some examples of what I call a multiperspectival social theory and media cultural studies.[13]

Contemporary societies require constant mappings and remappings because of the intensity of change and speed of current social transformations. We are living through an epoch of intense change, and many of the current theories of society describe aspects of this change, and are thus relevant in various specific contexts. No one theory, however, tells the whole story, and all contemporary theories have their limitations and blind spots, as well as their contributions. Consequently, I propose combining various contemporary social theories to provide some ways of illuminating and talking about phenomena and developments within the present age.[14] The mappings of each specific theory provide some novel insights, but usually are limited in specific ways. Some theories are thus useful for some tasks (i.e. Marxist ideology as a critique for analyzing class and hegemony), while other theories are useful for other tasks (i.e. feminism for interrogating gender, or queer studies for discussing the construction of sexuality and sexual preferences, and so on). No one theory could possibly address all topics or illuminate all features of social life. Thus, one must choose which theories one deploys, according to the specific tasks at hand.

For the purposes of this study, I shall therefore adopt a pragmatic contextualist approach to theory, using some critical theories for certain specific tasks and others for different ones. A multiperspectival approach holds that the more theories one has at one's disposal, the more tasks one can perform and the more specific objects and themes one can address. Further, the more perspectives that one brings to bear on a phenomenon, the better one's potential grasp or understanding of it could be. To be sure, a powerful and innovative single perspective (like psychoanalysis or feminism) might be more useful in illuminating or explaining certain phenomena than an eclectic combination of multiple perspectives, but combining powerful approaches like Marxism, feminism, post-structuralism, and other contemporary theoretical optics might yield more insightful and useful analyses than those produced by one perspective alone. Moreover, a Marxism informed by feminism and psychoanalysis is different and more useful than a theory innocent of such perspectives.

As I attempt to show in this collection, different topics and issues require varying methods and approaches. Indeed, throughout this book I attempt to flesh out my theoretical position, which is only suggested here, and believe that only through concrete studies can theories be developed and tested, and their hermeneutical and critical effectiveness validated. And the political efficacy of a theory can only be developed and tested through examination of its effects on practice. If a theory illuminates a phenomenon like MTV and produces altered reception of it (or perhaps rejection), or inspires the production of oppositional media practices, then the theory turns out to be valuable both in its theoretical and political effects.

The test of a theory is thus its use, its deployment, and its effects. From this perspective, theories are seen to be either useful or deficient through their application and effects. Contextual pragmatist and multiperspectival approaches thus work together to open up theoretical inquiry to a multiplicity of discourses and methods. Theories and discourses are more or less useful depending on the issue under question, the specific application of the theory in the theorist's hands, and the goals intended. In the next sections, I shall note which particular theories I and others engaged in the analysis of the intersection of culture, society, and politics that is cultural studies have found most useful. Yet I do not intend to provide a history or genealogy of the trajectories of cultural studies. I will not provide a summary of works of various traditions of cultural studies, but wish instead to intervene in contemporary debates, staking out my own positions within the field of current problematics. Accordingly, in the following discussion, I cite only positions that I feel are productive for a media cultural studies, or indicate positions from which I am distancing myself.[15]

APPROACHES TO CULTURAL STUDIES

The metatheory for and models of social theory and cultural criticism that I am proposing here have been especially influenced by the Frankfurt School, British cultural studies, and postmodern/post-structuralist theory. As I indicate below, the Frankfurt School inaugurated critical studies of mass communication and culture and developed an early model of cultural studies. There are indeed many traditions and models of cultural studies, ranging from neo-Marxist models developed by Lukàcs, Gramsci, Bloch, and the Frankfurt School in the 1930s to feminist and psychoanalytic cultural studies. In Britain and the United States, there is a long tradition of cultural studies that preceded the Birmingham school.[16] The major traditions of cultural studies combine – at their best – social theory, cultural analysis, history, philosophy, and specific political interventions, thus overcoming the standard academic division of labor by surmounting specialization which bifurcates the field of study of the media, culture, and communications. Cultural studies thus operates with a transdisciplinary conception that draws on social theory, economics, politics, history, communication studies, literary and cultural theory, philosophy, and other theoretical discourses.

Transdisciplinary approaches to culture and society transgress borders between various academic disciplines. In particular, they argue that one should not stop at the border of a text, but should see how it fits into systems of textual production, and how various texts are thus part of systems of genres or types of production and have an intertextual construction. *Rambo* is a film, for instance, that fits into the genre of war films and a specific cycle of return-to-Vietnam films (see the analysis in Chapter 2). One should not, however, stop at the borders of intertexuality, but should move from the text to its context, to the culture and society that constitutes the text and in which it should be read and interpreted. For *Rambo* also replicates the right-wing discourses concerning POWs left in Vietnam and the need to overcome the Vietnam syndrome (i.e. shame concerning the loss of the war and overcoming the reluctance to again use U.S. military power). Interpreting the cinematic text of *Rambo* thus involves the use of film theory, social history, political analysis and ideology critique, and other modes of cultural criticism, as I will illustrate in the next chapter.

Transdisciplinary approaches thus involve border crossings across disciplines from text to context, and thus from texts to culture and society.[17] Crossing borders inevitably pushes one to the boundaries of class, gender, race, sexuality, ethnicity, and the other characteristics that differentiate individuals from each other and through which people construct their identities. Thus, most forms of cultural studies, and most critical social theories, have engaged feminism and the various multicultural theories, enriching their projects with theoretical and political substance derived from the new critical and multicultural discourses that have emerged since the 1960s.

Transdisciplinary cultural studies thus draws on a disparate range of fields to theorize the complexity and contradictions of the multiple effects of a vast range of forms of media/culture/communications in our lives and demonstrate how these artifacts serve as instruments of domination, but also offer resources for resistance and change. In the following sketch, I first indicate how the Frankfurt School developed an early approach to media studies still worth attending to, though I also identify some of its limitations. I next discuss British cultural studies which currently rivals postmodern theory in popularity and attention as a critical approach to the study of culture and society, indicating its contributions, but also some of its restrictions. Then, I discuss the postmodern turn in social and cultural theory and also explicate some of the attempts to develop a postmodern cultural studies. In the following discussions, I will focus primarily on aspects of these traditions that I believe are useful today for cultural studies while noting some limitations that I think have vitiated certain forms of contemporary cultural studies.

THE FRANKFURT SCHOOL

The Frankfurt School inaugurated critical communications studies in the 1930s and combined political economy of the media, cultural analysis of texts, and audience reception studies of the social and ideological effects of mass culture and communications.[18] Its proponents coined the term "culture industries" to signify the process of the industrialization of mass-produced culture and the commercial imperatives which drove the system. The critical theorists analyzed all mass-mediated cultural artifacts within the context of industrial production, in which the artifacts of the culture industries exhibited the same features as other products of mass production: commodification, standardization, and massification. The products of the culture industries had the specific function, however, of providing ideological legitimation of the existing capitalist societies and of integrating individuals into the framework of mass culture and society.

Adorno's analyses of popular music, Lowenthal's studies of popular literature and magazines, Herzog's studies of radio soap operas, and the perspectives and critiques of mass culture developed in Horkheimer and Adorno's famous study of the culture industries (1972) provided many examples of the usefulness of the Frankfurt School approach. Moreover, in their theories of the culture industries and critiques of mass culture, they were the first to systematically analyze and criticize mass-mediated culture and communications within critical social theory. In particular, they were the first to see the importance of what they called the "culture industries" in the reproduction of contemporary societies, in which so-called mass culture and communications stand in the center of leisure activity, are important agents of socialization, mediators of political reality, and should thus be seen as major institutions of contemporary societies with a variety of economic, political, cultural and social effects.[19]

Yet there are serious flaws in the original program of critical theory which requires a radical reconstruction of the classical model of the culture industries (Kellner 1989a). Overcoming the limitations of the classical model would include: more concrete analysis of the political economy of the media and the processes of the production of culture; more empirical and historical research into the construction of media industries and their interaction with other social institutions; more studies of audience reception and media effects; and the incorporation of new cultural theories and methods into a reconstructed critical theory of culture and the media. Cumulatively, such a reconstruction of the classical Frankfurt School project would update the critical theory of society and its activity of cultural criticism by incorporating contemporary developments in social and cultural theory into the enterprise of critical theory.

In addition, the Frankfurt School dichotomy between high culture and low culture is problematic and should be superseded by a model that takes culture as a spectrum and applies similar critical methods to all cultural artifacts ranging from opera to popular music, from modernist literature to soap operas. In particular, the Frankfurt School model of a monolithic mass culture contrasted with an ideal of "authentic art," which limits critical, subversive, and emancipatory moments to certain privileged artifacts of high culture, is highly problematic. The Frankfurt School position that all mass culture is ideological and debased, having the effects of duping a passive mass of consumers, is also objectionable. Instead, one should see critical and ideological moments in the full range of culture, and not limit critical moments to high culture and identify all of low culture as ideological. One should also allow for the possibility that critical and subversive moments could be found in the artifacts of the culture industries, as well as the canonized classics of high modernist culture that the Frankfurt School seemed to privilege as the site of artistic opposition and emancipation.[20] In addition one should distinguish between the encoding and decoding of media artifacts, and recognize that an active audience often produces its own meanings and uses for products of the culture industries.

Yet precisely the critical focus on media culture from the perspectives of commodification, reification, ideology, and domination provides a framework useful as a corrective to more populist and uncritical approaches to media culture which tend to surrender critical standpoints. Although the Frankfurt School approach is partial and one-sided it does provide tools to criticize the ideological and debased forms of media culture and the ways that it reinforces ideologies which legitimate forms of oppression. As I argue in Chapter 2 and throughout the book, ideology critique is a fundamental constituent of cultural studies and the Frankfurt School is valuable for inaugurating systematic and sustained critiques of ideology within the culture industries.

Moreover, on the level of metatheory, the Frankfurt School work preceded the bifurcation of the field of media studies into specialized subareas with competing models and methods. This bifurcation is documented in the 1983 *Journal of Communications* issue on "Ferment in the field" (Vol. 33, No. 3 [Summer 1983]), where some of the participants in this discussion on the state of the art of media communications studies noted a bifurcation of the field between a culturalist approach that focuses primarily on texts contrasted with more empirical approaches in the study of mass-mediated communications. The culturalist approach at the time was largely textual, centered on the analysis and criticism of all forms of communication as cultural artifacts, using methods primarily derived from the humanities. The methods of communications research, by contrast, employed more empirical methodologies, ranging from straight quantitative research, ethnographic studies of specific cases or domains, to specialized historical research. Topics in this area included analysis of the political economy of the media, audience reception and study of media effects, media history, the interaction of media institutions with other domains of society and the like.

Some contributors to the 1983 *JOC* symposium suggested a liberal tolerance of different approaches, or ways in which the various approaches complemented each other or could be integrated. In overcoming the divide between cultural and communications studies, I would suggest that the Frankfurt School approach is valuable because it provides an integral model that transcends contemporary divisions in the study of media, culture, and communications.[21] Their studies dissected the interconnection of culture and communication in artifacts that reproduced the existing society, positively presenting social norms and practices, and legitimating the state capitalist organization of society. The Frankfurt School carried out analysis within the framework of critical social theory, thus integrating communication and cultural studies within the context of study of capitalist society and the ways that communications and culture were produced within this order and the roles and functions that they assumed. The Frankfurt School also made apparent the inappropriate nature of quantitative methods for qualitative relations and produced methods to analyze the complex relations between texts, audiences, and contexts, as well as the relationships between the media industries, state, and capitalist economies. Thus the study of communication and culture was integrated within critical social theory and became an important part of a theory of contemporary society, in which culture and communication were playing ever more significant roles.[22]

BRITISH CULTURAL STUDIES AND ITS LEGACY

The Frankfurt School developed their model of the culture industry in the decades from the 1930s through the 1950s, and then did not develop any significantly new or innovative approaches to media culture. British cultural studies emerged in the 1960s as a project of approaching culture from critical and multidisciplinary perspectives which was instituted in England by the Birmingham Centre for Contemporary Cultural Studies and others.[23] British cultural studies situates culture within a theory of social production and reproduction, specifying the ways that cultural forms served either to further social domination, or to enable people to resist and struggle against domination. Society is conceived as a hierarchical and antagonistic set of social relations characterized by the oppression of subordinate class, gender, race, ethnic, and national strata. Building on Gramsci's model of hegemony and counterhegemony, cultural studies analyze "hegemonic," or ruling, social and cultural forms of domination, and seek "counterhegemonic" forces of resistance and struggle.[24]

For Gramsci, societies maintained their stability through a combination of force and hegemony, with some institutions and groups violently exerting power to maintain social boundaries (i.e. the police, military, vigilante groups, etc.), while other institutions (like religion, schooling, or the media) serve to induce consent to the dominant order through establishing the hegemony, or ideological dominance, of a specific type of social order (i.e. liberal capitalism, fascism, white supremacy, democratic socialism, communism, or whatever).

Hegemony theory involved both analysis of current systems of domination and the ways that specific political groups achieved hegemonic power (i.e. Thatcherism or Reaganism) *and* the delineation of counterhegemonic forces, groups, and ideas that could contest and overturn the existing hegemony. British cultural studies was thus connected with a political project of social transformation in which location of forms of domination and resistance would aid the process of political struggle.

Richard Johnson, in discussions at a 1990 University of Texas conference on cultural studies, stressed that a distinction should be made between the postmodern concept of "difference" and the Birmingham notion of "antagonism," in which the first concept often refers to a liberal conception of recognizing and tolerating differences, while the notion of antagonism refers to structural forces of domination, in which asymmetrical relations of power exist in sites of conflict. There is indeed an important difference between mere oppositions and differences (such as up/down, day/night, 0/1) through which linguistic systems are formed and in which opposing terms are opposite and equal, as opposed to relations of antagonism (workers/bosses, men/women, whites/blacks) in which the terms of difference are of unequal power and exist in relations of inequality and antagonism. Within such relations, oppressed individuals struggle to overcome structures of domination in a variety of arenas.

The key point here is that it is struggles against domination, against subordination, which are the ones focused on by a critical cultural studies. Not just any struggle and resistance, but those against domination, against structural relations of inequality and oppression are the ones highlighted by the critical cultural studies that I am concerned to develop.

Cultural studies thus situates culture within a socio-historical context in which culture promotes domination or resistance, and criticizes forms of culture that foster subordination. In this way, cultural studies can be distinguished from idealist, textualist, and extreme discourse theories which only recognize linguistic forms as constitutive of culture and subjectivity. Cultural studies by contrast is materialist in that it focuses on the material origins and effects of culture and the ways that culture is imbricated in process of domination or resistance.

Cultural studies thus requires a social theory that analyzes the system and structure of domination and forces of resistance. Since capital and economic relations have played a key role in structuring contemporary societies (often referred to as "capitalist" or "democratic capitalist" societies), Marxism has played an important role from the beginning of cultural studies, though there have been fierce battles concerning *which* forms of Marxist theory and more recently there have been sharp rejections of Marxist perspectives (see Bennett 1992 and Fiske 1993).[25] Classically, however, cultural studies has seen society as a system of domination in which institutions like the family, schooling, church, workplace, media, and the state control individuals and provide structures of domination against which individuals striving for more freedom and power must struggle.

Cultural studies, therefore, like the critical theory of the Frankfurt School, develops theoretical models of the relationship between the economy, state, society, culture, and everyday life, and thus depends on the problematics of contemporary social theory. Yet cultural studies also draws significantly on theories of culture. Crucially, cultural studies subverts the high and low culture distinction – like postmodern theory and unlike the Frankfurt School – and thus valorizes cultural forms like film, television, and popular music dismissed by previous approaches to culture which tended to utilize literary theory to analyze cultural forms, or to focus primarily, or even solely, on the artifacts of high culture.

Yet, as Aronowitz has argued (1993: 127ff.), British cultural studies has tended to ignore high culture, erasing it, with few exceptions, from their field of inquiry. They might be contrasted in this regard with the Frankfurt School, which celebrated the oppositional qualities of certain sorts of high culture, especially critical modernism, and with postmodernism, an aesthetic reaction against high modernism that mixed features of so-called high and low culture. British cultural studies, however, have generally failed to engage modernism, or other forms of high culture, and thus overlook the potentials for opposition and subversion, as well as ideology, in the works which some of its practitioners dismiss as elitist high culture. This is curious since a group of theorists around the magazine *Screen*, which was of signal importance in developing cultural theory in Britain and elsewhere during the 1970s, celebrated the oppositional quality of modernism against forms of realism and media culture, thus replicating the Frankfurt split. In retrospect, it seems better to consider the conservative and oppositional force and effects of all forms of culture. Though one should also reject the rigid high/low culture split that vitiated the Frankfurt School and *Screen* theory, which reserved emancipatory effects solely for the products of oppositional modernism while dismissing all forms of popular or mass culture as mere ideology.

A question of terminology

The innovation of British cultural studies, then, was to see the importance of media culture and how it is involved in processes of domination and resistance. Yet there is some debate concerning the proper terminology to describe the objects of those forms of culture that permeate everyday life in the familiar form of such things as radio or television. Raymond Williams and the members of the Birmingham school were responsible for the rejection of the term "mass culture," which they argue, properly I believe, tends to be elitist, erecting a binary opposition between high and low, that is contemptuous of "the masses" and its culture. The concept of "mass culture" is also monolithic and homogeneous, and thus neutralizes cultural contradictions and dissolves oppositional practices and groups into a neutral concept of "mass."

I would also, however, reject the term "popular culture" which John Fiske (1989a and 1989b) and other contemporary practitioners of cultural studies have unproblematically adopted (i.e. Grossberg 1989 and 1992). The term "popular" suggests that media culture arises from the people. The term also covers over the fact that it is a top-down form of culture which often reduces the audience to a passive receiver of predigested meanings. As used by Fiske, Grossberg, and others, "popular culture" collapses the distinction between culture produced by the people, or "popular classes," contrasted to mass-produced media culture, thus revelling in a "cultural populism" (McGuigan 1992) that often uncritically celebrates media and consumer culture.

Initially, the term "popular" was used by two of the founders of British cultural studies to refer to a relatively autonomous working-class culture that was "of the people."[26] The discourse of the "popular" has also long been utilized in Latin America and elsewhere to describe art produced by and for the people themselves as an oppositional sphere to mainstream or hegemonic culture, which is often a colonial culture, imposed from above. Thus, in Latin America and elsewhere, "popular forces" describe groups struggling against domination and oppression, while "popular culture" describes culture of, by, and for the people, in which they produce and participate in cultural practices that articulate their experience and aspirations. Calling mass-mediated commercial products of the culture industries "popular culture" thus collapses a distinction between two very different sorts of culture.

The concept of "popular culture" also presents a celebratory gloss associated with the Popular Culture Association, which often engages in uncritical affirmations of all that is "popular." Since this term is associated in the U.S. with individuals and groups that often eschew critical, theoretically informed, and political approaches to culture, it is risky to use the term "popular culture," though Fiske has tried to provide it with an inflection consistent with the left-populist and socially critical approach of cultural studies. In a 1991 interview, Fiske defines the "popular" as that which audiences make of and do with the commodities of the culture industries (see also Fiske 1989a and 1989b). He argues that progressives should appropriate the term "popular," wresting it from conservatives and liberals, using it as part of an arsenal of concepts in a cultural politics of opposition and resistance (discussion in Austin, September 1990).

Consequently, even the vocabulary of cultural studies is contested, with no agreement on the basic terms used to describe its field. Indeed, in recent years, new schools of cultural studies have emerged in Australia, Canada, the United States and elsewhere, utilizing different methods, concepts, strategies, and approaches. There is thus a plurality of cultural studies and a series of debates over its methods, focuses, politics, whether it should or should not be institutionalized, and so forth.

Moreover, there are problems with some of the basic vocabulary of many contemporary versions of cultural studies and thus the key concepts are unstable, constantly being challenged and revised. In view of the contest over terminology, each intervention in the field of cultural studies needs to lay out and explicate its critical language, distinguish itself from other discourses, and clarify its own specific use of the vocabulary. In my view, more debate is needed as to whether using the term "popular culture" in any form risks blunting the critical edge of cultural studies, and whether it is thus simply better to avoid ideologically loaded terms like "mass culture" and "popular culture." A possible move within cultural studies would therefore simply be to take culture itself as the field of one's studies without divisions into the high and the low, the popular and the elite – though, of course, these distinctions can be strategically deployed in certain contexts. Thus, I believe that instead of using ideological labels like "mass" and "popular," one could simply talk of culture and communication and develop a "cultural studies" cutting across the full range of media and culture.

In this book, I am adopting the concept of "media culture" to delineate the subject matter of my investigations. The term "media culture" has the advantage of signifying both the nature and form of the artifacts of the culture industries (i.e. culture) and their mode of production and distribution (i.e. media technologies and industries). It avoids ideological terms like "mass culture" and "popular culture" and calls attention to the circuit of production, distribution, and reception through which media culture is produced, distributed, and consumed. The term breaks down artificial barriers between the fields of cultural, media, and communications studies and calls attention to the interconnection of culture and communications media in the constitution of media culture, thus breaking down reified distinctions between "culture" and "communication."[27]

In fact, the distinction between "culture" and "communications" is arbitrary and rigid, and should be deconstructed. Whether one takes "culture" as the artifacts of high culture, the ways in which people live their lives, the context of human behavior, or whatever, it is intimately bound up with communication. All culture, to become a social artifact, and thus properly "culture," is both a mediator of and mediated by communication, and is thus communicational by nature. Yet "communication," in turn, is mediated by culture, it is a mode through which culture is disseminated and rendered actual and effective. There is no communication without culture and no culture without communication, so drawing a rigid distinction between them, and claiming that one side is a legitimate object of a disciplinary study, while the other term is relegated to a different discipline is an excellent example of the myopia and futility of arbitrary academic divisions of labor.[28]

In any case, British cultural studies presents an approach that allows us to avoid cutting up the field of media/culture/communications into high and low, popular vs. elite, and to see all forms of media culture and communication as worthy of scrutiny and criticism. It allows approaches to culture and communication that force us to appraise their politics and to make political discriminations between different types of artifacts that have different political effects. Like other multicultural approaches, it brings the study of race, gender, and class into the forefront of the study of media culture and communication.[29] It also adopts a critical approach that, like that of the Frankfurt School, but without some of its flaws, interprets culture within society and situates the study of culture within the field of contemporary social theory and oppositional politics.

The term "media culture" also has the advantage of signifying that our culture *is* a media culture, that the media have colonized culture, that they are the primary vehicle for the distribution and dissemination of culture, that the mass media of communications have supplanted previous modes of culture like the book or spoken word, that we live in a world in which media dominate leisure and culture. Media culture is thus the dominant form and site of culture in contemporary societies.

A question of politics

Media culture is also the site where battles are fought for the control of society. Feminists and antifeminists, liberals and conservatives, radicals and defenders of the status quo, struggle for cultural power not only in the medium of news and information, but also in the domain of entertainment, as I shall demonstrate throughout this book. The media are intimately connected with power and open the study of culture to the vicissitudes of politics and the slaughterhouse of history. They help shape our view of the world, public opinion, values and behavior, and are thus an important forum of social power and struggle.

From the beginning, the work of the Birmingham group was oriented toward the crucial political problems of their age and milieu and focused intently on the politics of culture. Some of the first work which defined British cultural studies, such as Richard Hoggart's *The Uses of Literacy* (1958), indicated how individuals created their identities and lives through their cultural resources. The first half of Hoggart's book details how working-class communities in Britain traditionally created oppositional cultures to the mainstream, and then describes how they were being eroded by the development of a national culture and processes of cultural homogenization directed by the state, schooling, and the media. This was also a theme of such major early influences on British cultural studies as Raymond Williams (1958 and 1962) and E.P. Thompson (1963).

From the 1960s, British cultural studies began to indicate how media culture was producing identities and ways of seeing and acting that integrated individuals into the mainstream culture (Hall and Whannel 1964).The Birmingham group's early focus on class and ideology thus derived from their acute sense of the oppressive and systemic effects of class in British society and the struggles of the 1960s against class inequality and oppression. Studies of subcultures in Britain sought to search for new agents of social change when it appeared that sectors of the working class were being integrated into the existing system and conservative ideologies and parties. Their attempts to reconstruct Marxism were influenced as well by 1960s struggles and political movements. The turn toward feminism, often conflicted, was directly influenced by the feminist movement, while the turn toward race as a significant factor of study was fuelled by the antiracist struggles of the day. The move in British cultural studies toward focus on education and pedagogy was related to political concern with the continuing bourgeois hegemony despite the struggles of the 1960s. The right turn in British politics with Thatcher's victory led in the late 1970s to concern with understanding the authoritarian populism of the new conservative hegemony.

In other words, the focus of British cultural studies at any given moment was mediated by the struggles in the present political conjuncture and their major work was thus conceived as political interventions. Their studies of ideology, domination and resistance, and the politics of culture, directed cultural studies toward analyzing cultural artifacts, practices, and institutions within existing networks of power and of showing how culture both provided tools and forces of domination and resources for resistance and struggle. This political focus intensified emphasis on the effects of culture and audience use of cultural artifacts, which provided an extremely productive focus on audiences and reception, topics that had been neglected in most previous text-based approaches to culture.[30]

Yet, especially as it has developed in the United States, many current configurations of cultural studies are too one-sided, producing new bifurcations of the field and, in part, occluding the field of communications proper by focusing too intently on cultural texts and audience reception. In his study of Madonna, for instance, John Fiske writes:

A cultural analysis, then, will reveal both the way the dominant ideology is structured into the text and into the reading subject, and those textual features that enable negotiated, resisting, or oppositional readings to be made. Cultural analysis reaches a satisfactory conclusion when the ethnographic studies of the historically and socially located meanings that *are* made are related to the semiotic analysis of the text.

(Fiske 1989a: 98)

This focus on text/audience, however, leaves out many mediations that should be part of cultural studies, including analyses of how texts are produced within the context of the political economy and system of production of culture, as well as how audiences and their subjectivities are produced by a variety of social institutions, practices, and ideologies. Consequently, in the following studies, I introduce the term "media cultural studies" to describe the project of analyzing the complex relations between texts, audiences, media industries, politics, and the sociohistorical context in specific conjunctures. In the studies in this book, for instance, I focus on some dominant forms of culture within U.S. society from the early 1980s to the present.

I argue that focusing on texts and audiences to the exclusion of analysis of the social relations and institutions in which texts are produced and consumed truncates cultural studies, as does analysis of reception that fails to indicate how audiences are produced through their social relations and how to some extent culture itself helps produce audiences and their reception of texts. Indeed, there is the danger of the fetishism of the audience in the recent emphasis on the importance of reception and audience construction of meanings. Thus, there has been a large-scale shift in emphasis from focus on text and the context of its production to emphasis on the audience and reception, in some cases producing a new dogmatism whereby the audience, or reader, alone produces meaning. The texts, society, and system of production and reception disappear in the solipsistic ecstasy of the textual producer, in which there is no text outside of reading – resulting in a parody of Derrida's *bon mot* that there is nothing outside of the text.

Furthermore, there has been a fetishism of resistance in some versions of cultural studies. Within the tradition of cultural studies reception research, there has been a call to distinguish between dominant, negotiated, and oppositional readings (Hall 1980b: taken up in Fiske's work). This schema distinguishes between "dominant" readings, whereby audiences appropriate texts in line with the interests of the dominant culture and the ideological intentions of a text, as when audiences feel pleasure in the restoration of male power, law and order, and social stability at the end of a film like *Die Hard*, after the hero and representatives of authority eliminate the terrorists who had taken over a highrise corporate headquarters. An oppositional reading, by contrast, celebrates the resistance to this reading in audience appropriation of a text, as when Fiske (1993: 3ff.) observes resistance to dominant readings when, during repeated viewings of a videotape of the film in a shelter for the homeless, the inhabitants cheered the destruction of police and authority figures in the scenes in which the villains take over the building.

There is a tendency in cultural studies to celebrate resistance *per se* without distinguishing between types and forms of resistance (a similar problem resides with indiscriminate celebration of audience pleasure in certain reception studies). Thus, resistance to social authority by the homeless evidenced in their viewing of *Die Hard* could serve to strengthen brutal masculist behavior and encourage manifestations of physical violence to solve social problems. Violence, however, as Sartre, Fanon, and Marcuse, among others, have argued, can be either emancipatory, directed at forces of oppression, or reactionary, directed at popular forces struggling against oppression, or arbitrarily exploding in any direction. Many feminists, in turn, see all violence as forms of brute masculist behavior and many people involved in peace studies see it as a failed form of conflict resolution.[31]

Indeed, the resistance that Fiske valorizes in his *Die Hard* analysis is not resistance at all but a very conventional replication of pleasure in violence that eliminates those who one positions as "bad." Audiences are taught to get pleasure out of seeing "bad guys" violently eliminated and Fiske's homeless men are simply reacting to the codes and conventions of Hollywood entertainment. To be sure, they are reacting with pleasure to the violent actions of those coded by the film as "villains" against those coded as "good guys" or innocent victims, so there is a reversal of the usual "good" and "bad" conventions, but the audience reaction valorized by Fiske as "resistance" is simply a visceral response to preconditioned Hollywood mechanisms that produce pleasure in the violent elimination of those deemed to be "bad" and deserving to be targets of violence.

In fact, Fiske's celebration of *Die Hard* fails to contextualize it within the cycle of male rampage films analyzed by Susan Jeffords in *Hard Bodies* (1994). *Die Hard* was one of a cycle of compensatory male fantasies that responded to the emergence of feminism and the conservative male response which refused to share power with women and that resisted feminist ideas. A series of masculist ideological extravaganzas starring such ultra-macho men as Sylvestor Stallone, Arnold Schwarzenegger, and Bruce Willis featured male superheroes as the necessary solution to society's problems, thus promoting an ideology of male supremacy. As the "white male paranoia" and conservative response to feminism intensified, these masculist fantasies became ever more brutal with films like *Die Hard II*, *Young Guns II*, and the like doubling or even tripling the acts of redemptive male violence (see Gerbner 1992).

Moreover, unqualified valorization of audience resistance to preferred meanings as good *per se* can lead to uncritical populist celebrations of the text and audience pleasure in its use of cultural artifacts. This approach, taken to an extreme, would lose its critical perspective and would lead to a populist positive gloss on audience experience of whatever is being studied. Such studies also might lose sight of the manipulative and conservative effects of certain types of media culture, and thus serve the interests of the culture industries as they are presently constituted and those groups who use the culture industries to promote their own interests and agendas.

Accompanying the fetishism of resistance is the fetishism of struggle. Fiske, for instance, makes "the popular" a terrain of struggle where audiences resist domination, struggle to produce their own meanings and pleasures, and evade social control and manipulation (1989a and 1989b). Political struggle is thus displaced into "struggle" for meanings and pleasure, while "resistance" is equated with the evasion of social responsibility, as in Fiske's examples of youth in video arcades, hanging out on the beach, surfing, or loitering in malls. Modes of domination are occluded, and resistance and struggle are depoliticized and rendered harmless, thus providing an ideology of "popular culture" perfectly congruent with the interests of the powers that be. Such "resistance" does not really challenge the existing structures of power, nor does it alter the material conditions or ameliorate the structures of oppression of those "resisting" by producing meanings and pleasures in the domain of "popular culture."

I am also put off by what I take to be a fetishism of audience pleasure in some current versions of cultural studies. Reacting against a somewhat ascetic attitude toward certain types of culture in the older radical theory, arguments have been made that attention should be paid to people's pleasure in popular film, television, or other forms of culture, and that this pleasure should be positively appraised and appropriated. While this was a useful move in many ways, it has led, I fear, to valorizing certain forms of culture precisely because they are popular and produce pleasure. Such a sweeping and uncritical approach disdains distinguishing between types of pleasure and the ways that pleasure can bind individuals to conservative, sexist or racist positions, as when the *Rambo*, *Die Hard* or the *Terminator* films mobilize pleasure around extremely masculist and violent behavior.

Pleasure itself is neither natural nor innocent. Pleasure is learned and is thus intimately bound up with power and knowledge. Since Foucault, it has become a commonplace that power and knowledge are intimately intertwined and that pleasure is bound up with both. We learn what to enjoy and what we should avoid. We learn when to laugh and when to cheer (and laugh tracks on TV sitcoms and entertainment cue us in case we don't get it ourselves). A system of power and privilege thus conditions our pleasures so that we seek certain socially sanctioned pleasures and avoid others. Some people learn to laugh at racist jokes and others learn to feel pleasure at the brutal use of violence.

Pleasures are often, therefore, a conditioned response to certain stimuli and should thus be problematized, along with other forms of experience and behavior, and interrogated as to whether they contribute to the production of a better life and society, or help trap us into modes of everyday life that ultimately oppress and degrade us. Resistance and pleasure cannot therefore be valorized *per se* as progressive elements of the appropriation of cultural texts, rather one needs to describe the specific conditions that give rise to the resistance or pleasure at stake and their specific effects. If one wishes to maintain a critical perspective, one must also make difficult normative discriminations as to whether the resistance, oppositional reading, or pleasure in a given experience or artifact is progressive or reactionary, emancipatory or destructive. Critical practice must seek norms of critique and make critical discriminations in appraising the nature and effects of cultural artifacts and practices – a task that I undertake in different contexts in the following studies.

Earlier cultural studies wanted to balance the ideological and the resistant, the hegemonic/dominant and the oppositional. This balancing act is evident in Hall's articles (1980b and 1981) "Encoding/Decoding" and "Deconstructing the Popular," which acknowledge the power of the mass media to shape and enforce ideological hegemony, the power of the people to resist ideology, and the contradictory moments and effects of media culture. This form of cultural studies thus attempts to negotiate the split between manipulation theory, which sees mass culture and society in general as dominating individuals, and populist resistance theory which emphasizes the power of individuals to oppose, resist, and struggle against the dominant culture. Such a dual optic is also evident in the work of E.P. Thompson (1963) which stresses both workers' abilities to resist capitalist domination and forms of cooptation, and Dick Hebdige's *Subculture* (1979) which presents rock music styles and youth culture both as forms of refusal and as commerical modes of incorporation of subcultural resistance into the dominant consumer culture.

Thus one should attempt to avoid the one-sided approaches of manipulation and resistance theory in favor of combining these perspectives in one's analyses. In a way, certain tendencies of the Frankfurt School can correct some of the limitations of cultural studies, just as British cultural studies can help overcome some of the limitations of the Frankfurt School.[32] The Frankfurt School social theory always situated its objects of analysis within the framework of the development of contemporary capitalism. While this sometimes led to reduction of all culture to commodities, ideology, and instruments of ruling class domination, it also eluci- dated the origins of all mass-produced cultural artifacts within the capitalist production and accumulation process, and thus forced attention to the economic origins and ideological nature of many of the artifacts of media culture. Likewise, the Frankfurt School emphasis on manipulation called attention to the power and seductiveness of the artifacts of the cultural industries and the ways that they could integrate individuals into the established order. The emphasis too on how the cultural industries produce "something for everyone, so that none can escape," suggests how difference and plurality are utilized to integrate individuals into the existing society.

Difference sells. Capitalism must constantly multiply markets, styles, fads, and artifacts to keep absorbing consumers into its practices and lifestyles. The mere valorization of "difference" as a mark of opposition can simply help market new styles and artifacts if the difference in question and its effects are not adequately appraised. It can also promote a form of identity politics in which each group affirms its own specificity and limits politics to the group's own interests, thus overlooking common forces of oppression. Such difference or identity politics aids "divide and conquer" strategies which ultimately serve the interests of the powers that be.[33]

The Frankfurt School emphasis on cooptation – even of seemingly radical and subversive impulses – raises the question of the nature and effects of "resistant readings," beloved by some cultural theorists. It suggests that even production of alternative meanings and resistance to "preferred meanings" may serve as effective ways of absorbing individuals into the established society. Producing meanings can create pleasures that integrate individuals into consumer practices which above all profit media industries. This possibility forces those who valorize resistance to emphasize *what sort of resistance*, what effects, and what difference does the resistance make?

The Frankfurt School was excellent at tracing the lines of domination within media culture, but was less adept at ferreting out moments of resistance and opposition. Yet it always placed its analysis of media and audience within existing relations of production and domination, whereas many studies of the audience and reception often fail to situate the reception of culture in the context of social relations of power and domination. Furthermore, there remain text-centered approaches within cultural studies which engage in theoretically informed readings of texts without considering their production, reception, or anchorage in an institutional organization of culture that takes varying specific forms in different countries, or regions, at different times in history – which is to say that textualist approaches often avoid study of the production and political economy of culture and even the historical context of culture.

While emphasis on the audience and reception was an excellent correction to the one-sidedness of purely textual analysis, I believe that in recent years cultural studies has overemphasized reception and textual analysis, while underemphasizing the production of culture and its political economy.[34] While earlier, the Birmingham group regularly focused attention on media institutions and practices, and the relations between media forms and broader social forms and ideologies, this emphasis has waned in recent years, to the detriment of much current work in cultural studies, I would argue. For instance, in his classical programmatic article, "Encoding/Decoding," Stuart Hall began his analysis by using Marx's *Grundrisse* as a model to trace the articulations of "a continuous circuit," encompassing– production–distribution–consumption–production" (1980b: 128ff.). He concretizes this model with focus on how media institutions produce messages, how they circulate, and how audiences use or decode the messages to produce meaning. Hall claimed that:

> The abstraction of texts from the social practices which produced them and the institutional sites where they were elaborated was a fetishization. . . . This obscured how a particular ordering of culture came to be produced and sustained: the circumstances and conditions of cultural reproduction which the operations of the 'selective tradition' rendered natural, 'taken for granted.' But the process of ordering (arrangement, regulation) is always the result of concrete sets of practices and relations.
>
> (Hall 1980a: 27)

Against the erasure of the system of cultural production, distribution, and reception, Hall called for problematizing culture and "making visible" the processes through which certain forms of culture became dominant (ibid.).[35] Raymond Williams, one of the formative influences on British cultural studies, called for a "cultural materialism . . . the analysis of all forms of signification . . . within the actual means and conditions of their production" (1981: 64–5), focusing attention on the need to situate cultural analysis within its socio-economic relations. Moreover, in a 1983 lecture published in 1985/6, Richard Johnson provided a model of cultural studies, similar to Hall's earlier model, based on a model of the circuits of production, textuality, and reception, parallel to the circuits of capital stressed by Marx, illustrated by a diagram that stressed the importance of production and distribution. Although Johnson emphasized the importance of analysis of production in cultural studies and criticized *Screen* for abandoning this perspective in favor of more idealist and textualist approaches (pp. 63ff.), much work in cultural studies has replicated this neglect. One could indeed argue that most recent cultural studies have tended to neglect analyses of the circuits of political economy and production in favor of text- and audience-based analyses.

Furthermore, there is a danger that cultural studies in various parts of the world might lose the critical and political edge of earlier forms of British cultural studies. Cultural studies could easily degenerate into a sort of eclectic populism of the sort evident in some of the work of the Popular Culture Association which is largely celebratory and uncritical of the textual artifacts that it deals with. Neglecting political economy, celebrating the audience and the pleasures of the popular, neglecting social class and ideology, and failing to analyze or criticize the politics of cultural texts will make cultural studies merely another academic subdivision, harmless and ultimately of benefit primarily to the culture industries themselves. Avoiding such a conservative development of cultural studies, I submit, requires a multiperspectival approach that pays attention to the production of culture, to the texts themselves, and to their reception by the audience. This requires a variety of disciplinary and critical perspectives linking cultural studies, ultimately, to critical social theory and radical democratic politics.

The position that I take on media and culture throughout these studies could also be denoted a form of cultural materialism, a key term that I intend in two senses. With Raymond Williams, I see cultural materialism as "the analysis of all forms of signification . . . within the actual means and conditions of production" (Williams 1981: 64–5). This dictum suggests that to adequately analyze media culture we must situate the objects of analysis within the system of production, and I would add distribution and consumption, within which they are produced and received. A cultural materialist approach thus stresses the importance of the political economy of culture, of the system that constrains what can and what cannot be produced, that provides limits and possibilities for cultural production.

Media production is thus intimately imbricated in relations of power and serves to reproduce the interests of powerful social forces, promoting either domination or empowering individuals for resistance and struggle. But a cultural materialism also focuses on the material effects of media culture, insisting that its images, spectacles, discourses, and signs have material effects on audiences. For a cultural materialism, media texts seduce, fascinate, move, position, and influence their audiences. Media culture has its material effects, its effectivity, and it is one of the goals of cultural studies to analyze how specific texts and types of media culture affect audiences, what sort of actual effects the artifacts of media culture exercise, and what sort of potential counterhegemonic effects and possibilities for resistance and struggle are also found in the works of media culture.

I shall flesh out this approach and provide examples throughout the book. First, however, I want to engage a recent move within the field of cultural studies.

A POSTMODERN CULTURAL STUDIES?

Arguments have emerged in recent years for a postmodern cultural studies. Some theorists like Denzin (1991) and Grossberg (1992) aggressively link cultural studies to the postmodern turn, while many others simply assume that the terrain of cultural studies is an allegedly postmodern culture and society, without really defining the terms, noting what is at stake, or making an argument concerning why their method or subject matter is indeed "postmodern."[36] In fact, the term "postmodern" is perhaps one of the most abused and confusing terms in the lexicon of contemporary critical theory. The terms "modern" and "postmodern" are used to cover a bewildering diversity of cultural artifacts, social phenomena, and theoretical discourses, and the concept of the postmodern requires constant scrutiny, clarification, and criticism.

During a spring 1993 trip to England, for example, I discovered a newspaper article in the *Guardian* titled "The postmodern politician" and found that the topic was just another boring old conservative with no discernible claims to be "postmodern." Upon returning to the United States, I picked up a copy of the *Washington Post Weekly* and noted a headline describing the Clinton administration's Dee Dee Myers as "the postmodern press secretary" and a reading of the article suggested that she was allegedly "postmodern" because she arched her eyebrow and was ironic in her speech. And, *Newsweek* published an article on Bill Clinton, "The postmodern president," without any analysis of what made him postmodern, in which the term is simply used as a buzzword to catch attention (January 10, 1994).

But the prize caption is awarded to the *New York Times* (May 12, 1993) for a headline: "Forget the bologna on white, here comes the post-modern sandwich." Scrutiny of this article indicated that modern sandwiches featured fat chunks of meat while "post-modern constructions . . . rely more on roasted or marinated vegetables than meat and that stylishly recycle leftovers like grilled vegetables, lamb, chicken, or fish" (p. B1). One may laugh at such muddled pop media usages . of the discourse, but things are often not much clearer when we turn to the theoretical discourses of academic books or presentations. Frequently, academic commentators simply assume that we are in a postmodern age without any specific analysis. Often usage of the term "postmodern" points to phenomena that are arguably modern and the discourse is merely used as a synonym for the contemporary moment in which we live, or contemporary novelties, without substantive analysis. My favorite example concerns a sociology professor who in being asked to describe more clearly what he meant by the term "postmodern" answered that the best description of "our postmodern society" was found in the passage in "The Communist Manifesto" in which Marx and Engels describe a state "where all that is solid melts into air." Of course, as Marshall Berman has shown (1982), the "Manifesto" is a virtual hymn to modernity and is a key text of modern theory.

For other examples of undertheorized uses of the term "postmodern" as a synonym for our contemporary society, one might look at the Introduction to the anthology of collected papers from a 1990 University of Illinois conference on cultural studies written by the editors (see Grossberg *et al.* 1992). There are references to "our postmodern age" without any argument or clarification concerning what makes it "postmodern," what constitutes the break with modernity, and what are its new features (ibid., 2, 6). Moreover, in a long footnote near the end of the Introduction, the editors describe the grounding and trajectory of cultural studies as a response to modernity, modernization, and modernism (ibid., 15–16).[37] Yet the editors fail to note the paradox concerning the relevance of cultural studies in a postmodern era if it is a product of and expression of the modern era (which much postmodern theory claims is over, thus requiring new approaches to culture and society, new politics, new modes of thought, etc.). Various authors in the collection *Cultural Studies* use the discourse of the postmodern, but usually fail to provide a sustained discussion and use the term in a variety of conflicting ways. It is therefore not clear what imprecise and muddled use of the term contributes, and one suspects that ultimately the discourse of the postmodern has produced more confusion than clarity, more muddle than illumination.[38]

Many theorists of the postmodern, or those who systematically deploy the term, often merely list a set of arbitrary characteristics which are said to be "postmodern," illustrated by questionable examples. Many of these lists and examples also cite key modern characteristics or artifacts as examples of the "postmodern,"[39] and thus fail to adequately theorize the phenomena. Some who argue for a postmodern turn in cultural studies, like Denzin (1991) arguably overdefine the term, while others underdefine it. For Denzin, everything that occurs in post-World-War-II U.S. society is "postmodern" and he provides list after list of its defining features, many of which could easily be assimilated to lists characterizing modern phenomena.

One of the more interesting attempts to link cultural studies with postmodern theory is found in Dick Hebdige's *Hiding in the Light* (1988). Hebdige wishes "to explore the genuinely life-enhancing and positive dimensions" opened up by the various debates of the "post" and to assimilate its insights into a revitalized cultural studies. After a long list of some of the things described as "postmodern," Hebdige notes that the very multiplicity of phenomena designated as postmodern suggests that "we are in the presence of a buzzword." Yet rather than simply concluding that the term is meaningless, Hebdige prefers to believe, with Raymond Williams,

that the more complexly and contradictorily nuanced a word is the more likely
it is to have formed the focus for historically significant debates, to have
occupied a semantic ground in which something precious and important was felt
to be embedded. I take, then as my (possibly ingenuous) starting point, that the
degree of semantic complexity and overload surrounding the term 'postmodernism' at the moment signals that a significant number of people with conflicting
interests and opinions feel that there is something sufficiently important at stake
here to be worth struggling and arguing over.

(Williams 1988: 182)

After delineating some of the key positions of postmodern theory, Hebdige proposes the yoking of some new postmodern perspectives to the older neo-Gramscian
program of linking cultural studies to the project of promoting radical social and
cultural change, to advance new solidarities, new struggles, new movements to
promote the cause of progressive social transformation. But, as he points out, this
is a different program, a different version of Marxism, than the older more orthodox
socialist revolutionary programs of, say, an Althusser, which ultimately replicated
old-fashioned Marxist party politics. The neo-Gramscian program by contrast has
no guarantees, no teleologies, no grand narrative of emancipation, no totalizing or
reductive discourses or politics, no privileging of a class or social group, no home
or solid basis from which to struggle, but still holds out the hope that new
solidarities, new forms of struggles, will emerge and sees the need to foster hope,
to promote radicalism, to hold out the possibility of more radical change, to bring
the light of radical critique and politics to the blinding light of the media, to
revitalize radical theory and politics, however modestly and tenuously.

I too am attracted to such neo-Gramscian perspectives and share Hebdige's
desire to produce new syntheses of cultural studies with other major theoretical
discourses of the present. I am also sympathetic to Hebdige's sense that "it is only
by grounding our analysis in the study of *particular* images and objects" that we
can overcome the limitations of the highly theoretical discourses of the past decades
and "the vertigo of postmodernism" (1988: back cover). But in his concluding
appendixes, Hebdige moves back and forth from affirming and distancing himself
from postmodern positions and thus ultimately is unclear how he positions himself
toward the discourse of the postmodern.

In the studies that follow, I shall carefully interrogate various uses of the
discourse of the postmodern to see if the term clarifies or confuses understanding
of the phenomenon under question. Although the discourse of the "postmodern"
often muddles more than it illuminates, it has a certain symptomatic value. Superficial and sloppy usage of the term points to phenomena or topics that need to be
theorized and thus the term is often a sign that something is under- or poorly
theorized. Negatively, the term is often an empty signifier and sign that more
concrete theorization is being avoided and is needed. Such empty use of the
discourse is a sign of lazy theorizing, the avoidance of difficult thinking and
analysis, and the replacing of theoretical analysis with a popular buzzword. But,

positively, it is a sign that something is new and needs to be comprehended and theorized. Thus, the term "postmodern" is often a placeholder, or semiotic marker, that indicates that there are new phenomena that require mapping and theorizing. Use of the term may also be a sign that something is bothering us, that new confusing phenomena are appearing that we cannot adequately categorize or get a grip on.

Such under- or poorly theorized discourse reduces the "postmodern" to the status of a piece of jargon, an often confused attempt to distinguish oneself from the commitments of modern theory, or to appear hip and cool. Another problem arises in that more articulated and compelling discourses of the postmodern are themselves often in conflict with each other (see the discussion of different versions of postmodern theory in Best and Kellner 1991). Thus, there is no shared, or agreed upon, discourse of the postmodern, but rather a series of competing paradigms and discourses. Moreover, new phenomena are constantly emerging which are claimed to be "postmodern." Thus, whether one is attending to the more rarified theoretical discourses of the present, or often laughable popularizations of the postmodern, such as the "postmodern sandwich" that I referred to above, the phenomena and discourses of the postmodern are constantly changing, becoming more complex, requiring new mappings and analyses to chart their trajectories.[40]

In order, therefore, for the discourse of the postmodern to have any cognitive content, certain distinctions need to be made and the family of terms of the postmodern must be distinguished from the discourses of the modern. In previous texts, I distinguished between modernity and postmodernity, as two different historical eras; between modernism and postmodernism, as two different aesthetic and cultural styles; and between modern and postmodern theory as two different theoretical discourses (see Kellner 1988; Best and Kellner 1991). Building on these analyses and historical genealogy, I wish to offer some further conceptual clarifications to try to illuminate the complex field of discourse of the modern and postmodern.

To begin, the contemporary discourse of the postmodern first emerged in the fields of culture and in the present epoch the postmodern fever also began in this domain. In the 1960s, a "new sensibility" appeared that defined itself against the abstraction and elitism of modernist art and modern forms of literary criticism. This new sensibility celebrated emergent cultural practices which were characterized by, among other things, breaking down the distinction between high and low art, by incorporating within aesthetic forms a panoply of icons and images of media culture, and by challenging conventional barriers between artist and spectator. These new aesthetic forms – such as the paintings of Andy Warhol or the novels of John Barth and Thomas Pynchon – eventually became known as examples of "postmodernism," as part of new cultural configurations which rejected features of classical modernism.

It is within architecture that the term postmodern first gained widespread currency. Several theorists and architects contrasted new forms of postmodern architecture that rejected the sterile glass and steel buildings associated with the high modernist functionalism of Mies van der Rohe and the international style that championed the same forms everywhere. Building on Robert Venturi's *Learning from Las Vegas* (1972), postmodern architecture appropriated traditional forms, deployed decoration and color eschewed by high modernist architecture, and attempted to adapt architecture to local conditions.

Articulating differences between modernism and postmodernism in literature, cinema, dance, theater, and other arts has proven more difficult, though. The overlaps and continuities here are more striking, and it is difficult to point to specific features of postmodern literature and art that have not been anticipated by modernist forms. Yet while there is not the break or rupture evident in architecture, theorists like Jameson (1991) and Hutcheon (1989) have described constellations of culture that exhibit sufficient shared features for the concept of postmodernism within the arts to have analytic substance, as I shall show in the following studies.[41]

Postmodernism in the arts, however, was often discussed as an element of a new "postmodern culture," "postmodern scene," or "postmodern condition" and broader conceptions of a new era of *postmodernity*, a break with modernity, began emerging in the 1970s in the theories of Baudrillard, Lyotard, and others.[42] In the 1980s, there was a proliferation of discourses on various forms of postmodern culture and society, with Baudrillard claiming that we have entered a new postmodern historical era, a "postmodernity." It also became popular to label a wide range of thinkers from Foucault to Derrida to Baudrillard as "postmodern," as having broken decisively with the assumptions of modern theory, and a variety of types of postmodern theory emerged. There is indeed no one postmodern theory, or one definition of postmodernity as a historical epoch, or of postmodernism in the arts. Instead, these discourses are themselves contested and conflictual with different theorists imposing their own definitions on these concepts.

Thus, the discourse of the postmodern is a cultural and theoretical construct, not a thing or state of affairs. That is, there are no phenomena that are intrinsically "postmodern" which the theorist can then describe. The concepts are generated as theoretical constructs used to interpret a family of phenomena, artifacts, or practices. Thus, the discourses of the postmodern produce their objects, whether a historical epoch of postmodernity, or postmodernism in the arts. Obviously, there are social and historical phenomena from which theorists derive concepts like postmodernity, or practices, artifacts, and artists in the field of culture from whom one derives the term "postmodernism." Yet which phenomena, practices, artifacts, and so on are seen as "postmodern" are themselves a function of the theoretical discourse which denominates some things as "postmodern" and others not.

Consequently, the family of concepts of the postmodern are merely conceptual constructs meant to perform certain interpretive or explanatory tasks and are not transparent terms that merely reflect established states of affairs.[43] Thus, when we are dealing with the discourse of the postmodern, we are operating on the level of theory and discourse and need to make clarifications and distinctions on this level (unless, of course, we are merely using the term as a buzzword, as in the journalistic and theoretical discourses cited above). As Mike Featherstone reminds us (1991:

1ff.), journalists, cultural entrepreneurs, and theorists invent and circulate discourses like the postmodern in order to accrue cultural capital, to distinguish themselves, to promote specific artifacts or practices as being on the cutting-edge, and to circulate new meanings and ideas. The discourse of the postmodern especially attracts younger people on the make, or those who wish to distinguish themselves as avant-garde, although it has also attracted many who wish to revive flagging careers or libidos with sexy new discourse.

Indeed, the emergence of the postmodern has much to do with battles for cultural capital in the present age. One way of contesting previous theories, canons, and models is to declare their obsolescence, or to radically negate their claims to truth, excellence, utility, or whatever. One accrues cultural capital by distinguishing one's work and positions from others, from attaching oneself to popular phenomena, and by joining new theoretical and cultural movements that enable one to identify oneself as hip, cool, with it, and up to date. Joining the postmodern carnival can be fun, allowing one to engage in often promiscuous excursions in which the normal rules and conventions of the proper are put aside, as one seeks new rules or conventions or to escape rule and convention altogether.

But it would be a mistake to merely dismiss the discourse of the postmodern out of hand as a mere fad or ephemeral fashion. For as I write, the discourse has elicited intense attention and controversy for the past decade (1983–93) and there is no end in sight. Although many predicted that the phenomenon was over,[44] there continue to be waves of books, articles, conferences, and discussions of the many modalities of the postmodern. People continue to feel passionately about the postmodern and the discourse obviously speaks to important changes in our culture and society and by now has acquired a certain weight. Postmodern theory has penetrated almost all academic disciplines, producing critiques of modern theory and alternative postmodern theoretical practices in philosophy, social theory, politics, economics, anthropology, geography, and just about every academic field. Groups and individuals marginalized in the society, culture, and university have taken the term as their own and use it to oppose the established order of things. Since many of these individuals are younger, one expects that the discourse will continue to be used for some time to come.

It will be one of the purposes of the following studies to interrogate some dominant discourses of the postmodern to demonstrate confusion, sloppiness, and laziness in many symptomatic uses of the discourse. I will interrogate whether the discourse is useful or not in interpreting specific phenomena in our contemporary culture. Whether or not a discourse or theory is useful can be determined by whether it does or does not illuminate specific phenomena, and helps or hinders particular tasks. One of the aims of these studies is to illuminate and map our contemporary society and culture, so determining the usefulness or uselessness of the discourse of the postmodern will be one of the tasks of the following studies, especially those collected in Part II.

Although it is prudent to be skeptical of extreme postmodern claims that would render obsolescent the assumptions, values, categories, culture, and politics of the modern era, it must be admitted that significant changes are taking place and that many of the old modern theories and categories can no longer adequately describe our contemporary culture, politics, and society. And yet the extreme claims for a postmodern break and rupture do violence to our sense of enduring continuities with the past and the fact that many ideas and phenomena which are claimed to be "postmodern" have their origins or analogues precisely in the modern era. Consequently, I would suggest that we are living between a now aging modern era and a new postmodern era that remains to be adequately conceptualized, charted, and mapped. Historical epochs do not rise and fall in neat patterns or at precise chronological moments. Change between one era and another is always protracted, contradictory, and usually painful. The sense of "betweenness," or transition, requires that one grasp the continuities with the past as well as the novelties of the present and future. Living in a borderland between the old and the new creates tension, insecurity, and even panic, thus producing a troubling and uncertain cultural and social environment.

The following studies attempt to capture some of the tension in living in a situation whose contours are not yet apparent and in which intense conflict is occurring between those conservative forces who wish to maintain the established social order and those who wish to transform it. These cultural wars are replicated in what we might call theory wars between those competing voices who wish to map and guide the construction of the present and future. In the studies that follow, I intervene in this context and propose the development of cultural studies within the framework of critical social theory and radical democratic politics. Indeed, I believe that one cannot do cultural studies without a social theory and that one of the valuable effects of cultural studies is that it can in turn contribute to developing a critical social theory and politics for the present age. This is, of course, parallel to the Frankfurt School claim that a theory of society is needed to illuminate social, political, and cultural phenomena and development, while intensive research into the latter areas can in turn contribute to developing critical social theory. Consequently, I interpret media culture in the context of critical social theory and in turn use media culture to illuminate social phenomena and conditions. Thus, I ultimately intend my media cultural studies as an attempt to situate cultural artifacts within the broader economic, social, and political contexts from which they emerge and in which they have their effects.

NOTES

1 As I argue below, it is Baudrillard and his followers who posit the most extreme rupture between modern and postmodern societies. For discussions of his and other postmodern theories, see Kellner 1989b and 1989c, Best and Kellner 1991, and Kellner 1994a.
2 On "post-Fordism," see Harvey, 1989. On "disorganized capitalism," see Offe 1985 and Lash and Urry 1987. On the "risk society," see Beck 1992.
3 This picture of the leisure and consumer society may be ideological. Recent studies show that the amount of hours devoted to work in the United States is at an all-time high; see Schorr's study of *The Overworked American* (1992). Yet there are also technological

trends that might lead to diminution of the length of the workday. See Gorz 1982 and 1985 and an article in the *New York Times* (November 24, 1993: A1) which indicated that there was a serious movement abroad in Europe to limit work to four days a week.

4 See Kellner and Ryan 1988 for a study of the contest of representations between the mid-1960s and mid-1980s in Hollywood film, and Kellner 1990a for a study of the contested terrain of U.S. television. On the "right turn" in the United States, see Ferguson and Rogers 1986. On the triumph of Thatcherism in England, see Hall and Jacques 1983 and Hall 1990.

5 See Altermann 1992 and the *Newsweek* issue of March 29, 1993 on "White male paranoia" for evidence of the role of conservative think tanks and pundits in shaping public opinion and the continuing conservative offensive on talk radio, television, and other cultural domains.

6 Jeffords (1994) argues that U.S. culture and politics manifested trends toward a "remasculinization of America" after U.S. military defeat in Vietnam, and Faludi (1991) interprets the new masculist culture as a "backlash" against feminism.

7 Convinced against those who argue "against theory" (i.e. Rorty *et al.*) that theories are of use in illuminating our social world, throughout this book I shall reflect on the nature and function of social theories, for it is not at all agreed upon, or evident, what social theories are, what they do, and what are their value and limitations. The theoretical perspectives that I will sketch out are perhaps most influenced by the critical theory of the Frankfurt School (see Kellner 1989a and Bronner and Kellner 1989) and postmodern theory (see Kellner 1989b, 1989c, and Best and Kellner 1991), though I also draw heavily on feminism and multicultural theory, and attempt to develop some new theoretical perspectives to illuminate our present moment.

8 See Howard and Klare 1972. In Europe, by contrast, Marxism was part of the standard intellectual discourse, though it tended to be monopolized by the Marxist parties. On the impact of Marxism on a diverse range of academic fields in the United States, see Ollman and Vernoff, 1982. For Britain, see Anderson 1980 and Davies forthcoming.

9 On the successive waves of feminism that appeared beginning in the United States during the 1960s, see the account in Willis 1984; on feminism in the U.S. in the 1990s, see Faludi 1991 and Brenner 1993. On the unhappy marriage between Marxism and feminism, see Hartman 1981. For an example of psychoanalytic feminism, see Mitchell 1974. For feminism in Britain, see Barrett 1980.

10 John Fiske curiously ascribes the importation and popularity of European theories in the United States and elsewhere to a Reaganism that exposed the falsity of the liberal consensus and the reality of class divisions and inequalities, which supposedly finally rendered pragmatic Americans susceptible to European theories that stressed conflict, inequalities, and struggle (1993: 40). But, in fact, as my narrative argues, the importation of European theories began in the 1960s and intensified in the 1970s and 1980s, well before Reaganism exposed the lies of the liberal consensus.

11 Metaphors are often highly revealing and the shift from conceiving of theories as "weapons of criticism" to "tools in a toolkit" marks a shift from revolutionary theory to milder forms of pragmatism and contextualism. Blending these perspectives, I would argue that theories can be tools or weapons, depending on the context, intentions, and use – a contextualist theory, no doubt, but with radical intent.

12 See Ricoeur 1970; Simons 1990; and Lepenies 1988.

13 The notion of a multiperspectival social theory and cultural studies is sketched out in Kellner 1991; Best and Kellner 1991; and is elaborated throughout this book.

14 Jameson (1991) and Harvey (1989) combine Marxist theory with postmodern theory to provide novel perspectives on contemporary society, while other theorists take more univocal Marxian, Weberian, feminist, or other classical positions on contemporary society, or develop new theoretical models and perspectives; for an overview of contemporary perspectives in social theory, see Ritzer 1990.

15 Many studies exist on the history and genealogy of cultural studies; see Hall 1980a; Johnson 1985/6; Fiske 1986a; O'Connor 1989; Turner 1990; Grossberg 1989; Brantlinger 1990; Agger 1991; During 1993; and Aronowitz 1993. See also the articles in Grossberg *et al.* 1992 and During 1993.

16 On earlier traditions of cultural studies in the U.S., see Carey 1989, and Aronowitz 1993 and for Britain, see Davies forthcoming.

17 Raymond Williams was especially important for cultural studies because of his stress on borders and border crossings. Like the Frankfurt School, he always saw the interconnection between culture and communication, and their connections with the society in which they are produced, distributed, and consumed. Williams also saw how texts embodied the political conflicts and discourses within which they were embedded and reproduced.

18 On the Frankfurt School theory of the culture industries, see Horkheimer and Adorno 1972; the anthology edited by Rosenberg and White 1957; the reader edited by Bronner and Kellner 1989; and the discussion of the Frankfurt School approach in Kellner 1989a.

19 I have analyzed some of these effects from a reconstructed critical theory perspective in analyses of Hollywood film with Michael Ryan (1988), two books on American television (Kellner 1990a and 1992b), and a series of media cultural studies, some of which are collected here.

20 There were, to be sure, some exceptions and qualifications to this "classical" model: Adorno would occasionally note a critical or utopian moment within mass culture and the possibility of audience reception against the grain; see the examples in Kellner 1989a. But although one can find moments that put in question the more bifurcated division between high and low culture and the model of mass culture as consisting of nothing except ideology and modes of manipulation which incorporate individuals into the existing society and culture, generally, the Frankfurt School model is overly reductive and monolithic, and thus needs radical reconstruction – which I have attempted to do in work over the past two decades.

21 The field of communications was initially bifurcated into a division, described by Lazarsfeld (1941) in an issue edited by the Frankfurt School on mass communications, between the critical school associated with the Institute for Social Research contrasted to administrative research, which Lazarsfeld defined as research carried out within the parameters of established media and social institutions and that would provide material that was of use to these institutions – research with which Lazarsfeld himself would be identified. Hence, it was the Frankfurt School that inaugurated critical communications research and I am suggesting that a return to a reconstructed version of the original model would be useful for media and cultural studies today.

22 In the 1930s model of critical theory, theory was supposed to be an instrument of political practice. Yet the formulation of the theory of the culture industries by Horkheimer and Adorno (1972 [1947]) in the 1940s was part of their turn toward a more pessimistic phase in which they eschewed concrete politics and generally located resistance within critical individuals, like themselves, rather than within social groups, movements, or oppositional practices. Thus, the Frankfurt School ultimately is weak on the formulation of oppositional practices and counterhegemonic cultural strategies.

23 I have been immersed in the problematic of British cultural studies since 1975, when I was involved in a study group in Austin, Texas and wrote Stuart Hall of the Birmingham Centre for Contemporary Cultural Studies. He responded with a long letter describing the history of the Centre and sent me a set of their stencilled papers which our group carefully studied. Over the next years we read all of their studies, journal articles, and books, and thus the first U.S. cultural studies group emerged in Austin, Texas. See my review of the earlier stages of the Birmingham project in *Theory, Culture, and Society*, Vol. I, No. 1 (1980).

24 Gramsci 1971 and 1992 and Hall 1986a. I further elucidate and illustrate the concept of hegemony in the following chapters.
25 Many of Stuart Hall's programmatic pieces discuss the appropriation of Marxism in British cultural studies, and especially the Marxism of Gramsci and Althusser (see Hall 1980a; 1986a; 1986b; and 1992).
26 See Hoggart 1958 and Williams 1958, and the discussions of the "popular" in Hall 1980a; McGuigan 1992; and Aronowitz 1993.
27 On the need of combining these approaches and overcoming the current division in the field between the approaches of "cultural studies" and "communication studies," see Kellner forthcoming.
28 Although he works in a department of communications, Lawrence Grossberg (1992) begins his metatheoretical presentation of cultural studies by attacking the concept of communication and effectively removing it from the conceptual field (ibid., 37ff.), drawing upon an earlier attempt to deconstruct the concept of communication (Grossberg 1982). I would prefer, however, to dissolve binary oppositions between culture and communication, to refuse privileging one over the other, and to show how contemporary media culture and communications are interconnected in the products of the cultural industries. I would also argue that methods drawn from the humanities to study "culture" and methods from the social sciences that investigate "communication" are both valuable for cultural studies. Finally, it is also curious that some departments and disciplines use the term "communication" to describe the object of their study, while other departments and individuals use the plural "communication*s*." There are obviously different types and levels of communications in our culture, thus the plural has its uses and validity, though the singular also serves to note that the many varieties are all forms of communication; consequently, I will use both terms in different contexts to denote plurality or singularity.
29 The early focus in Birmingham studies was on class and subcultures, but the influence of feminism forced a focus on gender and sexuality, and the influence of people of color within the Centre forced focus on race and ethnicity (see the narrative in Hall 1986a and Gilroy 1991). In any case, by the 1980s cultural studies everywhere had a multicultural agenda, though the earlier focus on class has been displaced in recent versions, a neglect that I shall attempt to avoid in my studies.
30 Textualism was especially one-sided in North American "new criticism" and other literary approaches which for some decades in the post-World-War-II conjuncture defined the dominant approach to cultural artifacts in the United States. The post-structuralist approaches that developed in France in the 1970s and quickly disseminated throughout the world were also highly textualist. The British cultural studies focus on audience and reception, however, was anticipated by the Frankfurt School: Walter Benjamin focused on the importance of reception studies as early as the 1930s, while Adorno, Lowenthal, and others in the Frankfurt School carried out reception studies in the same era. See the discussion in Kellner 1989a: 121ff. Except for some exceptions, however, the Frankfurt School tended to conceive of the audience as primarily passive, thus the Birmingham emphasis on the active audience is a genuine advance, though, as I argue below, there have been some exaggerations on this issue and qualifications to the notion of the active audience are now needed.
31 In fact, Fiske's other oft-repeated example of resistance by homeless men is their smuggling in copies of *Hustler* which they insert within *Life* magazine (1993: 18, 22, 25). Although such behavior does exhibit resistance to middle-class norms, it is highly questionable from a feminist perspective. The problem is that Fiske has no way to distinguish progressive from reactionary, emancipatory from destructive, resistance and celebrates all resistance as positive, thus failing to discriminate and evaluate different modes and types of resistance. Such a failure could have the effect of depoliticizing this most important and empowering notion.

32 See Kellner 1989a, Chapters 5–8.

33 I discuss identity politics in more detail below in analysis of the films of Spike Lee (Chapter 4) and the Madonna phenomenon (Chapter 7).

34 Most North American cultural studies and other varieties of cultural studies which have been influenced by postmodern theory likewise neglect production and political economy. I am not sure whether this is the influence of Baudrillard's pronouncements on "the end of political economy" (1976), or just laziness and ignorance of the domain of political economy, or a certain softness in practitioners of cultural studies that are uncomfortable with the "hard" domains of production and economics.

35 Yet in another article from the same period, Hall (1986 [1980]), rejected the political economy paradigm as reductionist and abstract (46–7). But note that he is rejecting the most economistic base/superstructure "logic of capital" model and not the importance of political economy *per se* ("This approach, too, has insights which are well worth following through"). Yet from the late 1970s through the present the dimension of political economy has receded in importance throughout the field of cultural studies and I would argue for reinserting its importance – a position that McGuigan (1992) also takes in a critique of the "cultural populism" of British cultural studies and its American and other cousins.

36 Stuart Hall once stressed the significance of breaks within a problematic,

> where old lines of thought are disrupted, older constellations displaced, and elements, old and new, are regrouped around a different set of premises and themes. Changes in a problematic do significantly transform the nature of the questions asked, the forms in which they are proposed and the manner in which they can be adequately answered. Such shifts in perspective reflect, not only the results of an internal intellectual labour, but the manner in which real historical developments and transformations are appropriated in thought, and provide Thought, not with its guarantee of 'correctness' but with its fundamental orientations, its conditions of existence.
>
> (Hall 1986: 33)

I would argue that a postmodern turn is such a significant shift, though its significance hasn't been fully registered within the tradition of British cultural studies – or at least many aligning themselves with the earlier tradition simply refer to a new "postmodern" culture and society without theorizing the significance of the shift, or in the case of Grossberg (1992), carry out a rather striking post-structuralist and postmodern transformation of cultural studies without signalling or theorizing the break with the earlier tradition.

37 I would agree with this latter argument, but the editors offer a highly questionable explication of these terms, defining modernity, for instance, as "a structure of experience and identity," rather than as a socio-historical formation, as an epoch in history, which is how modernity is defined in classical social theory (see Antonio and Kellner 1994 and forthcoming). Modernization is defined by the editors in terms of a broad range of phenomena usually associated with modernity, rather than as a process in which the forces of modernity impinge on traditional and non-Western societies and cultures, producing a highly complex and contested process of modernization and Westernization. Modernism is defined as "the whole complex of responses to the changing historical landscape of the modern," rather than to the avant-garde artists, such as Baudelaire, and art movements that articulated certain modern impulses and that revolted against established forms of culture, attempting to produce innovations in art (and sometimes in life).

38 This tendency to assume that the terrain of cultural studies is "postmodern" culture or society without defining the term, or providing any arguments, is widespread. The editors of a 1993 collection of mostly Canadian papers on cultural studies also simply declare that: "Modernity has passed into postmodernity" (Blundell *et al.* 1993: 8) and

refer to contemporary societies as "postmodern" (ibid., 10). There is no argumentation and a highly complex and contested term is thus taken as a synonym for contemporary society. Likewise, Aronowitz (1993) has a chapter on "Cultural studies in postmodern America" (167ff.), without defining the term or making any argument – indeed, earlier in his book, he stated that for the purposes of his book, it mattered little whether modernity was not exhausted or whether "we pronounce the arrival of a postmodern condition with its renunciation of all universals" (ibid., 14).

39 Almost everyone who uses the term "postmodern" has different definitions, sometimes engaging in overkill where everything contemporary is "postmodern," while sometimes merely offering an arbitrary list of characteristics, many of which are arguably modern. Others undertheorize the term, privileging one or two characteristics as marks of the postmodern without establishing a really important or distinctive break from the modern.

40 In recent years, I myself have been trying to chart the vicissitudes of the postmodern and to appraise the insights and regressions of the discourses; see my book on Baudrillard (1989b), my edited volume on Jameson (1989c); my book on postmodern theory with Steve Best (1991); and my Baudrillard reader (1994a).

41 Jameson argued in the first published draft of his theory of postmodernism in the arts that:

> radical breaks between periods do not generally involve complete changes of content but rather the restructuration of a certain number of elements already given: features that in an earlier period or system were subordinate now become dominant, and features that had been dominant again become secondary.
>
> (Jameson 1983: 123)

42 Such theories of postmodernity were anticipated by historians such as Toynbee and social theorists such as C. Wright Mills (see the genealogical discussion in Best and Kellner 1991).

43 This is an obvious point, but one often neglected: most theorists of the postmodern, or those who use the word without theorizing it, assume that there is something out there which is called "postmodernism" which is merely waiting to be discovered or described. Rather, terms of this sort produce their objects, enabling some objects to be labelled "postmodern" and others not to be so labelled.

44 From the beginning, there were many individuals in every discipline who maintained that the postmodern turn was a mere fad that could easily be ignored, but the debates roared on without the participation of those who ignored the phenomenon. Some publishers have claimed that interest is waning in postmodern controversies, as has a bookstore owner; see Rosenthal 1992. And yet the game goes on . . .

Chapter 2

Media culture, politics, and ideology
From Reagan to Rambo

In the following studies, I draw on a multiplicity of traditions to keep the project of cultural studies open, flexible, and critical, refusing to fix any orthodoxies, or to close off the field in any premature way. The excitement of cultural studies is that it is a new and open field in the process of making and remaking, and any interventions should merely attempt to offer some new perspectives or analyses and not to try to effect any theoretical closures. Indeed, cultural studies is a contested terrain open to multiple interventions and developments. As noted, some groups and individuals have been using cultural studies to celebrate the popular and to legitimate the academic study of "popular culture," while others use it to criticize existing inequalities and domination, or to advance specific political and cultural agendas. Conservative groups in turn attack it as subversive of educational ortho-doxy (see the documentation in Aronowitz 1993) while education reformers attempt to use it to make contemporary education more relevant and attuned to the nature and vicissitudes of contemporary culture (Giroux 1994; McLaren *et al.* forthcoming).

Most recently, it is to feminist and multiculturalist theories of race, ethnicity, nationality, subalterneity, and sexual preference that we can turn for specific critiques of oppression and theories of resistance, and these groups have made important contributions to cultural studies. Their discourses root their theoretical perspectives in the struggles of oppressed people and thus politicize theory and critique with passion and perspectives from existing political struggles and personal experiences. Such perspectives enlarge the field of cultural studies and political struggle, expanding, for instance, the concept of ideology critique to include dimensions of race, gender, sexuality, ethnicity, and other factors, as well as class – relations which I take up in this and the following chapters. They also infuse cultural studies with political passion and intensity, breathing new life into its projects.

Building on this work, I argue in this chapter for the need to deploy Marxian theories of class, feminist concepts of gender, and multiculturalist theories of race, ethnicity, sexual preference, nationality, and so on in order to articulate the full range of representations of identities, domination and resistance that one finds structuring the terrain of media culture. The forms of media culture are intensely political and ideological, and thus those who wish to discern how it embodies political positions and has political effects should learn to read media culture politically. This means not only reading media culture in a socio-political and economic context, but seeing how the internal constituents of its texts either encode relations of power and domination, serving to advance the interests of dominant groups at the expense of others, or oppose hegemonic ideologies, institutions, and practices or contain a contradictory mixture of forms that promote domination and resistance. Thus, reading media culture politically involves situating it in its historical conjuncture and analyzing how its generic codes, its positioning of viewers, its dominant images, its discourses, and its formal-aesthetic elements all embody certain political and ideological positions and have political effects.

Reading culture politically also involves seeing how media culture artifacts reproduce the existing social struggles in their images, spectacle, and narrative. In *Camera Politica: The Politics and Ideology of Contemporary Hollywood Film* (1988), Michael Ryan and I indicate how struggles within everyday life and the broader world of social and political struggles are articulated within popular film, which in turn are appropriated and have their effects within these contexts. We indicated how some of the most popular Hollywood films and genres from the 1960s to the late 1980s "transcode" contending social and political discourses and represent specific political positions within debates over the Vietnam War and the 1960s, gender and the family, class and race, the corporation and the state, U.S. foreign and domestic policy, and other issues which preoccupied U.S. society over the past decades.[1]

For example, some 1960s films presented anti-war discourses and advanced the positions of the 1960s counterculture (i.e. *Vietnam: The Year of the Pig*), while others, like *The Green Berets* (1967) presented positive representations of the U.S. intervention in Vietnam and attacked the counterculture. Throughout the 1970s to the present, media culture in general has been a battleground between competing social groups with some artifacts advancing liberal or radical positions and others conservative ones. Likewise, some texts of media culture advance progressive positions and representations of such things as gender, sexual preference, race, or ethnicity, while others articulate reactionary forms of racism or sexism. From this viewpoint, media culture is a contest of representations that reproduce existing social struggles and transcode the political discourses of the era.

Furthermore, cultural studies examines the effects of media cultural texts, the ways that audiences appropriate and use media culture, and the ways that media images, figures, and discourses function within the culture. In the following pages, I articulate some theoretical perspectives on media culture, politics, and ideology which I illustrate with some examples drawn from Hollywood film in the Age of Reagan and Bush's New World Order. I also examine some effects of these films and the ways that they intersected with the political debates and struggles of the period. In these analyses, I defend the centrality of ideology critique within cultural studies, yet specify some problems with the classical Marxian conceptions of ideology and propose some perspectives that will help contemporary criticism overcome these limitations.

IDEOLOGY AND MEDIA CULTURE: CRITICAL METHODS

Within the Marxian tradition, Marx and Engels characterized ideology as the ideas of the ruling class which achieved dominance in a specific historical era. The concept of ideology set out in *The German Ideology* (in Marx and Engels 1975: 59ff.) was primarily denunciatory and was used to attack ideas which legitimated ruling class hegemony, which disguised particular interests as general ones, which mystified or covered over class rule, and which thus served the interests of class domination. In this view, ideology critique consisted of the analysis and demystification of ruling class ideas, and the critic of ideology was to ferret out and attack all those ideas which furthered class domination.[2]

The classical Marxism of Marx and Engels, the Second International, and the Third International tended to focus on the primacy of economics and politics and to refocus attention away from culture and ideology. However, during the 1920s, Lukács, Korsch, Bloch, and Gramsci emphasized the central importance of culture and ideology and the Frankfurt School and other versions of Western Marxism also took up the importance of the critique of ideology as an important component of the critique of domination.[3] British cultural studies too, in its formative period, made the concept of ideology central to the study of culture and society and one of their early collection of texts was titled *On Ideology*.[4]

Yet there were problems within the Marxian tradition of ideology critique that needed to be overcome. Some Marxian traditions, including orthodox Leninism, the Frankfurt School, Althusser, and others, tended to presuppose both a monolithic concept of ideology and of the ruling class which unambiguously and without contradiction articulates its class interests in a dominant ideology. This concept reduces ideology to defense of class interests and is thus predominantly economistic with ideology referring primarily, and in some cases solely, to those ideas that legitimate the class rule of the capitalist ruling class. Thus, in this conception, "ideology" is confined to those sets of ideas which promote the capitalist class's economic interests.

In the last two decades, however, this model has been contested by a variety of critics who have argued that such a concept of ideology is reductionist because it equates ideology solely with those ideas which serve class, or economic interests, and thus leaves out such significant phenomena as gender and race and other forms of ideological domination. Reducing ideology to class interests makes it appear that the only significant domination going on in society is class, or economic, domination, whereas many theorists argue that gender, sexuality, and race oppression are also of fundamental importance and indeed, some would argue, are entwined in integral ways with class and economic oppression (see Cox 1948; Rowbotham 1972; Robinson 1978; Said 1978; Barrett 1980; Sargent 1981; Marable 1982; Lorde

1984; Kellner and Ryan 1988; Spivak 1988; Fraser 1989; Eisenstein 1979; hooks 1990 and 1992 and Gilroy 1991).

Many critics have correctly proposed that ideology be extended to cover theories, ideas, texts, and representations that legitimate interests of ruling gender and race, as well as class powers. From this perspective, doing ideology critique involves criticizing sexist, heterosexist, and racist ideology as well as bourgeois-capitalist class ideology. Such ideology critique is multicultural, discerning a range of forms of oppression of people of different races, ethnicities, gender, and sexual preference and tracing the ways that ideological cultural forms and discourses perpetuate oppression. Multicultural ideological critique involves taking seriously struggles between men and women, feminists and anti-feminists, racists and antiracists, gays and antigays, and many other conflicts as well, which are seen to be as important and worthy of attention as class conflicts by Marxian theory.[5] It assumes that society is a great field of struggle and that the heterogeneous struggles are played out on the screens and texts of media culture and are the proper terrain of a critical media cultural studies.

With this view, one needs to see the importance of a multitude of struggles between various groups, including struggles between dominant and subordinate groups and between class sectors for control of society. In the U.S., this has involved struggles between liberals and conservatives for hegemonic power and between a wide range of dominant and subordinate groups. On one level, ideology mobilizes sentiment, affection, and belief to induce consent to certain dominant core assumptions about social life (i.e. such as the value of individualism, freedom, the family, the nation, success, and so on). These core assumptions, the "common sense" of a society, are deployed by groups, whereby, for example, groups and forces in struggle tend to deploy discourses of democracy, freedom, and individualism which they inflect according to their own ideological agendas and purposes. Sometimes, for example, a concept like empowerment, which began as a critical concept in the 1960s among progressives ("Power to the People," the "empowerment project," etc.), is appropriated by opposing groups, as when conservatives during the Reagan/Bush era deployed the rhetoric of empowerment to support government regulatory agencies and policies to "empower" individuals against the state ("getting government off our backs").[6]

Thus, while there is no one unified and stable dominant ideology, there are core assumptions that different political groups mobilize and deploy. Indeed, contemporary democratic capitalist societies have been extremely divided during the past decades with competing groups and political parties struggling for control over society. For example, in the United States during the 1950s, moderate conservatives controlled the economy, society, polity, and culture, establishing a hegemonic project, overturning the democratic-liberal hegemony which had ruled since 1932 in the form of FDR's "New Deal." In the early 1960s, Kennedy liberals attempted to forge a liberal consensus and for some years their New Frontier was a successful hegemonic project until the assassinations of John and Robert Kennedy (themselves victims of an attempt to re-establish rightist hegemony, if one believes, as I do, the conspiracy theories). Thereafter, intense struggles between liberals and conservatives broke out, capped by the victory of Ronald Reagan in 1980, which established over a decade of conservative hegemony.

Reagan, in turn, redefined "common sense," producing a political rhetoric that is still operative during the Clinton era: government must be limited and taxes reduced; business must be strengthened to create jobs and increase national wealth; government "red tape" (and thus regulatory policies) must be eliminated; individual entrepreneurialism is the best road to success and producing a strong society, therefore government should do everything possible to encourage such business enterprise; life is tough and only the fittest survive and prosper. Yet on many political, social, and cultural issues, the conservatives failed to gain hegemony, to redefine common sense, and thus "culture wars" continue to rage with conservatives attempting to root out remaining liberal and radical conceptions, practices, and policies (see Hunter 1991).

Media culture, as well as political discourses, helps establish the hegemony of specific political groups and projects. Media culture produces representations that attempt to induce consent to certain political positions, getting members of the society to see specific ideologies as "the way things are" (i.e. that too much government is bad, that government deregulation and free markets are good, that protecting the country requires intense militarization and an aggressive foreign policy, and so on). Popular cultural texts naturalize these positions and thus help mobilize consent to hegemonic political positions.[7]

Criticizing hegemonic ideologies thus requires showing how certain positions in media cultural texts reproduce existing political ideologies in current political struggles, as when some films or popular music articulate conservative or liberal positions, while others articulate radical ones. Moreover, doing ideology critique involves analyzing images, symbols, myths, and narrative, as well as propositions and systems of belief (Kellner 1978, 1979, 1982). While some contemporary theories of ideology explore the complex ways that images, myths, social practices, and narratives are bound together in the production of ideology (Barthes 1957; Jameson 1981; and Kellner and Ryan 1988), others restrict ideology to propositions stated discursively in texts.[8] Against this restrictive notion, I would argue that ideology contains discourses and figures, concepts and images, theoretical positions and symbolic forms. Such an expansion of the concept of ideology obviously opens the way to the exploration of how images, figures, narratives, and symbolic forms constitute part of the ideological representations of gender, sexuality, race, and class in film and popular culture.

To carry out a multicultural and figurative ideology critique of *Rambo*, for instance, it wouldn't be enough simply to attack its militarist or imperialist ideology, and the ways that the militarism and imperialism of the film serves imperialist interests by legitimating intervention in such places as Southeast Asia, the Middle East, Central America, or wherever. One would also have to criticize the discourses and figures that construct the text's gender and racial problematics to carry out a full ideology critique, showing how representations of women, men, the Vietnamese, the Russians, and so on are a fundamental part of *Rambo* and that a key element of the text is remasculinization and re-establishment of white male power after defeat in Vietnam and assaults on male power by feminist and civil rights movements. Consequently, reading the ideological text of *Rambo* requires interrogation of its images and figures as well as its discourse and language across a range of problematics while inscribing these problematics within the context of existing political struggles. Such an analysis, as I will argue below, suggests that the figure of Rambo represents a specific set of images of male power, American innocence and strength, and warrior heroism which serve as vehicles of masculist and patriotic ideologies which were significant during the Reagan era.

Such figural analysis is important because the representations of popular cultural texts constitute the political image through which individuals view the world and interpret political processes, events, and personalities. The politics of representation thus probes the ideological images and figures, as well as discourses, which transcode dominant and competing political positions in a society. In a mass-mediated image culture, it is representations that help constitute an individual's view of the world, sense of personal identity and gender, playing out of style and lifestyle, and socio-political thought and action. Ideology is thus as much a process of representation, figure, image, and rhetoric as it is of discourse and ideas. Moreover, it is through the establishment of a set of representations that a hegemonic political ideology is established, such as New Right conservativism. Representations thus transcode political discourses and in turn mobilize sentiment, affection, perception, and assent toward specific political positions, such as the need for male warriors to protect and redeem society.

Critical theories attempt to contribute to practice and a critical cultural studies seeks to empower individuals, by giving them tools to criticize dominant cultural forms, images, narratives, and genres. The studies in this book thus endeavor to teach how to read, deconstruct, criticize, and use media culture. It has been my experience in over twenty-five years of teaching that students and others are not naturally media literate, or critical of their culture, and should be provided with methods and tools of critique to empower them against the manipulative force of existing society and culture. On the other hand, many contemporary individuals have a deep involvement in the artifacts of media culture, are often eager to discuss their views, often have interesting insights, and should be encouraged to critically examine and analyze the culture in which they are so deeply immersed.

In line with this pedagogic intent, I am thus interspersing theory with concrete studies that illustrate my theoretical positions throughout the following pages. Indeed, I would hope that these studies contribute to the development of a critical media pedagogy that would empower individuals to discern the messages, values, and ideologies embedded in media culture texts.[9] When individuals learn to perceive how media culture transmits oppressive representations of class, race, gender, sexuality, and so on that influence thought and behavior, they are able to develop critical distance from the works of media culture and thus gain power over their culture. Such empowerment can help promote a more general questioning of the organization of society and can help induce individuals to join and participate in radical political movements struggling for social transformation.

Ideology assumes that "I" am the norm, that everyone is like me, that anything different or other is not normal. For ideology, however, the "I," the position from which ideology speaks, is that of (usually) white male, Western, middle- or upper-class subject positions, of positions that see other races, classes, groups, and gender as secondary, derivative, inferior, and subservient. Ideology thus differentiates and separates groups into dominant/subordinate and superior/inferior, producing hierarchies and rankings that serve the interests of ruling powers and elites.

Ideology is thus part of a system of domination which serves to further oppression by legitimating forces and institutions that repress and oppress people. Ideology itself forms a system of abstractions and distinctions within such domains as gender, race, and class, so as to construct ideological divisions between men and women, the "better classes" and "the lower classes," whites and peoples of color, "us" and "them," and so on. Ideology constructs divisions between "proper" and "improper" behavior, while constructing a hierarchy within each of these domains which justifies the domination of one gender, race, and class over others by virtue of its alleged superiority, or the natural order of things. For example, women are said to be by nature passive, domestic, submissive, and so on, and their proper domain is deemed to be the private sphere, the home, while the public sphere was reserved for, allegedly, more active, rational, and domineering men. People of color are often said to be lazy, irrational, and unintelligent, and thus inferior to the dominant white race.

Such sexist and racist thinking rests on a series of binary oppositions which a critical cultural studies attempts to subvert and undermine. The binary oppositions of ideology are rooted in a system of antagonisms between unequal forces and serve to legitimate the privilege and domination of the more powerful forces. The "norm" of ideology is usually white, male, and upper class and serves to denigrate and dominate non-white people, women, and working-class individuals. Ideology critique, however, interrogates the categories of whiteness, men, ruling class, heterosexuality, and other dominant powers and forms that ideology legitimates, showing the social constructedness and arbitrariness of all social categories and the binary system of ideology.

Thus feminism and the critique of racism is an integral part of a multicultural cultural studies. In the ideological operations which produce the likes of sexism, racism, and classism, we see *abstraction* at work: ideologies which legitimate the superiority of men over women, or of capitalism over other social systems, so as to attempt to justify the privileges of the ruling classes or strata – such patriarchal capitalist and racist ideologies abstract from the injustices, inequities, and suffering produced by the system of racist, patriarchal capitalism, such as the glaring inequities of power and wealth within a supposedly egalitarian society and the sufferings of subordinate groups and individuals.

Thus, abstraction is fundamentally related to the key features of ideology such as legitimation, domination, and mystification, and the drawing of *boundaries* (between allegedly inferior and superior systems, groups, values, and so on) also plays a fundamental role in this process. Boundary maintenance (between men and women, capitalists and workers, whites and nonwhites, Americans and the rest of the world, capitalism and communism, and so on) serves the interests of social domination, as well as the functions of legitimation and mystification of social reality. Thus, I am proposing that the "distortion," "mystification," "masking," and other occluding functions usually associated with ideology are related to a certain sort of abstraction and to a specific type of ideological boundaries, which legitimize the domination of ruling social groups.

A cultural studies that is critical and multicultural must therefore carry through a critique of abstractions, reifications, and ideology which traces reified categories and boundaries back to their social origins and which criticizes the distortions, mystifications, and falsifications therein. Thus, one of the functions of dominant media culture is to maintain boundaries and to legitimate the rule of the hegemonic class, race, and gender forces. Marxism, feminism, and multicultural theory, however, pursue a critique of boundaries, focusing on the binary system of oppositions that structure class, sexist, racist and other ideological discourses. All of these forms of critical theory are thus weapons of critique in the struggle for a more humane society and see ideology as providing theoretical underpinnings for systems of domination.[10]

Consequently, such variables as race, class, gender, sexual preference, and ideology are articulated in terms of the organization of the existing society and the struggles for power in the society. To illustrate such a multicultural approach and the need for expanding the concept of ideology critique, let us now undertake a reading of the Rambo films which emphasizes the ways that they transcode a certain Reaganite ideology and which analyzes the various dimensions and ideological strategies of the films, including their class, race, gender, and political ideology, as well as what I call the "Rambo effect."

At stake is developing a media cultural studies that can analyze, first, how media culture transcodes the positions within existing political struggles and in turn provides representations which mobilize consent to specific political positions through images, spectacle, discourse, narrative, and the other forms of media culture. And then the actual social effects of the phenomena should be traced. In the following sections, I undertake this inquiry through a close reading of media texts and analysis of their possible range of effects. Then I work through a study of the Rambo effect in order to provide some examples of the nature, functions, and effectivity of media culture within contemporary society.[11]

RAMBO AND REAGAN

The first Rambo film, *First Blood* (1982), presented the Vietnam veteran as a victim and merged an uneasy set of images that ascribed responsibility for his victimization to societal forces and that showed them driving him to violence. In the plot, Special

Forces veteran John Rambo (Sylvester Stallone) is searching for a member of his unit, who he discovers died of Agent Orange contamination, thus situating the Vietnam veterans as victims of their government. Unable to hitch a hide, Rambo walks into the small town of Hope, and is arrested by the sheriff who complains that he needs a haircut and bath. Mistreated by the sheriff and his deputies, Rambo escapes and wages war against the local and national guard law enforcement agencies, being positioned as a victim of oppressive authority and power. At the end, he surrenders to his former Special Forces commander Col. Trautman (Richard Crenna) and breaks down, crying that although he was a hero in Vietnam, he cannot even hold a job and is a figure of contempt and hatred, thus blaming all of society for making him an outcast.

In the second *Rambo* film (1985), Rambo is transformed into a superhuman warrior who rescues U.S. POW's still being held in Vietnam, thus transcoding the paranoia of contemporary conservativism concerning missing POW's in Vietnam.[12] The film is but one of a whole series of return-to-Vietnam films that began with the surprising success of *Uncommon Valor* in 1983 and continued with the three Chuck Norris *Missing in Action* films of 1984–6. All follow the same formula of representing the return-to-Vietnam of a team of former veterans, or a super-human, superhero veteran like Rambo, to rescue a group of American soldiers "missing in action" who are still imprisoned by the Vietnamese and their evil Soviet allies.

In general, media culture forms a system of culture organized according to various industries, types, genres, subgenres, and genre cycles. It follows the model of industrial production and is divided into genres with their own rules, conventions, and formulas. Film for instance, is divided into genres like the horror film, war film, musical, comedies, and so on, with their own distinctive conventions, forms, themes, and the like. Popular genres tap into concerns of the present and give rise to genre cycles attempting to emulate the success of popular artifacts.

The film *Rambo* synthesizes the "return-to-Vietnam" cycle with another cycle that shows returning veterans transforming themselves from wounded and confused misfits to super warriors (i.e. *Rolling Thunder, Firefox, First Blood*). All of these cinematic attempts to overcome the "Vietnam syndrome" show the U.S. and the American warrior hero victorious this time and thus exhibit a symptom of inability to accept defeat. They also provide symbolic compensation for loss, shame, and guilt by depicting the U.S. as "good" and this time victorious, while its communist enemies are represented as the incarnation of "evil" who this time receive a well-deserved defeat. In these cinematic fantasies, it is always the "enemy" that performs vicious and evil acts, while the Americans are virtuous and heroic. Cumulatively, the return-to-Vietnam films therefore exhibit a defensive and compensatory response to military defeat in Vietnam and, I would argue, an inability to learn the lessons of the limitations of U.S. power and the complex mixture of "good" and "evil" involved in almost all historical undertakings.

On the other hand, *Rambo* and the other Stallone-Norris meathead-hero films can be read as expressions of white male paranoia which present males as victims of foreign enemies, other races, the government, and society at large. The return-to-Vietnam films also exhibit an attempt at remasculinization, in which highly masculist male behavior is celebrated, as a response to feminism and other attacks on male power. In *The Remasculinization of America*, Susan Jeffords (1989) argues that Vietnam was a terrible blow to masculine pride, for which American males experienced great guilt and shame. A vast amount of Vietnam films and literature deal with this problem, she claims, attempting to heal the wounds and to reconstruct a damaged male psyche.

Yet the films can also be read diagnostically as symptoms of the victimization of the working class. Both the Stallone and Norris figures are resentful, inarticulate, brutal, and thus indicative of the way many American working-class youths are educationally deprived and offered the military, or activities like sports that channel violence into socially acceptable behaviour, as the only way of affirming themselves. Rambo's neurotic resentment is less his own fault than that of those who run the social system in such a way that it denies his class access to the institutions of articulate thought and mental health. Denied self-esteem through creative work, they seek surrogate worth in metaphoric substitutes like sports (*Rocky*) and war (*Rambo*). It is symptomatic that Stallone plays both Rocky and Rambo during a time when economic recession was driving the Rockys of the world to join the military where they became Rambos for Reagan's interventionist foreign policies.

The Rocky-Rambo syndrome, however, puts on display the raw masculism which is at the bottom of conservative socialization and ideology. The only way that the Rockys and Rambos can gain recognition and self-affirmation is through violent and aggressive self-display. And Rambo's pathetic demand for love at the end of the first two Rambo films is an indication that the society is not providing adequate structures of mutual and communal support to provide healthy interpersonal relationships and ego ideals for men in the culture. Unfortunately, the Stallone character intensifies this pathology precisely in its celebration of violent masculism and militarist self-assertion.

Reading *Rambo* politically

What is perhaps most curious, however, is how *Rambo* appropriates countercultural motifs for the right. On one level, the film is about the triumph of the individual over the system, continuing the dominant trope of individualism in American ideology, but giving the concept a particularly rightist and masculist twist after the 1960s appropriated individualism as social revolt and non-conformity. Moreover, Rambo has long hair, a headband, eats only natural foods (whereas the bureaucrat Murdock swills Coke), is close to nature, and is hostile toward bureaucracy, the state, and technology – precisely the position of many 1960s counterculturalists. This is an excellent example of how conservative ideologies are able to incorporate figures and fashion which neutralize and even reverse their original connotations as oppositional style and behavior. The film also incorporates radical anti-state discourses and images, for Rambo's real enemy is the "governmental machine, with its massive technology, unlimited regulations, and venal political motivations. Rambo is the anti-bureaucratic non-conformist opposed to the state, the new individualist activist" (Berman 1984: 145). Thus Rambo is a supply-side hero, a figure of individual entrepreneurialism, who shows how Reaganite ideology is able to assimilate earlier countercultural figures, much as fascism was able to provide a "cultural synthesis" of nationalist, primitivist, socialist, and racialist ideologies (Bloch 1991 [1935]).

This analysis suggests that Reaganism should be seen as revolutionary conservativism with a strong component of radical conservative populism, individualism and activism, and that this fits in with *Star Wars, Indiana Jones, Superman, Conan*, and other films and television series which utilize individualist heroes who are anti-state and who are a repository of conservative values. And, as Berman (1984) points out, this constitutes a major shift in the strategies of the culture industries which celebrated conformity and a beneficent state in the 1950s and which has shifted to valorization of nonconformity and individualistic heroism in the Reaganite age of entrepreneurial glory.

Yet the identification of Rambo with natural man against machine technology is problematized in that Rambo is also identified with technology, and specifically murderous military technology. Rambo's bow and arrow shoots missiles that explode with nuclear impact, thus merging nature and technology. Rambo's knife, a risible phallic symbol of aggressive masculinity, is also high-tech, enabling him to cut through barbed wire and to suture his wounds with a needle and thread conveniently stored in its butt. The knife also directs him with a compass, and, of course, provides him with a powerful weapon with which he can quickly and efficiently dispatch his adversaries. Moreover, Rambo is associated too with the power of helicopters, explosives, and other weapons, thus merging technology and nature in images of a pure "fighting machine."

Consequently, the images enact an implosion between body and technology, with the body itself, the figure of Rambo, being represented as a superweapon. "I am war," he says at one place and the cinematic images show him effortlessly gliding through nature, overcoming all adversity, and triumphing over his enemies. The spectacle of the film thus sutures the cultural opposition between nature and technology, via the lavishly displayed high-tech effects which overpower the spectator with sights, sounds, and the pleasures of the action/adventure genre. Thus, the technology appears to be a force of nature, just as Rambo appears to be war itself, rather than war, technology, and Rambo being perceived as socially constructed artifacts which are hardly "natural".

The film machine also mobilizes images and displays of gender and race to do its ideological work. In regard to gender, one might note that Rambo instantiates a masculist image which defines masculinity in terms of the male warrior with the features of great strength, effective use of force, and military heroism as the highest expression of life. Symptomatically, the women characters in the film are either whores, or, in the case of a Vietnamese contra, a handmaiden to Rambo's exploits who functions primarily as a seductive and destructive force. Her main actions are to seduce Vietnamese guards – a figure also central to the image of woman in *The Green Berets* – and to become a woman warrior, a female version of Rambo, who helps Rambo fight the bad guys. Significantly, the only (brief and chaste) moment of eroticism in the film comes when Rambo and his woman agent kiss after great warrior feats, and seconds after the kiss (of death) the woman is herself shot and killed. This renunciation of women and sexuality highlights the theme that the male warrior must go it alone and must thus renounce erotic pleasure. This theme obviously fits into the militarist and masculist theme of the film, as well as the genre of ascetic male heroes who must rise above sexual temptation in order to become maximally effective saviors or warriors.[13]

The representations and thematics of race also contribute fundamentally to the militarist theme. The Vietnamese and Russians are presented as alien Others, as the embodiment of Evil, in a typically Hollywood scenario that presents the Other, the Enemy, "Them," as the embodiment of evil, and "Us," the good guys, as the incarnation of virtue, heroism, goodness, innocence, and so on. *Rambo* appropriates stereotypes of the evil Japanese and Germans from World War II movies in its representations of the Vietnamese and the Russians, thus continuing a manichean Hollywood tradition with past icons of evil standing in for – from the Right's point of view – contemporary villains. The Vietnamese are portrayed as duplicitous bandits, ineffectual dupes of the evil Soviets, and cannon fodder for Rambo's exploits, while the Soviets are presented as sadistic torturers and inhuman, mechanistic bureaucrats.

And yet reflections on the representations of gender and race in the film make clear that these phenomena are socially constructed, are artificial constructs that are produced in such things as films and media culture. The stereotypes of race and gender in *Rambo* are so exaggerated, so crude, that they point to the artificial and socially constructed nature of all ideals of masculinity, femininity, race, ethnicity, and other subject positions. These representations are presented in cinematic terms which celebrate the white male power of Rambo against women and other races. Thus, to fully explicate filmic ideology and the ways that film advances specific political positions, one must also attend to cinematic form and narrative structure, to the ways that the cinema apparatus transcodes social discourses and reproduces ideological effects.

Film ideology is transmitted through images, figures, scenes, generic codes, and the narrative as a whole. Camera positioning and lighting help frame Sylvester Stallone as a mythic hero in *Rambo*; an abundance of lower camera angles present Rambo as a mythic warrior, and frequent close-ups present him as a larger-than-life human being. Focus on his glistening biceps, his sculptured body, and powerful physique presents him as a male sexual icon, as a figure of virility, which promotes both female admiration for male strength and perhaps homo-erotic fascination with the male warrior. Slow-motion travelling shots code Rambo as a force of nature, effortlessly gliding through the jungle, while triumphant music codes his accomplishments as superheroic. His regeneration into superhero are presented in shots where he magically leaps out of the water, purified and potent, poised to avenge and triumph.[14]

The action shots focus on his body as the instrument of mythic heroism, while the cutting creates an impression of dynamism that infuses Rambo with energy and superhuman power and vitality, just as slow-motion shots and lengthy takes which center on Rambo for long stretches of action tend to deify the character. When, by contrast, Rambo is tortured by villainous communists, the images are framed in the iconography of crucifixion shots with strong lighting on his head producing halo effects, as in medieval paintings, and the redder-than-red blood producing a hyperrealization, if I may borrow a Baudrillardian term (1983a), of heroic suffering. Close-ups on the communist villains focus on their sneering and sadistic pleasure in torturing Rambo, while the battle scenes depict the communists predominantly in long shots as insignificant and incompetent pawns in Rambo's redemptive heroism. And in one incredible scene, Rambo snaps off the head of the snake, evoking the myth of Adam and Eden, in which Adam cannot tame the serpent and must leave the Garden of Eden, whereby Rambo conquers it, demonstrating his power to rule the jungle.

William Warner (1992) has pointed out that the torture and suffering of Rambo, highlighted by the cinematography, enacts a sado-masochistic position whereby the spectator experiences the pain as just punishment for the guilt of the loss of masculinity and U.S. imperial power in Vietnam. Then, through a magical reversal, the subject attains the pleasures of the sadistic position by participating in Rambo's mastery and power over his adversaries. Such a scenario thus provides a psychic resolution to the trauma of loss in Vietnam and empowers spectators who are experiencing loss of power in the present hard times.

Jeffords (1994) reads the torture scenes in the *Rambo* films as demonstrating that the national body can recover from wounds and reconstitute itself as dominant, as powerful, as in control. The Rambo body also provides the norm of the powerful body that can protect us from harm and against which soft and weak bodies can be differentiated and seen as lacking. She argues that the inept sheriff and his deputies and the National Guard in the first *Rambo* represent the soft bodies that make the U.S. prey to foreign and domestic subversion. The Stallone, Norris, Schwarzenegger and other "Hard Bodies", by contrast, present the ideal man needed to preserve the existing society from its enemies and from internal decay and feminization.

In the case of Rambo, not only does the scenario of the film enact this redemptive drama of shame, humiliation, torture, and resurrection via an empowered subject, but the film spectacle enables the spectator to participate in the exciting experiences of Rambo effortlessly traversing the space of the jungle, blending in with nature. Spectators are invited to thrill in Rambo's destruction of his enemies, to experience redemptive violence, to triumphantly return with Rambo in a high-tech helicopter. Thus, the cinematic apparatus of spectacle contributes to the empowering experience. As with video games, the spectator is invited to achieve a position of mastery, to destroy enemies and to triumph over evil.

As Warner suggests (1992: 684–5), the spectacle of *Rambo* helps explain its appeal with young and international audiences.[15] Powerless spectators enjoy the thrill of identification with "natural" and technological power and magically overcome all adversity. The Hollywood special effects produce a spectacle whereby the audience is able to experience the power of decisiveiy defeating evil. The spectacle thus empowers audiences, providing a momentary sense of mastery and power, compensating for the decline of power in everyday life. In addition, media spectacles hide the ideological content, whereby fast editing, dazzling high-tech images, and narrative excitement overwhelm the viewer's critical faculties, thus subliminally conveying the ideologies through images and spectacle.

Furthermore, the "happy ending" closure situates the film as a return to the conservative Hollywood adventure tradition, and the victory over the evil communists codes *Rambo* as a mythic redemption of U.S. defeat in Vietnam by heroic action – a trope reproduced in the films of Stallone, Chuck Norris, and countless others, as well as in pulp novels and television shows. Such mythic redemption was carried out politically during the era in the actions of Ronald Reagan, Oliver North, and other "cowboys," who supported violence to resolve political conflict (Jewett and Lawrence 1988: 248f.). Not by accident did both the Hollywood heroes and the Hollywood president and his cronies act outside the law to carry out "heroic" actions constrained by the legal and political order.

Consequently, although the U.S. was denied victory in Vietnam, it has attempted to achieve it in media culture. This phenomenon shows some of the political functions of media culture which include providing compensations for irredeemable loss while offering reassurances that all is well in the American body politic – reassurance denied in less conservative films such as Oliver Stone's *Salvador*, *Platoon*, *Wall Street*, *Talk Radio*, *Born on the Fourth of July*, *Heaven and Earth*, and *Natural Born Killers*, which provide an instructive countercycle to the Stallone Rocky/Rambo cycles and which also testify to the conflictual nature of cinematic ideology in the contemporary period. For the Stone films demonstrate the pain of defeat and depict powerful institutions and social forces overshadowing individual ability to control the course of events. The conservative films, by contrast, celebrate the triumph of the will over adversity and their effects reveal the ludicrousness of claiming that the artifacts of media culture neither have powerful effects nor promote interests of domination. Instead, as the following study of the Rambo effect suggests, they are potent forces within contemporary culture that have a variety of discernible effects.

The *Rambo* effect

Rambo was one of the most popular films of its era. It opened at a record-breaking 2,074 theaters and had the third-largest opening gross in movie history – $32,548,262 in its first six days (*New York Times*, May 30, 1985). *Rambo* quickly became the number one film in box office receipts:

In its first 23 days of release, Rambo, which cost $27 million to produce, has grossed a phenomenal $75.8 million at the box office. Only two films in history, *Indiana Jones and the Temple of Doom* and *Return of the Jedi*, have had more successful launches.

(Time, June 24, 1985)

By the end of the summer, it had grossed over $150 million in the U.S. alone to become one of the most popular films of the day (*Business Week*, August 26, 1985). Moreover, it spawned a whole culture of "Rambomania" which:

> is spreading faster than the fire storms set by the hero's explosive warheads. Hollywood megahits of summers past have flooded the market with such whimsical souvenirs as furry Gremlins and cuddly E.T.s. This year stores are stocking up with war paraphernalia: a $150 replica of Rambo's high-tech bow and arrow, Rambo knives and an assortment of toy guns, including a semiautomatic job that squirts a stream of water 10 ft. Youngsters will soon be able to pop Rambo vitamins, and New Yorkers can send a Rambogram, in which a Stallone look-alike will deliver a birthday message or carry out a tough assignment like asking the boss for a raise. The U.S. Army has started hanging Rambo posters outside its recruitment offices, hoping to lure enlistees. Rambo fever is even spreading overseas. The film has already broken box-office records in Beirut and the Philippines, and 25 companies have signed contracts to distribute Rambo merchandise, even in countries where the film has not yet opened.

(Time, June 24, 1985)

Liberal critics described their horror over seeing the film with Rambomanaics who cheered the human killing machine's every exploit.[16] The film was quickly taken up by discussions and talk shows:

> Even a panel of political journalists on 'This Week with David Brinkley' last Sunday on ABC-TV pushed aside the President's tax plan, the SALT II negotiations and other heavyweight matters to talk about what the popularity of Sylvester Stallone's new action movie says about our national state of mind.

(Chicago Tribune, June 12, 1985)

The pundits concluded that its "message" was: "We should have won in Vietnam. We did win in Grenada. And now . . . on to Nicaragua!" (ibid.).

Columnist Ellen Goodman feared that Rambo's rescue of US POWs held in Vietnam would increase calls for military attempts to rescue hostages in Lebanon and elsewhere (*Chicago Tribune*, June 27, 1985) and soon after Ronald Reagan himself said:

> "Boy, after seeing *Rambo* last night, I know what to do next time." Reagan's remark came as he was preparing to address the nation on the freeing of 39 American hostages in Beirut. They were among 153 passengers on a TWA (Trans World Airlines) flight hijacked on June 14 as it headed for Rome from Athens.

(Reuters Ltd., June 30, 1985)[17]

Psychologists began describing war mania in young children,[18] and posters of the film, images of Rambo, and references to him appeared everywhere. Indeed, the term "Rambo" soon became a synonym for tough, macho, patriotic, and Reagan himself used the term "Ramboing" to describe an aggressive response to provocation. The film was endlessly discussed as expressing the signs of the times:

> Rambo has touched a raw nerve in America, a feeling that we should, in the words of Ronald Reagan, stand tall again. Ten years ago, after the collapse of Saigon and the anguish of the Watergate scandal, Rambo would have been laughed out of the movie theaters. The mood then was virulently antiwar, but today that's all changed.
>
> (*People*, July 8, 1985)

On the other hand, Vietnam veterans protested against the film all over the country, claiming that it provided distorted representations of both Vietnamese and American vets, while promoting violence, and they picketed theaters that ran the film. But Rambo had become a major figure in popular and commercial culture "heating up the poster, button and bumper sticker market." By mid-summer,

> more than 600,000 Rambo posters have been sold . . . There are 11 kinds of 'Rambo' buttons, with sales so far of 300,000. Next, bumper stickers. Among them: 'Need an Army? Hire Rambo'; 'Rambo – America's Newest Weapon'; 'Beware – This Vehicle Protected by Rambo'.
>
> (*Chicago Tribune*, July 11, 1985)

A novel based on the film sold over 800,000 copies (*Reuters North European Service*, July 31, 1985).

> T-shirts from *Rambo, First Blood, Part II*, have topped the 1.5 million mark (250,000 shirts). During the first five weeks of release, these shirts have outsold the previous record holder, the ever present M*A*S*H shirts . . . . Not only are millions viewing the film, but large numbers of viewers have decided to publicly identify and display themselves with an image of Rambo.
>
> (*Business Wire*, July 18, 1985)

A large number of Rambo toys, weapons, clothes, and other consumer items also saturated the market, and the next year a Rambo cartoon show opened. The film also inspired bizarre actions throughout the United States. A Rambo look-alike messenger, dressed in army fatigues and carrying a fake gun to deliver a Rambo-gram, led a policeman to shoot himself in the foot in pursuit of the messenger (*Proprietary to the United Press International*, August 19, 1985). And:

> Residents of a posh suburban Rochester neighborhood Thursday blamed a recent vandalism spree on "Rambo's Raiders," a group of adolescents emulating Sylvester Stallone's freedom-fighter movie character. Screens have been slashed, bushes and shrubs cut down and garden hoses turned on and aimed inside homes during the past few weeks in the Monroe County town of Penfield.

Sheriff's deputies said a group of teens who masquerade as Rambo in the quiet neighborhood may be responsible. Deputies this past weekend arrested two Stallone clones, who were dressed in camouflage fatigues, cut-off shirts and wore paint on their faces. "We understand that they wear army fatigues and carry knives," said JoAnne Cortese, whose home was vandalized. "It's almost like Rambo's Raiders. They feel that if Rambo can do it, they can do it."
(*Proprietary to the United Press International*, August 15, 1985)

Other reports surfaced of crimes, including murders, that were allegedly inspired by Rambo. The *Los Angeles Times* reported a murderer had used a knife like Rambo's and that the suspect was believed to have been inspired by the film (August 16, 1985).

A judge decried the glorification of Sylvester Stallone's Rambo film character in deciding the case against a 15–year-old boy accused of setting jungle-style booby traps in a park. Washington County Circuit Judge Jon B. Lund held Andrew S. Bene, Beaverton, accountable Tuesday on one count of recklessly endangering others but absolved him of three related weapons or assault charges.
(*Proprietary to the United Press International*, September 18, 1985)

And: "Police Monday charged a man with robbing a tavern and three customers while dressed as the movie character Rambo" (*Proprietary to the United Press International*, October 7, 1985). Most bizarrely:

A man who played a "Rambo" role for hero-worshipping teenagers was behind bars Saturday, accused of "brainwashing the kids" with commando warfare tactics and conspiring with one child to kill his parents. Wilmer Leonard McClinton Jr., 32, was held in the Mobile County Jail without bond on charges of selling firearms to minors, conspiracy to commit murder, criminal possession of explosives and contributing to delinquency of minors . . . . Lee said raids Friday on McClinton's home in Satsuma and former residence in Mobile produced knives, gunpowder and exploding arrows. Police said he used weapons and live ammunition to teach commando tactics to boys aged 11 to 15. "He took some of the kids to see the movie *Rambo* 10 times," said Juvenile Unit Sgt. James Huey.
(*Proprietary to the United Press International*, November 9, 1985)

The release of *Rambo* on video cassette multiplied the Rambo effect with many people purchasing or renting the film. The cassette sold 425,000 units the first day that it went on the market, breaking previous records (*PR Newswire*, January 14, 1986). Stories continued to circulate concerning the Rambo effect: "A teenager who defense attorneys said was under the delusion that he was John Rambo, a fictional Vietnam War veteran played by Sylvester Stallone, has been convicted of stabbing his mother's best friend" (*United Press International*, May 22, 1986). A young man "told police he played 'Rambo' with his 15-year-old neighbor the night the boy was killed . . . [He] was charged with the multiple stabbing death" of the boy

(*United Press International*, April 15, 1986). And: "A teenager authorities said shot himself in front of two friends after watching two violent films starring actor Sylvester Stallone was in critical condition" (*United Press International*, May 5, 1986). Rambo had firmly established itself within US folklore and the Rambo effect continued to circulate violence and reaction.

I earlier suggested how the spectacle of *Rambo* attracted international audiences and acclaim and indeed the Rambo effect circulated through the world. Reuters reported that in war-torn El Salvador, the film

> has broken box office records . . . where 20,000 people saw it on the day it opened . . . fights broke out among people lining up for tickets and [there were] several minor injuries after patrons stampeded to get in. Several officers and soldiers in the Salvadoran army have taken to wearing the same bandanna-style head-gear as the beefy, bare-breasted Rambo.
>
> (August 2, 1985)

The film also broke "box office records in South Africa, Hong Kong, Taiwan, Venezuela and elsewhere. It has even broken box office records in Israel and Lebanon" (*Reuters North European Service*, July 31, 1985)

There were efforts to ban the film in Britain,[19] but they failed and the film was also a great success throughout Europe.[20] "Rambo" thus became a figure of the global popular who mobilized identification around the figure.[21] *Rambo* also became embroiled in world politics and the contradictions of the Cold War. An official Soviet publication attacked the film and concluded:

> *Rambo* is not the only film of its kind. Similar Hollywood creations have been playing in American theaters for several years now. And many observers are forced to admit that this film serves another purpose – to influence public opinion in favor of military adventures, particularly in regard to Nicaragua. Even Stallone admitted in an interview that his film is 'a right-wing fantasy.' It would be more accurate to say that *Rambo* is a film that sows hostility and hatred. Its widespread popularity in America is lamentable.
>
> (*The Current Digest of the Soviet Press*, August 14, 1985)

But *Rambo* received a favorable review in the *Peking Evening News*: "This is a serious film with healthy content, profound social significance and a high degree of artistic material. An outstanding work in recent American cinema" (*The Washington Post*, August 8, 1985). And China's showing of the first Rambo film broke attendance records and produced "a Rambo craze" in China (*Proprietary to the United Press International*, September 25, 1985).

Yet, "Rambo" also became a figure of contempt and a negative discourse, as well as a positive one, emerged. A "Rambo" was coded negatively as someone who was excessively masculist, out of control, and potentially dangerous and violent. Feminists used the term to mock excessive male macho behavior and political liberals deployed it to attack the excesses of the conservative political establishment. The term became increasingly negative in political discourse, showing how such popular figures are themselves contested, part of a socially and politically constructed political discourse. Indeed, "Rambo" is a polysemic cultural construct which can be appropriated by opposing sides in political debate and struggle.

And so "Rambo" became a contested figure in U.S. cultural and political iconography and discourse. On one hand, there were Rambo bars (in Houston), Rambo fashion, Rambo weapons, and iconic images of Rambo on posters and other commercial paraphenelia. A U.S. mercenary recruited to aid the Nicaraguan contras was shown in a TV interview with a massive poster of Rambo behind him and the figure Rambo was assimilated to the aggressive conservative attempts at remasculinization and the re-assertion of U.S. military power during the epoch. Yet there were frequent attacks on Ramboism in the press and Warner counted twenty articles that equated Rambo with Oliver North in the Iran/Contra affair, references that were mostly negative (Warner 1992: 686), signifying male aggression out of control and out of the bounds of democratic propriety.

The popularity of the film *Rambo* and the Stallone, Chuck Norris, and other "action-adventure" vehicles suggests that the Hollywood President and large segments of the country had assimilated a manichean worldview from Hollywood movies whereby "the enemy" is so evil and "we" are so good that only violence can eliminate threats to our well-being. Thus, Reagan's most "popular" acts were his invasion of Grenada and bombing of Libya – precisely the sort of "action" celebrated in *Rambo, Top Gun, Iron Eagle*, and the other militarist epics of the Reagan era. Hollywood films therefore provided iconography which helped mobilize support for conservative and militarist political agendas. The images of helicopters landing in Grenada and Panama carried the same positive and exciting charge as images of military action in the Hollywood militarist films.

Consequently Hollywood films of the 1980s provided the iconography for the positive reception of images of "real" (i.e. as brought to you by television) aggressive military action. The presenting of "enemies" as absolutely evil and necessary to eliminate codes such U.S. military aggression as "good." Military heroes replicate the heroism in the Hollywood military spectacles and are infused with the same popular adulation as the Rambos of the film world. Moreover, *Rambo* and the return-to-Vietnam films thus articulate conservative imperialist/militarist fantasies which in turn transcode Reaganite anti-communist and pro-militarist discourses. Indeed, Reagan constantly employed Ramboesque solutions to the political challenges of the day, fighting secret wars all over the world and engaging in overt military actions, suggesting that the Hollywood President really believed that violence was the best way to solve conflicts.[22] Not by accident were Oliver North and other members of Reagan's secret government referred to as "Rambos" when they engaged in their illegal and criminal covert operations.

And so Hollywood film in the Age of Reagan enacted rites of mythical redemption in narratives which attempted to manage social anxieties, to soothe and alleviate the sense of shame associated with defeat in Vietnam, and to smooth away the rough edges of history (i.e. U.S. atrocities in Vietnam as depicted in *Platoon* and other antiwar films). In their mythical scenarios, Americans incarnate goodness and innocence, while communists represent pure evil – precisely the fantasy of Ronald Reagan in his pre-detente incarnation and precisely the mindset of the classical Hollywood cinema which Reagan embodied. This Hollywood/Reaganite mindset was hegemonic politically and culturally during Reagan's reign and requires analysis of the contemporary political context of Hollywood film to fully capture its ideological effects.

TOP GUN: REAGANITE WET DREAM

The Reagan era was one of aggressive military intervention in the Third World, with an invasion of Grenada, the U.S.-directed and financed Contra war against Nicaragua, the bombing of Libya, and many other secret wars and covert actions around the globe. Hollywood film nurtured this militarist mindset and thus provided cultural representations that mobilized support for such aggressive policy. Reagan's policies were continued by George Bush, who undertook an even more large-scale aggressive military action against Iraq. As an example of a media cultural studies that situates film in its socio-political context, I will next undertake readings of a series of Reaganite fantasies that legitimated the aggressive militarist policies of the Reagan and Bush Administrations and that provide a pool of cultural representations which could be mobilized to generate support for Bush's war against Iraq – an event that I interrogate in Chapter 5 below.

Top Gun (1986) was one of a series of films during the 1980s that encoded the Reaganite ethos of militarism, advocating a strong military while celebrating conservative and military values. Like *Rambo* and the other return-to-Vietnam films, *Iron Eagle*, *Red Dawn*, and other Reaganite fantasies, *Top Gun* celebrates individualistic heroism, military valor, and conservative American values. Like these other films, it operates in a binary universe where there is a struggle between good and evil in which the enemy is absolutely evil and Americans represent the embodiment of "goodness." Coming at the tail end of the Cold War with the Soviet Union, *Top Gun* is not as fiercely anti-communist as some of the films just mentioned, but its "enemy" seems to be Soviet communists, though the foreign Other to the good Americans is indeterminate enough to encompass Soviet allies like Libya or Iraq (i.e. the "enemy" flies MIGs, a Soviet plane, but is not identified as Russian, though the MIG fighter pilots have red stars on their helmets; yet, since this was the epoch in which Reagan bombed Libya, to the delight of his conservative brethren, the film's enemy could be read as Arab nations using Soviet MIGs and no specific anti-Soviet ideology is articulated in the film).

In many ways, *Top Gun* thoroughly embodies the social attitudes of Reaganism. Appearing in 1986, before the Iran/Contra crisis, the 1987 stock market crash, and exposés of the Savings and Loan scandals, *Top Gun* represents the ascendancy of a triumphant Reaganism at its last moment of supremacy before its fall from uncontested hegemony (obviously Reaganism had its comeback with the triumph of George Bush, Son of Teflon – but that's another story told in Kellner 1990a). The film was the most popular box office draw of the year, suggesting that it tuned into the social ethos of the epoch, and puts on display the central values of Reaganite conservativism.

Top Gun is primarily about competition and winning – women, military honor, sports, and social success. It unabashedly celebrates the value of being *top* gun, the elite, the best, the winner. The story features the exploits of Pete Mitchell, code-named Maverick, and winningly played by Tom Cruise in one of his string of Reaganite fantasies (*Risky Business*, *All the Right Moves*, *Cocktail*, and so on). Cruise's Maverick embodies the Reaganite/Yuppie values of winning at all costs, of putting competition at the center of life, and going all out to win in every domain of social existence from dating, to sports, to career.

The film opens with titles indicating that in 1969 the Navy Air Core set up a school to train elite aerial fighters, and in a later training session, it is announced that the U.S. needs to maintain its ratio of expert aerial fighter pilots in the contemporary world. The message is that even in a high-tech, computerized society, individual initiative and skill are crucial, indeed essential, to military survival. At one point, Maverick valorizes individual intuitive ability rather than cognitive abilities: "You don't have time to think up there. If you think, you're dead." The same anti-intellectual ethos pervaded the *Star Wars* films and inadvertently put on display the anti-intellectualism and thoughtlessness that was an essential part of Reaganism, promoted daily by President Feel-Good and by the commercial media which shared his values and anti-intellectualism (i.e. advertising, for instance, works by addressing and manipulating fears and fantasies, and not by utilizing rational discourse; Reaganism and media culture work, I suggest, in a similar fashion).

The opening title sequence through its montage of sound and images establishes the ethos of the film. As the titles cross the screen, eerie music provides a background to images of silhouettes slowly moving through a misty early morning dawn. The images of men are coupled with pictures of airplanes and the music shifts to more upbeat rhythms and the sounds of airplane motors and staccato radio messages produce a rich sound collage. A V-sign is flashed and a plane takes off from an aircraft carrier "somewhere in the Indian Ocean." The modernist image construction and collage of image and sound codes the fighter pilots with a mystical aura, drawing on the cultural codes of *Triumph of the Will*, which opened with a picture of an airplane magically moving through clouds to the accompaniment of martial music in a fusion of images of nature, technology, and clouds. *Top Gun* opens with a similar fusion and the project of the film will be to fuse high-tech imagery, mythical heroism, and masculinity into a figure of the "top gun" who succeeds in every walk of life and who will produce a proper role model for Reaganite youth.

The music track cuts to a rock background and two fighter planes and their crews take off for their daily mission. The fighter pilots and their planes have mythical names (Ghostrider, Merlin, Cougar, Maverick, and so on) and the image construction utilizes off-center framing, quick cutting, and high-tech sound montage to fuse the fighter pilots with awesome power and glory. Enemy MIGs suddenly appear and after ritualistic dogfighting, one of the fighter pilots, Cougar, loses control and Maverick must risk his life to escort his dazed comrade back to the destroyer where the planes are based. Cougar decides to quit and loses his status as "top gun" fighter, ineligible to go to the elite training school. Instead Maverick and his co-pilot Goose get their chances to prove themselves and enter the competition for the best of the best. In the Reaganite universe, only the elite succeed and the faint-hearted must fall by the wayside, deprived of the success and honor reserved for the top guns and top dogs in the deadly competition for wealth and power in which only the winners succeed and everyone else is a loser.

The clouds, fog, shiny planes, high-tech control centers, and handsome and heroic young pilots in the opening sequence code the naval aviators as modern heros, as quasimythical embodiments of the mystery and power of modern technology. Here high-tech image construction with the best cameras, editing equipment, and personnel invest the figures with aestheticized glory and the dazzling fight scenes and gee-whiz sound effects likewise encode the flight and fighting scenes with the awe and power of aestheticized technology. As with fascism as a political movement (see Benjamin 1969), military films like *Top Gun* aestheticize war and thus provide soft-core propaganda for the military. Indeed, the credits at the end provide "special thanks" to the pilots of the U.S. Navy F-16 aircraft and credit a large number of military officials and pilots who participated in the film, thus certifying its credentials as official, U.S. government approved propaganda.

One wonders how many pilots and soldiers who joined the military and fought in the Panama invasion, the Gulf War, and other military escapades of the era were influenced by such cinematic propaganda. Hollywood film, like the Hollywood President, are not innocent entertainment, but lethal weapons in the service of dominant socio-economic forces. *Top Gun*'s ideological project is to invest desire in the figure of heroic fighter pilots and high-tech war which it does with attractive star figures, cinematic high-tech wizardry and special effects, rock music and the sounds of speed and power, and, of course, the sophisticated planes and military gadgets. As noted, the images and spectacles of high-tech entertainment are semiotic vehicles that subliminally transmit ideological effects. During an initial Top Gun training session, one pilot whispers to another, when watching a video of a high-tech explosion/kill, "this gives me a hard-on." Indeed, this is the project of the film itself which turns on the spectator to the thrill of technological death, fusing Eros and Thanatos, libidinal energy and destruction, in images of technowar,[23] thus helping to produce the psychological disposition to thrill to images of technodeath in events like the Persian Gulf War against Iraq.

The scene cuts to Miramar, California, home of "Fightertown U.S.A," where the "top gun" school is found. Here, Maverick begins his competition with "Iceman," who is viewed as the top fighter pilot, the one to beat. Iceman and his partner "Slider" are your perfect all-American fraternity boy jocks, who reek with self-confidence, privilege, and the conviction that they are the best and deserve whatever they get. Maverick and Goose, by contrast, are more marginal characters and vaguely working class; they are the underdogs who will fiercely compete to become top dogs, celebrating the values and lifestyle of the dominant elites by their single-minded pursuit of the same values and goals.

It is soon clear that success with women is part of what it means to be "top gun." After their initial orientation session, the pilots go into a local bar, filled with attractive women coming on to the largely military male clientele. As the spectator voyeuristically enters the bar, one sees representations of female flesh and flashing smiles, projecting images of erotic paradise for the technowarriors of the Top Gun school. Media culture produces images that mobilize audience desire into certain modes of thought, behavior, and role models that serve the interest of maintaining and reproducing the status quo. Showing the pilots with beautiful women helps to invest the images of the military with erotic energy and turns on female spectators as well to equate sexual excitement with the military and uniforms, thus helping to supply the actual would-be warriors with the sexual prizes that serve as part of the stimulant for military service and heroism. In addition, women are objectified as sexual commodities, valued for good looks and readiness to serve and gratify men.

The message of the bar scene for women is that military men are exciting partners, thus positioning women to admire men in uniform. The message for males is that if you join the military, wear the uniform, and exhibit the marks of rank and honor, you'll score with the women, that, in short, military guys get the girls. As he enters the bar, Maverick quickly spots an attractive woman and makes his moves, singing to her, clowning, and coming on to her. She rejects him for an older man, but he follows her into the women's room where he continues his pursuit; competition and entrepreneurship demand innovation and courage to score the big bucks, glory, and girls promised by the conservative ideology of the era.

The next day as he enters his flight class, Maverick sees that the woman is his flight instructor and he cowers down beneath his dark glasses. The woman, Charlie (Kelly McGillis), is the perfect Reaganite female: competitive, out for promotion, and proper in her behavior. She incarnates a conservative appropriation of feminism in which women compete as equals with men while retaining their "femininity." "Charlie" has a man's name, but thoroughly feminine looks, sensibility, and behavior. She also represents the new woman in the military, and during a period in which the volunteer army depended on women recruits, her image of a successful and attractive military woman provides free recruitment advertisements for the volunteer army; many women probably found themselves in the deserts of Saudi Arabia during 1990, awaiting a violent war, as a result of appropriating positive images of women in military life promoted by films like *Top Gun*.

Top Gun also replicates conservative Hollywood cinematic and ideological codes. It utilizes the conventions of romance to validate Maverick as the prototype of the successful male. In subtle ways, the film also reinscribes the domination of women by men and the conventions of male-dominated romance. At first, Maverick finds himself subordinate to Charlie: she is his teacher, who has a Ph.D. in astrophysics, and is a figure of the new woman authority figure who is a threat to male power and domination. As their relationship evolves, it is she who initiates the romantic connection after his initial overtures. As the moment of their sexual involvement approaches, she states: "This is going to be complicated." By the end of the film, however, Charlie is rendered subordinate to Maverick. As he returns to the Top Gun flight school, a hero and now an instructor, the audience sees Charlie bestow upon Maverick an adoring glance; their eyes meet and this time it is Maverick who says, "This is going to be complicated," establishing himself as the initiator and the master of the relation. This narrative ploy not only utilizes the traditional Hollywood trope of the happy ending to mobilize audience pleasure in Maverick's total triumph, but also invests pleasure in his mastery of the strong woman.

The film provides as well positive images of family, father–son male bonding, and the continuity of generations – familiar conservative themes during an era in which such values had been strongly contested in the 1960s and 1970s. Maverick is the son of Duke Mitchell, a fighter pilot who had died under mysterious circumstances. In a key scene, Maverick visits Viper (Tom Skerritt) who tells him of his father's heroism and that his military record was stained because he, Viper, and others had strayed across the border to pursue the enemy (presumably in Laos or Cambodia) and thus had broken rules. Maverick talks of his family to Viper – presented himself as a good family man – and Viper comes to assume a surrogate father role to Maverick.

The images of Maverick's partner Goose also reinforce the family ideology. In one cafe scene, soon before Goose's death, Goose, his wife, and his children enjoy themselves with Maverick and Charlie. Goose plays the piano and sings "Great Balls of Fire," with the whole group energetically joining in. The singing of popular rock 'n' roll songs, and the ever-present rock soundtrack background, also invest the characters with positive energy, for their association with rock music associates them with the cultural signs of pleasure and sociality, aspects which are fused with images of family in this scene. The cafe scene ends with Goose's wife saying to him, "Goose, you great stud; take me to bed or lose me forever." For the top guns, therefore, marriage, good times, and intense sexuality come together in one convenient package and that package is marriage and family: the ultimate destination of Maverick and Charlie, with Charlie repeating the "take to me bed" phrase to Maverick soon after as they kiss on a moonlit night beside the bay as the scene cuts to black.

As in all good fantasies, the hero is tested and this happens when Maverick and Goose are engaged in a training exercise and their plane spins out of control; they are forced to evacuate and Goose is killed. Maverick feels guilty and resigns from the top gun school, though his father figure Viper talks him into returning to graduate. At the graduation ceremonies, there is a call for the top candidates to go immediately to a crisis assignment: Iceman, his partner Merlin, and Maverick are selected. The scene cuts to the "Indian Ocean, 24 hours later," where a communications ship is missing and must be rescued; MIGs are all around the area and there is a fear that the enemy will reach the ship first. Iceman and a partner and Maverick and the Iceman's former partner Merlin are sent out on patrol and encounter the enemy MIGs. Maverick saves Iceman and manages to knock out a series of MIGs, thus becoming the hero of his military peer group. These final battle scenes celebrate the vital role of the military and military heroism: the Top Gun shows that he has "all the right moves" and in "risky business" with the enemy he triumphs, blowing away MIG after MIG to the delight of the audience (I still recall with horror that Saturday afternoon when I saw the film with a thoroughly enraptured audience which roared with every kill).

I am aware that this reading of the manipulative effects of an ideology machine like *Top Gun* goes against the current emphasis on the active audience, constructing their own (oppositional) meanings from cultural texts. But some blockbuster films like *Top Gun* are carefully constructed ideological machines that celebrate and reproduce hegemonic political positions and attitudes. *Top Gun* positions the audience in ways to induce spectators to identify or sympathize with its politics; while many of us may resist these positions and may not buy into their ideologies, we must actively resist the text itself. Sure, spectators can produce any number of "oppositional" or "aberrant" readings, but we should also distinguish between texts that invite or facilitate oppositional readings and those that resist them, and we should recognize that some films succeed in pulling audiences into their ideological projects while others fail. Moreover, cultural studies should promote critical media literacy to help audiences resist ideological manipulation and this requires understanding of the ideological operations and effects of films like *Rambo* and *Top Gun*.

Like *Rambo*, *Top Gun* was one of the most popular films of its time, grossing over $130 million by the end of 1986, becoming the year's top-grossing film (*Time*, November 24, 1986). Like *Rambo*, it provided role models for identification and helped promote conservativism and militarism. *Time* reported that: "Its glorified portrayal of Navy life spurred theater owners in such cities as Los Angeles and Detroit to ask the Navy to set up recruiting exhibits outside cinemas where *Top Gun* was playing to sign up the young moviegoers intoxicated by the Hollywood fantasy" (November 24, 1986). It was later reported that the film made high school students dream of military life and contributed to a big jump in applications to military academies. Many students mentioned the film in their applications and a West Point captain agreed: "It doesn't hurt to have neat movies like *Top Gun* . . . I think everyone enjoyed the spill-off from that" (*The Washington Post*, January 19, 1987). A retired admiral noted that Tom Cruise and *Top Gun* "did a lot" for the Naval Academy. "They're still standing in line to become Naval aviators" (*The Washington Post*, June 24, 1987). The movie continued to be popular and Tom Cruise was named by students in grades eight through twelve as the person they most admired, according to a poll by the *World Almanac and Book of Facts* (*United Press International*, February 4, 1988). The film eventually took in over $350 million in box office receipts, had high video cassette rentals and sales, and entered U.S. folklore, with many Gulf War pilots and commentators referring to the film to describe U.S. military aviation exploits in the war against Iraq.

Such is the "genius" of *Top Gun* that it provides a relatively seamless narrative with few, if any, socially critical moments, polysemic meanings, discordant voices, or critical, marginal elements. The film rigorously privileges the position of Maverick, with whom the audience is invited to identify, and affirms without question his values and goals. Tom Cruise, of course, infuses his character with a winning smile and he is invested with romantic charm and attractiveness as he pursues and wins the flight instructor Charlie. Images of him playing volleyball, or undressing in the locker room or bedroom, present his body as hard, well-sculptured, and athletic, precisely the dominant figure of male virility and attractiveness.

Top Gun draws on cultural imagery from the last several decades to encode its hero with glory and positivity, and works to decenter and marginalize all oppositional readings. For instance, Maverick wears a black jacket and drives a motor-cycle, the image of 1950s rebellion; his name replays a popular television hero who was something of an oppositional, non-conformist – but safe – figure on 1950s TV (i.e. the cowboy gamblers Bart and Brett Maverick, resurrected in a 1994 film). With the Tom Cruise Maverick figure, however, these symbols of rebellion become icons of male fashion and virility. The soundtrack plays 1950s and 1960s rock music, which the characters sing at key junctures in the film. Here too symbols of non-conformity and individuality become symbols of group identity and cohesiveness. In fact, Maverick's "individuality" is thoroughly consistent with military group cohesiveness and is even functional for military purposes.

Thus, *Top Gun* utilizes dominant cultural imagery of the past decades to present a cultural synthesis of the present as the embodiment of everything that was best in the past: all oppositional meanings to potent cultural symbols are shorn away and they serve to celebrate the conservative present as the best of all possible worlds. Consequently, while the films of Robert Altman deconstruct Hollywood genres, American mythologies, and dominant ideologies in order to produce a complex text that problematizes our relation to dominant cultural forms, *Top Gun* exploits the images, symbols, and forms of the past to privilege conservative ideological positions in the present.

Top Gun's take on race is nowhere near the virulent racism that infected *Rambo*, *Iron Eagle*, and many other political films of the era. The "enemy" is faceless and though it is dangerous and must be destroyed, it is indeterminate and unnamed. Indeed, only one significant scene involves race in the whole film and it is a mark of the subtle racism practiced by conservative politicians and filmmakers when they couldn't get away with more blatant racism. After his partner Goose's death, a guilt-ridden Maverick finds it impossible to fly at his usual heroic level and when his new black partner chides him for failing to adequately perform during a flight exercise, Maverick grabs the black and rather nastily tells him: "I'll fire when I'm ready to fire. Have you got that?" This singular eruption of violence, the only time that Maverick loses his cool, functions to put an uppity and too-ambitious black in his place and puts on display white fears of blacks taking their positions or outperforming them.

Previously, the black pilot was a silent figure, frequently on the edges of the frames picturing the top guns. As a faceless figure depicted as part of the military team, he appears as an icon of the integrated military, which provides equal opportunity for whites and blacks and that provides blacks the possibility of advancement. Only in this one scene is the black given narrative prominence and here, he is coded negatively. Indeed, there is no reason why Maverick should have to remonstrate with a black partner, a white would have done just as well, except that the ideology machine *Top Gun* wants to exploit lingering hostilities toward people of color to gratuitously drive the audience to pity and sympathize with the temporarily limp hero.

Even more revealing, the black fighter pilot is the only main Top Gun trainee whose name is never mentioned or highlighted: his code name "Sundown" is faintly visible on the bottom of his helmet as he flies with Maverick, but his helmet is suddenly blank when he confronts Maverick on the ground, as if he has no personal identity and is merely a figure of the uppity black. Thus, while all the white pilots have their code names prominently displayed, the black is without significant identity. This omission (perhaps inadvertently) points to the inferior position of blacks who manage to become integrated into the white power structure and points to the complicity of popular Hollywood cinema in keeping blacks and people of color in a subordinate position. In fact, the codename "Sundown" connotes an absence of light, equating it with the color "black" that is negatively valorized in racist iconography. Indeed, *Top Gun* presents a primarily white elite, without the ethnicity that characterized the classical Hollywood war film or many contemporary war films (i.e. *The Boys in Company C*, *Platoon*, and *Heartbreak Ridge*).

Thus, through image and narrative construction, the Reaganism of the 1980s is ideologically infused with Tom Cruise's winning smile and military heroism is celebrated as the way to gain social acceptance and prestige. The military adventures of the Reagan and Bush regimes require willing accomplices and films like *Top Gun* help with recruitment and the production of proper attitudes. The society also needs highly competitive young people to spur the economy to new entrepreneurial heights and the film's celebration of competition and winning as the supreme value helps promote proper(ly capitalistic) social values, while perpetuating the myth of the American dream. Furthermore, it provides appropriate gender models too. Not surprisingly, Charlie appears back at the Top Gun school where the triumphant Maverick asked to be assigned after his heroic feats. They are obviously coupled at the end, so the narrative machine of the film satisfies all desire for closure: the hero wins his glory, gets the girl, and satisfies all of his goals. The traditional Hollywood happy ending thus serves to validate dominant sociopolitical values – as it always did. Conservative film form and conservative political values march together toward the American utopia that it was Reagan's political genius to sell to a public ideologically nurtured on Hollywood fantasies. Reaganite political discourse and Hollywood film thus provide complementary visions of a very specific ideological fantasy.

Thus, *Top Gun*'s conservativism is seamless and total: the film perfectly reproduces the conservative discourses of the period on winning and individual competition, the military, gender and heterosexual coupling, the family, patriotism, and race. The year's number one film thus allows analysis of the dominant ideology of the period which it serves to reproduce and strengthen. One of a series of popular conservative films, it anticipated the bombing of Libya and the Gulf War, while replicating the heroic fantasies of military success exposed in the Iran/Contra scandal: the revenge of the real which punctuated the military fantasies of the Hollywood White House. "It'll make a good movie someday," Reagan wistfully informed Oliver North when he was forced to dismiss him as the Iran/Contra scandal was exposed, and unless Tom Cruise continues his trek to the left (i.e. *Born on the Fourth of July*, *A Few Good Men*) perhaps Cruise himself will star in *Ollie North, Top Gun*, a potential cinematic replay of "Hollywood Politics, The Movie."

TO THE GULF WAR!

Top Gun, however, is only one of a series of conservative military films of the era (see Kellner and Ryan 1988; Britton 1986). Together, these films prepared the country for the Gulf War by celebrating the virtues of high-tech weaponry and military heroism, creating an Arab enemy to replace the Soviet nemesis, and promoting the specific foreign policy agendas of Reagan and Bush. Thus, just as late 1970s Hollywood films prepared the country for the conservative hegemony of the 1980s and early 1990s, so too did films of the Reagan and Bush era produce attitudes that would support the conservative and militarist policies of the hegemonic Republicans.

Iron Eagle I (1985) and II (1988) presciently anticipated the turn from a communist enemy to Arab nemesis. Together, the two *Iron Eagle* films portray the move toward detente with the Soviet Union and the production of a new superenemy which eventually found its incarnation in Saddam Hussein and Iraq, uncannily anticipated in *Iron Eagle I* and *II*. The *Iron Eagle* films contributed to the anti-Arab sentiments of the day by presenting negative images of Arab "terrorists" and regimes. The first *Iron Eagle* film was aided by the Israeli government which provided F-16s, Phantoms, pilots to fly the planes, and Israeli military advisors. The film was funded by a rich Texan who "had never invested in films before" and wanted "to make non-exploitation action films with pro-American sentiments", (*Los Angeles Times*, July 31, 1985). The film got poor reviews, but did well at the box office, leading to two sequels that also promoted anti-Arab politics. It is not by accident that Hollywood films follow the trajectory of U.S. foreign policy: films are highly capital-intensive and the producers of the culture industries closely follow political and social trends. They are especially sensitive to winds of change, so when detente with the Soviet Union appears as an important political development, Hollywood shifts its focus accordingly (leading to a box office problem for Sylvester Stallone's *Rambo III* which picked the Soviets as enemies in his Afghan epic at the very moment of detente). Yet Hollywood adventure films must have an Enemy, an evil "Foreign Other," and both Hollywood and Reagan and Bush turned to Arab "villains" for the political demonization necessary for the narratives of Hollywood film and U.S. politics at the moment when the Soviet Union was turning to Big Macs, pornography, crime, and capitalism.

The first *Iron Eagle* is more of a teen fantasy film than a full-blown military propaganda film *à la Top Gun* or an exercise in conservative ideological masturbation *à la Rambo*. The film opens with a high-tech air war between MIGs and U.S. fighter planes with a U.S. pilot shot down. An unnamed Arab country claims that the U.S. planes violated their air space, recalling the dogfighting between U.S. and Libyan fighter planes when Libya claimed air space for itself which the U.S. argued went beyond that allowed by international law. But in this version of the incident, the U.S. government covers over the capture and trial of the U.S. pilot, allowing him to languish in an Arab prison.

The son of the pilot is a would-be fighter pilot himself, deeply disappointed that he did not get admitted into the Air Force Academy because he failed a high school course during the time that he spent in Air Force flight simulators. The boy, Doug McMasters, his teenage friends, and a black retired pilot Chappy Sinclair (Lou Gossett, Jr.) conspire to save him. They use their airbase connections to get intelligence on the prison where the father is being held, steal two Air Force planes, and the son and Chappy undertake the father's rescue. In an incredibly hokey and implausible scenario, they do just that, knocking out half of the Arab army in the process.

Iron Eagle is extremely racist, portraying Arabs as subhuman sadists and villains. The Arab leader, who looks a lot like Saddam Hussein, is vicious and dictatorial. Arabs torture the captured U.S. pilot and sentence him to death arbitrarily and without any due process. In the final duel scene, the Arab leader himself commandeers a plane to fight the Americans after they liberate the captured pilot and the audience is positioned to cheer when the young teenager blows the Arab leader away. This scene replicates a disturbing trope, dominant in Hollywood adventure films from *Star Wars* to the present, in which audience pleasure is mobilized by images of total destruction. Such an audience is being preconditioned to crave the total obliteration of enemy countries like Iraq and such scenes thus produce pleasure in mass destruction – pleasure that would be mobilized by the computer videos of high-tech bombing in the Gulf War.

Iron Eagle II (1988) is more serious and more politically interesting. It enacts detente with the Soviet Union and the turn toward the Arab enemy. While the villain in *Iron Eagle I* looked like Saddam Hussein, the Arab enemy is obviously Iraq in the sequel. The plot involves a joint U.S./Soviet project to knock out an Arab secret nuclear bomb installation, fictively replaying the Israeli bombing of the Iraqi nuclear installation of 1981. Indeed, the film's credits end by giving "special thanks" to "the Ministry of Defense in the State of Israel" and thanks the Israeli Defence Forces and the Israeli Air Force. The film is an Israel–Canada co-production and if *Top Gun* can be legitimately seen as U.S. military propaganda, *Iron Eagle II* can be seen as Israeli propaganda.

The dramatic tension in the film is built around the conflicts between the U.S. and Soviet fighters, their surmounting of their former hostilities, and their pulling together to defeat the common enemy (a fantasy that Bush and his war team realized, with some success, in the war against Iraq). The successful conclusion is delayed by the machinations of a paranoid U.S. general who still hates and distrusts the Russians and who does everything possible to sabotage the mission (he attempted to ensure that the mission would fail initially by picking the worst possible misfits for the U.S. team). This general represents the lingering obstacle to detente and his defeat and humiliation represents the need for new military thinking, new enemies, and new strategies in the post-Cold-War world.

Not surprisingly, the Iron Eagle team triumphs, totally obliterating the Arab (read: Iraqi) nuclear installation, ending the threat of a sneak nuclear attack or nuclear blackmail. While the white and black Americans and Russians learn to work and cooperate together, they turn their hostility on villainous Arabs who are blown away with the body counts that Hollywood used to reserve for commies. In *Iron Eagle II*, however, the Arab enemies are voiceless and for the most part faceless, thus dehumanizing Arabs as ciphers who threaten, but are less than human.

Once again, Hollywood follows the trajectory of U.S. foreign policy, uncannily anticipating the war against Iraq. Indeed, in his Thanksgiving 1990 trip to visit the U.S. troops in Saudi Arabia, Bush expressed his concerns that Iraq had a nuclear capability that might be operative within a year as a justification for U.S. military action. This line was repeated by his administration officials over the next two days, but was dropped when every informed official indicated that it would be at least five to ten years before Iraq could obtain a credible nuclear facility (see Kellner 1992b, Chapter 2).

Other anti-Arab films of the Reagan/Bush era include *The Delta Force* (1986) which uses the format of the disaster film to vilify Arabs in a fictional account of a Palestinian hijacking of a passenger jet: the "terrorists" are thoroughly villainous and the film uses comic-book exaggeration to sketch out pictures of "good" Jews, Israelis, and Americans, menaced by the "evil" Palestinians. *Death Before Dishonor* (1987) portrays Arab terrorism against Israelis and then against the U.S. embassy and U.S. Marines in a fictional country of Jemel, thus linking the U.S. and Israel as common allies against Arab terrorism. *Steal the Sky* (1988) also positively portrays Israel, idealizing an Israeli attempt to steal a Soviet MIG from Iraq in the mid-1960s.

An ideologically bizarre fantasy film, *The Retaliator* (1986), also known as *Programmed to Kill*, portrays vicious Arabs who kill young tourists and then kidnap and torture American youths. A woman Arab sympathizer (Sandra Berdhahl) is captured by the U.S. forces and transformed into a robot, sent back to assassinate the Arab terrorist leader, her former lover. She does this, but then turns on the U.S. forces, obliterating several villainous Americans in a bizarre mixture of anti-Arab and anti-U.S. intelligence agency narrative. Such an ideologically contradictory scenario articulates populist fears both of evil foreign Others and of evil perpetuated by one's own government in a primarily paranoic imaginary that sees evil everywhere. It also displays fears of women getting out of control, in the image of the killer woman robot, who systematically murders terrorists and U.S. government agents alike.[24]

Navy Seals (1990) celebrates the high-tech commando forces which, according to one report, played a key role in the Gulf War (see *Newsweek* "Secret Warriors," June 17, 1991). Once again Arabs are dehumanized as fanatic terrorists, possessing deadly Stinger missiles which threaten innocent civilians. The SEAL team (named for their operations on SEa, Air, and Land) embody all the virtues of courage and efficiency and obliterate literally hundreds of Arabs, previewing the slaughter of the Iraqis by the high-tech military in the Gulf War. Like *Rambo*, *Navy Seals* and other anti-Arab films such as *Iron Eagle*, *The Delta Force* and *Death Before Dishonor* portray prolonged and detailed scenes of torture, to present Arabs as savage criminals and to position the audience against such villains.[25]

All of these films dehistorize actual historical conflicts and present struggles between Arabs and the West as a battle between civilization and barbarism in an indeterminate and mythical space. Prince (1993) documents how the anti-Arab thrillers "avoid locating the story in clear geographic terms" (ibid. 245). This indeterminacy functions to generally stigmatize Arabs and to provide villain scenarios that can be mobilized in any number of political interventions against, say, Iraq, Iran, Syria, Libya, or whoever. As Prince concludes:

> The vague geographical and political specifications accruing to the national and cultural conflicts dramatized in these films operates to render them in strongly ideological terms, in which the enemy occupies no terrain specifiable on a map's coordinates but is rather a hazy, nebulous, threatening Other, a projection of political and cultural anxieties that are stripped of their historical basis and are assigned to regions of the world in generalized, superficial and essentially mythological terms.
>
> (ibid.: 246)

These representations of Arabs in the contemporary Hollywood cinema are extremely racist and are disturbingly similar to perceptions of Jews in fascist films. In a variety of 1970s political thrillers, Arabs are portrayed as fanatic "terrorists" who coldly murder innocent victims (*Black Sunday*, *Nighthawks*) and lack human feeling. In corporate conspiracy films of the 1970s and 1980s, they are presented, or are alluded to, as greedy capitalists (*Rollover*, *Network*, *The Formula*, *Wrong is Right*, etc.). Thus, Arabs are serving as new villain stereotypes in Hollywood films and by the 1980s were the privileged target of Hollywood manicheanism (see Shaheen 1984).

Such stereotypes obviously dehumanize Arabs, presenting them as violent and villainous. In general, the anti-Arab films of the past years combine racist and chauvinist ideologies that present Arabs as the incarnation of evil and Americans as the embodiment of good. This vision replays what Edward Said (1978) described as "Orientalism" which establishes the virtues of the West by means of delineation of differences between the "civilized" West and the "savage" Orient which was portrayed as irrational, barbaric, underdeveloped, and inferior to the rational, refined, and humane West. In *Navy Seals*, the film opens with cuts between a terrorist attack on a U.S. Navy helicopter and a wedding scene in which a black member of the group is getting married. The images set the scene for contrast between representations of the civilized and personalized Americans and the savage and depersonalized Arabs. The black SEAL is killed and a long funeral underscores the value of life in the West, in contrast to the seeming disdain for life in the Middle East. The scenes also transfer racism from blacks to Arabs, presenting the black in positive terms against the viciously represented Arabs.

Arabs were thus the villain of choice for Hollywood adventure films and the conservative U.S. administrations. Hollywood orientalism helped produce negative images of Arabs that Bush could mobilize in demonizing the Iraqis in the Persian Gulf War. In these same adventure film scenarios, women tended to be decentered and a pornographic erotics of violence replaced sexual eroticism, much as the cool killers of the Persian Gulf War were shown pornography films before going out on their "turkey shoots" against the literally defenseless Iraqis, showering their bombs on military and civilian targets in spasms of ejaculatory violence lit up by flashing infra-red photos of anti-aircraft fire exploding in orgasmic splendor. This erotics of violence, visible daily in the Gulf War, was anticipated in the video games and war films of the preceding years and has helped produce a pornographic military culture that may produce even more monstrous films and foreign policy adventures in the years to come.

And yet critical examination of these pro-war and anti-Arab films exposes their simplicity and puerile childishness. *Iron Eagle*, for instance, is constantly deconstructing its conservative ideology. When the teenage son learns that his father is being held prisoner in the Middle East, his black teenage friend tells him not to worry, because "President Peanut" is out and the new President, "Ronald Raygun," will take decisive action and rescue his father. Well, the government does nothing, requiring the teen heroes to carry out the rescue mission themselves (the real Reagan would, of course, realize the fantasy of attacking Arab enemies in his Libya bombing of 1986). Thus the film inadvertently conveys the message that the current conservative government is incompetent and uncaring (approximately the truth in this case). Moreover, this rightist fantasy constantly portrays the military as a bunch of bunglers, who are constantly being manipulated by the teenagers who are able to steal crucial intelligence and two fighter planes for their mission.

Iron Eagle's scenario is so hyperbolic, so ridiculous, that it reveals itself as sheer nonsense, as a totally implausible teen fantasy picture that allows teenagers to be heroes, to identify with characters that carry out heroic actions that complacent adults are unable to do. This specific fantasy structure, though, limits its identity positions to teenagers and perhaps black men silly enough to identify with Cappy. No self-respecting adult, however, could identify with the fantasy or accept its narrative terms as plausible. *Iron Eagle* thus presents itself as an extremely limited teen fantasy, of limited ideological use.

Other anti-Arab films also deconstruct their own opposition between the "savage" Middle East and the "civilized" West. While the West supposedly values life and the Middle East devalues it, the films indulge in the slaughter of countless Arabs. One is supposed to cheer such slaughter as a cleansing of irredeemable evil, but the brutality and repetitiveness of the high-tech massacres indicate that the true savages are those in the West who make such simplistic barbaric films, which prepare the way for real life high-tech massacres, as the genocidal U.S. war against Iraq.

Read diagnostically, even right-wing films can be seen to expose their contradictions and to undercut the ideologies that they affirm. One could do a deconstructive reading of the rightist fantasy *Red Dawn*, that features a Soviet-led invasion of the U.S., which shows the ludicrousness of right-wing anti-communist fears and obsessions (see Kellner 1991). Such ideological fantasies may be of sufficient complexity, or riven by internal conflicts, to produce oppositional readings against the grain, while more modernist films like *Nashville*, *Blade Runner*, *Do the Right Thing* or *Zelig* may require multivalent readings to do justice to their complexity.

A film like *Top Gun*, by contrast, is an ideology machine that mobilizes desire into certain ideological positions and utilizes narrative to privilege some positions (i.e. success, winning, romance), while negatively presenting other positions (i.e. quitting, losing, not being a team player, etc.). The narrative attempts to position the audience to identify with certain characters and then produces obstacles to their attaining the goal that the audience is positioned to want them to obtain (i.e. getting the girl, becoming top gun). When the narrative allows the audience desire to be satisfied by producing the romantic couple and military heroism at the end, the audience is positioned to experience these victories as good and to identify with the values and behavior celebrated.

Yet some qualifications should be made. The audience may resist the attempt at manipulation and the text may fail to obtain its ideological ends. A film like *Top Gun* is successful, however, as attested to by its box office reception and positive reception by audiences. Some films may be more conflicted and contradictory than a successful ideology machine like *Top Gun*. Indeed, many Hollywood films are neither "conservative" nor "liberal" because they want to play it both ways, to gain the maximum possible audience by offending nobody. Predominantly conservative texts may contain liberal features or deconstructively undermine their own conservativism, and liberal films during the 1970s were constantly reproducing conservative discourses (see the discussion of corporate and political conspiracy films and the Jane Fonda films in Kellner and Ryan 1988). In any case, the artifacts of media culture should be read in their specific social contexts to decipher their meanings and messages and to appraise their effects. I amplify this notion of a diagnostic and contextual cultural studies in the following chapter, where I will also more fully elucidate and develop some of the theoretical categories introduced here as well as my conception of cultural studies.

NOTES

1 The process of "transcoding" describes how social discourses are translated into media texts, as when *Easy Rider* transcodes 1960s countercultural discourses of freedom, individualism, and community in cinematic images and scenes, when, for instance, the bikers drive through nature with the soundtrack playing "Born to be Wild," or "Wasn't Born to Follow." See the explication and use of the term in Kellner and Ryan 1988.

2 John Thompson (1984, 1990) examines classical and recent theories of ideology and finds that many of them sever the link between ideology and domination, and therefore rob ideology of the critical edge that it had in Marx and other neo-Marxists. I would therefore agree with Thompson on the need to link the concept of ideology with theories of hegemony and domination, and thus to delimit its application to ideas and positions which serve functions of legitimation, mystification, and class domination that assure the domination of the ruling class, gender, and race over other classes and groups within society, rather than equating *all* ideas or political positions with ideology (see Kellner 1978 for an earlier presentation of this position).

3 Attempts within cultural studies to downplay the importance of ideology critique, such as Fiske (1993), play into the hands of an establishment that has for decades attempted to abolish the concept of ideology as too political and politicizing. The "end of ideology" debate within the social sciences and apolitical approaches to literature, philosophy, and the other humanities have all attempted to banish the concept of ideology. Given the centrality of the concept of ideology to earlier traditions of cultural studies, it is ironic that some of those identifying with cultural studies are now trying to put aside one of its central and defining concepts.

4 The collection was first published as part of the series of *Working Papers on Cultural Studies* 10 (1977) and then republished.

5 *Camera Politica* (Kellner and Ryan 1988) took seriously this full range of struggles and attempted to demonstrate how the current struggles of U.S. society and politics were articulated in popular film. We also stressed the need to see that conflicts between liberals and conservatives for the control over society are highly important, as are the class conflicts that were the focus of the earlier moment of Marxian ideology critique.

6 In the *New York Times* (November 27, 1993: A1), there is a story concerning the emergence of a new conservative cable TV network that is called "National Empowerment Television." The conservatives organizing this project prefer the term "populist" to that of "conservative," thus attempting to coopt another term once (and still) deployed by the Left and progressives.

7 For more detailed discussions of ideology as hegemony, see Kellner 1978, 1979, 1990a, and 1992b. My studies here build on this earlier work where I explicate these concepts in more detail.

8 Thompson (1984) examines a large number of contemporary theories of ideology which want to fundamentally define ideology in terms of language and a discourse theory. Against this position I wish to include image, symbol, myth, and narrative in the repertoire of ideological instruments, and thus combine discourse theory with myth–symbol criticism and narrative analysis in order to note the ways that images, scenes, and narratives attempt to convey ideology. A more recent move in cultural studies, influenced by some off-the-cuff remarks by Foucault and arguments of Deleuze and Guattari, would reject the concept of ideology altogether on the grounds that it is reductive, economistic, and of less importance than the apparatus of domination and control – which is then concluded to be the proper target of radical critique; Fiske (1993) takes up this argument. Although it is surely valuable to analyze such institutions and practices that reproduce social domination, simply throwing out the concept of ideology critique is theoretically disabling. Moreover, ideology is involved in the reproduction and functioning of precisely these institutions, discourses, and practices that Foucault

and others wish to analyze. Instead of throwing the concept out, what is needed is reconstruction of the concept of ideology and expansion of ideology critique that traces its functions and effects in social life.

9   For recent works in critical pedagogy that stress the need for critical media literacy, see Giroux 1992 and 1994, and McLaren *et al.* forthcoming.

10 John Fiske (1993) develops a peculiar critique of what he calls "ideology" theory that he argues covers over the fact that it is "power" that actually oppresses people and not ideology. In fact, as Gramsci, the Frankfurt School, British cultural studies, and others have argued for decades, it is a combination of overt power (i.e. forces of violence and oppression) and ideology that maintains the existing social order and that serves interests of domination and oppression. Indeed, ideology arguably has power effects and to exclude culture/ideology from power, or to too sharply distinguish between the two, seems perverse from the Foucaultian perspectives that Fiske is pursuing in his latest work. In any case, by attempting to exclude ideology critique from cultural studies, Fiske weakens the project, depriving it of a crucial weapon of critique. Furthermore, by uncritically adopting a "post-structuralist" position on power (which rejects structural perspectives), Fiske covers over the fact that there are obdurate and oppressive *structures* that oppress women, people of color, and other oppressed groups and that ideology covers over, idealizes, or naturalizes these structures. Thus, while post-structuralist perspectives on power, such as Foucault's, can contribute to a more sophisticated social theory and cultural studies, simply throwing out structural analysis and ideology critique undermines the project of cultural studies which should draw on structuralist *and* post-structuralist theory, ideology critique *and* analysis of the institutions and practices of power and domination.

11 In some major recent examples of cultural studies published in the United States, one notes a dearth of close reading of actual media culture in Brantlinger 1990; Grossberg 1992; Aronowitz 1993; and Fiske 1993. There is almost no sustained reading of popular music in Grossberg 1992, despite the fact that the book purports to be about rock music; likewise Aronowitz's *Roll Over Beethoven* (1993) fails to concretely engage media texts in favor of discussion of theory and some of the theoretical and political debates around cultural studies. Although Fiske discusses the Elvis phenomenon (1993), he does not engage Elvis's music, nor does he really discuss the texts of media culture in any sustained fashion, or provide any close readings. Whereas decentering of textual analysis might be a useful corrective to cultural studies that in some forms were excessively textualist, I believe that it is useful to utilize textual analysis as an important part of cultural studies, and thus in the following chapters, there will be many close readings of cultural texts. I also attempt to illuminate the effectivity of media culture, whereas Fiske seems to think that media culture has no effects, that it is people's appropriation or use of media culture that is of crucial importance for cultural studies. I believe by contrast that analyzing the texts of media culture is useful in discerning their effects, though I admit that the audience is something of a sphinx and that it is impossible to ascertain precisely what effects the various domains and artifacts of media culture actually have on their audience. Moreover, general theories of media effects are probably empty and problematic, though one can trace the effects of some artifacts like *Rambo*, *Slacker*, *Beavis and Butt-Head*, rap, media representations of Gulf War, Madonna, and other key phenomena as I do in the following studies, in which I provide some new perspectives on the vexed question of media effects and a new research program to detect effects of media culture figures, texts, and spectacles.

12 As late as 1992 or 1993, a disinformation campaign took place alleging that a KGB file contained documents indicating that Vietnam had indeed purposely held U.S. POWs hostage after the war, a myth perpetuated for decades by Ross Perot, other paranoids on the right, and those who wanted to block normalization of relations with Vietnam as

revenge for U.S. military defeat in the region. For exposure of the 1992 disinformation campaign, see Bruce Franklin's article in *The Nation* (May 10, 1993: 616).

13 Jeffords notes that *Missing in Action* (1984) also shows the hero renouncing women and sexuality, inscribing the hero in the fascist scenario of sexual purity, subliminally identifying his efficacy with asceticism (1989: 132f.). Such representations point to parallels in Theweleit's analysis of male fascist warriors in Nazi Germany (1987).

14 Jeffords (1989: 130ff.) notes that there are four scenes where Rambo emerges from water to accomplish heroic action, thus enacting mythic purification rites, primal images also present in the slow-motion climax of *Missing in Action*, when Chuck Norris emerges from water, machine-gun blasting, to destroy his enemies.

15 "The Rambo films 'work' for American teenagers and children who have little or no knowledge or interest in its Reaganist statement. *Rambo*'s spectacular action seems, too, to have worked in tandem with its heroic masculinity in making it extraordinary popular from Iceland to Yugoslavia to Lebanon" (Warner 1992: 684–5).

16 "*Rambo* is the biggest crowd-participation movie in a long while. Audiences really scream when Mr Stallone's John Rambo is tortured. They cheer and cheer when he embarks on his revenge" (*New York Times*, May 30, 1985). And: "in the Loop's United Artists theater I witnessed a cheering of human carnage that would have embarrassed the Romans" (*Chicago Tribune*, June 12, 1985). As the summer progressed, enthusiastic audience response seemed even to increase: "In movie theaters, young enthusiasts jump to their feet chanting 'U.S.A., U.S.A.' as Johnny Rambo blasts another batch of the enemy to the world beyond" (*Reuters Ltd.*, July 27, 1985). Liberal critics, by contrast, counted the acts of violence and attacked the film.

17 In another sound-test warm-up for a radio address, Reagan had said: "'My fellow Americans, I am pleased to tell you I have just signed legislation which outlaws Russia forever. The bombing begins in five minutes.' The White House insisted that the quote was a joke and off-the-record. But press accounts of the comment infuriated Moscow, frightened Europeans and gave Democrats some unexpected political ammunition" (*Reuters Ltd.*, June 30, 1985).

18 One psychologist noted:

> In my psychiatric practice, I see more and more evidence among children of playing war. And I see more and more of it tied to television and the movies. I had a 15-year-old kid from Downstate Illinois in my office last week who'd seen 'Rambo' nine days in a row. He'd tried to sign up with the military, wearing a headband and an American flag like the character in the movie, and he was crushed when they wouldn't take him.
>
> *Chicago Tribune*, June 16, 1985)

19 As it turned out, the film was not banned, but predictions of the film generating violence materialized:

> A gang of youths fought with police inside a movie theater which was showing *Rambo*, police said today. About 50 youngsters forced their way into a theater in Gloucester, western England, through a fire exit. Fighting broke out when 22 police officers were called in to restore order, a spokesman said. Seven people were being detained, he added.
>
> (*Reuters Ltd.*, September 1, 1985)

20 *Rambo*

> is proving as successful in France as it was last summer in the United States, breaking opening day records in Paris. . . . *Rambo* opened to 342,082 admissions in France on 340 screens, another opening day record for the territory. A spokesman for Tri-Star Pictures said *Rambo* was also breaking records in other countries where it has opened.
>
> *Proprietary to the United Press International* (November 8, 1985)

21 Most curiously:

> Pirated videos of *Rambo* circulating in the Middle East carry French and Arabic subtitles with a different storyline. Set in the Philippines in 1943, the subtitled version has Rambo returning, after escaping two years earlier, to rescue World-War-II POWs still held by the Japanese. All dates are changed accordingly, despite action scenes with rocket-firing helicopters and other high-tech weaponry. As a U.S. Soldier tells Rambo on the English soundtrack 'you made a hell of a reputation for yourself in 'Nam', the subtitles read: 'You made quite a name for yourself in Guadacanal' (scene of a major pacific battle of World War Two). 'It's obviously been done for political reasons,' said a diplomat who viewed the pirated tape, noting that the subtitles delete all references to Vietnam and the Soviet Union. The manager of one of Cyprus' largest illegal video houses speculated the film had been 'sanitized' for distribution in Middle East countries like Syria which maintain close ties with the Soviet Union and might otherwise be offended by *Rambo*.
>
> (*Reuters North European Service*, August 26, 1985)

22 I sometimes give a very short lecture on the mind of Ronald Reagan, in which I point to the ways that he assimilated the generic codes and worldview of the Hollywood western, war film, melodrama, and other genres, that dichotomized the universe into the forces of good vs. evil, which presented "us" as "good" and "them" as "evil," and which thus repressed any negative and aggressive inclinations in one's own country and psyche.

23 On the concept of "technowar," see Gibson's (1986) description of high-tech systems of warfare in Vietnam; I draw on this concept in Chapter 5.

24 Some of Steven Seagal's films also villainize American officials who are shown to be duplicitous and criminal, operating outside the rule of law and engaging in criminal activities. In *Above the Law* (1988), U.S. government officials are shown involved in the sale of drugs and involved in terrorism, while *Under Siege* (1992) shows renegade military and intelligence figures leading an effort to take over a U.S. nuclear submarine, while the government officials themselves are shown as duplicitous and amoral. Such films transcode radical critique of U.S. foreign policy and the U.S. government and serve as counterpoles to the conservative films. Both, however, operate with the same comic-book manicheanism.

25 *Not Without My Daughter* (1990) presents Iranians and the Iranian revolution in totally negative terms, featuring the story of an American woman who married an Iranian. Her husband turns into a monster during a trip back to Iran in 1984 and the wife undertakes the difficult task of escape from her husband to flee the country with her daughter.

Chapter 3

For a cultural studies that is critical, multicultural, and multiperspectival

The artifacts of media culture are thus not innocent entertainment, but are thoroughly ideological artifacts bound up with political rhetoric, struggles, agendas, and policies. Given their political significance and effects, it is important to learn to read media culture politically in order to decode its ideological messages and effects. As I have argued so far, reading media culture politically requires expanding ideological criticism to include the intersection of gender, sexuality, race, and class, and to see that ideology is presented in the forms of images, figures, generic codes, myth, and the technical apparatus of film, television, music, and other media forms, as well as in ideas or theoretical positions.

Yet cultural texts are not intrinsically "conservative" or "liberal." Rather, many texts try to go both ways to maximize their audiences, while others advance specific ideological positions, but they are often undercut by other aspects of the text. The texts of media culture incorporate a variety of discourses, ideological positions, narrative strategies, image construction, and effects (i.e., cinematic, televisual, musical, and so on) which rarely coalesce into a pure and coherent ideological position. They attempt to provide something for everyone to attract as large an audience as possible and thus often incorporate a wide range of ideological positions. Still, as I have argued, certain media cultural texts advance specific ideological positions which can be ascertained by relating the texts to the political discourses and debates of their era, to other artifacts concerned with similar themes, and to ideological motifs in the culture that are active in a given text.

In this chapter, I will explicate my concept of cultural studies, the need for a contextual cultural studies, and the notion of diagnostic critique. I will first explicate my conception of a critical multiculturalism as a basis for cultural studies and then discuss my conception of a multiperspectival cultural studies. After explicating my conception of a contextual cultural studies, I indicate why it is important to utilize a dual optic that ferrets out both ideological and utopian moments from media culture. I also indicate how deconstruction and post-structuralist concepts can be deployed in cultural studies and explicate my conception of a diagnostic critique, which I illustrate with a reading of Oliver Stone's 1986 film *Platoon*.

FOR A CRITICAL MULTICULTURALISM

I aim at developing a cultural studies that is *critical* in that it probes forms of oppression and domination and articulates normative perspectives from which to criticize these forms. To develop a critical standpoint requires one to articulate the social constitution of the concepts of gender, class, race, ethnicity, and sexuality, and the ways that representations of these phenomena produce identities in contemporary societies, as well as how alternative representations produce new and different identities. Maintaining a critical standpoint also requires interpreting culture and society in terms of relations of power, domination, and resistance, as well as articulating the various forms of oppression in a given society via multicultural perspectives. Moreover, critical social theory and media cultural studies involves developing normative standpoints from which one can critically engage cultural texts. This requires spelling out specific values and validating them in concrete contexts.

Critical perspectives toward culture and society have long attacked domination and oppression while positively valorizing resistance and struggle which attempt to overturn these forces. This is true of British cultural studies, the Frankfurt School, feminism, certain forms of post-structuralism, and critical multiculturalism. Thus, values of resistance, empowerment, democracy, and freedom are adopted as positive norms, used to criticize forms of oppression and domination. Yet such values are adopted as conventions, as normative standards through which one can criticize specific examples of domination, oppression, and the ideologies that further such conditions, rather than as absolute moral principles. A broad range of contemporary theory thus renounces foundationalism, seeing concepts and norms as social conventions adopted to serve specific purposes.

A critical cultural studies adopts norms and values with which it criticizes texts, artifacts, and conditions that promote oppression and domination. It positively valorizes phenomena that promote human freedom, democracy, individuality, and other values that the project adopts, defends, and valorizes in concrete studies and situations. Yet a critical media cultural studies also intends to relate its theories to practice, to develop an oppositional politics aimed at producing a progressive turn in contemporary culture and society through contributing to development of a counterhegemony to the conservative hegemony of the past years. A critical perspective sees culture as inherently political and as, in many cases, promoting specific political positions and as aiding forces of domination or resistance. Such a perspective perceives existing culture and society as a contested terrain, and chooses to ally itself with the forms of resistance and counterhegemony against the forces of domination. Grounding its politics in existing struggles and social forces, it places social theory and cultural studies in the service of socio-cultural criticism and political change.

Furthermore, a critical cultural studies must relentlessly examine its own methods, positions, assumptions, and interventions, constantly putting them in question and revising and developing them. Critical social and cultural theories are thus open, flexible, non-dogmatic, and without guarantees. Recognizing that contemporary society and culture is a contested terrain, critical theories engage opposing theories and are not afraid to appropriate material from them and to reject aspects of their own theories shown to be problematic, or to question its own assumptions or values if they are shown to be questionable.

Both the Frankfurt School and the Birmingham group were constantly renegotiating their positions in relation to new historical conditions and theoretical developments, and this self-reflexivity and flexibility is an epistemological strength that other versions of cultural studies and social theory should emulate. The Birmingham group was constantly appropriating new perspectives, such as feminism and multiculturalist theories of race and nationality, as a result of criticisms of their previous positions. There was also constant reflection and debate over the methods and goals of cultural studies. This reflexivity and flexibility was also characteristic of certain stages of development of the Frankfurt School, though some of its positions hardened into an orthodoxy, resistant to new theoretical developments and unable to deal with new social conditions (see Kellner 1989a). There is always the danger that a powerful theory and method can degenerate and harden into an orthodoxy and only vigilant critique, openness, flexibility, and a commitment to revision and development can prevent such rigidity and dogmatism.

Maintaining a critical perspective also involves developing a critical theory of society to ground one's cultural analysis and critique. Critical social theory carries out a critique of existing systems of domination and points to forces of resistance and possibilities for radical social transformation. It reads media culture texts in the context of how they relate to structures of domination and forces of resistance and which ideological positions they advance within the context of current debates and social struggles. Thus, a critical cultural studies is not merely interested in providing clever readings of cultural texts, but is also interested in advancing a critique of structures and practices of domination and advancing forces of resistance struggling for a more democratic and egalitarian society.

A critical social theory and cultural studies that attacks oppression and strives for social equality is necessarily *multicultural* and seeks to attend to differences, cultural diversity, and otherness. I am using the term "multicultural" here as a general concept for those diverse interventions in cultural studies that insist on the importance of scrutinizing representations of class, gender, sexuality, ethnicity, subalterneity, and other phenomena often displaced or ignored in previous approaches to culture. A critical multicultural approach, in my conceptualization, involves analysis of relationships of domination and oppression, the way stereotyping works, resistance on the part of stigmatized groups to dominant representations, and the struggle of these groups to represent themselves, to counter dominant and distorting representations, and to produce more positive ones. "Multicultural" here thus functions as a general rubric for all those attempts to resist the stereotyping, distortions, and stigmatizing by the dominant culture. A critical multiculturalism also works to open cultural studies to analysis of the relations of force and domination in society and the ways that these are covered over and/or legitimated in dominant ideological representations.[1]

A critical multicultural perspective takes seriously the conjunction of class, race, ethnicity, gender, sexual preference, and other determinants of identity as important constituents of culture which should be carefully scrutinized and analyzed in order to detect sexism, racism, classism, homophobia, and other tendencies that promote domination and oppression. Multiculturalism recognizes that there are many cultural constituents of identity and a critical cultural studies indicates how culture provides material and resources for identities and how cultural artifacts are appropriated and used to produce individual identities in everyday life.

The multicultural project also validates the positive contributions to culture and society of diverse races, genders and sexual identities, ethnicities, and social classes and groups. It is often noted that the most exciting work in recent years[2] comes from feminist theory and those multiculturalists analyzing race, gender, nationality, and alternative sexualities. These new cultural theories gain inspiration from new social movements and have forced a sea change in how we look at and respond to texts. The canons of white male European culture have been challenged and a wide range of new voices and individuals have been encountered. In addition, the perspectives of oppressed groups present critical insights into mainstream culture, allowing us to see oppressive elements that we might overlook from our more privileged perspectives.

A critical cultural studies is allied with an insurgent multiculturalism (Giroux 1993) which supports the struggles of oppressed groups against domination and subordination, siding with those in struggle against inequality, injustice, and oppression. An insurgent multiculturalism (or cultural studies) does not just register differences (though this activity can be important), but analyzes relations of inequality and oppression that generates struggles. Moreover, it also positively valorizes representations that help promote the struggle of the oppressed against domination, while attacking representations that legitimate, naturalize, or cover over domination. An insurgent multiculturalism is thus part of the "pedogogy of the oppressed" (Freire 1972) which helps the oppressed see their oppression, name their oppressors, and articulate the goals and practices of liberation.

Thus whereas Fiske and others valorize resistance and struggle *per se*, an insurgent cultural studies only positively interprets struggle and resistance against oppression, against structural inequality, grounding its analyses in antagonisms between structural inequalities and oppression. An insurgent cultural studies enters into dialogue with members of oppressed groups in struggle and expands cultural studies to include voices usually excluded in more academic forms of cultural studies, thus striving for a more inclusive and political project.

The theories of interpretation, approaches to culture and society, and political interventions of a wide range of oppressed and multicultural groups have thus produced new perspectives and tools of criticism. Such groups have used cultural studies as a way of challenging canons and orthodoxies, legitimating the texts and voices of subordinate groups, and politicizing culture and education. Yet multiculturalism as a movement and ideology (in a broader sense than I am using the term) can easily be coopted by corporate forces that promote the term as a new front for melting-pot liberalism that helps individuals work and get along together through the promotion of toleration and acceptance of difference. Multiculturalism can also lead to in-group separatism and the various forms of identity politics, through which individuals identify with single-interest groups and construct their identities through identification with specific groups and categories and exclusion of others. Such single-interest politics fragment or block development of progressive blocs and alliances, and thus weaken the possibility of progressive social transformation.

Against such attempts to coopt the discourse of multiculturalism, or to use it as a badge of separatism that promotes special interests, I am using the term to encompass attempts to resist exclusion of specific issues and perspectives from the terrain of cultural studies. Indeed, multiculturalism, as I am using the term, demands openness to the discourses of all oppressed or subordinate groups and the need to perceive the importance of engaging a broader range of types of representation in order to produce fuller and more critical readings of texts. But a critical multiculturalism does not entail affirming that there are nothing but differences; rather it points out that there are common forces of oppression, common strategies of exclusion, stereotyping, and stigmatizing of oppressed groups, and thus common enemies and targets of attacks. It thus stresses commonalties as well as differences and insists on the articulation of how representations of such things as race, gender, and class are intertwined and function as vehicles for ideologies of domination which naturalize, legitimate, or mask social inequalities, injustice, and oppression.

Critical multiculturalism also sees differences in terms of contradictions between unequal forces, theorizing oppositions between the more powerful and subordinate groups in terms of relationships of domination which creates the possibility of resistance against all forms of oppression. It also articulates common goals in struggle whereby dominant representations, or other forms of social oppression, are resisted and struggled against. A critical multiculturalism thus allies itself with the struggles for emancipation and for the creation of a more free, just, and egalitarian social order.

A multiculturalist focus on the diversity of forms of oppression and resistance is connected to development of a multiperspectival social theory and cultural studies that draws on the wide range of work done in the field in recent years. A multiperspectival cultural studies attempts to avoid one-sidedness, orthodoxy, and cultural separatism by stressing the need to adopt a wide range of perspectives to understand and interpret cultural phenomena. As I have been arguing, gender, race, class, and other key cultural constructs are interconnected and reproduced in cultural forms and representations. To get a fuller picture of cultural texts and social phenomena, one must therefore grasp a wide range of constituent elements of cultural texts and practices. To do this properly, one needs to draw on a spectrum of critical methods, as some are better to grasp class, others to conceptualize gender and sexuality, and yet others to articulate race, myth and symbol, subliminal and latent dimensions of culture, and so on.

TOWARD A MULTIPERSPECTIVAL CULTURAL STUDIES

A cultural studies that is critical and multicultural should therefore also be "multiperspectival." This is a cumbersome and unattractive term, but remains the best concept that I have found to describe the sort of cultural studies that I am trying to develop. I shall elucidate this concept with some theoretical and practical analyses in this and in following chapters. Simply put, a multiperspectival cultural studies draws on a wide range of textual and critical strategies to interpret, criticize, and deconstruct the artifact under scrutiny. The concept draws on Nietzsche's perspectivism which holds that all interpretation is necessarily mediated by one's perspectives and is thus inevitably laden with presuppositions, values, biases, and limitations. To avoid one-sidedness and partial vision one should learn "how to employ a *variety* of perspectives and interpretations in the service of knowledge" (Nietzsche 1969: 119). For Nietzsche: "There is *only* a perspective seeing, *only* a perspective 'knowing'; and the *more* affects we allow to speak about one thing, the more complete will our 'concept' of this thing, our 'objectivity,' be" (ibid.). Expanding this call for multiperspectival interpretation in later aphorisms collected in *The Will to Power* (1968), Nietzsche argues: "every elevation of man brings with it the overcoming of narrower interpretations; that every strengthening and increase of power opens up new perspectives and means believing in new horizons" (1968: 330).

Applying these notions to cultural interpretation, one could argue that the more interpretive perspectives one can bring to a cultural artifact, the more comprehensive and stronger one's reading may be. I have been arguing that to capture the full political and ideological dimensions of the texts of media culture, one needs to view them from the perspectives of gender, race, and class. I am now suggesting that combining Marxist, feminist, structuralist, post-structuralist, psychoanalytic, and other critical perspectives will provide fuller, more complete, and potentially stronger readings. Combining, for instance, ideology critique and genre criticism with semiotic analysis allows one to discern how the generic forms of media culture, or their semiotic codes, are permeated with ideology. The conflict/resolution code of most television entertainment, for example, provides an ideological notion that all problems can be resolved within the existing society by following conventional behavior and norms. Advertising often deploys a similar model, showing a problem and that the product advertised provides the solution.

A perspective, in this analysis, is an optic, a way of seeing, and critical methods can be interpreted as approaches that enable one to see characteristic features of cultural artifacts. Each critical method focuses on specific features of an object from a distinctive perspective: the perspective spotlights, or illuminates, some features of a text while ignoring others. The more perspectives one focuses on a text to do ideological analysis and critique – genre, seniological, structural, formal, feminist, psychoanalytic, and so on – the better one can grasp the full range of a text's ideological dimensions and ramifications. It therefore follows that a multiperspectival approach will provide an arsenal of weapons of critique, a full range of perspectives to dissect, interpret, and critique cultural artifacts.

Some qualifications to this position should be made, however. Obviously, a single reading – Marxist, feminist, psychoanalytic, or whatever – may yield more brilliant insights for the study of some phenomena than combining various perspectival readings; more is not necessarily better. However, a variety of critical perspectives utilized in a proficient and revelatory fashion provides the potential for stronger (i.e. more many-sided, illuminating, and critical) readings. Secondly, a multiperspectival approach may not be particularly illuminating unless it adequately situates its text in its historical context. A text is constituted by its internal relations and its relations to its socio-historical situation and the more relations articulated in a critical reading, the better grasp of a text one may have. A multiperspectival method must necessarily be historical and should read its texts in terms of its socio-historical context and may also choose to read history in the light of the text.

Certain methodological strategies are, of course, incompatible and a multiperspectival approach must choose between competing perspectives in terms of what specific task is at hand and what specific goals one has. For some purposes, it may be useful to engage in a focused feminist reading, while for other purposes one might carry through multivalent readings, getting at a text from a variety of perspectives. A multiperspectival position, however, that is not a mere liberal eclecticism, or merely a hotchpotch of different points of view, should allow its various perspectives to inform and modify each other. For instance, a Marxism that is informed by feminism will be different from a one-dimensional Marxism innocent of feminism (and vice-versa). A Marxist-feminist position that is informed by post-structuralism will be different from a dogmatic Marxist-feminist perspective that reduces a film solely to class and gender problematics. For poststructuralism champions a multiplicity of perspectives, focuses attention on features ignored by some Marxist or feminist perspectives, and undermines naive beliefs that one specific interpretation is certain and true. Yet a poststructuralist perspective like deconstruction can itself become predictable and one-sided if it does not utilize other perspectives such as Marxism and feminism (see Ryan 1982 and Spivak 1988).

Each critical method has its own strengths and limitations, its insights and blindspots. Marxian ideology critiques have traditionally been strong on class and historical contextualization and weak on formal analysis, as well as gender and race; feminism excels in gender analysis but sometimes ignores class, race, and other determinants; structuralism is useful for narrative analysis but tends to be overly formal; and psychoanalysis calls for depth hermeneutics and the articulation of unconscious contents and meaning, but sometimes ignores sociological determination of texts and individuals. Thus, the more of these critical methods one has at one's disposal, the better chance one has of producing reflexive and many-sided critical readings.

Of course, a reading of a text is only a reading from a critic's specific position, no matter how multiperspectival. Any critic's specific reading is only their own reading and may or may not be the reading preferred by audiences (which themselves will be significantly different according to class, race, gender, region, ethnicity, sexual preferences, ideologies, and so on). There is thus a split between textual encoding and audience decoding and always the possibility of a multiplicity of readings and effects of specific texts (Hall 1980b). One way to discover how audiences read texts is to engage in ethnographic surveys (see the Appendix to Kellner and Ryan 1988), but even then one is not sure how texts affect audiences and shape their beliefs and behavior. Thus, one needs to study which images, figures, and discourses of media culture become dominant and trace their effects through a variety of circuits, as I do in this book.

Although all texts are polysemic and subject to multivalent readings depending on the perspectives of the reader, I am not advocating an "anything goes" liberal pluralism. All of the critical methods that I have mentioned are deployed by a critical cultural studies to interpret the text and its effects within the existing system of domination and oppression and use critical social theory to contextualize the artifact and the reading in relation to existing social struggles. The critical cultural studies that I am delineating takes the side of progressive forces struggling against domination and attacks structures, practices, and ideologies of domination and oppression. Thus, the various methods and perspectives used are deployed within a critical social theory that attacks a system of domination and that struggles for a more democratic and egalitarian social order.

A multiperspectival approach thus multiplies both theoretical perspectives and the perspectives from which cultural phenomena are viewed and interpreted. Within the history of cultural studies, the project has been driven to appropriate new weapons in its theoretical arsenal, as new movements produce new theories and discourses. Cultural studies is now genuinely international and multicultural, and this has greatly expanded the perspectives from which we can view and appraise dominant, marginal, and oppositional cultures. And, as noted in Chapter 1, the struggles and turbulence of the past decades have also generated a proliferation of theories and methods which we can deploy as instruments and weapons in developing more multiperspectival visions and methods. Each theory and perspective is to some degree a product of a social struggle and can be adopted as a weapon of critique in the struggle for a better society. It is the project of critical cultural studies to adopt such weapons and to employ them in specific projects and domains.

Consequently, I am deploying cultural studies and critical social theory both to analyze hegemonic forces of domination and counterhegemonic forces of resistance. There are always controlling forces and blocks in society that form a hegemonic project, as well as forces struggling against this hegemony. During the conservative hegemony of Reagan and Bush, for example, conservative forces dominated the economy, polity, society, and culture, but there were always forces in struggle against this hegemony, ranging from liberals fighting for political power to black single mothers struggling for welfare rights. The forces of domination find articulation in media cultural texts, as do forces of resistance and the voices of individuals oppressed by the existing social system.

For example, films like *Rambo* and *Top Gun* mobilized desire into subject positions congruent with the Reaganite military build-up and interventionist foreign policy, while male hero films mobilized desire and fantasy into a remasculinized male subject that was part of a backlash against feminism (see Faludi 1991 and Jeffords 1994). Yet films like *Casualties of War* and *A Few Good Men* mobilized its audiences against the sort of military heroism celebrated in the conservative films and positively valorized individuals with a conscience who would stand up to the pressures from conservative authority to "do the right thing." These liberal individuals with a conscience were also more sensitive than the hard-bodied heros of the Stallone–Norris–Willis–Schwarzenegger conservative films. In the cultural wars between liberals and conservatives of the period, media culture thus intervened on different sides, producing opposing identities, models of masculinity, and gender politics for its audiences.

A critical cultural studies thus demonstrates how cultural texts produce social identities and subject-positions and contrasts opposing positions. It analyzes media messages and effects, and attempts to show how certain figures, models, and discourses undermine the values and ethos of a pluralistic, egalitarian, democratic, and multicultural society, whereas other figures and models may promote the creation of a more egalitarian and democratic society. A cultural studies that is critical and multicultural thus intervenes in the cultural wars of the period and uses its analyses of media culture to promote social change toward a more democratic society, fighting forms of media culture that promote oppression while linking more progressive media culture with political movements struggling for freedom and democracy.

TOWARD A CONTEXTUAL CULTURAL STUDIES

The critical, multicultural, and multiperspectival conception of cultural studies that I am sketching draws on Antonio Gramsci's theory of hegemony (1971) which presents culture, society, and politics as terrains of contestation between various groups and class blocs (see Boggs 1984 and Kellner 1990a). From this perspective, cultural critique should specify which contests are going on, between which groups, and which positions, with the cultural analyst intervening on what is perceived as the more progressive side. Expanding on Gramsci, a variety of individuals have attempted to develop a more differentiated concept of ideology which pays more attention to emergent, residual, and hegemonic ideologies within contemporary neo-capitalist (or state socialist) societies (see Williams 1977; Kellner 1978 and 1979; Hall 1987). This expansion of the concept of ideology anchors ideology critique more securely in concrete and historically specific socio-political analysis and thus grounds ideology critique in the context within which political conflict actually occurs.

Thus, I see media culture as a *contested terrain* reproducing on the cultural level the fundamental conflicts within society rather than as an instrument of domination. Examination of Hollywood film from 1967 to the present (Kellner and Ryan 1988), for example, reveals that U.S. society and culture were torn apart by a series of debates over the heritage of the 1960s, over gender and sexuality, over war, militarism, and interventionism, and over a great variety of other issues. On one hand, *Rambo, Red Dawn, Missing in Action, Invasion U.S.A, Top Gun*, and the like represent aggressively right-wing positions on war, militarism, and communism that served as soft- and hard-core propaganda for Reaganism and a distinctly right-wing interventionist and militarist agenda.

On the other hand, *Missing, Under Fire, Salvador, Latino*, and other left or liberal films sharply contested the rightist vision of Central America and U.S. interventionism in that area by representing the U.S. and ruling bourgeois cliques as "bad guys" in generic scenarios that are primarily sympathetic to rebels and those struggling against U.S. imperialism. Against *Rambo* and other return-to-Vietnam films, *Platoon, Full Metal Jacket*, and *Casualties of War* subvert the right-wing version of Vietnam, as films like *M.A.S.H., Catch-22, Soldier Blue*, and others previously attacked right-wing versions of militarism and U.S. foreign policy in earlier debates over Vietnam. And in the domain of sexual politics, antifeminist films like *Ordinary People, Kramer versus Kramer, An Officer and A Gentleman, Fatal Attraction, Basic Instinct, The Hand That Rocks the Cradle, Shiver, The Temp*, and *Body of Evidence* can be contrasted with more feminist films like *Girlfriends, Desperately Seeking Susan, Working Girls*, and *Desert Hearts*, which present women struggling for independence and equality. The latter films advance various feminist positions, while the former are part of the backlash against feminism analyzed by Faludi (1991). U.S. society has been deeply divided in the realm of sexual politics and various artifacts of media culture take opposing positions in the culture wars of the present age and thus should be analyzed in terms of their positions and effects within existing social struggles.

It should be noted, however, that mainstream Hollywood is severely limited in the extent to which it will advance socially critical and radical positions. Hollywood film is a commercial enterprise and it does not wish to offend mainstream audiences with radical perceptions and thus attempts to contain its representations of class, gender, race, and society within established boundaries. Radicals are thus usually excluded from Hollywood film, or are forced to compromise their positions within accepted limits. Moreover, the generic codes and conventions of Hollywood film tend to limit its discourses and effects. The conventionality of focused stories with individual characters, the use of close-ups and shot-reverse shots, that cut from one character to another, the use of recognizable and popular stars, and other elements of conventional Hollywood film tend, for example, to limit Hollywood films to the parameters of individualism, thus precluding positive portrayals of political groups or collectivities struggling for change. Thus, it is the independent film movement to which one must look for the most progressive political interventions within the terrain of American film culture (Kellner and Ryan 1988).

In any case, films and other forms of media culture should be analyzed as

ideological texts *contextually* and *relationally*, seeing some texts as more progressive radical or liberal responses to rightist artifacts and ideological positions,
rather than, say, just dismissing all media culture as reactionary and merely
ideological, as certain monolithic theories of the "dominant ideology," such as the
classical critical theory of Horkheimer and Adorno (1972), many Althusserians,
some feminists, and others, are wont to do. A contextualist cultural studies reads
cultural texts in terms of actual struggles within contemporary culture and society,
situating ideological analysis within existing socio-political debates and conflicts
rather than just in relation to some supposedly monolithic dominant ideology, or
some model of mass culture that is simply equated with ideological manipulation
or domination *per se*.

One way to delineate the ideologies of media culture is to read the artifact
relationally, situating films, for example, within their genres or cycles, as well as
within their historical, socio-political, and economic context. Reading films contextually involves seeing how they relate to other films within the set, and how the
genres transcode ideological positions. This would involve reading *Rambo* in terms
of the return-to-Vietnam cycle which can be situated within the whole genre of
Vietnam films and debates over the U.S. intervention in Vietnam and its aftermath.
It would involve reading *Top Gun* in the context of the series of films dealing with
military life in the period (i.e. *An Officer and a Gentleman, Iron Eagle, Heartbreak
Ridge*, and so on), in which some of the films treat military life in a celebratory
fashion, while others present more critical visions.

While *Top Gun* and *Iron Eagle*, for example, present a utopia of military life,
more realist war films like *Platoon, Full Metal Jacket*, or *Casualties of War* show
the actual consequences of military life when actual war breaks out. Likewise, while
Heartbreak Ridge has a generally positive view of military life, with some criticism
of elite officers, it shows the dangers and anxieties involved in even a minor military
excursion like the Grenada invasion, though ultimately it transcodes Reaganite
triumphalism, presenting the Grenada invasion as a U.S. victory. *Taps, Lords of
Discipline, Brainstorm, War Games, The Dogs of War, Blue Thunder, A Few Good
Men*, and others present a more critical vision of the U.S. military, while *Up the
Academy, Tank, Deal of the Century, Spies Like Us* and the other satirical films
present more critical visions of the U.S. military and of the national security state.

By relating specific films to other generic examples and to the range of current
debates which the genres address, right-wing films can be read, for instance, as
responses to actual threats to conservative hegemony, and thus as testimonies to
current social conflicts and contradictions. Or liberal films can be read as contest-
ations of conservative hegemony, rather than just as wimpish variations of the same
dominant ideology. From this contextualist perspective, ideology critique thus
involves doing ideological analysis within the context of social theory and social
history. Reading films politically, therefore, can provide insight not only into the
ways that film reproduces existing social struggles within contemporary U.S.
society, but can also provide insight into the social and political dynamics of the
era. Even highly ideological films like *Rambo* point to social conflicts and to forces

that threaten conservative hegemony, such as the liberal antiwar, antimilitary position which *Rambo* so violently opposes. Thus, ideology can be analyzed in terms of the forces and tensions to which it responds while projects of ideological domination can be conceptualized in terms of reactionary resistance to popular struggles against traditional conservative or liberal values and institutions.

Thus, rather than just conceptualizing ideology as a force of domination in the hands of an all-powerful ruling class, ideology can be analyzed contextually and relationally as a response to resistance and as a sign of threats to the hegemony of dominant group, sex, and race powers. Consequently, 1960s films can be read as a resistance to the social conformity and conventional cinema of the earlier era, while *Dirty Harry* can be interpreted as a response to the radicalism of the 1960s and the recent triumphs of liberalism within criminal law. Sexist and reactionary films like *Straw Dogs* or *The Exorcist* can be read as responses to feminism and the resistance of women to male domination. Blaxploitation films like *Shaft* or *Superfly* can be read as signs of resistance to black subservience to whites and as a reaction against black stereotypes in Hollywood films. And the racism of films like *Rocky* can be read as articulations of white working-class fears of blacks and as testimonies to increased cultural and political power of blacks in U.S. society, while the relative absence of dramatic Hollywood narrative films about blacks in the Reagan era can be interpreted as the resistance of conservatives to black demands for racial equality and increased power. Or, *Top Gun*, *Rambo*, and the return-to-Vietnam films can be read as responses to U.S. defeat in Vietnam, to challenges to imperialism, and to those who would curtail the military and limit U.S. military power.

Drawing on studies of the relationships between social ideologies and movements and their environments by sociologist Robert Wuthnow (1989), I want to utilize the categories of *social horizon, discursive field*, and *figural action* to describe some of the ways that cultural texts transcode and articulate social images, discourses, and conditions and in turn operate within their social field. The term "social horizon" refers to the actual experiences, practices, and features of the social field of media cultural texts which help structure the universe of both the media culture and its reception. The social horizon of the 1960s, which provided the backdrop of films like *Easy Rider* or *Woodstock*, was the emergence of the counterculture with its own style of dress, behavior, music, language, and culture – a *counter*culture that defined itself against mainstream "establishment" culture during a period of intense social turmoil and contestation. The "sixties" thus provides the social horizon of films of the period which in turn are transcoded, or articulated, within specific discursive fields.

The discursive field of *Easy Rider* and *Woodstock* was sixties' countercultural music, language, lifestyle, and practices which attempted to innovate cultural production and to produce alternative forms of life, ways of living. The content of the social horizon was articulated into specific discursive fields in films like *Easy Rider* which utilized a rock music soundtrack, eccentrically cut images of bikers riding through nature, and deployed figure/ground images that framed the bikers against the desert, mountains, sky, and sun to transcode sixties' ideologies of freedom, individualism, harmony with nature, emancipation through technology, and so on. *Woodstock* used triple-screen division, cutting between stage and audience, tight close-ups interwoven with long shots, and so on to cinematically transcode the tight connection between rock concert audiences and the musicians during the period. The film *Woodstock* thus transcoded the sixties' discourses of community, love, freely expressed sexuality, individualism, and revolt through the discursive field of its cinematic images and discourses.

Thus, media culture articulates a complex set of mediations. It transcodes 1960s discourses like the counterculture, or feminism, as well as competing mainstream liberal or conservative discourses. Some texts of media culture that projects positive images of women transcodes feminist discourses (i.e. *Girlfriends*, *Desert Hearts*, *Working Girls*, etc.), while the antiwomen images and discourses that have returned with a vengeance in the 1990s (i.e. *Basic Instinct*, *Falling Down*, *The Hand That Rocks the Cradle*, and so on) articulate the antifeminist discourses and backlash against feminism described by Faludi (1991) and others. The competing array of social discourses at a given moment is thus articulated in media culture which draw upon and in turn circulate competing social discourses of the moment, thus intervening within social struggles and conflicts.

Media culture also articulates social experiences, figures, events, and practices, as well as discourses. Fashion style, contemporary looks and artifacts, and other signs of the contemporary, all suture or weave the audiences into the cinematic texts. Indeed, for media culture to work for its audiences it has to resonate to social experience, to "fit in" with the social horizon of audiences, and so popular media culture taps into existing fears, hopes, fantasies, and other concerns of the day.

The figural action in films like *Easy Rider* involved celebatory presentation of the figures of the bikers who incarnated the countercultural ethos and ideology of freedom and individualism of the period. The figure of the fighting machine *Rambo* by contrast embodies the militarist and masculist discourses of the 1980s, though as noted, he also incorporated countercultural images of individualism and the natural to articulate the militarist/masculist ideology of the era. The figural action of *Woodstock* involved the rock musicians as godlike cultural heroes, the promoters as benevolent facilitators of counterculture, and the audience as hip participants in countercultural community and rebellion. These cinematic innovations also formally enact the cultural revolution that the film depicts in its celebration of the Woodstock festival and counterculture. Just as the actual counterculture attempted a revolution of everyday life and to produce new forms of culture, so too did contemporary filmmakers attempt to produce new cinematic forms, bringing an innovative modernist impulse into Hollywood film, challenging and subverting its conventions and producing new forms of cinematic language.

The films, rock music, and counterculture of the 1960s in turn had their own figural and discursive effects, disseminating countercultural images and ideologies as audiences appropriated the images, style, fashion, and attitudes into their own lives. In particular, films like *Easy Rider* and *Woodstock* not only strengthened the countercultural convictions of its audiences, but incorporated new recruits into the counterculture by promoting its style, fashion, and rebellious alternative culture. On the other hand, reducing 1960s activism and rebellion to cultural style made it easy to incorporate and coopt the counterculture within mainstream U.S. culture and the images of *Easy Rider* and *Woodstock* facilitated this process of cooptation and exploitation which eventually led to the death of the counterculture as a genuinely oppositional culture.

In the last chapter, I indicated some of the discursive and figural effects of *Rambo* and the ways that the figure and film were embedded in a struggle over its meaning, providing semantic and imagistic resources that could be articulated in diverse ways. In recent years, there has been a trend to study the effects of media culture through audience ethnography, studying either fan behavior or the ways that audiences, such as homeless men watching *Die Hard* (Fiske 1993), use the artifacts of media culture. While these studies often provide valuable, if limited, insight into the effects of media culture, I would suggest that there are other ways to study its effectivity. One can study the reception of media culture by analyzing its reviews, criticism, and the ways that the texts become embedded in popular discourses and generate a multiplicity of diverse effects. This mode of reception studies was advanced by Walter Benjamin in the 1920s and 1930s and has been taken up by literary theorists like Jauss who have developed literary reception studies to delineate how literature has been received by various publics.

New computer data-bases, like Dialog and Lexis/Nexis, make it possible to do a new type of reception studies, such as I am doing in this book. One can type in code words like "Rambo" and "Reagan" to see some of the ways that the figure of Rambo was articulated within popular political discourses. The result was literally hundreds of references which I drew upon in the previous chapter in my study of "the Rambo effect," and I did similar data-base searches concerning all the major films that I am analyzing, as well as the Gulf War, rap music and hip hop culture, *Beavis and Butt-Head*, *Miami Vice*, MTV, cigarette advertising, Madonna, and cyberpunk fiction. One finds literally thousands of references which enable one to trace the effects of texts that enter into media culture through a wide range of social discourses that articulate a variety of diverse effects.

On the other hand, although figures like Rambo and Madonna can generate powerful direct effects, it is rare that single films, popular songs, television programs, and so on directly influence their audiences. Yet some examples of the *global popular* attain the status of directly influencing thought and behavior by producing models of gender, style, or action. Such powerful images are emulated throughout the world and often directly affect their audiences. Yet, on the whole, it is the cumulative effects of 1960s films and music that articulate countercultural ideologies which serve to promote certain movements and which affect the ways that people see, talk, and behave. Or it is the cumulative effects of racist images of Arabs in Hollywood movies and television news and entertainment that makes it possible to mobilize anti-Arab discourses in political events like the Gulf War. And so while the very figure of a Rambo may have a massive range of effects, some of which I documented, it is the cumulative impact of all of the anti-Arab images of film and television that negatively constituted images of Arabs, rather than a single film or artifact alone.

Critical cultural studies is concerned with analyzing certain *resonant images* (Kellner 1990a) which is one of the keys to ferreting out media effects. Certain images resonate to our experiences and stick in the mind, moving us to later thought and action. Sometimes pop figures like a Rambo, a Madonna, a Beavis and Butt-Head become highly resonant, mobilizing thought and behavior, so that one wants to be a Madonna, imitating her style of dress and image moves; one wants to be a Rambo, imitating his macho behavior; one emulates Beavis and Butt-Head, replicating their laughs, their ways of speaking, and perhaps even their asocial behavior.

In the 1950s, resonant images of non-conformist rebels and bikers (Marlon Brando, Elvis Presley, James Dean, or beatnik writers like Jack Kerouac) became highly influential, modelling style, thought, and behavior; in the 1960s, counter-cultural figures became resonant images. Occasionally, a resonant image might be detached in effect and memory from its narrative structure and while the textual message may be "crime does not pay," or "adultery brings unhappiness," it is the memory of the criminal or the adultery that remains in one's mind, that influences thought and behavior. This was possibly true of 1930s crime dramas in which the energy and power of a Cagney or Bogart might have been what stuck in one's mind, producing rebellious or criminal behavior, rather than their getting caught or murdered. Likewise Mario van Peeble's *New Jack City* (1991) might attempt to convey an antidrug message and develop a narrative in which crime is punished and does not pay, yet perhaps the images of the drug dealers leading the high life are what resonates and what influences later behavior.

Likewise, paleosymbolic scenes (Kellner 1979) may be vehicles of powerful media effects, as scenes of communal fun in films like *Easy Rider* or *Woodstock* might promote the ideologies and lifestyle of the counterculture with their images of nude swimming, easy sex, getting high, and participating in social ritual. The preface "paleo" signifies a sort of "before symbolism" or "underneath symbolism." Paleosymbols are tied to particular scenes that are charged with drama and emotion. For example, Freud found that certain scenic images, such as a child being beaten for masturbation, or discovering his parents having sex, have a profound impact on subsequent behavior. The images of these scenes remain as paleosymbols which control behavior, for instance, producing guilt accompanying masturbation, or infusing sex with great fascination and attraction, or fear and repulsion. Paleosymbols are not subject to conscious scrutiny or control; they are often repressed, closed off from reflection, and can produce compulsive behavior. Thus Freud believed that scenic understanding was necessary to master scenic images, and, in turn, this mastery could help in understanding what the scenic images signified and how they influenced behavior.

Paleosymbolic scenes may deeply influence one's perceptions of members of opposite genders, races, and classes, and may shape gender behavior and style. Media representations of blacks as violent and threatening may produce negative images of members of this race. Such images are often presented in gripping and dramatic scenes and the images are thus likely to stay in the viewer's mind. Likewise, images of violence as the way to solve problems and exert power may create strong paleosymbolic residues that shape violent attitudes and behavior. Or the paleosymbolic scenes of *Rambo* may stick in one's mind, leading one to engage in body-building, arms training, and perhaps violent action, as with the examples noted in my discussion of the Rambo effect.

Likewise, paleosymbolic images of predatory and violent women, such as the vampire-like predators of *Fatal Attraction* and *Basic Instinct* which I will discuss below, or the monstrous women of horror films, might produce fear of women. Or pornography or scenes that degrade, brutalize or mutilate women may produce violence against women. Media culture provides powerful images and scenes for identification that may directly infuence behavior, providing models of action, fashion, and style.

In appraising the effects of media culture, one must avoid the extreme of either romanticizing the audiences of media culture, or of reducing them to a homo-geneous mass incapable of critical thought or action. One needs to grasp the contradiction that the media do manipulate people and yet people also manipulate and use the media. British cultural studies tries to capture this contradiction in the distinction between encoding and decoding, whereby the texts of media culture may be encoded as the most crass, ideological and banal artifacts and yet audiences can produce their own meanings and pleasures out of this material. Yet it is a mistake to go too far toward the active audience, as Fiske and others have done, and to exaggerate the power of audiences against media culture. The media are tremendously powerful forces and underestimating their power does not benefit critical projects of social transformation.

In any case, the effects of media culture are highly complex and mediated, and require study of the origin and production of media culture texts, their distribution and reception by audiences, and the ways that individuals use cultural texts to produce meaning, discourses, and identities. Such effects can best be discerned by concrete studies of how popular cultural artifacts like the *Rambo* films, rap music, or *Beavis and Butt-Head* circulate and gain effectivity within media culture and everyday life. I will thus continue to engage in such concrete studies later in this and the following chapters, but first want to introduce some more theoretical material concerning some of the ways that one can learn to read media culture critically and thus increase one's media literacy.

IDEOLOGY AND UTOPIA

Because of the closeness of popular media texts to their social conditions, they provide privileged access to the social realities of their era and can thus be read to gain insight into what is actually going on in a particular society at a given moment. Consequently, the ideologies of media culture should be analyzed within the context of social struggle and political debate rather than simply as purveyors of false consciousness whose falsity is exposed and denounced by ideology critique. Although demystification is part of ideology critique, simply exposing mystification and domination isn't enough; we need to look behind the ideological surface to see the social and historical forces and struggles which generate ideological discourses and to examine the cinematic apparatus and strategies which make ideologies attractive.

Furthermore, on this model, ideology criticism is not solely denunciatory and should seek socially critical and oppositional moments within all ideological texts – including conservative ones. As feminists and others have argued, one should learn to read texts "against the grain," yielding progressive insights even from reactionary texts. One can also attend to the possibility of using more liberal or progressive moments or aspects of a film against less progressive moments as when Jameson (1979, 1990) extracts the socially critical elements from films like *Dog Day Afternoon* or *Jaws*, which are contrasted with more conservative positions and used to criticize aspects of the existing society.

Furthermore, radical cultural criticism should seek out those utopian moments, those projections of a better world, that are found in a wide range of texts (Bloch 1986). Extending this argument, one could claim that since ideology contains rhetorical constructs that attempt to persuade and to convince, they must have a relatively resonant and attractive core and thus often contain emancipatory promises or moments. Specification of utopian moments within the most seemingly ideological artifacts was the project of Ernst Bloch whose great work *The Principle of Hope* was translated into English in 1986 (see Kellner 1994b). Bloch provides a systematic examination of the ways that daydreams, popular culture, great literature, political and social utopias, philosophy and religion – often dismissed *tout court* as ideology by some Marxist ideological critique – contain emancipatory moments which project visions of a better life that put in question the organization and structure of life under capitalism (or state socialism).

Throughout his life, Bloch argued that Marxism was vitiated by a one-sided, inadequate, and merely negative approach to ideology. For Bloch, ideology is "Janus-faced," two-sided: it contains errors, mystifications, and techniques of manipulation and domination, but it also contains a utopian residue or surplus that can be used for social critique and to advance political emancipation. Bloch believed that even ideological artifacts contain expressions of desire and articulations of needs that socialist theory and politics should heed to in order to provide programs and discourses which appeal to the deep-seated desires for a better life within everyone. Ideologies thus provide clues to possibilities for future development and contain a "surplus" or "excess" that is not exhausted in mystification or legitimation. And ideologies may contain normative ideals whereby the existing society can be criticized, as well as models of an alternative society.

Drawing on Bloch, Jameson has suggested that mass cultural texts often have utopian moments and proposes that radical cultural criticism should analyze both the social hopes and fantasies in the film, as well as the ideological ways in which fantasies are presented, conflicts are resolved, and potentially disruptive hopes and anxieties are managed (Jameson 1979, 1981, 1990). In his reading of *Jaws*, for instance, the shark stands in for a variety of fears (uncontrolled organic nature threatening the artificial society, big business corrupting and endangering community, disruptive sexuality threatening the disintegration of the family and traditional values, and so on) which the film tries to contain through the reassuring defeat of evil by representatives of the current class structure. Yet the film also contains utopian images of family, male bonding, and adventure, as well as socially critical visions of capitalism which articulate fears that unrestrained big business would inexorably destroy the environment and community.

In Jameson's view, mass culture thus articulates social conflicts, contemporary fears and utopian hopes, and attempts at ideological containment and reassurance. Consequently, cultural criticism requires a "double hermeneutic" that attends to ideology and utopia. For Jameson:

> works of mass culture cannot be ideological without at one and the same time being implicitly or explicitly Utopian as well: they cannot manipulate unless they offer some genuine shred of content as a fantasy bribe to the public about to be so manipulated. Even the 'false consciousness' of so monstrous a phenomenon of Nazism was nourished by collective fantasies of a Utopian type, in 'socialist' as well as in nationalist guises. Our proposition about the drawing power of the works of mass culture has implied that such works cannot manage anxieties about the social order unless they have first revived them and given them some rudimentary expression; we will now suggest that anxiety and hope are two faces of the same collective consciousness, so that the works of mass culture, even if their function lies in the legitimation of the existing order – or some worse one – cannot do their job without deflecting in the latter's service the deepest and most fundamental hopes and fantasies of the collectivity, to which they can therefore, no matter in how distorted a fashion, be found to have given voice.
>
> (Jameson 1979: 144)

Top Gun is, of course, a conservative utopia that uses the military as a scene for utopian images of community, romance, male heroism, and self-affirmation. Films like *Jaws*, by contrast, might use utopian images to provide a critique of the loss of community, and its destruction by commercial interests. Popular texts may thus also contain social criticism in their ideological scenarios and one of the tasks of radical cultural criticism is to specify utopian, critical, subversive, or oppositional meanings, even within the texts of media culture (see Kellner 1979). For these artifacts may contain implicit and even explicit critiques of capitalism, sexism, or racism, or visions of freedom and happiness which can provide critical perspectives on the unhappiness and unfreedom in the existing society. *The Deer Hunter*, for instance, though an arguably reactionary text (Kellner and Ryan 1988), contains utopian images of community, working-class and ethnic solidarity, and personal friendship which provides critical perspectives on the fragmentation, alienation, and loss of community in everyday life under contemporary capitalism.

The utopian images of getting high and horsing around in the drug hootch in *Platoon* provide visions of racial harmony and individual and social happiness which offer a critical perspective on the harrowing war scenes and which code war as a disgusting and destructive human activity. The images of racial solidarity and transcendence in the dance numbers of *Zoot Suit* provide a utopian and critical contrast to the oppression of people of color found in the scenes of everyday and prison life in the film. And the transformation of life in the musical numbers of *Pennies From Heaven* provide critical perspectives on the degradation of everyday life due to the constraints of an unjust and irrational economic system which informs the realist sections of the film.

In addition, Hollywood films, even conservative ones, put on display hopes and fears that contest dominant hegemonic and hierarchal relations of power (Ryan 1989: 111ff.). Ideological texts thus put on display both the significant dreams and nightmares of a culture and the ways that the culture is attempting to channel them to maintain its present relations of power and domination. *Top Gun*, for example, exhibits the need for individual achievement, recognition, community, and love. It presents the (dubious) argument that these needs can be satisfied by military life. Other films show that the present society cannot satisfy existing needs, or assuage existing fears, as when *Thelma and Louise* (1991) suggests that women must take radical action to maintain their autonomy in existing patriarchal society. And a documentary like *Roger and Me* (1990) shows the destruction of working-class communities as multinational corporations close down their plants.

From this perspective, a critical cultural studies should not only critique dominant ideologies, but should also specify any utopian, oppositional, subversive, and, emancipatory moments within ideological constructs which are then turned against existing forms of domination. This procedure draws on the sort of immanent critique practiced by the Frankfurt School in the 1930s, when they turned earlier forms of democratic bourgeois ideology against current, more reactionary, forms in fascist society. An immanent critique of contemporary society thus turns its own values against current social forms and practices that deny or contradict widely recognized values such as freedom or individualism (see Kellner 1984, 1989a). Thus, while bourgeois ideologies of freedom, individualism, and rights are to some extent ideologies which mask class rule and domination, they also contain critical and emancipatory moments which can be used to criticize the suppression or curtailment of rights and freedom under capitalist society. The practice of what the Frankfurt School called "immanent critique" thus turns ideology against ideology, using more rational and progressive ideologies against more repressive and reactionary ones (i.e. turning liberalism against fascism or New Right conservativism). The Frankfurt School critical theorists, however, never engaged in such an immanent critique of media culture and I am proposing here that such a project could be of use to cultural studies today, replacing earlier denunciatory models.

Consequently, sharp distinctions between ideology and science or theory, or ideology and utopia, should be deconstructed.[3] Ideology has to have some cognitive and utopian features in order to appeal to individuals. If ideology were nothing more than lies and mystification, it would have no hold on an individual's experience of life, and if it had no attractive features it would not appeal to people. Thus ideological texts often have some cognitive content and utopian moments that cultural studies should examine and discuss. But ideology critique is also interested in how ideology tricks individuals into accepting contemporary social conditions and ways of life. Ideology presents historically constructed conditions as natural, as common sense and the way things are, as if it were natural for Rambo to slaughter hundreds of individuals and then to turn on the state and its computers.

Ideology also presents the specific interests of groups as universal, as in everyone's interests, as if it was in everyone's interests to intervene in foreign countries and to kill communist or Arab "enemies." Ideology transforms negative conditions and forces into positive ones, as if it were good that the U.S. employs mercenaries and undercover agents to carry out its dirty work. Ideology thus represents the world upside down, with culture and the historically contingent appearing as nature and the eternal; with particular class interests appearing as universal; with highly political images, myths, and stories appearing as apolitical.

Ideology is thus a rhetoric that attempts to seduce individuals into identifying with the dominant system of values, beliefs, and behavior. Ideology replicates their actual conditions of existence, but in a mystified form in which people fail to recognize the negative, historically constructed and thus modifiable nature of their societies. Yet the work of ideology is very complex and it is to 1970s French theories that we turn for new perspectives on culture and ideology that can be of use to cultural studies.

HEGEMONY, COUNTERHEGEMONY, AND DECONSTRUCTION

Developments of new ways of reading and criticizing texts by so-called New French Theory also has some important implications for the project of cultural studies. Various French post-structuralists have contested the somewhat simplistic Marxian belief that ideology resides in and constitutes the center of texts, and that ideology critique simply involves refutation and demolition of the central ideological proposition of the text. Against this procedure, theorists like Roland Barthes, Pierre Macheray, Jacques Derrida, and other post-structuralists propose new ways of reading texts and engaging in ideology critique. Texts, in the post-structuralist view, should be read as the expression of a multiplicity of voices rather than as the enunciation of one single ideological voice which is then to be specified and attacked. Texts thus require multivalent readings, and a set of critical or textual strategies that will unfold their contradictions, contestatory marginal elements, and structured silences. These strategies include analyzing how, for example, the margins of texts might be as significant as the center in conveying ideological positions, or how the margins of a text might deconstruct ideological positions affirmed in the text by contradicting or undercutting them, or how what is left unsaid is as important as what is actually said.

Such a strategy involves paying attention to the margins, to seemingly insignificant elements of a text, as well as to the specific ideological positions affirmed. *An Unmarried Woman*, for example, presents the ideology of liberal feminism whereby Erika (Jill Clayburgh) is able to develop herself more fully both in terms of relations and career after her husband leaves her for a younger woman. At the end of the film, she prances merrily down a Manhattan street with a giant painting just given to her by her lover (Alan Bates), whose offer to go with him immediately to New Hampshire she rejected so that she could also pursue a career. As Erika crosses the street, three black and Latino working women stop to look at her and the frame freezes on their faces, undercutting the film's ideological affirmation of liberal feminism by showing that most women cannot afford the luxury, or have the privilege, of making choices available to upper-class women like Erika.

Thelma and Louise, by contrast, exhibits a more radical feminism in its critique of male brutality, forcing the female protagonists to violence and a life of crime. Yet the ending could be read as undercuting an affirmation of sisterhood and the triumph of women by showing the protagonists driving off a cliff, as if attempts at women's liberation and solidarity were impossible. Yet the ending could also be read as an affirmation of their solidarity and an indication that women cannot achieve liberation in the existing society of male violence and power, and must radically transform the society and culture before real liberation is possible. Obviously, films do not have one simple message and can give rise to a multiplicity of readings, depending on what aspects of a film the critic chooses to focus on and the complexity of the text itself.

Marginal elements in films might be important in other ways as well. In the opening title sequence of *Beverly Hills Cop* we get rather realistic pictures of the black Detroit ghetto – precisely the world that the ideological project of the film attempts to erase, as the action shifts to the upper-class world of Beverly Hills. Although *Cruising* is arguably a homophobic attack on gay male life, it shows the sexual ambivalence of the male cop (played by Al Pacino) and, indirectly, the excitement of the gay scene in some of the cinematic representations. Some cinematic texts are, as Robin Wood argues, inherently incoherent and contradictory (Wood 1986). In these cases, ideology critique would put on display the central ideological contradictions, or would attempt to show how what appears to be the central ideological position or argument is itself put into question and undermined by contradictory or marginal elements within the text. This procedure would thus show how ideologies may come into contradiction with themselves or fail, and thus demonstrates the cracks and fissures, vulnerabilities and weak points, and gaps within hegemonic ideology itself.

One should also pay attention to what is left out of ideological texts, for it is often the exclusions and silences that reveal the ideological project of the text. For instance, *The Deer Hunter* and the return-to-Vietnam films leave out U.S. atrocities against the Vietnamese (portrayed in films like *Platoon* and *Casualties of War*) and present U.S. soldiers as innocent victims of evil Vietnamese and communists. Ideological presentations of women in contemporary society in Hollywood films often leave out the ways that women are bonding together to fight male oppression, not only via friendship, *à la* Thelma and Louise, but also by means of group organization and associations. Hegemony thus works by exclusion and marginalization, as much as by affirming specific ideological positions.

Such methods of ideology critique therefore encourage the critic to be as much interested in *how ideology fails* as in how it succeeds, in how ideological texts are sites of tensions and dissonance even when they seem most harmonious and ideologically successful. Although the first *Dirty Harry* film, for example, is obviously a right-wing call to law and order, it displays a conflict between liberal and conservative views of law enforcement and while it attempts to privilege the conservative version, it depicts a society so ridden with crime, corruption, and hopeless inertia that a critical reading could demonstrate that *both* liberal and conservative solutions to crime are inadequate and that *only* radical social restructuring can address the problems that the film presents. Inadvertently, perhaps, the conclusion of the first *Dirty Harry* film, where Harry throws his badge away, points to a society so corrupt that even the right-wing solution to crime must inevitably fail. The conservative individualist hero walks away alone into (pure) nature in the film, but conservative economic interests are themselves destroying the nature yearned for by its fantasists, thus showing the classical conservative solution to be increasingly untenable in the modern world.

Deconstructive criticism thus shows how ideological projects fail, or undercut their own messages and intentions. Media culture texts are complex and require multivalent readings. Yet they are not so polysemic that they can mean anything and audiences are positioned to accept certain positions via the deployment of the apparatus of the cinema, television, or whatever form. Although audiences can resist "dominant" readings, it is not certain that they always resist these meanings and there is little evidence for the belief that audiences always read texts against the dominant culture, as Fiske comes close to claiming. Indeed, the studies in this book undermine his claim that: "there can be no popular dominant culture, for popular culture is formed always in reaction to, and never as part of, the forces of domination" (Fiske 1989a: 43). As our studies of *Rambo*, *Top Gun*, and other militarist, sexist, and racist films suggest, media culture sometimes legitimates forces of domination and induces audiences to gain pleasure in assent to ideological positions, sometimes fails to do so, and sometimes provides pleasure in opposition to dominant ideologies and institutions.[4] Ethnographic interviews with audiences concerning their interpretations of media culture and attempts to analyze media effects must deal with the fact that many messages of media culture are subliminal and perhaps not consciously perceived. A diagnostic critique thus assumes a depth dimension to media culture and uses methods of myth and symbol interpretation to ferret out hidden, latent, and subliminal meanings.

Applying psychoanalytical methods to reading *Top Gun*, for instance, suggests that the film is about phallic power and the threats to masculist values in the 1960s and 1970s and their reassertion during the 1980s. Being "top gun" obviously means being top stud as well as top fighter pilot and the two competencies are related throughout the film. When Maverick is triumphant in his military exploits he gets the girl and when he fails she leaves him; when he triumphs at the end, she is there to validate his victory. *Top Gun* is full of phallic symbols and power, images of male potency, from the first images of the phallic airplanes to the closing battle scenes. Thus, the psychoanalytic perspective strengthens the feminist one and not by accident have many feminists adopted psychoanalytic perspectives.

Read diagnostically, *Top Gun* articulates fears that male power is being threatened by women in the current society and enacts its re-privileging. A number of films of the 1980s and 1990s also present phallic women as a threat to male power and familial domesticity. Part of what Susan Faludi diagnosed as backlash in the media (1991), films like *Fatal Attraction* and *Basic Instinct* portray strong, single, independent successful women in an extremely negative light. *Fatal Attraction*'s (1986) villainess, a single and successful editor named Alex played by Glenn Close, seduces a married male, Dan Gallagher (played by Michael Douglas), and then proceeds to obsessively pursue him, seeking to destroy his marriage and to possess him for herself.

Faludi points out how the film was initially intended to be a sympathetic portrayal of the dilemmas of a single independent woman and how the original version makes her a tragic victim of her situation, showing her committing suicide alone in a bathtub. But the film revises that ending, having the wife shoot the single woman, who the film positions the audience to hate, with its contrasts of the happy family life and the evil threats to it represented by Alex. One key scene shows her voyeuristically watching a happy family scene in which Dan gives his daughter a rabbit, while his wife looks on with affection. Alex is shown outside looking in during a scene that dramatizes precisely what this single career woman is missing and she vomits as she realizes all that she lacks.

The other side of *Fatal Attraction* is that it provides a morality tale for men, warning that if they stray from matrimonial monogamy – even once – it could wreak disaster and destroy what is presented as most important in life. *The Hand That Rocks the Cradle* (1992) contains similar problematics in favor of the traditional family and traditional women's roles at the expense of single women. In its melodramatic plot, a happily married woman, Claire Bartel (played by Annabella Sciorra), reports that her gynecologist sexually molested her; other women report the same and he commits suicide, causing his wife Peyton (played by Rebecca De Mornay) to have a miscarriage. In a hyperbolic revenge plot, Peyton enters the Bartel home as a nannie to their two children and proceeds to attempt to destroy the wife, thereby wreaking revenge for her husband's death.

And so once again men are warned that if they stray from matrimonial fidelity disaster will ensue and women are shown descending into madness and violence without a man to take care of them and enable them to realize their feminine nature. In one scene, Peyton is caught breast-feeding the Bartel's new-born baby by a black handyman, who she gets fired with false accusations that he sexually molested the young daughter. The image of the woman with child represents the norm for women which is denied Peyton, who is subsequently driven to psychotic extremities to try to fulfill this role. And in both films it is the wife who, in fighting for her family, kills the evil threat to their familial happiness.

Fatal Attraction and *The Hand that Rocks the Cradle* contrast bad and good women, with traditional women represented as good and the sort of independent professional woman celebrated by certain versions of feminism, or single women *per se*, depicted as lacking and driven to vile and destructive behavior. *Basic Instinct*, by contrast, simply vilifies women as such in its story of a successful woman writer (played by Sharon Stone) whose family, lovers, and enemies are shown as mysteriously murdered. The striking thing about this film is the extent to which it vilifies *all* of its women characters. Its convoluted plot makes it ambiguous as to whether the woman writer, or a woman police psychologist obsessed with the writer, are really guilty of the crimes. Two other major women characters, the writer's lesbian lover and an older woman, are also revealed to be mass murderers who killed their families, thus representing women *per se* as evil and vicious – traditional sexist stereotypes.

Basic Instinct also vilifies lesbians as perverted and predatory, and portrays women as wanting to assume male phallic power and control. Indeed, the film can be read as an alarmist allegory concerning what women would do if they were to assume phallic power. Both the writer of *Basic Instinct* and Alex of *Fatal Attraction* can indeed be read as derisive vehicles of phallic power run amok with knives and ice-picks, used as murder weapons of choice, serving as crudely Freudian symbols of the violent phallus.

A diagnostic critique, such as I will illustrate and develop in the following studies, uses history to read texts and texts to read history. Such a dual optic allows insight into the multiple relations between texts and contexts, between media culture and history. My diagnostic critique of contemporary media culture will suggest that ideological hegemony in U.S. society today is complex, contested, and constantly being put into question. Hegemony is negotiated and renegotiated, and is vulnerable to attack and subversion. In recent years, for instance, the New Right political hegemony of the Reagan years passed over to a more centrist conservatism of the Bush regime that in turn became increasingly militarist in the wake of the Panama invasion and Persian Gulf War. Yet, despite the seeming popularity of the Gulf War, Bush's hegemony turned out to be vulnerable, shaky, and subject to overthrow and reversal – as indeed happened in the 1992 Presidential election.

Reading media culture diagnostically thus presents insights into the current political situation, into the strengths and vulnerabilities of the contending political forces, and into the hopes and fears of the population. From this perspective, the texts of media culture provide important insights into the psychological, socio-political, and ideological make-up of a specific society at a given point in history. Reading media culture diagnostically also allows one to detect what ideological solutions to various problems are being offered, and thus to anticipate certain trends, to gain insights into social problems and conflicts, and to appraise the dominant ideologies and emergent oppositional forces. Consequently, diagnostic political critique enables one to perceive the limitations of mainstream conservative and liberal political ideologies, as well as helping to decipher their continuing appeal. It enables one to grasp the utopian yearnings in a given society and challenges progressives to develop cultural representations, political alternatives, and practices and movements which address these predispositions.

Such diagnostic reading thus helps with the formulation of progressive political practices which speak to salient hopes, fears, and desires, and the construction of social alternatives that are grounded in existing psychological, social, and cultural matrixes. Consequently, diagnostic film critique does not merely offer another clever method of reading films but provides weapons of critique for those interested in producing a better society.

PLATOON: A DIAGNOSTIC CRITIQUE

Almost two decades after the fall of Saigon to communist forces, Vietnam continues to be a hotly contested topic in American culture and politics. As J. William Gibson (1986) indicates in his book *The Perfect War: Technowar in Vietnam*, liberals from the beginning presented Vietnam as a series of "tragic mistakes," while conservatives blamed defeat on the politicians and excessive "restraint" in the use of military force. In the aftermath of Vietnam, liberals and leftists claimed that the debacle demonstrated the limits of U.S. military power, the impossibility of policing the world and stopping liberation movements everywhere. For conservatives, on the contrary, the "Vietnam syndrome" represented a failure of will, liberal cowardice and defeatism, which should be overcome with renewed military build-up and intervention. With Ronald Reagan's Presidential victories in 1980 and 1984, the rightist version became official policy, and Reagan's problems with the Iran/Contra scandals can arguably be traced to the right's inability to accept the limits of U.S. power and its obsessive drive to stop communism, to defeat the Foreign Other, to reassert U.S. military might all over the world.

The battle between left and right over Vietnam, war, and militarism has taken place within Hollywood film and U.S. popular culture as well as within the political arena. Although John Wayne's ultra right-wing fantasy *The Green Berets* (1968) was the only actual fictional film which dealt with U.S. involvement in Vietnam during the years of American intervention, many films like *M.A.S.H.*, *Catch-22*, *Soldier Blue* and others could be read as attacks on U.S. involvement in Vietnam, and as ripostes to right-wing versions of militarism and U.S. foreign policy within the context of the debates over Vietnam in the late 1960s and early 1970s.[5] After the U.S. pulled out of Vietnam and the communist forces won, the Hollywood debate on Vietnam finally emerged front and center. Left-liberal films like *Coming Home*, *Who'll Stop the Rain* (both 1978), *Cutter's Way* (1981), and *Born on the Fourth of July* (1989) sympathetically presented vets as victims of a misguided war, while *Go Tell the Spartans* and *The Boys From Company C* (both 1978), and *Hamburger Hill* (1987) presented combat films located in Vietnam that criticized U.S. involvement, and that therefore raised questions about imperialist intervention in the Third World.

The two major 1970s films in Hollywood's debate over Vietnam, however, *The Deerhunter* (1978) and *Apocalypse Now* (1979), both used a "heart of darkness" scenario to present racist visions of "innocent" Americans thrown into violent warfare in the "mysterious" and "savage" East. Both films presented mythical visions of male heroism that tried to salvage some redeeming virtues from U.S. defeat in Vietnam, and both dishonestly evaded the causes, history, and actual trajectory of the Vietnam war (i.e. both were more about "manhood" and "heroism" than Vietnam itself).

During the Reagan era, such ideological extravaganzas as *Rambo, Red Dawn, Missing in Action, Top Gun,* the TV mini-series *Amerika,* and other artifacts of media culture represented aggressively right-wing positions on war, militarism, communism, and so on. These films and others like *An Officer and a Gentleman, Star Wars, Indiana Jones, ad nauseam* served as soft and hard core propaganda for Reaganism and a distinctly right-wing interventionist and militarist agenda. In this context, *Platoon* can be seen as a left-liberal intervention in the Hollywood debate over Vietnam.

Oliver Stone's *Platoon* is arguably the most realistic and critical Vietnam combat film yet to appear.[6] The story – based on Stone's experiences in Nam during 1967–8 – deals with the experiences in Vietnam of a young army volunteer Chris Taylor (Charlie Sheen), who is obviously Stone's alter ego. The young soldier emerges out of darkness from the bowels of a military transport vehicle into dusty, gold-yellow (and highly filtered) light and the sound of helicopters in a dramatic introduction to Vietnam, presented as an exotic Otherness. He and his fellow soldiers see corpses in body bags, and are immediately transported to the jungle for combat duty, thus thrusting the viewer into the reality of combat without any preparation or background.

Chris himself has obviously landed in Vietnam without any real knowledge of what is going on there and what he is getting himself into. On the initial hike, the heat, the insects, the foreign jungle terrain, and the fear cause him to throw up, and a sympathetic officer agrees to carry some of the excessive baggage which he has brought with him. Chris tries to explain his motivations and experiences in voice-over narrations which summarize his letters to his grandparents, though he is soon overwhelmed by his experience, which can no longer be expressed in conventional terms, and halts this activity.

As soon as Chris and his platoon reach his camp "somewhere near the Cambodian border," he is assigned night patrol, and soon thereafter Chris and the audience are initiated into the rituals of search-and-destroy patrol duty, night watches, and fire fights in which deadly explosives suddenly flash, maim, and kill. The key combat episodes – which shed most critical light on U.S. involvement in Vietnam – include the torching of Vietnamese villages, and an all-out "enemy" assault which traps the American forces who are cut off from supply and support forces. The village scene provides a powerful depiction of U.S. atrocities. The U.S. troops enter a village suspected of harboring Viet Cong, and brutalize women, children and animals in the process, after which they torch the village. In a key narrative device, the "humane" Sgt. Elias (Willem Dafoe) prevents the more brutal Sgt. Barnes (Tom Berenger) from killing a young girl after he had already killed a woman and other villagers. Chris, who had begun participating in the atrocities, looks on intently and shortly thereafter breaks up the rape of a village teenager by other soldiers.

The scene recalls My Lai and other U.S. war crimes, and thus both realistically points to the brutalizing effects of the Vietnam War while disallowing the traditional war film conventions that depict "our boys" as good, and the "enemy" as evil. Likewise, the concluding massacre scene shows the victimization of U.S. soldiers who are used as bait to attract an enemy assault which would allow the U.S. army to use its superior fire power and conventional weapons and strategies that were precluded by the conditions of jungle warfare. The U.S. captain eventually orders an air attack on the region which indiscriminately destroys U.S. and Vietnamese troops.

The social horizon of *Platoon* was obviously the Vietnam War itself, the experiences of the U.S. soldiers, and the tumultous debate over the war in the U.S. The discursive field of the film was the anti-war discourses that questioned U.S. motives and actions in the Vietnam War, undercutting rationales that legitimated the U.S. intervention. The war is put in question by Chris's narrative questioning of the war, the violent deaths of the U.S. soldiers in the platoon, and the brutal actions against the Vietnamese. The figural action privileged in the film involved the activity of the soldiers in battle, on patrol, and in camp. The dominant figures, however, as I argue below, constituted a clash between "good" and "bad" soldiers which defocused attention on the irrationality of the U.S. intervention and presented the action as a symbolic morality tale playing out opposing images of soldiers and manhood.

Most of the movie deals with the fear, the uncertainty, and the brutalization undergone by young Americans thrown into the jungles of Nam. Although there is some focus on the drug culture which provided a break and an escape from combat, there is very little of the clichéd conversation, obligatory love or personal emphasis, or celebrations of male heroism and bonding that is typical of the Hollywood war films. *Platoon* has an hallucinatory intensity about it, and it powerfully recreates the experience of being at war in a completely hostile and alien environment. Oliver Stone's focus in the film is on the experience of combat, and the film brilliantly recreates the environment and atmosphere within which U.S. troops fought in Vietnam. The film also makes clear from the beginning that it is for the most part poor white working-class people and people of color who are drafted and sent to Vietnam, and that the war certainly does not serve their own interests in any way whatsoever. Indeed, *Platoon* deglamorizes warfare by showing how it brutalizes young men and inevitably brings out the worst in their natures.

On the other hand, *Platoon* neither presents the Vietnamese as autonomous subjects with their own point of view and reasons for fighting, nor does it illuminate U.S. involvement in Vietnam and the imperialist nature of the intervention. Like most other Hollywood Vietnam war films, *Platoon* focuses almost exclusively on the U.S. troops and their experiences, and presents the Vietnamese as objects of either fear (in the combat scenes) or pity (in the atrocity scenes). Indeed, in many ways *Platoon* shares the conventions and masculist ideologies of a tradition of Hollywood war films. The plot development is structured as Chris Taylor's initiation into both knowledge and "manhood," and masculinity is defined (as in the most reactionary Hollywood traditions) as the ability to commit violence. For Chris is clearly transformed from a naive "greenie" into an experienced and effective killing machine who comes charging out of a foxhole in the final battle scene to kill dozens of Vietnamese in a way that would have made Audie Murphy and John Wayne proud.

The central symbolic trope of the film which contrasts the "evil" soldier Sgt. Barnes to the "good" Sgt. Elias is equally problematical. From the beginning, Barnes is a hard-assed disciplinarian and brutally effective leader who showers Chris with obscenities and tells him to get his sorry ass moving when he is about to collapse on his first march. Elias, by contrast, takes some of the books and excess gear from his pack and offers to transport it himself. As the story unfolds, one group of soldiers identify around Barnes, whereas others associate with Elias, delineating what Stone saw as a fundamental division in the Vietnam army between hard-core militarist regulars (boozing rednecks) and more humane countercultural types (blacks, Hispanics, and the hippie drug culture).[7] Stone and the film perceive one group as the good guys and the other as the bad guys – reproducing the manichean vision which runs throughout the Hollywood war film.

This moralistic division allows Stone to celebrate Elias (and ultimately Chris) as the "good" soldier, while negating Barnes and his cohorts as bad soldiers. Elias is thus presented as more "humane" and "moral" than Barnes, but he also calls Vietnamese "dinks" and seems to get pleasure from killing scores of "enemies" and going on dangerous missions. Stone allows him almost superhuman heroics and a redemptive death scene where he stumbles in slow motion as he is shot repeatedly by the Vietnamese after Barnes had attempted to assassinate him, and dies with his arms reaching up to heaven.

Consequently, because of the intense focus on combat and moral conflict, there is really no political analysis of U.S. involvement in Vietnam, nor does the film deal on any level with the question of "why were we in Vietnam?" Stone's vision is really no different than the earlier critical Vietnam films *Go Tell the Spartans* and *The Boys in Company C* (both 1978). Like *Spartans*, *Platoon* shows the U.S. blundering into a military adventure with no clear objectives and with no sense of the terrain and situation. Like both *Spartans* and *Boys*, *Platoon* draws a firm boundary between "good" and "bad" wars, and "good" and "bad" soldiers, rather than carrying out a more penetrating critique of war, militarism, and U.S. foreign policy.

Consequently, political issues are displaced by moral issues centering on the moral struggle between Barnes, who represents brutal efficiency, and Elias, who represents idealistic humanity trying to preserve respect for human life in difficult circumstances. At the end of the film, the young narrator Chris refers in a voice-over to Barnes as "our Captain Ahab," and of "Barnes and Elias fighting for possession of my soul." In a rather masculist concluding gesture, Chris kills Barnes, thus symbolically purging his soul of the evil and brutality which he was confronted with in Nam.

Thus, *Platoon*'s symbolism overpowers its realism, but despite its failings, there are some quite powerful critical visions of U.S. involvement in Vietnam in the film. The brutality of the U.S. platoon in the Vietnamese village is as stomach-churning a presentation of U.S. atrocities in Vietnam as Hollywood is likely to produce, and such powerful scenes subvert the ideological manicheanism of the traditional Hollywood war film that sees U.S. soldiers as "good" and the "enemy" as "evil." The final combat scene illustrated how some platoons served as bait to attract the Vietnamese into open fire, and the slaughter of both the U.S. and Vietnamese forces provide powerful indictments of the futility and brutality of the war.

In its political context, *Platoon*'s critical vision of U.S. intervention countered the rightist discourse on Vietnam of Rambo, Reagan, and others who refused to see that the Vietnam War was fundamentally and morally wrong. Moreover, its graphic demonstrations of the horrors of war mobilized subject positions against fantasies of military heroism promoted in the comic-book militarism of films like *Rambo*, *Top Gun*, and other militarist extravaganzas. In this context, *Platoon*'s Academy Awards and its critical and commercial success helped turn Hollywood away from the Reaganite entertainment and mindless militarism that was dominant in Hollywood during the Reagan years.

Thus, some media culture promoted prowar feelings, while other artifacts promoted antiwar positions. A diagnostic critique reads films politically in order to analyze the opposing political struggles and positions and their relative strengths and weaknesses. It attempts to discern how media culture mobilizes desire, sentiment, affect, belief, and vision into various subject positions, and how these support one political position or another. A diagnostic critique thus indicates how the texts of media culture help to produce political identities and criticizes those identities and effects which are counter to democracy and that support the forces of domination and oppression.

Politics, however, pervades everyday life, as well as the great political battles that dominate media news and information. A diagnostic critique thus also probes the politics of everyday life and its struggles around issues like race, gender, and class. From this perspective, media cultural texts articulate the fears and hopes, the dreams and nightmares, of a culture and thus are a source of novel and important socio-psychological insights, displaying what audiences are feeling and thinking at a given moment. This explains why psychoanalysis continues to be of importance for cultural studies. Against the notion of the depthlessness and surface of contemporary cultural texts claimed by postmodern theory, I would argue that many cultural texts today continue to be bearers of meaning and to require depth-hermeneutical models to ferret out their meanings and the range of their possible effects. The studies in the following chapters will pursue these topics, showing how cultural studies can contribute to presenting diagnostic insight into the struggles of everyday life, as well as the major political and media events of the era.

NOTES

1 I am thus appropriating the term multiculturalism for my agenda of cultural studies and am not intervening in the debates over multiculturalism in education in which, as Giroux (1992), McLaren (1993) and Scatamburlo (forthcoming) argue, there are a diverse range of corporate/conservative, left-liberal, and more critical multicultural projects. I am associating these cultural studies with what Giroux, McLaren, and Scatamburlo describe as critical multiculturalism.

2 For some of my earlier work in developing multiperspectival theory, see Kellner 1991 and 1992a, and Best and Kellner 1991.

3 Althusser wants to contrast science to ideology, as its radical other, whereas Mannheim, Bloch, Ricoeur, and others oppose ideology to utopia. I would suggest that one should not make such tight distinctions, that ideology and science, as well as ideology and utopia, are interconnected. Yet I see the concept of culture as wider than ideology, and believe that one can, on an analytical level, counterpoise various discourses to ideology. One can also contrast ideological discourses and criticize one ideology from the standpoint of another, as when one attacks fascism from the standpoint of liberal humanism. Theories that might be ideological, in the sense of legitimizing a dominant social order, in one context, can be critical and subversive in another, as when Marxism provided conservative social functions in legitimizing the former Soviet Union, while presenting radical critical perspectives on actually existing capitalist societies. Thus, all discourse and critique is contextual, using norms in specific contexts, rather than positing absolute standards of critique.

4 See the appendix to *Camera Politica* that discusses interviews with audiences concerning the political messages and effects of popular films. The survey displays a range of reactions to and readings of the politics of popular films (Kellner and Ryan 1988), many that follow the ideological encoding of the films while others resist it, or offer their own readings.

5 On Hollywood's presentation of Vietnam, see Britton 1986; Wood 1986; and Kellner and Ryan 1988.

6 Most reviews highlighted *Platoon*'s alleged realism and praised its honesty, verisimilitude, and so on (the film poster and advertisements for the film were full of such comments). Likewise, reflections on the film by veterans and political commentators tended to stress its realism and accurate representations of the war and the experience of fighting; see, for example, the pieces in the *New York Times* by correspondent David Halberstam and Marines veteran David Trainor (March 15, 1987). I shall dissent from this position here and generally perceive realism as a set of conventions which construct a picture of the world rather than as a way of imitating the world or providing access to the real.

7 Oliver Stone sets forth his dualistic and dichotomizing vision in an article in *American Film* where he writes that *Platoon* "mirrored the very civil war that I'd witnessed in all the units I was in – on the one hand, the lifers, the juicers and the moron white element (part Southern, part rural) against, on the other, the hippie, dope-smoking, black, and progressive white element . . . Right versus Left" (Oliver Stone "One from the Heart," *American Film* (January–February 1987): 19). This article and the extended interview in *Film Comment* (February 1987): 11–20, 60, presents Stone as the left wing of the Hollywood boy's club, and although Stone's films have their limitations, taken cumulatively, such films as *Salvador, Born on the Fourth of July, Talk Radio, JFK* and *Heaven and Earth* present something of a left-progressive intonation within the voice of U.S. media culture.

Part II

Diagnostic critique and cultural studies

Chapter 4

Social anxiety, class, and disaffected youth

In the previous chapters, I delineated aspects of my method and model of cultural studies and in the rest of the book will apply it to concrete studies, to doing cultural studies. In the previous chapter, I introduced the concept of diagnostic critique which uses history and social theory to analyze cultural texts and uses cultural texts in turn to illuminate historical trends, conflicts, possibilities, and anxieties.[1] My conceptions of a contextual cultural studies and the notion of diagnostic critique will be illustrated in this chapter, first, by study of some horror and fantasy films that articulate the social anxieties of working- and middle-class people in an era of economic insecurity in the United States and elsewhere. In Chapter 2, I interrogated how Hollywood films transcoded the political discourses of the era, while the studies in this chapter will probe the anxieties of ordinary people in the terrain of everyday life during the same period. Cultural studies can thus use its methods to probe events, discourses, and social trends on both the macro and micro level, engaging both the defining political trends and events of the era, as well as the texture and travails of everyday life.

I will argue that the *Poltergeist* and other horror films articulate fears of downward mobility in the contemporary era and provide allegories concerning social anxiety over losing one's job, home, and family. Next, I interrogate the situation of contemporary youth through analysis of the film *Slacker* and the MTV-series *Beavis and Butt-Head*. Throughout this chapter, I will suggest that media culture provides social allegories which articulate class and social group fears, yearnings, and hopes.[2] Decoding these social allegories thus provides a diagnostic critique with insight into the situation of individuals within various social classes and groups, like youth. Thus, fantasy and entertainment may be the vehicle of deadly serious diagnoses of the contemporary era which cultural studies should analyze and interpret.

POLTERGEISTS, GENDER, AND CLASS IN THE AGE OF REAGAN AND BUSH

During the past two decades, the horror-occult genre was one of the most popular and successful Hollywood genres.[3] Horror films have traditionally dealt with universal and primal fears (i.e. fears of dying, aging, bodily decay, violence, sexuality, etc.). However, the most interesting contemporary horror films (*The Exorcist, The Texas Chainsaw Massacre, Carrie, Alien, The Shining,* and so on) have presented, often in symbolic-allegorical form, both universal fears and the deepest anxieties and hostilities of contemporary U.S. society. A subtext of these films is the confusion and fright of the population in the face of economic crisis, accelerating social and cultural change, a near epidemic of cancer, industrial diseases, and AIDS, political instability, and fear of nuclear annihilation. The wide range and popularity of post-1970s Hollywood horror films suggests that something is profoundly wrong with U.S. society and a probing of these films may help reveal something about the source of contemporary fears.

The 1980s was also the era of Reagan and Bush and in this study, I wish to relate the social anxieties of the era to the conservative hegemony and will argue that these phenomena are interconnected. The 1980s was an unprecedented era of class warfare with massive redistribution of wealth from working and middle-class sectors to the rich and an era of high fear of unemployment, downward mobility, and crisis for the working classes.[4] While the 1970s saw a wave of popular films dealing with the working class (Kellner and Ryan 1988), it was rarely featured in 1980s Hollywood films which focused more on middle- and upper-class families and individuals. Yet the working class was often presented as threatening others to middle-class life and, as I attempt to demonstrate below, was often negatively stigmatized in genres like the horror film.

The broad panorama of popular horror films attests to a resurgence of the occult in contemporary society which suggests that individuals are no longer in control of everyday life. When individuals perceive that they do not have control over their lives and that they are dominated by powerful forces outside themselves, people are attracted to occultism. Consequently, during eras of socio-economic crisis when individuals have difficulty coping with social reality, the occult becomes an efficacious ideological mode which helps explain unpleasant circumstances or incomprehensible events with the aid of religious or supernatural mythologies.

In the crisis of German society after World War I, for instance, there was a proliferation of horror films and the first great wave of American horror films appeared in the midst of the 1930's depression. After the explosion of the atomic bomb and with the heating up of the Cold War and arms race in the 1950s, another wave of occult horror films appeared, featuring visions of mutant animals and humans, or apocalyptic holocausts. Over the years, media culture has accumulated a rich treasure house of occultist lore to draw upon, and in the 1970s and 1980s Americans turned to occultism for experiences and ideas which helped them cope with economic crisis, political turmoil and cultural malaise. In this resurgence of the occult, repressed fears and irrational forces sought symbolic expression which often served as vehicles for reactionary ideologies in contemporary film (i.e. *The Exorcist* trilogy, *The Omen* trilogy, and a variety of monster films, demonic possession films, and other occult thrillers).

Whereas conservative horror films provide fantasies of reassurance that existing authorities and institutions can eliminate evil, many contemporary horror films do not provide reassurance that historically specific or universal evils can be suppressed and contained. Instead, they reveal a society in crisis, where destructive forces are rampant and conventional authorities and values are incapable of defeating and eliminating the evils afoot. Consequently, these films often do not legitimate contemporary American institutions and values but show horrific violence and social disintegration to be ubiquitous and powerful forces in the contemporary social order. This is true to some extent of films that rely on religious institutions to defeat "evil" (i.e. *The Exorcist* and to a greater extent the more nihilistic films of George Romero, Tobe Hooper, Wes Craven, Larry Cohen, and others that show contemporary institutions and ways of life to be the source of horror).[5]

In the following discussion, I shall disclose how the *Poltergeist* series negotiates middle-class fears and insecurities concerning race, gender, and class in the contemporary era. I'll interpret these films allegorically as articulating deep-rooted fears that are often explored in genres like the horror film rather than realist films, where they might be too painful to confront and explore. Horror films are a reactionary genre to the extent that they blame occult forces for societal disintegration and a life out of control, thus deflecting attention from the real sources of social suffering. Yet they also offer the possibility of radical critique by presenting suffering and oppression as caused by institutions that need to be reconstructed.

1970s horror films, for example, saw monsters being produced by families, and thus could be taken as socially critical, cinematically articulating the critiques of the family in 1960s political movements. Films like *The Texas Chain Saw Massacre*, *Motel Hell*, and so on presented the family as monstrous, as the source of monsters, thus replicating feminist critiques of the patriarchal family. But films like *Poltergeist* show good families being attacked by monsters, and thus serve as ideological defenses of the middle-class family, which transcode cinematically the conservative pro-family discourses of the 1980s. Yet, read diagnostically, even conservative horror films reveal contemporary anxieties concerning the family, downward mobility, and homelessness in an uncertain economy and deteriorating social order. In the following diagnostic reading, I accordingly discuss the *Poltergeist* films as indicators of social anxiety and disintegration in contemporary U.S. society.

Poltergeist and social anxiety

Among the wave of 1980s occult-horror films, *Poltergeist* (1982), directed by Tobe Hooper and co-authored and produced by Steven Spielberg,[6] is especially interesting because it articulates the underlying anxieties of the new middle class in the Age of Reagan. *Poltergeist*, along with Spielberg's *E.T., The Extra-Terrestrial* (1982), explores with sympathy and even affection the environment and lifestyle of the new affluent, suburban middle class and presents symbolic projections of its insecurities and fears. While *E.T.* presents an optimistic and charming allegory of suburban middle-class life, *Poltergeist* presents its shadow-side and nightmares in a story where the Other, the Alien, is not a friendly extra-terrestrial who comes from outside the society to help it, but threateningly emerges from *within* the socio-economic system and social subconscious to terrorize the ordinary middle-class people who are the subject of the film. Thus, whereas *E.T.* is Spielberg's childlike fantasy of hope, *Poltergeist* is a symbolic probing of universal and specifically American fears that takes the form of an allegorical nightmare, the decoding of which should tell us something about everyday life during the Reagan era.

Poltergeist features the adventures with the occult of the Freeling family which discovers that its house is built on top of a Native American graveyard whose spirits seek revenge against the intruding family. In another plot twist, evil spirits attempt to seduce the clairvoyant five-year-old daughter, Carol Anne into the spirit world. Her parents try to rescue her and are forced to turn to parapsychologists and a diminutive woman medium for help.

The family unit in *Poltergeist* contains a father, Steve Freeling (Craig T. Nelson), his wife Diane (Jobeth Williams), a teenage daughter Dana (Dominique Dunne), a young boy Robbie (Oliver Robins) and little Carol Anne (Heather O'Rourke), who is the first to make contact with the poltergeists. The Freelings live in one of the first houses built in Phase One of a housing project called Cuesta Vista. The father is a successful real estate agent who has sold 42 percent of the housing units in the area – which his boss tells him represents over seventy million dollars worth of property. As a reward for his heroic efforts, he has all the commodities desired by the new affluent middle class. Depiction of this class and its fears of losing their home, family, and property is a central focus of the *Poltergeist* films.

The name "Freeling" evokes the dominant ideology of freedom and from this perspective a "freeling" is a free being, a member of a class and society free from basic worries and cares, free to celebrate and live the American middle-class dream. "The Star-Spangled Banner," referring to the "land of the free," plays in an opening segment and refrains later in the film, which presents iconic images of American flags throughout. Yet *Poltergeist* deals with the threats to freedom and loss of sovereignty in contemporary middle-class life, and the all-too-real prospects of downward mobility in an American dream gone sour and become a nightmare.

The film opens with display of the new icons and objects of upper-middle-class status and provides a charming look at the new affluent consumer environment with its split-level houses, omnipresent multichannelled TV, electronic gadgets, boun-tiful toys for the kids, dope and sex for the parents, and a treasure house of commodities for every conceivable purpose. The opening images show the father asleep on his couch in front of his television. To the tune of the national anthem, we see configurations of television dots forming the scene of marines putting up the flag on a hill of Iwo Jima, evoking America's heroic past. But the present is troubled. The camera pans from room to room in the affluent house showing the family members asleep. The TV goes off and static fills the screen. Carol Anne, the youngest member of the household, gets up, goes downstairs, and stands in front of the TV talking to the strange lights dancing about in the static. The entire family comes down and looks at her in amazement. Throughout the film, the TV static will signal bizarre happenings and menace.

After the opening scene, *Poltergeist* presents some comic tableaux of suburban life. A heavy-set man drives down the street on a bicycle carrying a case of beer precariously balanced on the handlebars. Some playful kids aim their electronically directed toys at him and he falls off the bike. The beer cans spill and explode and he desperately carries the remaining, and still exploding, cans into the house where a group of middle-aged and middle-class men are watching a football game on TV. The pleasures of communal TV football in suburbia are soon disrupted: the next door neighbor's television set is plugged into the same remote control frequency and the kids next door have switched the channel to *Mr Rogers* to the dismay of the football fans. The husband runs out to negotiate a peaceful settlement with the neighbor who insists on the rights of his children, and the two fathers blast their remote control devices at each other's TVs, switching the channel from the football game to *Mr Rogers* to the alternating consternation and joy of the football audience and the kid show audience.

The opening scenes depict images of technology getting out of control that will permeate the *Poltergeist* films. Technology out of control serves as a trope for fears of loss of sovereignty and power over one's immediate environment. In particular, there was fear of television taking over leisure activity and young people's minds during the 1980s and *Poltergeist* articulates this fear in a parable whereby young Carol Anne is sucked into a television set that is the portal to the "other world" of spirits. The young girl talks to the "TV people" in the opening sequence in which her hands lightly rest upon the static-filled TV screen at the end of the day's broadcasting. As the film proceeds, the television will play a major part in the plot.

The scenes of the Freeling's television and the family's and then neighbor's interaction with it also ironically depict the dialectic between public and private space in the contemporary suburban environment. Suburban Americans share the public space of television, mass communications, and consumer culture, yet for the most part participate in the shared culture in the private space of their own home. The community portrayed is a leisure community bound together by the objects of play and entertainment: toys, television, sports, beer and other common commodities. This community is a fragile one: without the TV, for instance, the weekend football watching community dissolves. Most suburbanites do not know their neighbors, unless they share leisure activities in common. The "remote control television" scene shows how shared suburban space overlaps and produces conflicts, as well as how weak, or non-existent, "neighborliness" is in the suburbs. It also depicts a new communications environment and technology which individuals do not yet understand and do not fully control.

Crucially, we watch the family withdraw from their suburban community and turn in on themselves when the poltergeist crisis unfolds. Their neighbors are of little help and only appear when the poltergeists destroy the Freeling's house and threaten the neighborhood. In fact, *Poltergeist* projects a view that the most organic, solid and viable social unit and institution in suburban life is the middle-class nuclear family. Spielberg and his co-workers present very positive and affectionate scenes of middle-class family life without the satirical or ironic distance of many contemporary filmmakers (Altman, de Palma, Woody Allen, and other liberal and radical critics of the family).

After introducing the Freeling family, in another key scene, the kids are tucked away in bed and Steve and Diane are alone in their bedroom. The wife holds a marijuana cigarette and talks and giggles about past memories, taking us back from the 1980s to the 1960s. The scene suggests that the flower children are grown up, married, and heads of families. The husband, however, is engrossed in a biography about *Ronald Reagan: The President, The Man*. The husband eventually drops the book and starts fooling around with his wife. He plays wild animal, whispers in her ear and Diane sighs, "Oh, I just love it when you talk dirty!" The scene cuts to the children in their bedroom: they are awake in fear during a thunderstorm. In addition to the thunder and lightning, a gothic tree casts weird shadows throughout the room, a clown grinningly menaces (an iconic image from Tobe Hooper's previous film *The Funhouse*, which will periodically reappear as a sign of menace), and the poltergeists begin knocking things around.

The next night during an even more powerful thunderstorm, branches of a giant tree take the young son Robbie out of the bedroom window and his parents desperately retrieve him from the forces of raging nature. At this point, Carol Anne disappears, the family enters a state of panic, and the film enters the realm of occultist allegory. *Poltergeist* presents allegorical spectacles of a family holding together in the face of adverse experiences that threaten to pull it apart. The scenes of separation throughout the movie express fear of impending disintegration of the family and fear of separation from the haven of the family. As the poltergeists become more destructive, Carol Anne is spirited away to a nether world, the teenage daughter spends more and more time with her friends, and the young boy and his dog are sent away to his grandparents. The father too is pulled away by the demands of his job, but eventually he chooses the family over his job (i.e. he finally quits his job and moves away with his family). There are frequent affirmations of love and strong portrayals of family bonds. The mother, especially, is the moral and physical center of the family and shows herself ready to risk her life for her children, while retaining courage in the face of adversity.

Moreover, unlike typical horror films where individuals frequently blunder into disaster, in *Poltergeist* the individuals act rationally, cooperatively, and courageously. The father goes to Stanford and summons a group of parapsychologists who come to investigate the phenomena and they in turn call in a diminutive woman spiritualist, Tangina (Zelda Rubinstein), who tells the family how to deal with the poltergeists and how to get their daughter back. With the spiritualist's guidance, the mother enters the spirit world to retrieve her daughter – revealing the depth of her love and concern for her child. Significantly, it is the women who play the key role in rescuing Carol Anne – reinforcing traditional images of women as protectors and nurturers of children.

In addition to representing fears of the family being torn apart, *Poltergeist* deals with anxieties about losing one's home, or watching it fall apart. The American dream has traditionally focused on buying and owning one's own home and in an era of accelerating unemployment, a weak economy, and diminishing discretionary income, fear of losing one's home, or not being able to maintain it, accelerated during the 1980s. Stephen King, author of such popular books as *Carrie, The Shining, The Stand*, and so on – which themselves are a fertile source of symbolic allegories about contemporary American anxieties – writes of *The Amityville Horror*, a gothic, occult precursor to *Poltergeist*:

> the picture's subtext is one of economic unease . . . .Little by little, it is ruining the Lutz family financially. The movie might as well have been subtitled 'The Horror of the Shrinking Bank Account'. . . .*The Amityville Horror*, beneath its ghost-story exterior, is really a financial demolition derby.[7]

Poltergeist too shows a house gradually but inexorably falling apart. Rooms become uninhabitable, machines and technology either do not work or operate out of the family's control, commodities and toys fall apart. Finally, the house literally collapses and the family must flee. This allegory of the home under siege is part of the reason that the film was so effective in manipulating its audience: viewers can identify with this very average middle-class family in a house that constantly gives them troubles and is eventually taken away from them. *This* is a contemporary horror story for current and would-be home owners, many of whom lost their homes during the Age of Reagan and Bush.

The social horizon of *Poltergeist* is thus the loss of homes and breaking up of families during an era of economic insecurity and social fragmentation which saw many people losing their homes, a divorce-rate of over 50 per cent, and middle- and upper-class people falling into lower-class strata. The discursive field of the film is both pro-family discourses and the articulation of social anxieties concerning home and family. The threats to middle-class security are, however, projected onto the figures of poltergeists which allegorically serve as vehicles of the socio-economic forces that were pulling families apart and causing many to lose their homes and fall into downward mobility.

As it turns out, the source of the poltergeist disturbance is the result of a decision of the land developing company, for which the father works, to build their project on top of a graveyard after removing the headstones, but without removing the corpses. In zombie scenes reminiscent of the horror classic *Night of the Living Dead*, the dead arise from the earth and terrorize the neighborhood. The film thus plays on fears that land developers will destroy the environment and upset delicate ecological balance – another contemporary worry that is the site of current struggles to limit growth and suburban development.

Yet the poltergeists also represent fear of racial otherness, and the films can be read as fear of racial invasion and destruction of suburban middle-class utopia. The monsters in *Poltergeist* appear as dark-skinned monstrosities, an otherness to white middle-class "normality." Fears of racial others are linked to fears of working-class others in *Poltergeist*. Some workers appear early in the plot to toil on a family swimming pool, itself a symbol of middle-class affluence. The workers are slightly dark-skinned ethnic types, and appear somewhat uncouth and vaguely threatening. Two male workers leer at the teenage daughter who responds with obscene gestures to the mother's amusement. Soon after, one worker opens the window to drink the mother's coffee and snack on some food laying on the drainboard. The mother catches him and good-humoredly chastises the vaguely threatening worker who she calls "Bluto" (an odd name, perhaps after the menacing working-class character in *Popeye*); a name appropriated by the John Belushi character in *Animal House* as well.

Horror films thus mobilize fear of the other and draw lines between normality and abnormality, good and evil. Goodness resides in middle-class familial normality and Otherness resides in the working-class and racial Others like Native Americans in the *Poltergeist* films. From this perspective, the threatening monsters stand in allegorically for race and class forces threatening middle-class stability. Such cinematic representations transcode the conservative, yet anxious, pro-family discourses of the era in their celebration of the family and negative stigmatizing of otherness.

Another major subtext of the film is fear of television. Carol Anne first comes under the spell of the poltergeists through the TV set and then disappears – indeed, how many American children have disappeared into the TV set! The poltergeists and the disembodied voice of the little girl after she is spirited away communicates through the TV set just as so many Americans receive their communication from the outside world through TV. As noted, television static is an iconic image of disturbance throughout the film, and the television is on constantly. During the scenes in which the parapsychologists attempt to analyze the situation, state-of-the-art video cameras and recorders are placed throughout the house. The poltergeists are actually recorded and played back on a video-recorder demonstrating the mechanical reproducibility of everything in media society and the possibility of instant replay.

The images of video surveillance may also articulate fears that Big Brother is watching, that new technologies will invade privacy, that a new technological panopticon is on the way.[8] We see here, symbolically portrayed, the power of television to captivate audiences, spy on people, and become an organizing center of leisure. The fear that television might eventually totally replace cinema is certainly one of Hollywood's greatest fears and perhaps a concern of Spielberg and his collaborators. In the final scene, when the family has left their ill-fated house and checks into the Holiday Inn, we see them taking out the TV set and putting it on the balcony. The audience laughs and claps and the filmmakers grin and everyone goes home, and sooner or later, probably sooner, turns on the TV.[9]

The Holiday Inn site at the end reveals the underlying theme of security vs. insecurity in the film. What could be more secure than the Holiday Inn, that icon of middle-class sameness where one knows in advance that one will receive the same room and furnishings anywhere in America? *Poltergeist* points to intense middle-class insecurities in the Age of Reagan with growing fears of unemployment, losing one's home, and losing control over one's life and possessions. It contains a panorama of fears of growing powerlessness in the face of corporate power and greed, an economy out of control and rapid cultural change. It reproduces the fears of the disintegration of the family exploited by Reagan and the New Right, as well as fears of television and losing control over one's children. It reveals the Age of Reagan to be an era of fear and trembling for both the middle and the working classes faced with intensifying threats to their livelihood and well-being.[10]

Poltergeist also lightly plays on fears of teenage sexuality in the scene near the end when the teenage daughter appears with a large hickey on her neck, which reflects back on a scene preceding it, when she responds to the news that her family is going to spend the night at a Holiday Inn with a knowing remark: "Oh, I remember that place," and her mother looks on with amused tolerance.[11] Earlier, in the marijuana/bedroom scene, the mother recalls being examined for hickeys and bruises by her father. Thus, in opposition to the attack on teen sexuality by sectors of the New Right, *Poltergeist* seems to project a liberal view of easy sexual tolerance and acceptance.[12]

Poltergeist confronts primal fears of bodily disintegration and death as well as fears specific to the present era. All horror films play on anxieties over rapid change in which life goes out of control and either multiplies or mutates at a rapid pace, or disintegrates and falls apart with frightening speed and intensity. Horror films present horrifying images of life gone berserk and manipulate fears that we have of disease, bodily disintegration, and death. One striking sequence in *Poltergeist* allegorically confronts a contemporary version of the universal fear of bodily mutation: fear of cancer in an age where one out of four people will fall prey to this dread disease, and one out of five will die from it. Many contemporary horror films play on this fear by showing bodies rapidly mutating, decaying and changing abnormally. The prevalence of images of rapid bodily mutation in recent horror films symbolically portrays, I believe, representations of cancer at work in speeded up motion like those Walt Disney nature films that used to show the growth of plants and animals with time-lapse photography. If this intuition is correct, then deep-rooted fear of cancer and bodily disintegration accounts for part of the fascination and horror with which the audience watches bodies bizarrely mutate during horror films. *Poltergeist*, for instance, shows a young Stanford scientist go to the kitchen and take a steak out of the refrigerator. We see the piece of meat undergo cancerlike metastasis, spewing out bizarre growths and organs before our eyes. The frightened scientist goes into the bathroom and washes his face, then looks into the mirror only to see his face mutate into rotting flesh. Although this hallucination disappears, he leaves the house and does not return.

Likewise, the most spectacular scenes of the dead returning to life in *Poltergeist* confront us with disintegrating flesh that literally embody fears of death and disintegration. We also see the mother grey prematurely after her trip to the spirit world – another symbolic presentation of fear of rapid aging. Finally, the film plays on hopes for afterlife and fears that it may be hellish – one of the sources of power of fundamentalist religion – by depicting an afterlife and showing that it is populated by monsters who torment those who are not the elect and do not make it to the realm of spiritual salvation which the film holds out as a blissful reward for the saved.

Poltergeist thus presents a panorama of symbolic images of contemporary American nightmares. It achieves its power by drawing on real fears which it presents in symbolic form that allows people to experience their subconscious anxieties in the safe medium of film in an ideology machine that smoothes over and tranquilizes their fears by showing the family pulling through. *Poltergeist* presents the landscape of contemporary consciousness more powerfully than the fairy tale *E.T.*, revealing the contours of American consciousness in the Age of Reagan to be fearful, consumer and family oriented, and ready to believe and do anything in order to survive.

Although *Poltergeist* hints that corporate capitalism is rapacious, destroying the earth, exploiting people, and even threatening human survival, the real source of contemporary anxieties is displaced onto the occult. Hence, while *Poltergeist* and other recent horror films contain allegories about contemporary anxieties, the audience is directed by the film toward spectacles of occult horror rather than the horror show of contemporary life in the United States. The irrationalist-occultist metaphysics in films like *E.T.* and *Poltergeist* therefore weaken the social insights present in the films and strengthen the rampant irrationalism in U.S. society manifest in religious revivalism, cults, new age spiritualism, and so on.

In fact, several of Spielberg's major films are permeated with the fuzzy-minded occultism that T.W. Adorno shrewdly characterized as "the metaphysics of dopes" (1974: 24). Although Spielberg and company's excursions into the supernatural allow individuals to experiences anxieties in a symbolic form that they might not be able to face in a more realist narrative form, his 1980s films tend to project real fears onto threats by evil spirits, and focus hope on deliverance by some beneficent extra-terrestrials (*Close Encounters, E.T.*), or superheroes like Indiana Jones in *Raiders of the Lost Ark*. Spielberg's ideology machines all too often summon his audience to escapist fantasies, conservative affirmation of middle-class values, traditional mythic heroes, and the forms of traditional popular culture. Unlike the more critical Hollywood filmmakers who dissect dominant myths and question dominant values (i.e. Altman, Scorsese, Allen, and so on), Spielberg is a storyteller and mythmaker who affirms both the opposing poles of middle-class values and lifestyles as well as a transcendent occultism.

The turn to the occult in post-*Exorcist* (1973) Hollywood film represents an ideological crisis in American society by presenting a society in crisis whose institutions are under attack by a variety of forces. Some of the most popular horror-occult films (*The Exorcist, The Omen, Carrie, The Amityville Horror, The Shining*, and so on) portray a disintegrating society incapable of dealing with the evils presented in the films. If there is any salvation, or a solution to the problems depicted, in most of these and other Hollywood "blockbuster" films, it appears transcendentally in the form of aliens or extra-terrestrials, the church or the spirit world, or superheroes from other worlds or other times like Superman, Batman,

Conan, or Indiana Jones. The appeal to the past, or to the transcendental, for heroes, values and legitimation does not, however, effectively legitimate the institutions of the existing society, and points to a legitimation crisis in contemporary American society (Habermas 1975).

Poltergeist, it is true, does attempt to positively portray the family and middle-class lifestyles, but there are ideological contradictions in Spielberg's work between attempts to celebrate existing middle-class institutions and values in contrast with the search for salvation from extra-terrestrials, or spiritualism. There are also hints in his films that existing institutions and values lack vitality. In *Close Encounters*, the husband abandons his family to pursue his fantasy of making contact with the aliens in the U.F.O.'s; in *E.T.*, the absence of the father (separated from the mother and in Mexico with a new girlfriend) can be seen as a psychological reason for the boy to turn for friendship and love to the extra-terrestrial; and while in *Poltergeist*, we have a particularly strong portrait of the family as a viable institution, the rest of the dominant institutions, and especially the corporation, are presented in a critical light.

Thus, although an ideology of the family emerges from *Poltergeist*, the film does not provide ideological legitimation of the American political economy. In this light, the turn to the occult and transcendent-spiritual values in recent Hollywood films discloses a failure of the culture industries to provide effective ideological legitimation for contemporary American capitalism. Nonetheless, whatever one thinks of Spielberg's occultism, or his affirmation of middle-class values, his work is valuable for shedding light on contemporary U.S. society and revealing the fears, hopes, and fantasies of the new affluent, suburban middle class. In Steven Spielberg, the new middle class has found its storyteller and ideologue. His fantasies are permeated with ideologies that should be probed, decoded and criticized by those interested in understanding U.S. society and culture in the contemporary era.

Poltergeist II and the crisis of patriarchy

The original *Poltergeist* is brilliantly produced, combining Tobe Hooper's taste for the macabre and striking images with Spielberg's cinematic talents. The fluid camera is constantly moving throughout the film, producing striking images and juxtapositions; the lighting creates some stunning effects of the supernatural; editing is fast-paced, and the film is gripping throughout. Brian Gibson's *Poltergeist II: The Other Side* (1986), by contrast, is cinematically mediocre and its contrived "plot" travels further into the occult and supernatural. Yet the film's silly occultism provides an allegory of middle-class fears and I interrogate it from this perspective.

Carol Clover (1992) points out how women are privileged in the first *Poltergeist* film. The daughter and mother are presented as possessing more intuitive and clairvoyant powers, the chief parapsychologist is a woman, as is the medium, presenting women as the more powerful figures. The father is shown to be helpless, and is usually depicted looking on from the sidelines, while the women control the discourse and events (only the women, for instance, participate in a long discussion of death and the afterlife). Clover fails to analyze, however, how the film articulates a crisis of patriarchy brought about by the strong women who threaten the power of the father, providing a need for him to reaffirm his power and overcome the crisis of patriarchy in the second *Poltergeist* film. Her intent focus on the important role of gender in the contemporary horror film also occludes the importance of the role of class and race, just as her argument that the horror film often privileges women over men covers over the importance of the resurrection of male power in *Poltergeist II*.[13]

Indeed, whereas the father was rather marginal in the first *Poltergeist*, he is central to the second one. The film opens a year later, with the father out of work and the family living with his wife's mother. The father indicates how much he misses his job and how he wishes that they could return to their home. He complains about the failure of the insurance company to reimburse them for the loss of their house, articulating contemporary anxieties concerning bureaucratic institutions and corporations. He also jokes about his "downward mobility," yet he is portrayed as being completely ineffectual and pathetic, unable to better himself. Hence, the family is forced to live in the mother-in-law's house and the father seems to be unable to do anything to get the insurance company to reimburse them for the loss of their house, nor is he able to get back his old job. Thus, the family represents a thoroughgoing crisis of patriarchy and articulates male fears of losing house, job, and self-respect in a declining economy and disintegrating social order.

In the narrative of the film, the Freeling family is once again threatened by the loss of their daughter, this time through the intervention of a mysterious preacher named Kane, played by Julien Beck, who was at the time dying of cancer and projected a gaunt, haunting, ghastly figure.[14] Kane is represented as an evil demon who is trying to abduct Carol Anne into the spirit world, and he is representative of an uneducated and malevolent working-class figure, a cross between the shyster preacher played by Robert Mitchum in *Night of the Hunter* and the southern thug who threatens the middle class in standard Hollywood horror and crime dramas.

In the occult plot, Kane is a cult religious leader who led a group of fundamentalist fanatics to California during the last century. They dwelled in a cavern, underneath the current Freeling house, believing that the world was coming to an end. The members of the religious sect, however, had a collective change of mind and attempt to climb out of the cave when the predicted end of the world passed, but they were trapped as Kane had sealed the entrance with a stone. The sect was rumored to have been killed by Native Americans, but, in the occult plot, their spirits continue to reside fitfully in the cave beneath the graveyard over which the Freeling's house was built, unable to go to "the other side." The spirits are attracted to Carol Anne, who they see as good and innocent, and able to lead them "into the light," to take them to "the other side." By comparison, the evil Kane – presented as a devil figure – seems to want to spirit Carol Anne into the poltergeist world in order to use his power over her to regain control over his "flock." From this perspective, Kane represents the irrational, authoritarian working-class patriarchy that Steve Freeling must overcome to be a good middle-class father and husband.

Read allegorically, the poltergeist disturbances are thus overdetermined, focusing on spirits of the dead angry over the desecration of the burial site in the first *Poltergeist*, and on poor whites in the second. The images of the poor white religious sect members, trapped in the cave, represent the fears of the middle-class, anxious that downward mobility might push them into a similar forlorn state. The flashback images of the poor whites thus subliminally warn the audience that they too could fall into this condition. Cumulatively, the images of the spirits of poor whites and the dead haunting the white middle class transcode its fears and anxieties in an era of economic and social insecurity of invasion by other races and classes.

Poltergeist II thus continues the probing of contemporary fears concerning race, class, gender, and sexuality, even more starkly and extravagantly than the first *Poltergeist*. The film was released in 1986, during a Reagan recession in which fear of unemployment, of losing one's home, and of loss of control over one's life was growing. Once again, technology is shown out of control, with an early scene showing a vacuum cleaner refusing to behave, and throughout the film, the father's car is breaking down, perhaps articulating fears of loss or failure of one's automobile, a special token of prestige and power for the middle class. Now the family is threatened both by the spirits of the poor whites wanting out of their spirit dimension and the spirits over whose graveyard the house was built. Together, the *Poltergeist* films thus allegorically represent fears that monsters from lower classes and other races will destroy middle-class suburban utopia.

Once again, the poltergeists come to haunt the family and once again it is the women that are in touch with the spirit world. The film introduces the grandmother (played by Geraldine Fitzgerald), whose house the Freelings are living in, who also possesses occult power and communicates throughout the film from "the other side" with Carol Anne after her death. But this time the father too must deal with the spirits and prove himself "man" enough to lead the family. At one point, the preacher Kane shows up, and rants at Steve:

> "Who do your wife and family turn to with their problems? They turn to *him* [Taylor], now don't they? They don't trust you any more, and what you fear is that you're not *man* enough to hold this family together! Now, let me in. *Let me in!*"

The father is aided by Taylor, a Native American (Will Sampson) who appears as a "magic helper" (a traditional fairy tale motif) and who lectures him on his responsibilities and need to take charge. In one scene, the father goes off to a "sweat lodge" ceremony with the Native American, a scene of male bonding where the father presumably retrieves some of his lost patriarchal power. He is given a feather, which he proudly displays as a totem of his lost and hopefully to be regained patriarchal power.[15]

Yet the father is still lacking power and resolve and in one key scene he turns to the spirits of alcohol, getting drunk on a bottle of tequila, the type with the worm in the bottle. In the occult plot shift, Kane inserts himself into the worm, to use the weak father to spirit away his daughter. The father swallows the worm and becomes demonically "possessed." The possession takes the form of a violent desire to have sex with his wife, whom he attempts to rape when she declines. In a violent struggle with the monster, the worm comes out of the father's mouth, now in the form of a giant snake, who – after a grotesque birthing metamorphosis – assumes the form of Kane! The figure of the worm/snake/monster/Kane symbolizes dangers of out-of-control working class sexuality and equates Kane with monstrous and threatening power.[16]

The father, however, eventually redeems himself and once again takes control of his family. The family bonds together to return to Cuesta Verde, the scene of their destroyed home. They go together in the cave under their house where Kane and his followers are trapped. The evil spirits seize Carol Anne and her mother, but with the help of the Native American, Taylor, the father and the son go to "the other side" to retrieve the mother and daughter. The father thus proves that he is worthy of re-assuming patriarchal power and restores the family to unity. After escaping the cave, the family is shown once again in their old neighborhood, presumably to resume their happy and affluent suburban life.

The father has thus reconstituted his identity as leader of the family and re-established a male authority in touch with the irrational, traditional, and heroic to become a proper middle-class patriarch. Likewise, the family is reconstituted as a positive and integral unit, overcoming threats and challenges to its integrity. Unlike the horror films of an earlier era that showed the family producing monstrosities and horror, the family in the *Poltergeist* films survives threats from the monsters who are outside "others" and threats to middle-class normality. Such films thus present ideological defenses and celebrations of the middle-class nuclear family.[17]

DIAGNOSTIC CRITIQUE: FROM *POLTERGEIST* TO *SLACKERS* AND *BEAVIS AND BUTT-HEAD*

In my reading of the *Poltergeist* films, the poltergeists represent threatening class and racial others who menace middle-class normality and the films articulate contemporary fears of the middle-class family in an uncertain economy and disintegrating social order. The two films show middle-class life as out of control and threatened with dissolution. Yet the re-establishment of patriarchal order brings the family back together. The most poignant images of *Poltergeist II* show the family framed together in single shots, bonding collectively as a united familial unit. Both of these films show families being torn apart and coming back together, a cinematic fantasy in an era in which real families *were* torn apart by a disintegrating economy and social order. Indeed, losing one's house and job and being threatened by crime and downward mobility were and still are all-too-real fears in the contemporary United States, so perhaps audiences could symbolically confront such fears only in genres like the horror film, rather than realist drama. Indeed, who would want to watch a drama of a family losing job, home, and then being torn apart, an event which has become all too familiar during the past decade of permanent economic crisis.

From another perspective, the *Poltergeist* films, like conservative films such as *The Big Chill*, represent the end of the 1960s. In the first *Poltergeist*, the mother and father smoke dope and make love in one scene; the 1960s generation has grown up, married, and now live affluent lifestyles in the suburbs. In *Poltergeist II*, the wife tells the husband that "You were never a hippie," that the husband just assumed hip attitudes to impress another girl. A significant scene revolves around the mother cutting roses in the garden and remembering planting the roses with her mother when she was a girl – a poignant image of the continuity of the generations which some 1960s radicals wanted to rupture. In the *Poltergeist* films, the 1960s are now dead and buried: relentless traditionalism and celebration of the family have returned with a vengeance and Hollywood is only too happy to return to conservative institutions like the middle-class family which it has traditionally celebrated.

Yet all is not happy in the home of the brave and the land of the free and to discover articulations of contemporary class dynamics in the Hollywood cinema, one must deal with genres like the horror and fantasy film to fully experience the vicissitudes of class in the contemporary era and the deep anxieties around class downward mobility, perhaps *the* American nightmare. Horror and fantasy can deal with thematics too painful and disturbing to be confronted in social realist genres. But while horror and fantasy can be deployed to criticize existing institutions, they can also deflect attention from the real sources of contemporary suffering onto occult figures. This is the ideological function of the *Poltergeist* films which are conservative celebrations of middle-class normality that, read diagnostically, can reveal the threats to the family which it is the purpose of the film to patch over. The project of the *Poltergeist* films is thus ultimately to suture the spectator into desire for typical middle-class life after allowing experience of threats to it to be played out. The films are thus symptomatic of the right turn in U.S. culture after 1960s radical critique and political movements put in question institutions such as the family and patriarchy.

The *Slacker* effect

And so where does this situation leave the younger generation? For insight into the plight of contemporary youth, one can look to Richard Linklater's *Slacker* (1990) and *Dazed and Confused* (1993) and to the 1993–4 MTV phenomenon *Beavis and Butt-Head*. *Slacker* is probably the quintessential cinematic dissection of the plight of the twenty-something post-1960s generation of disaffected youth, bombarded with media culture and alienated from the conservative hegemony of "straight" middle-class society. The youth of *Slacker* all live on the margins of society and pursue off-beat lifestyles, refusing to play the game of academic success, career, marriage, and family espoused by the mainstream, and celebrated in the *Poltergeist* films.

The film pursues a day in the life of Austin, Texas youth during the late 1980s. The narrative opens with director Rick Linklater arriving in Austin on a bus. He embarks at the bus station and gets into a taxi where he proceeds to recount the "weird" dream he has just had and philosophizes concerning the possibility of alternative universes and lives, consisting of choices not made, which he had just read in a book. The film then pursues an aleatory itinerary in which one character accidentally encounters another and the narrative proceeds to trek each new character, leaving the previous ones behind. The result is a vision of youth leading aimless, disconnected lives, wandering from one scene and situation to another without specific goals, or purpose.

Yet the young slackers are in a totally media-saturated society in which the products of media culture provide the basis of their conversations, fantasies, and lives. A political conspiracy buff tells of government conspiracies and cover-ups from the space program, referencing *World Weekly News*; another speculates on *Live Elvis*; an agitated young woman tries to sell Madonna's pap smear, complete with black pubic hair; another slacker recounts statistics indicating the lack of a genuine mandate for Bush in the 1988 presidential election, which it turns out, come from the *Dallas Morning News*; a young black sells "Free Mandela" T-shirts and pamphlets, while doing a political rap derived from media cliches; a video artist/activist has a room full of TV sets and videotapes, trying to capture everything on tape; the local music scene is a major sources of interest and entertainment, as are movies and television; two slackers philosophize about the cartoons Scooby Doo and the Smurfs in a cafe; and many of the characters spout fragments of pop philosophy derived from media culture.[18]

The slackers, however, appropriate media culture for their own ends. turning articles from conservative media sources into material for radical social and political critique, while using media technology for their own purposes (as does obviously director Linklater and his team). The slackers are not passive products of media effects, but active participants in a media culture who use media to produce meaning, pleasure, and identity in their lives. The ubiquitous T-shirts often have logos or images derived from media culture, and TV and music are constant backgrounds for the cinematic events of the film.

Thus, the media form the very fabric of the slackers' lives and allow diagnostic critique to discern that for many segments of youth today media culture *is* their culture. Previous studies of media effects were too restricted in their (pseudo)scientific research methods and thus failed to see how media culture circulates images, artifacts, information, and identities which are appropriated by audiences which use the media culture to create their pleasures and identities. Researchers concluded too quickly that media culture had no discernible and measurable effects because their experimental situations were too artificial and their methods inappropriate to tap into the texture of everyday life to see how people actually use the media to produce meanings, pleasures, and identities.

Slacker thus allows a diagnostic critique of how media culture saturates contemporary youth culture and provides the materials from which young people produce meanings, identities, and bondings. In a sense the film presents a "postmodern" vision of the plight of contemporary youth.[19] The youth are lost in the moment and seemingly live completely fragmented and disconnected lives, going from one activity to another through largely accidental mediations. No one seems to have any long term plans or projects, and all seem to only live for the moment, drifting through life as if in a dream with no dreamer.

Yet as the characters in the film wander from one scene to another, and as some characters leave the frame, while others enter, one gets a sense of something of a Slacker community in which the Slackers are connected to each other, even if temporarily or minimally. Yet the community consists of nomadic wanderings, accidental connections, unstructured comings and goings, and a vision of life as consisting of disconnected moments of euphoric intensity, punctuated with periods of banality and meaninglessness.

The style of *Slacker* thus utilizes the postmodern strategy of fragmenting and disconnecting narrative unity, presenting a series of slices of barely connected lives, meandering through the surface of things, without any depth or deeper meaning. A young man picks up a young woman outside of a music club, takes her home, and we see her get out of bed and leave the next morning, while the roommate watches TV in the same room, without any dialogue shown passing between the characters.

The film thus explores surfaces and while there are moments of great humor and intense conversation, there is no character development, plot development and resolution, or the production of deep meanings that link sequences, or tie the narrative strands together. Moreover, Linklater pastiches modernist movies, as where he draws on Luis Buñuel's modernist film *The Milky Way* (1969) as the principle of narrative (dis)organization of the film (I define modernism in more detail in Chapter 5). Buñuel's film presented the voyage of religious pilgrims on their way to Spain in a timeless space and placeless time, in which the main characters encounter one eccentric figure after another, who soon disappear as another strange person enters the narrative sequence. *Slacker* also presents a world of accidental connections and absurdist juxtapositions, though while Buñuel's film had some main characters who remained in the narrative, and utilized allegorical probing of Christian myths, *Slacker* has no main characters, with each slacker disappearing after her/his few moments of narrative focus, and the film eschews allegory or symbolic meaning.

Slacker's concluding sequence plays with Godard's *One Plus One*, substituting for Godard's black revolutionaries proclaiming revolution a "Post-modern Paul Revere" (as described in the titles) riding in a car with loudspeakers, describing a government weapons program. And while the end of Godard's film shows his camera apparatus on the beach, scooping up his then wife Anne Wiazemsky and raising her to the sky in a fade-out, in a delirious romantic image of transcendence through love and cinema, *Slacker* shows a group of all-night party animals driving up to Mount Bonnell, the highest point of Austin, with a movie camera which they throw off the cliff. The camera pans to the cover of Paul Goodman's book *Growing up Absurd* before spiralling images of the camera swirling down the cliff cut to black in a nihilistic conclusion that nothing really matters in a totally absurd world, neither love, nor cinema, nor creativity, nor transcendence of any sort.

Yet in another sense, *Slacker* represents a modernist auteur with a distinctive vision and style which adds up to a sharp, insightful view of the plight of contemporary youth, alienated from the American dream and traditional American values, floating on the media surfaces of contemporary life with their attention focused and shaped by media culture. The film was financed on a very low budget and shares the innovative ethos of the independent film. In an early scene in an Austin coffee house, a student picks up a copy of Hal Foster's collection of essays on postmodern culture, *The Anti-Aesthetic* (1983), and a copy of Marshall Berman's book on modernity and modernist culture, *All That is Solid Melts Into Air* (1982), is visible on a table. The two books articulate opposing contemporary aesthetic evaluations (i.e. modernism vs. postmodernism). I would argue that Linklater combines modernist and postmodernist aesthetic strategies and that the film is thus between the modern and the postmodern.[20]

Moreover, *Slacker*'s vision of multiple possibilities of life, with a wide range of individuals producing their own meanings, might have emancipatory effects. The characters are not conforming or submitting to an over-arching structure of domination, and while they all get opinions and images from the media, they process them in their own individual and idiosyncratic ways. Such a vision especially appealed to young audiences and *Slacker* was felt deeply, producing distinctive "Slacker effects" (see my earlier study of the Rambo effect). The film became a cult favorite throughout the country and indeed the world. During the past few years wherever I go to lecture, someone, upon learning that I live in Austin, mentions *Slacker* and how much they love the film. Moreover, in 1993, city officials in Austin were worried about the large number of homeless youth on the streets and margins of the city, many of whom had seen *Slacker* and came to Austin in search of like-minded cohorts and to pursue the "Slacker" lifestyle, now identified with Austin.

Thus, *Slacker* articulated experiences of disaffection of youth from contemporary U.S. society and produced a new concept to describe contemporary youth, mythologizing the lifestyles of slackers in Austin, Texas. It obviously tapped into deep feelings of contemporary youth, striking a highly responsive chord in its audiences who used the film to articulate their own experiences and feelings. The success of the film also won Linklater a $6 million Hollywood contract to make another youth film, *Dazed and Confused* (1993), which traced a day in the life of Austin highschool students on graduation day of 1976. Linklater's "Hollywood" film presents graduating seniors who also lack any guiding purposes or goals and who are alienated from their parent's "straight" middle-class world.

Thus, Linklater's films present a diagnosis of the situation of youth in an absurd society in which traditional norms and values no longer have any hold on many of the young. They present the opportunity for a diagnosis of the situation of contemporary youth in the U.S.A and suggest that large numbers of young people are disconnected and alienated from the mainstream culture celebrated by network television and conservative Hollywood film. The cult TV show of 1993–4, *Beavis and Butt-Head* also presents the opportunity for a diagnostic critique of the plight of the current generation of youth in a situation of downward mobility.

Beavis and Butt-Head: no future for postmodern youth

Animated cartoon characters Beavis and Butt-Head sit in a shabby house much of the day, watching television, especially music videos, which they criticize in terms of whether the videos are "cool" or "suck." When they leave the house to go to school, to work in a fast food joint, or to seek adventure, they often engage in destructive and even criminal behavior. Developed for MTV by animated cartoonist Mike Judge, the series spoofs precisely the sort of music videos played by the music television channel.[21] *Beavis and Butt-Head* quickly became a cult favorite, loved by youth, yet elicited spirited controversy when some young fans of the show imitated typical Beavis and Butt-Head activity, burning down houses, and torturing and killing animals.[22]

The series provides a critical vision of the current generation of youth raised primarily on media culture. This generation was possibly conceived in the sights and sounds of media culture, weaned on it, and socialized by the glass teat of television used as pacifier, baby sitter, and educator by a generation of parents for whom media culture, especially television, was a natural background and constitutive part of everyday life. The show depicts the dissolution of a rational subject and perhaps the end of the Enlightenment in today's media culture. Beavis and Butt-Head react viscerally to the videos, snickering at the images, finding representations of violence and sex "cool," while anything complex which requires interpretation "sucks." Bereft of any cultivated taste, judgment, or rationality, and without ethical or political values, the characters react in a literally mindless fashion and appear to lack almost all cognitive and communicative skills.

The intense alienation of Beavis and Butt-Head, their love for heavy metal culture and media images of sex and violence, and their violent cartoon activity soon elicited heated controversy, producing a "Beavis and Butt-Head" effect that has elicited literally thousands of articles and heated debates, even leading to U.S. Senate condemnations of the show for promoting mindless violence and stupid behavior.[23] From the beginning, there was intense media focus on the show and strongly opposed opinions of it. In a cover story on the show, *Rolling Stone* declared them "The Voice of a New Generation" (August 19, 1993) and *Newsweek* also put them on its cover, both praising them and damning them by concluding: "The downward spiral of the living white male surely ends here: in a little pimple named Butt-head whose idea of an idea is, 'Hey, Beavis, let's go over to Stuart's house and light one in his cat's butt'" (October 11, 1993). "Stupid, lazy, cruel; without ambitions, without values, without futures" are other terms used in the media to describe the characters and the series (*The Dallas Morning News*, August 29, 1993) and there have been countless calls to ban the show.

Indeed, a lottery prize winner in California began a crusade against the series,

after hearing about a cat that was killed when kids put a firecracker in its mouth,
imitating Beavis and Butt-Head's violence against animals and a suggestion in one
episode that they stick a firecracker in a neighbor boy's cat (*The Hollywood
Reporter*, July 16, 1993). Librarians in Westchester, New York ranked *Beavis and
Butt-Head* high "on a list of movies and television shows that they think negatively
influence youngsters' reading habits," because of their attacks on books and
frequent remarks that books, or even words, "suck" (*The New York Times*, July 11,
1993). Prison officials in Oklahoma banned the show, schools in South Dakota
banned clothing and other items bearing their likeness (*Times Newspapers Limited*,
October 11, 1993), and a group of Missouri fourth graders started a petition drive
to get the program off the air (*Radio TV Reports*, October 25, 1993).

Yet the series continued to be highly popular into 1994, and it has spawned a
best-selling album of heavy metal rock, a popular book, countless consumer items,
and movie contracts in the works. *Time* magazine critic, Kurt Anderson, praised
the series as "the bravest show ever run on national television" (*The New York
Times*, July 11, 1993) and there is no question but that it has pushed the boundaries
of the permissible on mainstream television to new extremes (some critics would
say to new lows).

In a certain sense, *Beavis and Butt-Head* is "postmodern" in that it is purely a
product of media culture, with its characters, style, and content almost solely
derivative from previous TV shows. The two characters Beavis and Butt-Head are
a spin-off of Wayne and Garth in *Wayne's World*, a popular *Saturday Nite Live*
feature, spun off into popular movies. They also resemble the SCTV characters Bob
and Doug McKenzie, who sit around on a couch and make lewd and crude remarks
while they watch TV and drink beer. Beavis and Butt-Head also take the asocial
behavior of cartoon character Bart Simpson to a more intense extreme. Their
comments on the music videos replicate the popular Comedy Central Channel's
series *Mystery Science Theater 3000*, which features two cartoon stick figures
making irreverent comments on god-awful old Hollywood movies and network
television shows. And, of course, the music videos are a direct replication of MTV's
basic fare.

Beavis and Butt-Head is interesting for a diagnostic critique because the main
characters get all of their ideas and images concerning life from the media and their
entire view of history and the world is entirely derived from media culture. When
they see a costumed rapper wearing an eighteenth-century-style white wig on a
music video, Butt-Head remarks: "He's dressed up like that dude on the dollar."
The 1960s is the time of hippies, Woodstock and rock 'n' roll for them; Vietnam
is ancient history, collapsed into other American wars. Even the 1950s is nothing
but a series of mangled media cliches: on Nelson, the twins of 1950s teen idol Ricky
Nelson, Butt-Head remarks that: "These chicks look like guys." Beavis responds:
"I heard that these chicks' grandpa was Ozzy Osbourne." And Butt-Head rejoins:
"No way. They're Elvis's kids."

The figures of history are collapsed for Beavis and Butt-Head into media culture and provide material for salacious jokes, which require detailed knowledge of media culture:

> Butt-Head: What happened when Napoleon went to Mount Olive?
> Beavis: I don't know. What?
> Butt-Head: Pop-Eye got pissed.

Moreover, Beavis and Butt-Head seem to have no family, living alone in a shabby house, getting enculturated solely by television and media culture. There are some references to their mothers and in one episode there is a suggestion that Butt-Head is not even certain who his father is, thus the series presents a world without fathers.[24] School is totally alienating for the two, as is work in a fast-food restaurant. Adult figures who they encounter are largely white conservative males, or liberal yuppies, with whom they come into often violent conflict and whose property or goods they inevitably destroy.

There is a fantasy wish-fulfillment aspect to *Beavis and Butt-Head* that perhaps helps account for its popularity: kids often wish that they had no parents and that they could just sit and watch music videos and go out and do whatever they wanted to (sometimes we *all* feel this way). Kids are also naturally disrespectful of authority and love to see defiance of social forces that they find oppressive. Indeed, Beavis and Butt-Head's much maligned, discussed, and imitated laughter ("Heh, heh, heh" and "Huh, huh") may signify that in their space *they rule*, that Beavis and Butt-Head are sovereign, that they control the television and can do any damn thing that they want. Notably, they get in trouble in school and other sites of authority with their laugh, but at home they can laugh and snicker to the max.

And so the series has a utopian dimension: the utopia of no parental authority and unlimited freedom to do whatever they want when they want to. "Dude, we're there" is a favorite phrase they use when they decide to see or do something – and they never have to ask their (absent) parents' permission. On the other hand, they represent the consequences of totally unsocialized adolescent behavior driven by aggressive instincts.[25] Indeed, their "utopia" is highly solipsistic and narcissistic with no community, no consensual norms or morality to bind them, and no concern for other people. The vision of the teenagers alone in their house watching TV and then wreaking havoc on their neighborhood presents a vision of a society of broken families, disintegrating communities, and anomic individuals, without values or goals.

Beavis and Butt-Head are thus left alone with TV and become couch-potato critics, especially of their beloved music videos. In a sense, they are the first media critics to become cult heros of media culture, though there are contradictions in their media criticism. Many of the videos that they attack are stupid and pretentious, and in general it is good to cultivate a critical attitude toward culture forms and to promote cultural criticism – an attitude that can indeed be applied to much of what appears on *Beavis and Butt-Head*. Such critique distances its audience from music video culture and calls for making critical judgments on its products. Yet Beavis and Butt-Head's own judgements are highly questionable, praising images of violence, fire, naked women, and heavy metal noise, while declaring that "college music," words, and any complexity in the videos "suck."

Thus, on one level, the series provides sharp social satire and critique of the culture and society. The episodes constantly make fun of television, especially music videos, and other forms of media culture. They criticize conservative authority figures and wishy-washy liberals. They satirize authoritarian institutions like the workplace, schools, and military recruitment centers and provide critical commentary on many features of contemporary life. Yet, the series undercuts some of its social critique by reproducing the worst sexist, violent, and narcissistic elements of contemporary life, which are made amusing and even likeable in the figures of Beavis and Butt-Head.

Consequently, *Beavis and Butt-Head* is surprisingly complex and requires a diagnostic critique to analyze its contradictory text and effects. There is no denying, however, that the *Beavis and Butt-Head* effect is one of the most significant media phenomena of recent years.[26] Like Linklater, Judge has obviously tapped into a highly responsive chord and created a media sensation with the characters of Beavis and Butt-Head serving as powerfully resonant images. In 1993, while lecturing on cultural studies, wherever I would go audiences would ask me what I thought of *Beavis and Butt-Head* and so I eventually began to watch it and to incorporate remarks on the series into my lectures.[27] If I was critical or disparaging, young members of the audience would attack me and after a lecture at the University of Kansas, a young man came up, incredulous that I would dare to criticize the series, certain that Mike Judge was a great genius who understood exactly how it was for contemporary youth, with no prospects for a job or career, and little prospect for even marriage and family and a meaningful life. In this situation, I was told, what else can young people do except watch MTV and occasionally go out and destroy something?

In a sense, the series thus enacts youth and class revenge against older, middle-class and conservative adults, who appear as oppressive authority figures. Their neighbor Tom Anderson – depicted as a conservative World War II and Korean war veteran – is a special butt of their escapades and they cut down trees in his yard with a chain saw, which, of course, causes the tree to demolish his house, assorted fences, power lines, and cars. They put his dog in a laundro-mat washing machine to clean it; they steal his credit card to buy animals at the mall; they lob mud baseballs into his yard, one of which hits his barbecque; and otherwise torment him. Beavis and Butt-Head also blow up an Army recruiting station with a grenade, as the officer attempts to recruit them; they steal the cart of a wealthy man, Billy Bob, who has a heart attack when he sees them riding off in his vehicle; and they love to put worms, rats, and other animals in the fast food that they are shown giving to obnoxious white male customers in the burger joint where they work.

Beavis and Butt-Head also love to trash the house of their "friend" Stewart whose yuppie parents indulgently pamper their son and his playmates. Stewart's permissive liberal parents are shown to be silly and ineffectual, as when his father complains that Stewart violated his parents' trust when he let Beavis and Butt-Head in the house after they caused an explosion which blew the wall out. The mother gushes about how cute they are and offers them lemonade – in fact, few women authority figures are depicted.

The dynamic duo also torment and make fun of their liberal hippie teacher, Mr Van Driessen, who tries to teach them to be politically correct. They destroy his irreplaceable eight-track music collection when he offers to let them clean his house to learn the value of work and money. When he takes them camping to get in touch with their feelings and nature, they fight and torment animals. In fact, they rebel against all their teachers and authority figures and are thus presented in opposition to everyone, ranging from conservative males, to liberal yuppies, to hippie radicals.

Moreover, the series presents the revenge of youth and those who are terminally downwardly mobile against more privileged classes and individuals. Like the punk generation before them, Beavis and Butt-Head have no future. Thus, while their behavior is undeniably juvenile, offensive, sexist, and politically incorrect, it allows diagnosis of underclass and downwardly mobile youth who have nothing to do, but to destroy things and engage in asocial behavior.

From this perspective, *Beavis and Butt-Head* is an example of media culture as popular revenge:[28] Beavis and Butt-Head avenge youth and the downwardly mobile against those oppressive authority figures who they confront daily. Most of the conservative men have vaguely Texan, or Southwestern, accents, so perhaps the male authority figures represent oppressive males experienced by Judge in his own youth in San Diego, New Mexico and Texas. Moreover, Beavis and Butt-Head's violence is that of a violent society in which the media present endless images of the sort of violent activities that the two characters regularly engage in. The series thus points to the existence of a large teenage underclass with no future which is undereducated and potentially violent. The young underclass Beavis and Butt-Heads of the society have nothing to look forward to in life save a job at the local 7–Eleven, waiting to get held up at gunpoint. Consequently, the series is a social hieroglyphic which allows us to decode the attitudes, behavior, and situation of large segments of youth in contemporary U.S. society.

For a diagnostic critique, then, it is wrong to simply excuse the antics of Beavis and Butt-Head as typical behavior of the young. Likewise, it is not enough simply to condemn them as pathological.[29] Rather the series reveals how violent society is becoming and the dead-end futures of downwardly mobile youth from broken homes who are undereducated and have no real job possibilities or future. Indeed, the heavy metal culture in which Beavis and Butt-Head immerse themselves is a way for those caught up in deadend lives to blot everything out, to escape in a world of pure noise and aggression, and in turn to express their own aggression and frustrations through heavy metal "head-banging." Thus, when Beavis and Butt-Head play the "air guitar," imitating heavy metal playing during the music videos, they are signalling both their aggression and the hopelessness of their situation.

Beavis and Butt-Head's narcissism and sociopathic behavior is a symptom of a society that is not providing adequate nurture or support to its citizens. It is indeed curious that many of the most popular media culture figures could easily be clinically diagnosed and analyzed as narcissistic: Rush Limbaugh, Andrew Dice Clay, Howard Stern, and other popular media figures are examples of empty, insecure, and hostile individuals who resort to extreme behavior and assertions to call attention to themselves. In turn, they tap into audience aggression and frustrations and become popular precisely because of their ability to articulate inchoate social anger. Indeed, compared to a Rush Limbaugh, Beavis and Butt-Head are relatively modest and restrained in their narcissism.

Beavis and Butt-Head, Rush Limbaugh, and other figures of contemporary U.S. media culture also think they know things, but are know-nothings in the good old tradition of American anti-intellectualism. These figures are basically buffoons, sometimes entertaining and often offensive, who in the classical syndrome of narcissism are empty, insecure, and aggressive. They masquerade their emptiness and insecurity in verbal bravado and aggressiveness and attention-seeking action. They also display classic symptoms of fear of women, who they continually objectify, and engage in puerile and infantile sexual jokes and gesture. Beavis and Butt-Head are classic teenagers whose hormones are out of control and who cannot control them, and their elders like Howard Stern and Andrew Dice Clay exhibit similar symptoms. These figures of popular entertainment are all white boys, incapable of taking the position of the other, of empathizing with the other, or of respecting differences. They are all extremely homophobic, though Beavis and Butt-Head are obviously repressing homosexual proclivities signalled in all the "butt" jokes, "suck" references, and Butt-Head's injunction: "Hey, Beavis pull my finger."

In a sense, *Beavis and Butt-Head* is an example of what has been called "loser television," surely a new phenomenon in television history. Previous television series tended to depict wealthy, or secure middle-class, individuals and families, often with highly glamorous lives. It was believed that advertisers preferred affluent environments to sell their products and so the working class and underclass were excluded from network television for decades. Indeed, during the Reaganite 1980s, programs like *Dallas, Dynasty*, and *Life Styles of the Rich and Famous* celebrated wealth and affluence. This dream has been punctured by the reality of everyday life in a downsliding economy, and so a large television audience is attracted to programs that articulate their own frustration and anger in experiencing downward mobility and a sense of no future. Hence, the popularity of new "loser television," including *The Simpsons, Roseanne*, and *Beavis and Butt-Head*.

Thus, the MTV show *Beavis and Butt-Head* allows a diagnostic critique of the plight of contemporary youth in disintegrating families, with little education, and with no job possibilities. Beavis and Butt-Head's destructiveness can be seen in part as an expression of their hopelessness and alienation and shows the dead-end prospects for many working-class and middle-class youths. Moreover, the series also replicates the sort of violence that is so widespread in the media from heavy metal rock videos to TV entertainment and news. Thus, the characters' violence simply mirrors growing youth violence in a disintegrating society and allows the possibility of a diagnostic critique of the social situation of contemporary youth.

Yet the show *is* highly violent and has already had spectacular violence effects. In the *Liquid Television* animated short that preceded the series, Judge shows Beavis and Butt-Head playing "frog baseball," splattering frogs and bashing each other with baseball bats (an image immortalized on one of many Beavis and Butt-Head t-shirts). In other shows, they use lighters to start fires, blow up a neighbor's house by sniffing gas from the stove and then lighting it, and engage in multifarious other acts of mayhem and violence. A Los Angeles area school teacher discovered that about 90 percent of her class watched the show and invited a local fire department official to speak to her class

> after several students wrote about playing with fire and explosives in their autobiographical sketches. Some examples: "A major 'Beavis and Butt-Head' fan, Jarrod Metchikoff, 12, used to 'line them (firecrackers) up in a tube and shoot them in the sewer pipe' until his mother found out. Brett Heimstra, 12, said he set off firecrackers in manholes and sewers until his mother discovered them and he 'heard some stuff about how it's dangerous.' Elizabeth Hastings, 12, said she knows a boy who lights firecrackers in portable toilets.
>
> (*Los Angeles Times*, October 16, 1993).

The fire official told the students "about a 10-year-old Orange County boy who lost use of his hand after an explosion caused by WD-40 and a cigarette lighter" (ibid.). After the initial reports of cruelty to animals and fans of the show starting fires (see note 22), many more such reports came in. The fire chief in Sidney, Ohio, "blamed MTV's cartoon for a house fire started by three girls" (*The Plain Dealer*, October 14, 1993). Further: "Austin, Texas, investigators say three fires started by kids may have some connection to the show" (*U.S.A Today*, October 15, 1993). And Houston teenage fans of the show were blamed for setting fires near the Galleria mall (*Radio TV Reports*, October 25, 1993).

Intense criticism of the show's violence – and Congressional threats to regulate TV violence – led MTV to move back its playtime to later in the evening and there was a promise not to replay the more violent episodes, or to show Beavis and Butt-Head starting fires, or Beavis shouting "Fire! Fire!" but the series had already become part of a national mythology and its popularity continued apace.[30] Indeed, media culture is drawn to violence and taboo-breaking action to draw audiences in an ever-more competitive field. Thus, the program's excesses are directly related to a competitive situation in which commercial media are driven to show ever more violent and extreme behavior in the intense pressures for high profits – a trend that many believe will accelerate as the number of TV channels grows and competition becomes fiercer.

And so we see how media culture taps into its audience's concerns and in turn becomes part of a circuit of culture, with distinctive effects. Media cultural texts articulate social experiences, transcoding them into the medium of forms like television, film, or popular music. The texts are then appropriated by audiences, which use certain resonant texts and images to articulate their own sense of style, look, and identity. Media culture provides resources to make meanings, pleasure, and identity, but also shape and form specific identities and circulate material whose appropriateness may insert audiences into specific positions (i.e. macho Rambo, sexy Madonna, disaffected Slackers, violent Beavis and Butt-Head, and so on).

The *Beavis and Butt-Head* effects were particularly striking. Not only did the show promote acts of violence and copious discussion of media effects, but the characters became models for youth behavior, with young people imitating various of their tics and behavior patterns. Of course, the series generated a large consumer market of "Beavis and Butt-Head" products, which in turn proliferated its images and effects. For example: "Mask-maker Ed Edmunds of Distortions Unlimited says he's sold 40,000 Beavis and Butt-Head masks, his top sellers for this Halloween season." (*U.S.A. Today*, October 26, 1993). In 1994, Beavis and Butt-Head combs, calendars, and even day-planners were on the market.

The show also strongly influenced musical tastes and sales, providing a boon for heavy metal rock. Studies showed that sales jumped of every video played on the show, including ones Beavis and Butt-Head panned.[31] The *Beavis and Butt-Head* effect even became part of political contestation:

> It was only be a matter of time before "Beavis Clinton" and "Butt-Head Gore" T-shirts began appearing on the streets of Washington. The hapless, ugly, dumb cartoon characters have been altered to look like the leaders of the free world, thanks to local political entrepreneurs and T-shirt creators Kathleen Patten, Beth Loudy and Chris Tremblay. On the shirts, Beavis is sporting a Fleetwood Mac T-shirt and is seen asking Butt-Head, "Eh, do you think we'll get re-elected?" To which the veep, wearing the Greenpeace whale logo, says: "Huh . . . nope".
> (*Washington Times*, October 26, 1993)[32]

Previous studies of media effects seem blind to the sort of complex effects of media culture texts of the sort I have discussed in analyses of the *Rambo* effect, the *Slacker* effect, and the *Beavis and Butt-Head* effect. In each case, figures and material were taken from these texts and were used to produce meaning, identities, discourse, and behavior. The media provide symbolic environments in which people live and strongly influence their thought, behavior, and style. When a media sensation like *Beavis and Butt-Head* appears, it becomes part of that environment, and in turn becomes a new resource for pleasures, identities, and contestation.

Thus, it is totally idiotic to claim that media culture has no discernible effects, as in the dominant paradigm from the 1940s, which lasted several decades.[33] Yet it is equally blind to blithely claim that audiences simply produce their own meanings from texts and that the text's do not have their own effectivity. As my discussions have shown, media culture has very powerful effects, though its meanings are mediated by audiences and even a figure like Rambo can be a contested terrain in which different groups inflect its meanings in different ways.

The *Slacker* and *Beavis and Butt-Head* effects that I have just discussed crystallize the experiences and feelings of alienation and hopelessness produced by a disintegrating society and shape these experiences into identification with slackers, rockers, heavy metal and nihilistic violence of the sort engaged in by

Beavis and Butt-Head. Popular media texts tap into and articulate feelings and experiences of their audiences and in turn circulate material effects that shape thought and behavior. The texts of media culture thus have very powerful and distinctive effects and should thus be carefully scrutinized and subject to diagnostic critique – a project that I will continue in the following chapters.

NOTES

1   This dual optic of reading history through texts and using history and theory to read texts was that of T.W. Adorno and Walter Benjamin; see the discussion in Kellner 1989a and the development of diagnostic critique in Kellner and Ryan 1988.

2   I should acknowledge the influence of Fredrick Jameson. For his use of allegory, which I draw upon here, see Jameson 1979, 1981, 1990 and 1991 and on Jameson see my study in Kellner 1989c.

3   *Variety* claimed that in 1980 horror and sci-fi films would generate more than one-third of all box-office rentals and predicted that by 1981, the figures would reach 50 percent. See "Horror Sci-Fi Pix Earn 37 percent of Rentals--Big Rise During 10-Year Period" (January 3, 1981). *Cinefantastique* (Vol. 9, Nos. 3–4 (1980): 72) reported in a decade re-cap that half of the top ten money making films of all time are horror and science fiction films. The popularity of the horror film has continued to the present.

4   As Ferguson and Rogers argue:

> The combination of social-spending cuts, other budget initiatives, and the massively regressive tax bill produced a huge upward distribution of American income. Over the 1983–1985 period the policies reduced the incomes of households making less than $20,000 a year by $20 billion, while increasing the incomes of households making more than $80,000 by $35 billion. For those at the very bottom of the income pyramid, making under $10,000 per year, the policies produced an average loss of $1,100 over 1983–85. For those at the top making more than $200,000, the average gain was $60,000. By the end of Reagan's first term, U.S. income distribution was more unequal than at any time since 1947, the year the Census Bureau first began collecting data on the subject. In 1983, the top 40% of the population received a larger share of income than at any time since 1947.
>
> (Ferguson and Rogers 1986: 130)

5   On "subversive" and "critical" moments in these and other contemporary filmmakers' works, see the studies in Britton, Lippe, Williams, and Wood 1979; Kellner and Ryan 1988.

6   *Poltergeist* is credited as a Tobe Hooper film and Hooper is credited as director, while Spielberg is credited as producer, source of the story, and one of the writers. There have been many discussions concerning alleged tensions between Hooper and Spielberg during the filming, as well as debate over whose film it really is – as if a collective enterprise "belonged" to one person or another. In fact, the film itself is an amalgam of the cinematic styles and concerns of Hooper and Spielberg. This film exhibits Hooper's flair for the suspenseful, odd and horrific, and Spielberg's affection for the middle class, fuzzy minded occultism, and technical skill.

7   Stephen King, "Why We Crave Horror Movies," *Playboy* (January 1981): 237.

8   In *Discipline and Punish*, French theorist Michel Foucault (1979) analyzed the apparatus of surveillance developed in the early nineteenth century by Jeremy Bentham, which he called a "panopticon," describing an architectural structure whereby prisoners, students, workers, or others could be constantly surveyed. New technologies present the possi-

bilities that new high-tech surveillance could create a frightening panopticon society, *à la* Orwell's *1984*.

9 Fear of television has been an obsession of Spielberg's in his recent films. Early in *Poltergeist*, the children are told not to play so roughly and Carol Anne is directed to watch TV: she flicks it on and a violent Western is playing! In *E.T.*, when the alien watches television for the first time, he communicates his thoughts and feelings to the young boy at school (they have apparently achieved a "mind-meld," to use *Star Trek* lingo, sharing each other's minds). When E.T. watches a violent scene on TV, the boy is then violent at school; E.T. watches John Wayne kiss Maureen O'Hara and the boy kisses a little girl at school. The fear that children will imitate what they see on TV is widespread in U.S. society today, and is symbolically portrayed in *Poltergeist* and *E.T.*. – the concern has emerged in contemporary discussions of media violence and the impact of shows like *Beavis and Butt-Head* on the young. Not accidently, when the little boy in *E.T.* succeeds in his ploy to stay home from school to be with his new companion, the mother warns: "And no TV!"

10 Of course, the industrial working class, more than the middle classes, faced economic disaster during the de-industrialization of America, but this situation, as I suggest later, was probably too *really horrible* for Hollywood to deal with, thus working-class and middle-class fears were projected into horror films dealing with predominantly middle-class families.

11 In cinematic folklore surrounding the film, the young actress playing the teenage daughter died a violent death (she was murdered by a jealous boyfriend), giving rise to rumors of supernatural complicity – rumors which multiplied when Heather O'Rourke who played Carol Anne also died some years later.

12 The stalker films presented a more concerted attack on teen sexuality, invariably killing the young teens after a sexual encounter; the stalker films contain a curious mixture of modern sexual titillation and traditional punishment of "immoral" sexual behavior; they also contain a mixture of pro- and anti-woman aspects, as when they target young women for punishment, but show some strong women fighting back as survivors.

13 Clover (1992) fails to see that *The Exorcist* and many contemporary horror films are anti-feminism and anti-independent and strong women, preferring to see the genre as strongly pro-women; in fact, like most genres, it has its reactionary and progressive wings, as I shall show in this discussion.

14 Beck, of course, was the founder of the avant-garde Living Theater and was himself a life-long radical.

15 Clover presents the Native American Taylor as representative of a more feminine nature which the father must get in touch with (1992: 94), but she misses the significance of the crisis of patriarchy that Steve must overcome and the motif of resurrection of male power; she also fails to read the retreat to the sweat lodge as male bonding that resurrects male power. Rather than representing the feminine *per se*, Taylor represents a more traditionalist supernatural wisdom against "normal" science and reason, so the message is ultimately that Steve must become more masculine and more wise to reassume the phallic power under threat.

16 Clover (1992: 106f.) sees the birthing segment as a positive expression of the transgression/mixing of gender identities and generally valorizes the frequent birthing images in the contemporary horror film as evidence of the positive and strong role of women in the genre. But these images of monstrous births – which run through horror films like the *Alien* series, *The Thing*, and many others – can be seen as extremely negative images of biological processes and thus as anti-women, as projecting negative images of birth as monstrous and women as bearers of monstrosities.

17 I am leaving *Poltergeist III* (1988) out of my discussion, since it does not deal with the Freeling family, showing instead Carol Anne visiting relatives in Chicago and the return of Kane to try to abduct her again. The film is so bad that it could be taken as symptomatic

of the decline of the horror genre in the contemporary era, though part of the problem with the vague and unresolved plot might be due to Heather O'Rourke's death, who was then unavailable to shoot scenes necessary for coherence and resolution. O'Rourke's death, following upon that of Dominique Dunne, the young woman who played her teenage sister in *Poltergeist I*, fuelled occultist folklore concerning the revenge of evil spirits, a focus that should have been levelled at the nature of a violent society with inadequate medical care (Dunne was killed by a jealous boyfriend, and O'Rourke's family sued for medical malpractice, claiming that her daughter's ailment was misdiagnosed and that she was therefore given medical advice and treatment that led to her death at 13).

18 On the other hand, unlike *Beavis and Butt-Head*, which I discuss below, the slackers also read books, referencing Tolstoy, Dostoyevsky, de Sade, and various other writers and poets, though the differences between books, TV, and movies seem to be levelled, with the various characters reducing everything to sound bites and clichés.

19 The conception of "postmodernism" that I am using here is that of Jameson (1991) who focuses on flat, one-dimensional experiences or images, disconnected and fragmented, but punctuated by moments of euphoric intensity. This concept describes both the form of the film *Slacker* and the texture of its characters' experiences and lifestyle.

20 Coincidentally, I was teaching a course on modernity/postmodernity the semester of the film's shooting, was using the two books in the coffee house in my course, and several of my students were in the film. Thus, aesthetic debates concerning modernism and postmodernism were in the air during the period, and Linklater, who I have known for years, obviously picked up on these ideas, blending them in an innovative fashion in his film.

21 *Beavis and Butt-Head* was based on an animated short by Mike Judge, in which the two characters play "frog baseball," shown at the Sick and Twisted Animation festival and taken up by MTV's animated series *Liquid Television*. The series itself premiered in March 1993, but because there were only four episodes, the show went on hiatus, returning May 17 after Judge and his team of creative assistants put together thirty-two new episodes (*The San Francisco Chronicle*, June 29, 1993). The series tripled MTV's ratings and MTV ordered 130 more episodes for 1994 (*The New York Times*, October 17, 1993).

22 An October 9, 1993, story in the *Dayton Daily News* reported that a five-year-old boy in Dayton, Ohio, ignited his bedclothes with a cigarette lighter after watching the pyromaniac antics of Beavis and Butt-Head, according to his mother. The boy's younger sister, aged 2, died in the ensuing blaze. The mother said her 5-year-old son had become "obsessed" with *Beavis and Butt-Head* and imitated the characters' destructive behavior. I provide more examples of the *Beavis and Butt-Head* effect throughout this section.

23 An October 23, 1993, Senate Hearings on TV violence focused media attention on the show, though U.S. Sen. Ernest Hollings (D-SC) botched references to it, saying: "We've got this – what is it – Buffcoat and Beaver or Beaver and something else. . . . I haven't seen it; I don't watch it; it was at 7 o'clock – Buffcoat – and they put it on now at 10:30, I think" (*The Hartford Courant*, October 26, 1993). Such ignorance of media culture is often found in some of its harshest critics.

24 Their family genealogy in a book on the series puts a question mark in the place of both of their fathers (Johnson and Marcil 1993). So far, their mothers have not been shown, though there are some references to them. It is also unclear exactly whose house they live in, or are shown watching TV in, and whether they do or do not live together. One episode suggests that they are in Butt-Head's house and that his mother is (is always) out with her boyfriend, but other episodes show two beds together in what appears to be their highly messy bedroom and as of early 1994, their parents have never been shown.

25 Psychoanalysts like to identity Beavis and Butt-Head with the Freudian Id, with

uncontrolled aggression and sexual impulses that they cannot understand or control (they were often shown masturbating, or talking about it, and Beavis uncontrollably "moons" attractive female singers while watching music videos). There is also a barely repressed homo-erotic element to their relationship, expressed in the endless "butt" jokes and references, their constant use of "sucks," and other verbal and visual behavior ("Hey Beavis, pull my finger!").

26   Margot Emery was taking a midterm examination in a mass communications theory course for master's degree candidates at the University of Tennessee at Knoxville when she found, on the last page, a question about . . . Beavis and Butt-Head. Novelist Gloria Naylor, Hartford Stage Company artistic director Mark Lamos and other distinguished panelists were discussing stereotypes in art, especially the depiction of Jews in 'The Merchant of Venice,' when unexpectedly the talk swung around to . . . Beavis and Butt-Head. Fred Rogers of 'Mister Rogers' Neighborhood' was being honored for his work by the Pittsburgh Presbytery and wound up discoursing upon . . . Beavis and Butt-Head. Thomas Grasso, a prisoner whose main problem these days is deciding whether he'd rather have the state of Oklahoma execute him or the state of New York imprison him for a very long time, recently wrote a poem comparing Gov. Mario Cuomo and a New York corrections official to . . . Beavis and Butt-Head. In fact, it has become so rare to read 10 pages of a magazine, to browse one section of a newspaper or to endure 30 minutes of television or radio talk without bumping into some knowing reference to the animated MTV dullards.

(The Hartford Courant, October 26, 1993)

27   Via MTV marathons of the series in summer 1993, January 1994, and Steve Best's collection, I was able to see almost every episode of the series. I also did extensive Nexis data-base searches for mainstream media references to and debates over the series and through the Fall of 1993 and into 1994, there were literally hundreds of references to the series. There also appeared a best-selling album of the heavy metal that Beavis and Butt-Head celebrate, a best-selling book, and movie deals in the works. Consequently, one can also easily speak of the *Beavis and Butt-Head* effect.

28   On this concept and a wealth of examples, see Kellner 1978.

29   After a Washington, D.C. psychologist said that Beavis and Butt-Head's humor sounded like the antics of normal youth, she frantically called back the reporter after seeing that night's episode, leading her to comment on voice mail: "I totally condemn this program. I do not see any shred of normal adolescent behavior here. It's one of the most sadistic, pathological programs I've ever seen. I would not recommend it to anyone of any age" *(The Washington Times,* October 17, 1993). The same story noted that an advocate of People for the Ethical Treatment of Animals stated: "Psychiatrists will tell you that almost every major serial killer has animal abuse in their background. Beavis and Butt-Head not only torture animals, but they are preoccupied with fire, and those are two of the three predictors of adult criminal behavior."

30   MTV's parent company Viacom was engaged at the time in a much-publicized battle to merge with Paramount and the conglomerate obviously did not want too much bad publicity. Thus, MTV had to walk the line between preserving its most profitable and popular product and avoiding excessive media criticism. The result was compromises that softened the edge of *Beavis and Butt-Head,* while attempting to preserve the show's popularity. As of spring 1994, the MTV strategy has worked with the show continuing to be highly popular with controversy diminishing.

31   The group White Zombie's album *La Sexorcisto: Devil Music Vol. 1,* for example,

wasn't selling enough to make the nation's Top 100 charts, averaging only about 2,000 copies a week. But the group's video has been a fixture on "Beavis and Butt-Head" since the summer, and the exposure – along with the bratty teens' words of praise – have propelled the album into the national Top 30. Estimated sales now: more than 500,000 copies. . . . Rick Krim, MTV's vice president of talent and artists relations, explains the response to the "Beavis and Butt-Head" exposure. 'We had liked the 'Thunder' video and supported it with play on the various specialty shows,' he says. 'That never really sparked significant album sales, the 'Beavis and Butt-Head' exposure sure did. The sales response was pretty immediate. . . Almost everything that gets played on the show gets some sort of sales bump from it"

(*Billboard*, September 4, 1993).

32 Such an anti-Clinton move could backfire as younger voters might interpret the association to suggest that Clinton and Gore are "cool" are thus come to support them.

33 I am speaking of Lazarsfeld's "two step flow" model which claimed that media culture had no direct effects, that its effects were modest and minimal, and mediated by "opinion leaders" who had the more important effects on consumer and political behavior, social attitudes, and the like (see Katz and Lazarsfeld 1955 and the critical discussion of its effects in Gitlin 1978).

Chapter 5

Black voices from Spike Lee to rap

In this chapter, I will use rap music and the films of Spike Lee to provide a diagnostic critique of the situation of African-Americans in the United States today.[1] Black rap artists and filmmakers have used media culture to articulate their visions of contemporary U.S. society and have used media culture to resist the culture of racial oppression in the United States and to articulate their own forms of resistance and oppositional identities. I will accordingly probe the aesthetic strategies and politics of some recent productions by black popular artists to delineate the resources for social critique and political action found in their work.

Indeed, media culture reproduces existing social struggles and discourses, articulating the fears and sufferings of ordinary people, while providing material to produce identities and make sense of the world. When members of oppressed groups gain access to media culture, their representations often articulate alternative visions of society and give voice to more radical perceptions. Yet a diagnostic critique is also interested in the limitations of these works in order to advance the interests of the oppressed in future struggles.[2]

Despite the continued oppression of blacks and people of color and growing violence against African-Americans, black culture has produced extremely important works in the last decades in the fields of literature, film, music, theater, and a full range of arts.[3] Cultural expression has always been a way of resisting oppression and articulating experiences of resistance and struggle. Gospel, blues, jazz, rock, and other forms of music have traditionally articulated African-American struggle and resistance. Black literature has also been a rich source of original voices, articulating the vicissitudes of the African-American experience and their culture of resistance. During the past decade, new African-American voices have appeared in the realms of film, hip-hop culture, and rap music, and these black incursions into media culture will be the focus of this chapter.

THE FILMS OF SPIKE LEE

During the 1980s, Hollywood joined Ronald Reagan and his administration in neglecting black issues and concerns. Few serious films during the decade featured blacks who were mostly stereotypically portrayed in comedies, often with black comics like Richard Pryor or Eddie Murphy playing against a white buddy (Guerrero 1993b: 113ff.). Within this context, Spike Lee's films constitute a significant intervention within the system of Hollywood film. Addressing issues of race, gender, and class from a resolutely black perspective, Lee's films provide insights into these explosive problematics missing from mainstream white cinema. Starting with low-budget independent pictures like *Joe's Bed-Stuy Barbershop: We Cut Heads* (a 1983 student film) and *She's Gotta Have It* (1986), Lee moved to Hollywood financing of his films starting with *School Daze* (1988), a focus on black college life that spoofed the college film genre and the musical. His next film, *Do the Right Thing* (1989), was immediately recognized as an important cinematic statement concerning the situation of blacks in contemporary U.S. society and the films that followed (*Mo' Better Blues, Jungle Fever, Malcolm X,* and *Crooklyn*) won Lee recognition as one of the most important cineastes at work in the United States today.

Moreover, the success of Lee's films helped open the door to financing a wide range of other films by young blacks in the 1990s. The profits made by Lee's films produced on a low budget showed that there was an audience for black films dealing with contemporary realities. Estimates suggest that from 25–30 percent of the U.S. film audience are black Americans (overrepresenting their 13 percent of the population), and Hollywood calculated that there was a significant audience for black-oriented films (Guerrero 1993b).[4] Moreover, the profits that Spike Lee made on his early films, produced on a low budget, procured continued financing of his own films and opened the door for a renaissance of films by, usually young male, African-Americans during the 1990s.[5]

In the following study, I examine Spike Lee's aesthetics, conception of morality, and politics, arguing that his aesthetic strategies draw on Brechtian modernism and that his films are morality tales that convey ethical images and messages to their audiences. I also discuss Lee's politics, focusing on the figure of Malcolm X in Lee's work and his sometimes contradictory identity politics, in which politics is subordinate to creating one's identity and identity is defined primarily in terms of cultural style. I argue that despite their limitations, Lee's films push key buttons of race, gender, sexuality, class, and black politics, thus providing a compelling cinematic exploration of the situation of blacks in contemporary U.S. society and the limited political options which they have at their disposal in the current organization of society. I begin with a reading of *Do the Right Thing* (hereafter *DRT*), turn to *Malcolm X* (hereafter *X*), and conclude with more general comments on Lee's gender politics, his identity politics, and his aesthetic strategies.[6] I then go on to probe the voices of black ghetto radicalism in the arena of rap music and examine some of the controversies concerning it, concluding with some reflections on oppositional culture and counterhegemony.

Do the Right Thing as a Brechtian morality tale

DRT (1989) takes place in a Brooklyn ghetto on the hottest day of the year. Mookie, a young black man (played by Spike Lee), gets up and goes to work at Sal's Pizzeria on a Saturday morning. Various neighborhood characters appear as Lee paints a tableau of the interactions between blacks and Italians, and the Hispanic and Korean residents of the Brooklyn ghetto of "Bed Stuy." Conflicts between the blacks and Italians erupt and when a black youth is killed by the police, the crowd destroys the pizzeria.

Lee set out to make a film about black urban experience from a black perspective and his film transcodes the discourses, style, and conventions of African-American culture, with an emphasis on black nationalism that affirms the specificity of black experience and its cultural differences from mainstream white culture. Lee presents black ways of speaking, walking, dressing, and acting, drawing on black slang, music, images, and style. His films are richly textured ethnographies of urban blacks negotiating the allures of the consumer and media society, and the dangers of racism and an oppressive urban environment. The result is a body of work that represents uniquely black perspectives, voices, styles, and politics.

Yet Lee also draws on the techniques of modernism and produces original innovative films that articulate his own individual vision and aesthetic style. In particular, like the German theater artist Bertolt Brecht, Spike Lee produces a cinema that dramatizes the necessity of making moral and political choices.[7] Both Brecht and Lee produce a sort of "epic drama" which paints a wide tableau of typical social characters, shows examples of social and asocial behavior, and conveys didactic messages to the audience. Both Brecht and Lee utilize music, comedy, drama, vignettes of typical behavior, and figures who present the messages desired by the author. Both present didactic learning plays, which strive to teach people to discover and then do "the right thing," while criticizing improper and antisocial behavior. Brecht's theater (as well as his film *Kuhle Wampe* and his radio plays) depict character types in situations that force one to observe the consequences of typical behavior. Lee, I would argue, does the same thing in *DRT* (and most of his other films), depicting typical work, familial, and street scenes and behavior. In particular, the three street-corner philosophers, who offer comic commentary throughout, are very Brechtian, as is the radio DJ, Mister Señor Love Daddy, who tells the audience not only to do the right thing throughout the movie ("and that's the truth, Ruth"), but he repeatedly specifies "the right thing," insisting that the ghetto population: "Wake Up!," "Love one another," and "Chill!"

DRT posits the question of political and social morality for its audience in the contemporary era: what is "the right thing" politically and morally for oppressed groups like urban blacks? The film is arguably modernist in that the question of the political "right thing" is left open in the film. By "modernist," I refer, first, to aesthetic strategies of producing texts that are open and polyvocal; that disseminate a wealth of meanings without a central univocal meaning or message; and that require an active reader to produce the meanings.[8] Second, I take modernism to be an aesthetic tendency dedicated to the production of unique works of art that bear the vision and stylistic imprint of their creator. Third, the type of modernism associated with what Peter Bürger (1984) calls the "historical avant garde" attempts to produce serious works that change individuals' perceptions and lives and strive to promote social transformation. Movements like futurism, expressionism, Dada, and surrealism meet these criteria, as do the works of Brecht and Lee, though I ultimately argue that Lee's films contain a unique mixture of American popular cultural forms and modernism, inflected through Lee's African-American experience.[9]

Thus, I am claiming that in a formal sense the works of Spike Lee are in accord with these modernist criteria and that his aesthetic strategies are especially close to those of Brecht. Lee's texts tend to be open, to elicit divergent readings, and to generate a wealth of often divergent responses. He is, in this sense, an "auteur" whose films project a distinctive style and vision which cumulatively exhibit a coherent body of work with distinctive features and effects. His work is highly serious and strives for specific transformative moral and political effects. Yet there are also ambiguities in Lee's work. While the disk jockey, Mister Señor Love Daddy, serves as a voice of social morality (*Sittlichkeit*, how to treat others) in *DRT*, it is an open question what, if any, political position Lee is affirming. Does he agree with the politics of Malcolm X or Martin Luther King? Is he advocating reform or revolution, integration or black nationalism, or a synthesis of the two?

Throughout the film, Public Enemy's powerful rap song "Fight the Power" resonates, but it is not clear from the film *how* one is supposed to fight the power, or what political strategies should be employed to carry out the struggle. Indeed, one could read *Do the Right Thing* as a postmodern evacuation of viable political options for blacks and people of color in the present age.[10] That is, one can read the film as demonstrating that, politically, there is no "right thing" to do in the situation of hopeless ghetto poverty, virulent racism, and the lack of viable political options and movements. In this postmodern reading, the film projects a bleak, nihilistic view of the future, marked by hopelessness and the collapse of modern black politics. In this context, political reformism and Martin Luther King's nonviolence appear questionable as viable instruments of change. But it is not clear that violence is an attractive option and one could even read the film as questioning social violence, demonstrating that it ultimately hurts the people in the neighborhoods in which it explodes. (One could read the events in Los Angeles, which Lee's film uncannily anticipates, in a similar light).

On this postmodern reading, it is not clear what the power is that one is supposed to fight, what instruments one is supposed to use, and what one's goals are supposed to be. This nihilistic postmodern reading suggests that modern politics as a whole is bankrupt,[11] that neither reform or revolution can work, that blacks in the U.S. are condemned to hopeless poverty and the subordinate position of an oppressed underclass without the faintest possibility of improving their situation by any means whatsoever. Yet one could also read *DRT* as a modernist film that forces the viewer to compare the different politics of Malcolm X and Martin Luther King and to decide for his or her self what the "right thing" is for blacks in the contemporary era. In the following analysis, I'll interrogate whether *Do the Right Thing* is a modernist or postmodernist film in both its style and politics, and whether Lee privileges Malcolm X or Martin Luther King in the film. But first I want to interrogate the cultural politics of *DRT*.

Cultural politics in *Do The Right Thing*

The characters in *DRT* are portraits of distinctive neighborhood African-, Hispanic-, Italian-, Anglo-, and Korean-American individuals and Lee depicts typical modes of their behavior and their conflicts with one another. Race for Lee is presented in *DRT* in terms of cultural identity and image, especially cultural style. As Denzin points out (1991: 125, 130ff.), the characters wear T-shirts that identify their cultural politics and style. Mookie, the black worker in Sal's pizzeria, wears a Jackie Robinson baseball jersey, symbolizing the position of a black who breaks the colorline in the white man's world (as Lee himself has done). While working, Mookie also wears a shirt with his name on it and the logo of "Sal's Pizzeria," signifying his position between the two worlds. Radio Raheem, whose radio blasts out "Fight the Power" which provokes the confrontation with Sal, wears a T-shirt proclaiming "Bed-Stuy or Die." This message identifies him as a figure who asserts black solidarity and rebellion to preserve the community.

Lee also deploys color-coding symbolism in the wearing of T-shirts, with Pino, Sal's racist son, wearing white, while Vito, his son who gets along with blacks, wears a black T-shirt. Sal's clothes code him as the boss/worker who drives up to his pizzeria in a Cadillac, but he dons an apron to make the pizzas, presenting him as a petit-bourgeois small businessman. Other shirts identify the wearer with white or black cultural heroes. A young white man who has just purchased a ghetto apartment wears a Larry Bird Boston Celtics' jersey, while a young black man wears the L.A. Lakers' jersey of Magic Johnson. The Hispanics wear sleeveless colored T-shirts, while the older black men wear sleeveless white T-shirts, conventional single-colored shirts, or go topless. Most of the young women wear tube tops, though Mookie's sister Jade sports designer clothes.

Clothes and fashion accoutrements depict the various characters' styles and identity. Buggin' Out, an angry young black youth, wears a yellow African kente shirt with a gold chain around his neck and a gold tooth. He also wears Nike Air Jordan shoes (that Lee does commercials for), and explodes with anger when the Celtic fan accidentally soils them. Radio Raheem wears the same type of shoes himself and his ghetto-blaster and rap music establishes his cultural identity (he only plays Public Enemy). He also displays a set of gold brass knuckle rings, engraved with "love" and "hate": supposedly the two sides of the sometimes gentle and sometimes violent Raheem.[12] Mookie too sports a gold tooth and earring, marking him as a participant in black urban cultural conventions.[13] The three black street-corner philosophers, discoursing on the current situation of blacks, are casually dressed, while the alcoholic Da Mayor (Ossie Davis) wears old and dirty clothes, coding him as an example of failed black manhood. Mother Sister (Ruby Dee) dresses conventionally and represents traditional matriarchal black values, disapproving of Da Mayor and "shiftless" young blacks.

In fact, *DRT* influenced fashion trends itself: "the summer of 1989 saw millions of young people wearing Mookie-style surfer baggies over lycra bike shorts" (Patterson 1992: 125). Indeed, Spike Lee himself opened a fashion store in Brooklyn, designing his own T-shirts and clothes, and he produced and acted in commercials for Nike Air Jordan shoes. He thus depicts a society in which cultural identity is produced through style and consumption and himself contributes to this trend through his films and commercial activity.[14]

The ways that mass cultural images pervade style and fashion suggest that cultural identity is constituted in part by iconic images of ethnic cultural heros, which are badges of identity and forces of division between the races. Sal has pictures of famous Italian-Americans (his "Hall of Fame") on the wall of his pizzeria, and Buggin' Out's demand to put pictures of blacks on the wall and Sal's vehement refusal to do so precipitates the attempted boycott and the subsequent violence. A stuttering and perhaps mentally retarded young Black, Smiley, is selling pictures of Malcolm and Martin,[15] who appear as icons of black politics, and references to Jessie Jackson and Al Sharpton appear in graffiti, constituting black political leaders as cultural heroes, along with sports and music stars.

These scenes suggest how media culture provides the material for identity and how different subcultures appropriate different images to provide identities. Identity is thus formed on a terrain of struggle in which individuals choose their own cultural meanings and style in a differential system that always involves the affirmation of some tokens of identity and rejection of other ones. Social institutions individuate people with social security numbers, voting registration, consumer lists, data-bases, police and academic records, and so on, but producing one's individual identity means refusing to be defined by these determinations and choosing other forms of identity. More and more, it is the case that media culture provides resources that are appropriated by audiences to make meanings, to create identities, as when teenage girls use Madonna as a model, or blacks emulate African-American cultural heroes, or aspiring Yuppies look to professionals on TV shows like *LA Law* for patterns of identity.

Identity is thus mediated by mass-produced images in the contemporary media society, while image and cultural style is becoming ever more central to the construction of individual identities – as I am indicating in this discussion and will take up again in the following chapters. Media culture provides a powerful source of new identities, replacing nationalism, religion, the family, and education as sources of identity. As Benedict Anderson argued (1983), nationalism provided a powerful imaginary community and identities, and the forms of media culture provide surrogates for both individuals and groups who are able to participate in imaginary communities through cultural style and consumption and who can produce individual and group identities through the appropriation of media cultural images.

Media culture also provides modern morality tales that demonstrate right and wrong behavior, that show what to do and what not to do, that indicate what is or is not "the right thing." Media culture is thus an important new force of socialization and it is one of the merits of *DRT* to put this process of the creation of identity through image and cultural style on display in a fashion which shows as well how different identities are produced in opposition to each other and represent a terrain in which social conflicts are played out.

DRT shows how cultural identity is also articulated through music and expressive styles. The black DJ and Radio Raheem play exclusively black music, while the Puerto Rican street teens play Spanish-inflected music. A scene where Radio Raheem and the Puerto Ricans duel each other with loud playing radios signifies the cultural clash and divisions in the ghetto community. In addition, Sal provokes Radio Raheem by ordering him to "turn that jungle music off. We ain't in Africa," while Buggin' Out replies: "Why it gotta be about jungle music and Africa?"

Thus, different cultures use popular music to establish their cultural identities and different styles of music divide the community. But it is the racial epithets that most pungently articulate the contemporary social conflicts and tensions. At a key juncture in the film, in modernist and Brechtian fashion, Lee interrupts his narrative and has the characters look into the camera and spit out vicious racial slurs, with Mookie attacking the Italians ("Dago, Wop, guinea, garlic breath, pizza slingin', spaghetti bender," etc.). Pino, the racist son, replies to the camera, assaulting blacks: "Gold chain wearin' fried chicken and biscuit eatin' monkey, ape, baboon, fast runnin', high jumpin', spear chuckin', basket ball dunkin' titso spade, take your fuckin' pizza and go back to Africa."

A Puerto Rican attacks Koreans in similar racial terms and the Korean grocer attacks Jews. This scene, thoroughly Brechtian, brilliantly shows the racial differences encoded in language, but tends to equate all modes of racism as logically equivalent, whereas one could argue that the institutional racism against blacks is far more virulent than the variegated cultural racisms articulated and that Lee never really catches the reality of racism as part of a system of oppression.[16] From this perspective, the existing society especially oppresses people of color: it is, then, not just the case that there is racism, and racial hatred, among all the races and ethnicities, but there is an unequal distribution of power and wealth in contemporary U.S. society, in which blacks and people of color tend to suffer disproportionately from systemic racial and class oppression. Put otherwise, Lee does not understand that capitalism is a system of oppression, which especially exploits and oppresses its underclass, particularly people of color.

Lee, however, presents racism in personal and individualist terms as hostility between different members of different groups, thus failing to illuminate the causes and structures of racism. Moreover, the film effectively denigrates political action, caricaturing collective action and the tactic of the economic boycott which served the civil rights movement so well. As Guerrero puts it:

> by constructing Buggin Out and Radio Raheem as supercilious and unreasonable characters, advocating the most effective social action instrument of the civil rights movement, the economic boycott, and then having the possibility of social

action dismissed by the neighborhood youth for the temporary pleasures of a good slice of pizza, the film trivializes any understanding of contemporary black political struggle, as well as the recent history of social movements in this country. This dismissal of collective action is further accented by contrasting Buggin Out and Raheem with the character of Mookie, the film's calculating middle-man, positioned between Sal and the community. For it is through Mookie's aloof, individualist perspective that much of the film is rendered.

(Guerrero 1993b: 149)

In addition, Lee is constantly celebrating consumerism, the center of much of the film's focus and affective investments, rather than depicting how consumerism has come to centrally organize ghetto existence. Much affective investment is placed on the eating of pizza, ice cream, ice cones, drinking beer, and displaying consumer items. As I noted, there is a strong emphasis on the construction of identity through clothes and style and no one questions consumerist practices.

Yet Lee does incisively show how clothes, music, language, and style separate the various ethnic groupings in his vision of a divided ghetto community. Such a situation is ripe to explode into violence and *DRT* presciently anticipated the L.A. uprisings that erupted in May 1992, after a white jury acquitted the policemen who were videotaped viciously beating Rodney King. *DRT* is thus properly read as a cautionary tale warning what might – and did – happen if relations between the races continue to worsen.

Thus, *DRT* has its insights, as well as its limitations, and a diagnostic critique can read the film as articulating some of the conditions that produce violence in the ghettoes.The film is particularly strong in depicting the ghetto explosion that erupts after Radio Raheem is killed by white policemen when he and Sal start fighting. Lee has his own character Mookie throw a garbage can through the window of Sal's Pizzeria and violence breaks out that destroys the establishment. A close viewing of Mookie's action suggests that it was a conscious, deliberate act and that Lee *was* presenting it as "the right thing." The camera zooms in on Mookie deliberating about what to do after the police have accidentally choked Radio Raheem to death in a fight that began when Sal smashed his beloved radio. Lee then pans a long and slow shot of Mookie methodically walking away to pick up a garbage can and then returning to throw it through the window of the pizzeria, starting the riot that ends in its destruction. It is clear that he is doing it because of rage over Radio Raheem's death and that Lee is depicting the act as a conscious, deliberate act on Mookie's part.[17]

On this reading, Lee is privileging human life over property and is suggesting that violence against property is a legitimate act of retaliation. One could also argue that Mookie is directing the mob's violence against the pizzeria and away from Sal and his sons, thus ultimately protecting them against the mob's wrath.[18] It is, of course, debatable whether the act of violence was "the right thing," though it is a rejection of King's philosophy of non-violence. Yet it is not clear that this act produces anything positive for Mookie or the black community; one could indeed argue the opposite.[19] Smiley puts the picture of Malcolm X and Martin Luther King standing side by side on the wall, thus fulfilling Raheem's desire to have black images in the pizzeria. But they are shown burning in the wall, raising the question of whether this can be read as a sign of the futility of black politics in the present age, allegorically enacting the fading away of the relevance of Malcolm and Martin in the current moment.

In any case, the (white conservative) critique that *DRT* was "bad" because it was likely to produce violence and increase race hatred is misplaced. Rather, Lee's film reveals the living conditions and the racial tensions and conflicts that are likely to produce racial and other forms of urban violence. That is, *DRT* explores the social environment that produces violence and urban explosions. In interviews after the film, Lee protested that he was only depicting existing urban situations and not offering solutions, and this position seems wholly reasonable.

Yet one could still criticize Lee for deconstructing modern politics as futile or irrelevant, thus giving voice to a postmodern nihilism.[20] However, certain aspects of the film counter this reading of *DRT* as an expression of a bleak, postmodern pessimism which would affirm the obsolescence of a modern black politics of the sort typified by Malcolm X and Martin Luther King. Lee himself later claimed that he is affirming a politics that would embrace aspects of both King and Malcolm X, that would use both men's philosophies and strategies for social change in different contexts. He calls attention to the still picture put on the wall of the Pizzeria as it burns:

> Malcolm X and Dr King are shaking hands and smiling. So when I put those two quotes there, it was not a question of either/or, not for me, anyway, just a choice of tactics. I think they were men who chose different paths trying to reach the same destination against a common opponent.

> (Lee and Wiley 1992: 5)

Thus, the seemingly opposing quotes of King and Malcolm X that close *DRT* both, on this view, articulate valid positions and it would thus be a question of context and tactics concerning which view was most appropriate. Yet the scenario of the film itself seems to privilege Malcolm X, who would eventually be the topic of Lee's major film epic to date. Indeed, the vision of *DRT* is in some ways consistent with Malcolm X's black nationalist teachings and thus does affirm certain modern political positions. One of the street-corner philosophers expresses wonder and chagrin that the Korean grocer can turn a boarded-up building into a successful business, while blacks cannot. Surely this is a nod toward Malcolm X's views on black self-sufficiency and economic independence, and certainly Spike Lee has enacted this philosophy as successfully as anyone in the black community. It is clear that Mookie is going to get nowhere working in Sal's Pizzeria and the other home-boys in the movie are also rapidly going nowhere. "Time to wake up, brothers, and get your shit together," is an arguable message of the film.

Likewise, Malcolm X put a heavy emphasis on black manhood, standing up to the white power structure, fighting back, and acting decisively to maintain one's self-respect. In that sense, Mookie's violent action instantiated certain of Malcolm's teachings, though one could raise the question whether this was in fact "the right thing." One could also raise some questions concerning whether Malcolm X did or advocated the "right thing" politically at various phases of his life and what his legacy is for us today. I will interrogate *X* from these perspectives, arguing that the film, like *DRT*, is ultimately a morality tale and that Lee's politics slide into a black identity politics that can neither be pinned down to specific modern positions (i.e. Martin or Malcolm), nor to postmodern nihilism.

Malcolm X as a morality tale

From the perspective of my reading of *DRT*, one could argue that *X* can be read as a morality tale interrogating what is the "right thing" for blacks in contemporary U.S. society in both the individual and the political sense. In this reading, it is the figure of Malcolm X that is the center of the film and the key transitions involve his transforming himself from criminal to dedicated black nationalist working for the Nation of Islam, and then transforming himself again into a more secular internationalist. The key, then, is Malcolm X as moral ideal, as a model of a black transforming and making something of himself, becoming self-sovereign, rather than any specific political position or message that Malcolm X taught.

Although Lee strongly affirms Malcolm X's politics, he is not, I believe, an uncritical sycophant and hagiographer, and puts in question some of Malcolm X's views, while forcing the audience to decide whether the actions of Malcolm or other characters in his films are indeed "the right thing." I thus see *X* and *DRT* as political morality plays and believe that Spike Lee was perfectly justified to tell black and other children to skip school to see the film *X*. Not only does one learn a great deal about one of the most important figures of our time, but one is forced to reflect upon what is the "right thing" for individual and political morality. Yet I would argue that Lee's film on Malcolm X focuses more on Malcolm as a role model for blacks, making it a morality tale for contemporary individuals. The life of Malcolm X is certainly exemplary as an example of a figure able to undergo profound self-transformation and to forge his own individual identity under difficult circumstances (the delineation of such righteous models is also congruent with Brechtian strategy).

The first part of *Malcolm X*, arguably, shows what the wrong thing is for blacks today, that is, to engage in a life of crime, drugs, and shallow materialism.[21] Yet Lee invests so much time and energy to this phase of Malcolm's life that it makes the one-time criminal Malcolm Little almost attractive and certainly sympathetic. Malcolm X himself in his autobiography presents Malcolm Little as a very bad dude and negative figure (Haley and X 1965), though it does not seem that this image emerges from Lee's film. Denzel Washington creates an engaging character and Lee's use of comedy and melodrama invests the Malcolm Little character with positive energies. So although he is caught in criminal activity and goes to jail, the film puts a positive spin on his early life, full of high times with white women, drugs, exciting high jinks, and good buddies.[22]

Lee uses the strategy of epic realist historical tableaux in this sequence, heavily seasoned with comedy, satire, and music. As always, music is extremely important in Lee's films and *X* can be seen and heard as a history of black music over the decades and how it was an integral part of the texture of everyday life. Once again, parallels with Brecht are obvious, as Brecht used music to capture the ethos and style of an age and as a way of making, or highlighting, certain didactic points. Moreover, it is clear that Lee is presenting certain forms of black behavior, such as "conking" hair, as bad and the early sequences contain the obvious moral that a life of crime leads to jail. The message concerning black men involving themselves with white women is less clear, though Lee tends to present interracial relationships negatively in *X* and other films such as *Jungle Fever*.[23]

The prison sequence shows Malcolm Little refusing to submit to the humiliations of prison life and then being broken by solitary confinement. But he is also shown coming to accept black Muslim teaching and bettering himself through study. It is one of Lee's pervasive messages that education is the way to "uplift the race" (one of the mottos of *School Daze* and the title of the book on that film), and certainly Malcolm X embodies a positive model of this philosophy, as he is shown learning to study and to gain knowledge. Indeed, Malcolm X emerges from prison a totally changed man and an exemplar of an individual who undertakes to transform himself successfully.

So far, the aesthetic strategies of *X* can be read as a Brechtian epic drama, as a Brechtian morality tale which embodies specific lessons for blacks and others through showing tableaux of social and asocial behavior which contrasts positive and negative values and behavior. Lee deploys a variety of genres and styles, and mixes in music, comedy, and dramatic flashbacks into key episodes of Malcolm X's early life (the mixing of genres is also Brechtian). The last third of the film continues this strategy, though it is too dense and compressed to present adequately Malcolm X's teaching and the complexity of his later positions. The key episode is the shift from Malcolm X's adherence to the teachings of Elijah Muhammad and the Nation of Islam to his radical activist social philosophy. Yet there was, arguably, too much of the religious and dubious racial teachings of the Nation of Islam and not enough of Malcolm X's late social philosophy, which many believe is his most valuable radical legacy.[24]

In Lee's defense, he does spend much energy trying to make clear the reasons for Malcolm X's break with the Nation of Islam and shows that Malcolm underwent a very significant transition to a radically new position, thus again making the point concerning the importance of radical self-transformation. Lee also dealt with the complexity of Malcolm X's assassination and the strong possibility that both the Nation of Islam and U.S. government agencies were involved in his murder – as opposed to just pinning it on the Nation of Islam. He also strongly emphasized that the "mature" Malcolm saw that all colors were equal in his experiences in Mecca. In fact, I am bracketing the question of historical accuracy in my discussion (upon which much of the critique of the film has focused, both from Lee's friends and enemies) and am focusing instead on the issue of aesthetic strategy and the politics of the film.[25]

In any case, Lee's film on Malcolm X raises questions concerning his own politics – a topic I take up in the next section.

Lee's cultural politics

In this study, I have focused on Lee's cultural politics and use of Brechtian aesthetic strategies. Yet there are some major differences between Brecht and Lee. Brecht was a convinced communist with very specific political values and a fairly specific Marxist political agenda (though there is some debate about this; see Kellner 1981). Lee, by contrast, does not seem to have as focused a political agenda. His politics appear more vague and indeterminate than those of Brecht, thus perhaps coding Lee as somewhere between a high modernist position that refuses any determinate political position; a more pragmatic contextualist politics, that draws on disparate sources for specific political interventions in concrete political situations; and an identity politics, in which politics is defined primarily through the production of cultural identity.

The social horizon of Lee's films is the oppression of African-Americans in a highly racist society and their resistance to oppression through production of distinctive cultural styles and identities. Lee's films transcode the discourses of black pride and affirmation, and present figures of strong blacks resisting racism and struggling to create their own identities. On the whole, Lee privileges cultural politics over the struggles of political movements and actions. His films focus on the specificity of African-American oppression and resistance, and present a distinctive African-American cultural style and identity as key constituents of a politics of identity that focuses on the affirmation of black pride and the positivity of black culture. Such cultural politics are valuable for providing awareness of the distinct forms of oppression suffered by specific groups and for making the production of an independent cultural style and identity an important part of the struggle against oppression. But cultural politics deflects attention from pressing political and economic issues and may well produce a separatist consciousness that undermines a politics of alliance that would mobilize distinct groups against oppressive forces, practices, and institutions.

Hence, I wish to qualify my presentation of Lee as a Brechtian for I do not think that Malcolm X plays the role that Marx played in Brecht's work, nor, for that matter, does the black radical tradition as a whole play such an important role in Lee's work as the Marxian tradition played in Brecht's work. Lee's politics are, for the most part, culturalist, focusing on black identity and moral decisions concerning race, gender, and personal identity. This was evident in *DRT* where Lee interrogated the visible badges of cultural politics and presented the conflicts of the community in primarily cultural terms. Lee excels in presenting small group dynamics and has not been successful in articulating the larger structures – and structural context of black oppression – which impact on communities, social groups, and individual lives. Thus, he does not really articulate the dynamics of class and racial oppression in contemporary U.S. society.

This leads to related questions about representations of gender, race, and class in Spike Lee's films. *DRT* focuses more on gender and race than class, seeing the antagonism between the Italians and blacks more as a racial conflict than a class conflict. While the small businessman Sal can be seen as a representative of the class system that oppresses blacks, he is, like the Korean grocer, really part of the ethnic working class himself, even though he owns a small business. Lee claims that he intended to deal with the black working class in *DRT*, writing: "In this script I want to show the Black working class. Contrary to popular belief, we work. No welfare rolls here, pal, just hardworking people trying to make a decent living" (Lee and Jones 1989: 30).

This passage, written before he actually made the film, is curious because the only blacks shown working are the DJ, Mookie, and a black cop. Mookie's sister is said to work, but it isn't clear if any of the other blacks are working or not. And although the neighborhood depicted is one that is inhabited by what could be called the black underclass, there is no exploration of their oppressive living and working conditions in the film. All of the characters define their identity in terms of fashion, consumption, and cultural style. Only the old drunk, Da Mayor, dresses slovenly, while all of the other characters seem to be full-scale participants in the consumer society (much of the film, in fact, concerns consumption of pizza, ice cream, ice cones, beer, and other drinks, food, and various consumer goods, for which everyone always seems to have the money).

Consequently, as I noted earlier, Lee tends to celebrate consumption and to define cultural identity in terms of style and consumption patterns. Moreover, he fails to address the reality and dynamics of class oppression. In fact, Lee does not really explore black underclass exploitation and misery in his films. Reflecting his own middle-class perspective, most of Lee's characters are middle-class and upwardly mobile blacks. The protagonists of *She's Gotta Have It* are middle-class and although some of the students in *School Daze* are represented as of different classes and status groups, they are at least upwardly mobile. The one scene in a fastfood chicken restaurant, in which the students confront working-class blacks, suggests hostility and difference between these sectors of contemporary African-Americans, but the differences are not adequately explored in Lee's films. *Mo' Better Blues* (1990) and *Jungle Fever* (1991) focus on black professionals and while the latter has powerful images of a crack house and degradation through drug addiction, neither explores the reality of black underclass oppression.

Thus, even though all of the characters of *DRT* are ghetto-dwellers, the phenomenon of class and class oppression is not really explored, nor is it in his other films, including *X*. The ghetto blacks in the beginning of *X* are shown getting zoot suits, hair-conked, and dancing in dazzling ballrooms where they can pick up white women. In one scene, where Malcolm is working on a train and fantasizes about pushing food into the face of an obnoxious customer, it is more race than class hatred that is shown. Lee shows Malcolm getting into a life of crime in the next scene, where he encounters a Harlem crime lord, who takes him on, suggesting that it is race hatred, rather than class oppression, which pushes blacks into crime. And nowhere does Lee adequately explore the world of class difference and exploitation.

The Malcolm who converts to Islam takes on resolutely middle-class values and the black underclass almost disappears from the film once he leaves prison and becomes a major political figure. Thus, Lee fails to depict class oppression and projects his own black middle-class values into the characters in all of his films. Amiri Baraka claims that Lee "is the quintessential buppie, almost the spirit of the young, upwardly mobile, Black, petit bourgeois professional" (Baraka 1993: 146) and argues that these values permeate his films.

Yet gender, like race, *is* a major focus of all of Lee's films, although he has been sharply criticized by black feminists for his treatment of the topic. bell hooks, for example, criticizes Lee's conventional construction of masculinity and his stereo-typical, usually negative, images of women (hooks 1990: 173ff.). His male characters often define themselves through acts of violence and typically engage in extreme macho/masculist behavior. The women are generally more passive and powerless, though, occasionally, as with Mookie's sister Jade and his Puerto Rican wife Tina, they verbally assault the male characters. Indeed, these examples show Lee's proclivity toward utilizing images of stereotypical female "bitchiness," although Jade, played by his sister Joie Lee, is a strongly sympathetic character.

As Michelle Wallace notes, Lee privileges conventional heterosexual relation-ships and negatively stigmatizes oral sex, which Wallace argues demeans gays, as well as negatively portraying "the rest of the vast range of illicit sexual practices and psychosocial developments beyond the pale of compulsory heterosexuality, in which such perverse passions as interracial sex and drug addiction are included" (Wallace 1992: 129). In fact, I think that part of the underlying problem with Lee's gender politics are his proclivities to use Brechtian "typical" characters to depict "typical" scenes. The "typical," however, is a close breath away from the stereo-typical, archetypical, conventional, representative, average, and so on, and lends itself to caricature and distortion. Lee's characters thus often embody gender or racial stereotypes. He is only a "realist" in Brecht's sense of trying to depict "real" situations, but he does not engage the realities of underclass life or of gender oppression to any great extent. Indeed, like Brecht, he uses comedy, aesthetic interruption, satire, farce, and other devices to confront the problems of race, gender, and sexuality. These are hot issues of the present, and much of the interest in Lee's work resides in his pushing of these buttons. Yet one could question whether Lee interrogates gender and sexuality any more seriously or successfully than he interrogates class.

As noted, in all of his films, Lee depicts certain characteristic types of gender behavior and interaction between the sexes, but often does so in stereotyped ways. He also puts a heavy stress on skin color, dividing blacks in *School Daze* according to the color of their skin. In *Jungle Fever* too, there are constant contrasts between light- and dark-skinned blacks, and the wives of the two main black characters are extremely light-skinned. Both *Fever* and *X* fetishize the white skin of women, showing them to be both an intense object of black male desire and a route to black male downfall. One of the jazz musician's girlfriends in *Mo' Better Blues* is light-skinned, while the other is dark black. Most of the sex scenes in Lee's films are shot at night and the lighting exaggerates skin color differences, highlighting the almost obsessive focus with skin color in Lee's films.

Yet as hooks (1990), Wallace (1992), Guererro (1993b), Reid (forthcoming b), and others have argued, Lee seems to rule out the possibility of healthy romantic relationships between people of different color – a quasi-segregationist position that a more progressive multi-culturalist vision would reject. There are also stereotypical doublings of women between "good" and "bad" in Lee's films, especially evident in *X*, where Malcolm's girlfriend Laura goes from good to bad. Laura is first depicted as Malcolm's good girlfriend, contrasted to the white woman Sophia. Laura, however, becomes a junkie and a whore, and thus the good/bad opposition with Laura is reversed. Eventually, Malcolm's wife Betty appears as the ultimate good woman, against whom all previous and other women appear as "bad." Yet this replicates the stereotypical "madonna" and "whore" opposition which has dominated a certain type of classical Hollywood cinema. A possible exception to these stereotypes in *X* are the Muslim sisters who are seduced and made pregnant by Elijah Mohammed, but they too are ultimately presented as victims, as helpless objects of male desire and as breeding machines to perpetuate male patriarchy.

Moreover, in all of Lee's films women are relegated to the sphere of private life, while men are active in public life. This is most striking in *X*, where Malcolm X's wife is primarily depicted as a dutiful spouse, raising his children and standing passively beside him. Thus, there are few positive images of women in Lee's films, or of egalitarian relationships between men and women.[26] Malcolm is shown as a harsh patriarch who seems to want a wife primarily for breeding. Flipper in *Jungle Fever* abandons his black wife for a white woman and then this relationship is shown to fail. Nola Darling in *She's Gotta Have It* plays off three black men against each other and the resulting tension harms all her relationships. The jazz musician has two girlfriends in *Mo' Better Blues* and, once again, this situation is shown as untenable; the main character marries the more conventional woman, has a family, and gives up his jazz career. Thus, one rarely sees in Lee's films strong, independent women, egalitarian relationships, or men who treat women with genuine respect and care.

In part, Lee's sexual politics fall prey to the stereotypes of the classical Hollywood cinema and do not transcend this level. But they also reflect the male chauvinism in the black and other minority communities and the intensity of conflict between male and female – explosive tensions also articulated in rap music. But his cinema does not explore the causes of these tensions, or propose any solutions. Likewise, he ultimately fails to address the causes or propose solutions to the political oppression of blacks.

For the most part, Lee privileges morality over politics in his films which are best viewed as morality tales rather than political learning plays in Brecht's sense.[27]

Although his early musical *School Daze* thematizes class to some degree, on the whole Lee's films deal more with race and gender than class (which is, of course, a major focus of Brecht's Marxian aesthetic).

Before making my final criticisms, however, I want to stress the progressiveness and excellence of Lee's films in relation to other products of the Hollywood cinema. His films are far and away superior to most other Hollywood films and it is good that Lee is able to use media culture to articulate African-American perspectives which are then disseminated through his films and his energetic promotion of them. Both aesthetically and politically his works are so far superior to most Hollywood films that it seems unfair to criticize him. Yet it is through critique and self-critique that cultural and political progress are made, and Lee has been criticized from within the black community for not taking more specific political positions, for being politically vague and indeterminate, and for replacing nitty-gritty issues politics with cultural politics.[28]

Thus, Lee tends to reduce politics to cultural identity and slogans. *School Daze* ends with the message "Wake Up!" proclaimed by the black activist hero of the movie and *Do the Right Thing* begins and ends with the DJ Mister Señor Love Daddy proclaiming this. Fine, wake up. But to what, and what does one do when one is awake? Such concrete politics seem beyond the purview of Lee's vision and suggest the limitations of his politics.

Moreover, he seems to be primarily concerned with the situation and oppression of blacks and does not explore the oppression of other groups. This could be excused on the grounds that it is useful to have someone undertaking this effort, yet there are limitations, as I have been noting, concerning Lee's exploration of black oppression, which tends to ignore how a system of exploitation oppresses blacks and other people of color and oppressed groups. Indeed, Lee's color fetishism aids a divide and conquer perspective which, in essence, blinds the colonized and prevents solidarity among the oppressed. As Cornell West puts it:

> As long as we simply hide various particularisms . . . there cannot be a radical democratic project. So there must be strategies and tactics that cut across identity politics, cut across region, and gender, race, and class. Class is still around even though it's been unable to constitute an identity that has the saliency and potency of the other identities. And we must attempt to think about how we create and sustain organizations that acknowledge this. Because we're in the bind we're in partly because we've been unable to generate the transgendered, transracial, transsexual orientation of social motion, social momentum, social movement. And if we can't do that, then there will be many, many more David Dukes by the end of the twentieth century, even while we engage in our chatter about identity.
>
> (West 1992a: 23)

Thus, identity politics helps keep oppressed peoples apart and tends to reduce politics to the search for a cultural identity and style. Lee never portrays political movements in any serious fashion. He fetishizes leaders, which, as Adolph Reed puts it:

> also reflects an idea of politics that is antidemocratic and quietistic. Great Leaders don't make movements. Insofar as they aren't just the work of clever publicists, they are in most important respects holograms created by movements. Understanding politics as a story of Great Leaders produces nostalgia and celebration, not mobilization and action.
>
> (Reed 1993: 19)

Although there is a conflict in Lee's work between his affirmation of Malcolm X's modern politics and evocation of a postmodern political pessimism, it seems to me that the central problem with Lee's politics is that he ultimately comes down on the side of a culturalist identity politics, which subordinates politics in general to the creation of personal identity. Identity for Lee is primarily black identity and he constantly operates with a binary opposition between black and white, and "us" and "them." Lee's identity politics, moreover, are primarily culturalist, in which identity is defined by "image" and cultural style. This was clearly the case in *DRT*, where every character's politics were defined in terms of cultural style. None of the various characters were involved in any political organization, movement, or struggle, and Buggin' Out's boycott of Sal's Pizzeria is a pathetic caricature of the real struggles by people of color for rights and survival.

Concrete issues of black politics in *DRT* were reduced to graffiti on walls where one read slogans like "Tawana Told the Truth," "Dump Koch," or "Jesse," referring to Jesse Jackson's 1988 run for the Presidency. Yet here too black politics are sublimated into slogans and images, and Lee's culturalist identity politics never really rise beyond this level. As bell hooks notes, Lee never explores alliance politics and fails to realize that:

> Combatting racism and other forms of domination will require that black people develop solidarity with folks unlike ourselves who share similar political commitments. Racism. . . is not erased when we control the production of goods and services in various black communities, or infuse our art with an Afrocentric perspective. Nostalgia for expressions of black style are less and less accessible to black folks who no longer live in predominantly black communities.
>
> (hooks 1990: 183–4)[29]

hooks also argues (1993) that Malcolm X becomes reduced to an image in Lee's presentation, both, I would add, in *DRT* and *X*. Spike Lee thus ultimately falls victim to a consumerist image culture, in which value, worth, and identity are defined in terms of images and cultural style, in which one's image determines who one is and how one will be received. Film, to be sure, is at its best a feast of images, but critical film interrogates these images, deconstructs those that serve the interests of domination, and develops alternative images, narratives, and aesthetic strategies. Lee, however, does not rise above the repertoire of dominant images already established and reproduces many questionable images of men, women, blacks, and other races.

Although his films show that cinema can address issues of key political importance and generate interesting discussions that may have progressive political effects, so far, his films, whatever their merits, are limited, specifically in their identity politics.

Yet his films do attack at least some of the many forms of sex, race, gender, and class oppression. While they might not ultimately provide models of a "counter-hegemonic cinema" as bell hooks and other black radicals desire, they provide some engaging and provocative cinematic interventions that are far superior to the crass genre spectacles of the Hollywood cinema.

RAP AND BLACK RADICAL DISCOURSE

African-Americans have traditionally used music and musical idiom as a privileged form of resistance to oppression. Gospel emerged as response to the oppression of slavery, while the blues articulated a response to institutional racism, and so both articulated suffering produced by oppression and resistance to it. Ragtime and jazz drew on African-American experiences, seeking a musical idiom to articulate suffering and joy, collective agony and individual expression, domination and resistance. As African-Americans moved from the South to northern industrial cities, they created new forms of music to express their experiences, producing, among other forms, rhythm and blues. Such African-American music and culture was often limited to black enclaves and was primarily disseminated through live performance.

During the 1950s, R. & B. mutated into rock and roll music and black artists like Fats Domino, Chuck Berry, Little Richard, and others entered into mainstream culture. White artists, however, like Pat Boone, quickly began covering and exploiting the African-American songs, though genuine rock culture contemptuously dismissed such "poaching" and most rock fans preferred the black musical artists who entered the mainstream of American culture. It was especially significant that black music made use of media culture to disseminate its meanings, music, and voices. The 1950s was an era of proliferation of radio stations and new recording technologies made available cheap recordings for the booming hi-fi/stereo industry. Tape recorders, car radios, and eventually cassettes helped make music an even more central part of media culture and it was probably professional sports and rock music that did as much as anything to promote civil liberties for blacks, to show whites that blacks were cool, to demonstrate that they were human beings who deserved the full range of civil liberties available.

Much of the black rhythm and blues that migrated into rock and roll was an urban, ghetto product, and African-American culture quickly assimilated music into the texture of urban life. Radios, stereos, walkman radio/cassettes, and ghetto-blasters transmitted the sounds of black culture throughout country, city, and suburb. New musical developments were quickly assimilated into African-American musical idiom. Reggae music provided both new sounds and a new politicization of music. Black rappers in the 1970s, like Gil Scott-Heron and

Grandmaster Flash, developed new forms of political music, articulating the experiences of oppression and struggle in the black urban environments.[30]

In the 1970s and 1980s, black urban hip hop culture developed new forms of music, dancing, and singing, appropriate to African-American experience and culture[31] – urban graffiti, break-dancing, black radio, club scenes with D.J.'s who practiced sampling (i.e. taking popular songs and overlaying them with rapping and electronic sounds), scratching (i.e. moving the needle rapidly over the disk), and punch-phrasing (i.e. deftly shifting from one turn-table to another). Rap thus started as a performance art, in club scenes, or rap parties, but the explosion of rap CD's and music videos made rap and hip hop culture highly visible, producing new forms of identities and experiences. Popularized in films like *Beat Street*, *Breakin'* and *Wild Style*, and played more frequently on BET (Black Entertainment Television) and MTV, rap became increasingly visible and popular – and controversial – as the decade moved on.

RAP is a form of talking or rapping music with the R signifying rhyme and rhythm and the P poetry – and in some cases politics. In the following discussion of this highly controversial form, I want to argue that rap itself is best seen as a cultural forum for urban blacks to articulate their experiences, concerns, and politics. As a cultural forum, rap itself is a contested terrain between different types of rap with competing voices, politics, and styles. It is thus a mistake to generalize concerning rap as the differences between different rappers are extremely significant. Thus, as we shall see, whereas some rap glorifies a gangster lifestyle, drugs, and misogynist attitudes, other rap artists contest these problematical interventions, using rap to articulate quite different values and politics.

Although there were rap artists in the 1970s, it was in the 1980s that it became visible and massively popular. The 1980s was a period of decline in living conditions and expectations for blacks under conservative administrations who shifted wealth from the poor to the rich, cut back on welfare programs, and neglected the concerns of blacks and the poor. During this period, the standard of living and job possibilities for African-Americans declined and living conditions in the inner-city ghettos deteriorated with growing crime, drug use, teen pregnancies, AIDS and sexually transmitted diseases, gangs, and urban violence.

Rap music articulated the experiences and conditions of black Americans living in violent ghetto conditions and became a powerful vehicle for political expression, articulating the rage of African-Americans facing growing oppression and declining opportunities for advancement, in which bare survival became an important issue. The music struck a responsive chord and rap songs and albums went to the top of the charts, leading record companies to produce more and more rap albums. During the 1980s and 1990s, new rap artists like N.W.A. (Niggers With Attitude), Public Enemy, Ice-T, Ice Cube, Sister Souljah, Queen Latifah, and 2 Live Crew won notoriety and fame for their increasingly radical, shocking, and sometimes outrageous rap music.

Rap confronts its listeners with a collage of urban sounds, combining sampling from radio, television, popular records, and other familiar sounds, ratched up to a high decibel level punctuated by the discourse of distinctive, aggressive voices. Voice is very important with distinct lyrics, articulating experiences and often messages. Rap is a mode of talking, not singing, and utilizes often complex, though unorthodox, rhyming schemes. Rap is usually delivered in a fast, staccato style and the often complex patterns of rhyme and rhythm can create tensions between the spontaneity of the performance and the fixity of the lyrics. Rap songs are often long and sometimes convoluted, continuing an African-American tradition of long and complex stories with individual variations and the solo riffs of rag-time, jazz, and the blues. The rapper is often like a minister in the black church, with a message for the audience, which the rapper conveys in distinctive ways, and like the chorus in the black church, rappers often have choral background.

Rap music usually utilizes an electronically produced sound track and the music often has a very rapid beat; Chuck D of Public Enemy noted that his group accelerated the beats per minute in typical rock productions, thus upping the speed. But rap is also dance music and the rappers often call on the audience to dance, to shake and move their arms, sometimes to raise a clenched fist or express defiance, or to in some ways participate in the musical performance. Queen Latifah frequently commands her audiences to "dance for me," and Ice-T explains that the rapper "won't be happy till the dancers are wet" with sweat, "out of control," and "possessed" by the beat and music (cited in Shusterman 1991: 628).

The affectivity of rap, the pleasures it produces and somatic effects, are thus related to the conjunction of the voice, music, spectacle, performance, and participation. Of course, some of these elements are not present in listening to records of rap music, though some of the somatic effects are present in the sound alone. Videos of rap concerts, however, or music videos of the albums or specific songs, help replicate some of the affective pleasures and live performances and in some cases multiply the visual pleasures by quick cuts and edits, and quite striking images. Ice-T's video version of "Original Gangster," for instance, is a visual tour de force with brilliant cinematography and many of Public Enemy's music videos, available in video rental stores but rarely shown on TV, also effectively combine visual montage with the music, generating a complex wealth of cognitive, visual, and somatic effects.

Rap also depends on technological virtuosity, with the DJ, who manipulates the electronic sounds, an important part of the rap crew. Rap therefore combines African-American oral traditions with highly sophisticated technological modes of reproduction. Moreover, rap sounds are often transgressive sounds, breaking the rules of propriety and acceptable discourse. They are often disorderly sounds, with the noise of police cars, helicopters, bullets, glass breaking, and urban uprisings in the soundtrack. Rap sounds are especially disturbing when played on loud "ghetto-blasters" in public spaces, announcing that the enemy is within, that the society is divided and facing explosive conflicts.

There are also frequent references to current events, such as the 1992 Rodney King shootings and the L.A. uprising, mentioned on many rap albums, which often use a collage of sounds of the ghetto, electronically bolstered. Rap develops a lexicon of distinctive language, political references, and iconic sounds, mixing them together and often repeating discourse or sound on other albums, as when Ice T's song "Mind Over Matter" reprises Public Enemy's use of the phrase. There is thus a common social, political, and cultural context to rap music which is highly intertextual (there are also attacks on other rap or black musical artists who abandon rap, or compromise, as I note below).

Rap music is, however, centered on the rapping, sometimes by a single rapper, often overlaid by choruses or repartee with others, and sometimes by entire groups who take the mike one after the other. One of the first things that one notices when listening to contemporary rap is how it is a form of articulating identity and self-assertion in an environment increasingly hostile to African-Americans. The rap artists frequently call attention to themselves and use their music to affirm their own identity. This may border on narcissism and a materialism that brags of its record sales and material possessions, but is also a mode of self-assertion in an environment hostile to any form of African-American self-expression. The rap artists are saying: Hey, we're here! Listen to us and hear what we are telling you!

The frequently collective nature of rap groups, on one hand, decenters individualism for group identity, but often affirms both the individual and group identity, as individual rappers call attention to themselves as distinct voices, but then re-submerge themselves into groups. Like graffiti artists, who took on nicknames, rap artists often utilize a pseudonym, like Chuck D or Snoop Doggie Dogg, to signify either the anonymity of black voices, or the need to take on another persona to express their concerns. The name serves as a mask in the tradition of African culture and signifies, on some occasions, that the rapper is speaking for the group, or community, as well as themselves.

Rap thus gives expression to very specific voices who have been left out of mainstream culture and the rap artists are concerned to tell you who they are, to let you know where they are coming from and what they have on their mind. Public Enemy's music constantly refrains the group's name in the background of the songs, and their group name itself is an expression of their outsider status and rebellion against mainstream culture. It plays on the sense that black youth are perceived as a "public enemy" in the society at large. Their name also signifies that they are emerging into the public sphere, into mainstream culture, as an enemy, as an outsider, as a disruptive force. They also frequently affirm themselves as "Public Enemy Number One," calling attention to themselves as a threat and danger to the mainstream.

Ice-T and Ice Cube adopt the "ice" metaphor, signifying their absolute coolness and hardness. Ice-T constantly evokes his own name, sometimes embellished with the refrain, "Ice, mother-fucking T," describing himself as the "original gangster." Ice Cube describes himself as "America's Most Wanted" and choruses taunt "Fuck you Ice Cube" as he raps his radical lyrics. Queen Latifah is a Queen, she-royalty, and African royalty at that, so show a little respect brothers! Sister Souljah appropriates the term "soul sister," given an African inflection with "Souljah," which also positions her as a "sister soldier," a militant in the cause of black radicalism, and choruses on her songs chant her name as she belts out her aggressive lyrics.

The Sister Souljah effect: during the 1992 Presidential election, candidate Bill Clinton, in an opportunistic and effective gesture, attacked the violence of rap lyrics, in the presence of Jesse Jackson and other blacks, singling out for censure Sister Souljah. The rap singer got her fifteen minutes of media fame and Clinton got a lot of publicity as a candidate not afraid to speak out on crime and violence, and to put blacks in their place – an opportunistic appeal to so-called "Reagan Democrats," telling them, in effect, that he was no panderer to special interests like blacks. For a diagnostic critique, however, it showed that Clinton was precisely an opportunistic panderer to conservative white interests and fears.

Clinton's rating got a quick bump and he went on to win the presidential election. Earlier, President George Bush attacked rap artist Ice-T for his song "Cop Killer." Bush followed the police and right-wing groups in making highly publicized attacks on rap music, thus both presidential candidates chose to attack rap. Meanwhile, rap became more aggressive and more controversial, articulating the correct perception by blacks that they were going to continue to be left out of the action, that the new Democratic Party administration would be no more sympathetic to their concerns than the Republican administrations of Bush and Reagan. The result was an increase in violence and provocation in rap music and continual violence in the increasingly explosive ghettos.

Indeed, the use of obscenity, terms like "nigger," and other shock techniques used by rappers are both a mode of self-expression and articulative of the actual language and violence of urban ghetto culture. Use of the term "nigger" to describe themselves and their group is an attempt to take a term of racist insult and to transform it into a badge of racial pride. Use of the terms "bitches" and "ho's," used to describe women in a derogatory fashion, replicate the sexism in the black community and the high level of tension in relations between the sexes. By 1993, male rappers were vociferously attacked by women in their community and elsewhere for use of such sexist terminology. Queen Latifah, for instance, in her 1993/4 hit music video and song "U.N.I.T.Y." calls for unity and derisively says: "Who you calling a bitch?!" A chorus tells the black woman audience, "You ain't a bitch and a 'ho'" and: "You gotta let 'em know." The video portrays street harassment of women and shows how to "dis" such foul behavior.

Indeed, 2 Live Crew and some other rap groups are consistently derogatory toward women, portraying them as good only for sex and otherwise as useless, nagging, dumb "bitches."[32] This sexism has caused quite a stir in the black community and has promoted much discussion that probably helps clarify relations between the sexes. Thus, for a diagnostic critique, the sexist songs themselves are an index of the deep hostility between the sexes and the need for restructuring relations between men and women.[33] This is not to excuse the sexism of the lyrics, but to combine critique with diagnosis, attempting to discern what such attitudes tell us about contemporary social realities and what needs to be done to address the problem.[34]

The use of terms like "nigger" and the frequent obscenity are indexes of the violent and conflicted relations between African-American men and women, blacks and whites, and other societal forces within the tense and deteriorating ghettoes of fortress America. Ghetto life *is* violent and rappers insist that their music and language simply articulates experience of the ghettoes, unembellished and "in your face." There is indeed often a sense of place central to rap music, with Ice-T and Ice Cube, for instance, locating South Central Los Angeles as the site of their musical expressions. Rap music videos often take place in urban ghetto environments with some ventures out into the more familiar iconic public spaces of places like Los Angeles or New York.

Chuck D of Public Enemy described rap as the CNN of the African-American community, as its source of news concerning what's coming down in the community, what people are feeling and thinking, and what's on the horizon. Indeed, the albums of Public Enemy, Ice-T, Ice Cube, and other rapper groups anticipated in an eery fashion the actual L.A. uprisings in May 1992, when the L.A. police who beat Rodney King were found not guilty by a suburban California jury (despite a videotape of the beating that showed in graphic detail the excessive violence used to "restrain" King).[35] There are constant references, usually highly derogatory, to U.S. political figures, like George Bush or Bill Clinton, or to officials like former Los Angeles police chief Darryl Gates.

Thus rap articulates a very distinct sense of place and time. Rappers often state both where they are rapping from and the date in their albums ("Ice-T, 1991, mother fucker, you should have killed me last year"). They are frequently asking the question "What time is it?" and answering: Time to Wake Up! Spike Lee, as I noted, constantly used the phrase Wake up!, almost as an emblematic motto to his films. Yet, it was not clear from his films what one what supposed to wake up and do. Rap clues you in. Rap tells it like it is and gives some good hints about What is to Be Done. Rap tells you that it is the time of conflicts between races, sexes, and classes. It is the time of the fire, the fire this time and once again, the time of urban violence and explosion. It is the time of buck-wilding, of wild sexuality, of STDs, HIV, and AIDS, of drugs, of crime, of gangs. It is a violent time, a time that will take many victims, especially young black males.

It is also a time to do something, a time to get educated as to what is happening, time to think and act for oneself. "Don't believe the hype!" Public Enemy shouts and rap music systematically attacks media culture, while contributing to the development of an alternative culture. Indeed, in a way rap music incarnates what Herbert Marcuse (1964) described as "the great refusal," refusing to submit to domination and oppression. Rap songs frequently invoke groups that *are* doing something, as well as the black radical heroes and traditions of the recent past. Public Enemy and other rap groups frequently refer to Malcolm X, the Black Panthers, R. Rap Brown, and others in the black radical tradition and themselves articulate its radical critiques of racial oppression and refusal to submit to domination. Public Enemy performs in quasi-military regalia and, following the Black Panthers, have their "Ministers" of information, education, and defense, as well as their "assault technician" to produce the electronic sounds, using military and revolutionary metaphors to describe themselves.

It's also the time of the apocalypse for black people, time that they'd better do something, or pay the price. Sister Souljah sings of "The Final Solution, Slavery's Back in Effect," telling how the President just announced that he, Vice-President Duke, and the Congress have just declared slavery back into effect because black people have not advanced technologically, their education testing scores are in decline, they are on welfare and having too many children, and so on. In her apocalyptic vision, the fascist government has ordered all blacks to report to designated camps. Ice Cube describes himself as "Amerikkka's Most Wanted," using the fascist code "Amerika" to describe the United States, punctuated by a triple "K", signifying the Ku Klux Klan, and he and other rappers frequently evokes pictures of a present and future fascist America.

Other rappers also project an apocalyptic future where violence is directed against blacks. Indeed, for many rappers, the apocalypse is now. Many blacks believe that HIV and AIDS is a government conspiracy to kill blacks, that drugs are encouraged and allowed by the government to destroy the black community and black youth, and that the power structure has no more use for black labor in a technological society and wants to exterminate them. And they are also aware that blacks are killing themselves in record numbers and that the violence threatens the very existence of the black community. The question then is: What can be done?

In such an apocalyptic situation, only radical solutions and politics have any meaning. Whereas Spike Lee is a voice of black nationalism, identity politics, and self-pride, much rap music is an articulation of the voice of black radicalism. As noted, there are frequent references to icons of the black revolutionary tradition and the use of the radical political discourse of the 1960s. Yet there is also a strong component of black nationalism and identity politics in rap music, which links rap to Spike Lee.[36] Indeed, there are frequent positive references to Lee in rap music. Public Enemy's "Burn Hollywood Burn!" (illustrated in a powerful music video) praises the films of Spike Lee in opposition to Hollywood stereotypical treatment, or neglect, of blacks. Lee, of course, featured Public Enemy's "Fight the Power" in *Do the Right Thing*. Ice Cube in turn used the Italian's litany of racial epithets from *DRT* in one of his songs to remind blacks what whites really think of them. And Ice-T includes images of Spike Lee in his music video version of "Original Gangster."

Both rap and Spike Lee thus tend to a form of identity politics, though there is some debate over the parameters of identity. Ice-T, for instance, has a song where he equates all people of color and oppressed people with "niggers," identifying Mexicans, Koreans, and other people of color with those oppressed by a white racist society. Ice Cube and other rappers, however, sometimes have derogatory references to Korean-Americans and other racial minorities in their songs, restricting the proud badge of "nigger" to black African-Americans as the privileged group of identity. And X-Klan and other rap groups advocate an Afrocentric black nationalism that privileges visions of a black nation.

Indeed, much rap music affirms the strands of radical black politics, ranging from Malcolm X to the Black Panthers to Louis Farrakan and Elijah Muhammad.[37] Public Enemy and other rappers often sample Malcolm X speeches and reference other black radical groups and figures. Ice-T sings openly of black revolution and while he sometimes celebrates the joys of consumer materialism (i.e. his house, car, possessions, etc.), he also frequently attacks capitalism as an economic system, whereas Spike Lee, as I have argued, tends to support a form of consumer capitalism where blacks have their piece of the action. Moreover, Chuck D of Public Enemy sees the system as a structure of oppression and many rappers call for the end of oppression and advocate radical political change.

Some rap music openly calls for violent revolution, while Lee advocates at most liberal reform. Public Enemy's music video flashes images of black oppression and struggle and then flashes the message, "Where are the revolutionaries? Shut it down!" Yet there is another strand in rap that stresses the urgency of mere survival, as when Grandmaster Flash states in his 1982 hit "The Message":

> Don't push me cuz, I'm close to the edge,
> I'm trying not to lose my head.
> It's like a jungle sometimes, it makes me wonder
> how I keep from going under. . .
> broken glass everywhere,
> people pissing on the stair,
> you know they just don't care.
> I can't take the smell, I can't take the noise.
> Got no money to move out,
> I guess I got no choice

Throughout the past years, there have been heated debates within the black community and mainstream media culture concerning the alleged celebration of gangs, violence, and drugs by rappers. Indeed, there are examples of such celebration, or naturalization, throughout rap music, but the major artists usually have a more nuanced position. As early as 1987, rap groups organized in a "Stop the Violence Movement," which produced a collective statement, song and video titled "Self-Destruction" (George 1988). Public Enemy, Ice-T, and other groups have been sharply critical of drug use as a poison to enslave and destroy black people. When they and other groups adopt "gangsta" and gang metaphors, they are often referring metaphorically to their own group, to their "crew." As noted, there is a strong component of group identification within rap, wherein one finds their own identity within broader communities. Although such celebration of group ethos and adoption of gang metaphors can support the existence of street gangs, it also promotes more benign forms of community that serve as a positive pendent to the narcissistic individualism endemic in contemporary U.S. society.

Indeed, there is a strongly moralistic and didactic streak in many rap groups. A close listening to Ice-T's *Original Gangster* notes moralistic condemnation of those who devote themselves to a life of crime and drugs, as well as to those blacks who sell out and distance themselves from their own people. A song titled "Ed" describes the life of a homeboy who drank a lot, did drugs, gambled, and blew all his money on women.

> One night he got drunk
> And started drivin real fast . . .
>
> . . .
> . . . Ed's dead

Ice-T's "Midnight" tells of the all-night adventures with violence and police of a gangsta crew and although the rapper character got home safely, he went off to sleep and at six in the morning the police broke through his door – riffing off the message that the gangsta life don't pay. "House" describes parents in a home down the street who drink and abuse their child and Ice-T tells the neighbors that they should "act like they give a damn!" and "Do something, call a cop." Ice-T's "Escape From the Killing Fields" provides a harrowing picture of violent ghetto life, punctuated with the chorus: "Ya gotta get out! Ya gotta get out!" His "Body Count" describes the violence of ghetto life and desperately calls out for the need to address the problems and find solutions.

Although Ice-T presents a macho, sometimes violent persona, he also constantly attacks drug use and indicates the consequences of violence, so it is simply wrong to claim that all rap celebrates such things, when some of the more popular rapsters clearly do not. And in "Keep your head up," 2 Pac tells his brothers to treat their women with more respect and that men who knock up women and then abandon them are "not real men." Ice Cube warns of the dangers of sexually transmitted diseases, as does Sister Souljah and other female rappers. Moreover, Sister Souljah, stupidly condemned by Bill Clinton, passionately tells her people to quit engaging in destructive and amoral behavior. In a song "Nigga's Gotta," she raps:

> Nigga's keep dying, mother keep crying
> I ask why
> Why we don't open our eyes 'cause
> Nigga's keep killing, illin' and thrilling
> No time, nigga's still chillin'
>
> Nigga's still drinking, boozing and stinking
> St Ides[38] big banking and nigga's not thinking
> Nigga's still smoking, gagging and choking
> Counting pennies and broke
> And still nigga's joking
>
> Nigga's still fucking, humping and sucking
> Family gone broken, father out buggin'
> Ask a nigga something he replies nothing
> Grabs his balls and keeps walking
>
> Nigga's grow bolder, wild with no order

Time grows shorter, father raped the daughter
Father up and left her, though he shouldn've kept her
Reverend should've blessed her, instead he tripped and slept her
Nigga's sink deeper

Nigga's still sittin', eating and shittin'
Roots cut off, forgotten and forgetting
Wanting for plenty ain't got any, needing for many
I wonder when we gonna get up, get serious
Nigga's got to do better

Niagga's too lazy, confused and crazy
Having more babies, no answers for the maybes
Gave up too easy, minds too weak, see . . .
Nigga's gotta do better.[39]

All the motifs that we have so far discussed are fully evident in Ice Cube's *Death Certificate* (1991). The text is a highly complex modernist collage of contemporary sounds and voices, condemning the society that offers blacks a quick death certificate with their birth certificates. The album opens by evoking a "state of emergency" and Ice Cube says that the "Death Side" presents a "mirrored image of where we are today" while the "Life Side" presents "a vision of where we need to go so sign your death certificate" – implying that black revolution will eliminate the supremacy of the white race. The inside cover liner says that "the best place for a young black male or female is the Nation of Islam" and a picture shows Ice Cube reading the *Nation* newspaper with a headline "Unite or Perish," while neatly dressed black youth and uniformed men from the Nation stand in the background.

The Death Side opens with a musical collage of a funeral of a young black and quickly cuts to a defiant Ice Cube warning not to go after him because he's "the wrong nigga to fuck wit." The opening stanzas of the song warn against "fucking" with him and threaten anyone who tries in violent terms, sprinkled with obscenities. He then brags up his rap crew as number 1 in the area, a typical self-aggrandizing move of rappers, rooting his music in South Central L.A., and noting that: "In '91, Ice Cube grew stronger and bigga." The last stanza announces that it is "payback" time and the lyrics threaten L.A. police chief Darryl Gates, warning him that if he comes up against Ice Cube, he'll be "goin' up against a Zulu." Deploying the macho bravado typical of certain strands of rap, Ice Cube warns Gates that he'll: "Break his spine like jellyfish" and "Kick his ass til I'm smellin' shit," concluding "Mess with Ice Cube ya get punked quick–pig!"

The macho bravado and violence is only comprehensible in the context of the tense conditions between L.A. blacks and the police, in which former police chief Darryl Gates has become a symbol of white racism and violence against blacks. Ice Cube is warning that there will be a payback and articulates black rage against the L.A. police. In another song, a cop bellows out that "We're gonna treat you like a king," and Ice Cube replies: "What goddamn king?" The policeman answers:

"Rodney King! Martin Luther King! And all the other goddam kings from Africa!" and then shoots him. The references to "King" refer both to the white violence against black leaders and ordinary blacks, but also to white violence against blacks in Africa, including kings, and transcodes the popular black nationalist discourse that blacks were once a nation of kings and princes.

The album is highly moralistic, as well as politically radical, telling blacks to give "up the nappy" and constantly attacking black "sellouts" and "Toms." A song "Look Who's Burning" warns about venereal disease and there are admonitions for safe sex throughout the album. While earlier Ice Cube refused to malign drug use, he now, perhaps following the line of the Nation of Islam, also attacks drug use in the community and warns blacks that their very survival is at stake.

Several other songs on the Death Side describe the death of young blacks and many express black rage at oppressive ghetto conditions. The Life Side opens with sounds of a birth and cuts to "I Wanna Kill Sam," where Ice Cube commences with an angry threat to kill Sam "cause the shit he did was uncalled for." In the second stanza, he describes the rape of a black mother and then capture and incarceration in a place where they were forced to "work all day" – presumably slave plantations, though the stanza could describe blacks thrown in prisons and work camps today. The result was the breaking up of black families and breaking down of black willpower, until blacks surrendered and prayed to the white God for mercy and relief.

Cutting to the present, Ice Cube complains that today the U.S. government wants to tax him, execute unruly blacks, spread drugs and HIV, and make people of color fight their wars. The song concludes with the phrase that Ice Cube wants to kill Sam "cause he ain't my muthafuckin' uncle," suggesting that blacks are aliens in the United States. In this song, Ice Cube's rage overflows, his words fly out like bullets, and his bitterness and anger are obvious in every line.

Turning more mellow and cautionary to black youth in "Doing Dumb Shit," Ice Cube tells of how as a fourth grader he pulled girl's hair, taunted the school bully, played the class clown, made dumb jokes, shot his b-b gun, knocked on people's doors and ran away, played hide and go get it, "til I got my ass whopped when I was ten years old, doing dumb shit." As a young teenager, he fell in love, started having sex, put rubbers on the wrong way, and woke up one morning with a bad case of the clap cause he was "doing dumb shit." As an older teenager, he got a VW, did drag racing, hung with the OGs (original gangsters) and got some street knowledge, and got in trouble "doing dumb shit" – but he survived.

Today, when seeing young black males doing the same dumb shit, going through the same stage of growing up – but dying young, Ice Cube is outraged at the culture that is killing them, but at the same time he warns his young audience that today "doing dumb shit" can get you killed and that its time they started wise up. The song ends with the refrain "dumb, dumb, dumb" and its corollary is that young blacks should get smart and stop engaging in dumb things like gangs, drugs, crime, and the violence that is killing off young black males at an alarming rate.[40]

In "Us," Ice Cube opens with a young black boy's fantasy of wealth and consumer goods and cuts to condemnation of blacks who refuse to invest in their communities. Ice Cube reiterates the messages that "there is no one to blame but us," concluding with the warning that "nobody gives a fuck about. . ." (cutting off sharply before saying "us"). Thus his message is that of black unity, self-sufficiency, and independence, not relying on any white benevolence or government handouts. This nitty-gritty street realism pervades rap and at least one wing moralistically condemns all the practices that keep blacks divided, oppressed, addicted, and subordinate.

Moreover, there is a positive emphasis on the need to work for change within the community. A radio voice-over indicates that Ice Cube himself has stayed in his community, invests in it, and tries to work for change. Indeed, in "Vaseline" he bitterly attacks members of his former group N.W.A. for leaving the community, hanging with whites, and selling out on their black radicalism (less palatable is his homophobic attack on their Jewish manager, indicating that "Easy E turned faggot" and that his former crew are now "getting fucked with no vaseline").

Ice Cube's bitter and violent attacks on his former crew and black sellouts indicate the deep divisions within the rap community and the tremendous differences between the groups. Indeed, there is a big distinction between rappers and those who engage in rock, soul, or mainstream popular music. There is also a difference between those ghettocentric groups who call for reform or revolution within their communities, and Afrocentric groups who call for a separate African nation. There are different levels of radicalism in rap, often delineated by live performances which tend to be most raw and extreme, to albums, sometimes not played on the radio because of their radicalism, to rock videos that tend to be the most benign because of television censorship.[41]

There are also many other differences between the various groups in terms of style, political ideology, and personalities. But the competition between groups also points to the habit and game of "dissing" (i.e. disrespecting) one's opponents, which builds on Jamaican and other African-American games and traditions, and which is also perhaps a function of heavy competition between the groups. There is also a drive among the various groups to be the best, though rappers often refer to each other positively as well, with Ice-T devoting a whole song to references to other rappers and groups who were "Players." In early 1994, several of the most popular rap songs played on BET (Black Entertainment Television) refer back to Public Enemy, which has become an icon of political rap.

Indeed, there is now a coherent tradition of rap with its icons, hierarchies, typologies, legends, and villains. Rap has a private language and slang with its homies or homeboys (pals from the neighborhood), crews and posses (i.e. the rap team), technical music lingo, expressions like "dope" and "fly" (which are positive), and often ritual obscenity and insider pejoratives. Terms like "gangs" often function metaphorically to describe the crew of the rap group and terms like "bad" signify "cool," or "good," thus reversing its ordinary connotations. Such a complex linguistic form requires learning a language and interpreting the many layers of meaning and signification.

In a sense, it is surprising how long the form has maintained its popularity, surviving as highly popular for at least fifteen years. Although rap music emerged in the 1970s, it did not hit the charts and public notice until the late 1970s and exploded into popularity in the 1980s. It seems to be even more popular in the 1990s, obviously articulating experiences of alienation and rage among large segments of youth and urban blacks. It has also become increasingly controversial in the past years, as I shall indicate in the next section, after indicating the sense it which it can and should not be described as "postmodern."

Houston Baker is constantly describing rap as "postmodern" by virtue of its "nonauthoritative collaging or archiving of sound and styles that bespeaks a deconstructive hybridity. Linearity and progress yield to a dizzying synchronicity" (Baker 1993b: 89). Rap does assemble a collage of contemporary sounds and pastiches previous forms in its sampling. But the sampling is sometimes deconstructive (as when a lyrical pop song is sampled in a violent context that undermines its ethos), though sampling can also be positive, as in the frequent homages to James Brown and other classics of R. & B., or to Public Enemy by current young rappers, as well as the sampling of Malcolm X. In any case, whether the sampling is positive or negative, it tends to recontextualize rap in new configurations of signification and thus against one-dimensional postmodernist texts that "stop making sense," that resist meaning and interpretation, rap music is often a meaning machine that demands interpretation, that multiplies meaning, signification, and political messages.

In the sense that I am using "postmodernism" (roughly that of Jameson 1991), rap is arguably modernist. Rap is a highly expressive form and rappers have distinct voices, styles, and messages, often related to modern politics. In opposition to fragmentary, disconnected, flat, and one-dimensional postmodern texts, which only refer to themselves or lack depth of meaning, the collaging of most rap music often adds up to a political statement, rather than fragments of nonsense or minimalist meaning. Rap often identifies with specific politics like 1960s black radicalism or Afrocentrism, rather than the evacuation of politics, as in some postmodern texts.[42]

The rap albums of a Public Enemy, Ice-T, Ice Cube, or Sister Souljah add up to an often coherent statement and, as noted, the music is often highly intertextual, producing a collectivity and distinctive codes of rapping, rather than extreme postmodern fragmentation. In fact, rappers like Ice Cube and Ice-T often follow rather conventional linear story or narrative lines in their rapping, which often have a narrative closure (though Public Enemy often operates with more complex forms).

Yet, there are also arguably postmodern features to rap, such as the recyling appropriation and sampling of previous forms,

the eclectic mixing of styles, the enthusiastic embracing of the new technology and mass culture, the challenging of modernist notions of aesthetic autonomy and artistic purity, and an emphasis on the localized and temporal rather than the putatively universal and eternal.

(Shusterman 1991: 614)

Schusterman demonstrates the presence of these features of postmodern aesthetics in rap and my only difference with him is that he begins his definition of rap, claiming that it is characterized by a "recycling appropriation rather than unique originative creation" (ibid.: 614).

By contrast, I have been arguing that rap music is often highly original, is expressive of a distinctive and strong voice, often has distinct messages and coherent narrative structures, proliferates meanings, requires an active audience, and in these senses shares key features of modernism. I would thus conclude that rap is between the modern and postmodern and draws upon both modernist and postmodernist aesthetic strategies. Description of these aesthetic categories is, of course, contested, but I would argue that rap is not a primarily postmodernist form, or, rather, is not fundamentally defined by its use in some rap artists of postmodern aesthetic strategies.

Rap is, to be sure, a hybrid form, combining African-American traditions with contemporary style, mixing the human voice and technology, found sounds and media snippets, music and discordant noise. But collage and hybridity are themselves features of modernist movements like cubism, surrealism, dada, and futurism. But most importantly, rather than deconstructing identity à la postmodernism, rap music is about creating identities. The rappers themselves establish their identities through their music and their audiences identify with oppositional culture and the critical attitudes and postures of rap, thus producing oppositional identities. Indeed, rappers are Gramsci's "organic intellectuals," who articulate the experiences of oppression of their community and focus attention on the causes and possible solutions for solving the problems articulated in the music. This brings us to the hotly debated issue of the effects of rap and the question of constituting counterhegemonic, alternative communities and cultural forms in the present moment.

RESISTANCE, COUNTERHEGEMONY, AND EVERYDAY LIFE

Thus rap music constitutes a culture of resistance against white supremacy and oppression. Resistance by African-Americans not only takes the form of musical and cultural expression, but also takes multiple forms of resistance in everyday life through language, style, attitude, and social relations. African-American expression through cultural artifacts is evident in the forms of media culture studied in this chapter, but also finds articulation in more avant-garde forms of culture. Within film, for instance, Marlon Riggs' *Tongues Untied* (1989) articulates the experience of black gay males, their oppression in the hands of mainstream culture, and Riggs' contradictory attitudes toward whites and whiteness. Julie Dash's *Daughters of the Dust* (1991) captures black history and women's experience from the point of view of a young black women visiting an island off the coast of Georgia that was once a refuge for runaway slaves, which forces her to rethink her position in U.S. society. The film also interrogates the tensions between tradition and modernity in the African-American experience.

The curious thing about black rap music is that precisely the more radical products seem to be the big sellers, though it is estimated that white male teens buy over half of the product. Music is less capital-intensive than film and has a high rate of return that makes it possible to quickly produce and sell its product. Film and more capital intensive forms of culture make it difficult for blacks to gain entry, though, as noted, the success of the films of Spike Lee helped make it possible for a number of young black film-makers to intervene in media culture.

This brings us to the issue of how rap music can be coopted into a consumer culture. As noted, the mega-best sellers of rap are often consumed by young middle-class whites and it is not clear what effects rap has on these groups. During 1994, MTV advertised a rap-oriented journal called "Vibe," and the advertisement appeared to transform rap into a consumer fetish for buppies, yuppies, and young consumers. And the type of rap played on MTV, BET, and other television networks is usually the more watered-down pop version of rap.

Thus, rap can thus easily become a commodity fetish and mode of assimilation. Rap has also been assimilated to advertising with shoes, cars, and even food storage ads (the Reynolds [w]rap campaign), have used rap techniques. Yet all popular commodities have a double-edged, or even multiple, effects. The commodity rap can circulate oppositional thought and action, and can empower people to struggle against the system of oppression. And it can function merely as titillation and entertainment and be coopted for conservative ends.

Moreover, the rap evocation of history and politics might have contradictory effects. On one hand, it is salutory that rap returns to the black radical tradition and deploys images of Malcolm X, the Black Panthers, Martin Luther King, and black political heroes in their lyrics and videos. And yet such appropriation also has the effect of transforming complex historical persons and positions into images, into easily consumed icons of radicalism that lack real political substance. The politics of rap can thus contribute to reducing politics to slogans and clichés, thus aiding in the evacuation of politics of the genuine sufferings and struggles of people. Such reduction of politics to image and cliché also aids the transformation of contemporary politics into a battle of images and a form of media sound-biting.

But it is a mistake both to dismiss all media culture because it is circulates in the commodity form and can be easily coopted into consumer culture, just as it is a mistake to believe that all so called "popular culture" empowers people by producing meanings, pleasures, and identities that somehow enable people to control their lives and to resist domination. In particular, it is important to see that even an overtly oppositional form like rap can be easily coopted, but can also radicalize and provoke oppositional behavior. Difference sells, but the difference can provoke effects different than mainstream culture, such as the production of oppositional identities and practices.

Indeed, during the past few years there has been furious debate about the effects of rap. When N.W.A. released their song "Fuck the Police" in the late 1980s, the FBI wrote threatening letters to their record label and the issue was widely discussed in the media. In 1990, there was a veritable assault on rap in the media with Tipper

Gore writing a widely circulated and syndicated piece attacking Ice-T and other rappers (*Washington Post*, January 8, 1990).[43] The *Los Angeles Times* published a long article highly critical of rap (February 11, 1990), as did many other daily newspapers. *Newsweek* published a long assault on rap's "attitude" (March 19, 1990) and *U.S. News and World Report* (March 19, 1990) also published an attack on rock and rap. The rap effect: the more records rap artists sold, the more worried parents became, the more the media attacked its excesses, and the more crimes and violence were pinned on rap.

In 1992 Ice-T formed a group "Body Count" which released an album with the title song "Cop Killer." As noted, President George Bush attacked Ice-T, FBI officials wrote to Warner Brothers to indicate that they did not appreciate the song, as did many police officials and citizens, possibly mobilized by conservative groups. Ice-T first agreed to take the song off of the album, though he replaced it with a powerful rap in favor of freedom of speech. He then, for reasons not fully specified, left Warner Brothers, probably because of pressure to further censor his outspoken radical views. The issues were played out in the mainstream press which continued the heated debate over the effects of rap, with efforts to censor it and ban it intensifying.

Since then the rap effect has continued to produce a wealth of claims that specific acts of violence and crime were caused by rap music and there have been many calls to ban and censor it. By 1993, many in the black community were attacking rap and some black radio stations agreed not to play so-called "gangsta rap," which allegedly promoted sex, drugs, obscenity, and violence. The same year, rappers like Flavor Flav of Public Enemy and Tone Loc and Snoop Doggie Dogg were arrested on crime charges. And so by 1994, rap was a music form under siege – though it continued to sell well and be highly popular, perhaps in part because of the furious controversy.

The assault on rap is perhaps unprecedented in media history. Probably never before has a cultural form been under such heavy assault. During the last months of 1993 and early 1994, literally hundreds of articles appeared each month on the topics of rap and violence and night after night attacks on rap appeared on television – enough material for a separate book on the topic. The hysteria is surely a sign of public panic concerning the rise in crime and a scapegoating of rap as a cause of the rising violence and public disorder. It is also symptomatic of the negative attack on young black men in contemporary U.S. society, surely the most stigmatized group of the present moment.

There is no doubt but that rap has powerful effects, but they are complex and many-sided. One also needs to see the diversity of views and positions within the rap community with some groups and individuals openly promoting crime, drugs, misogynony, anti-Semitism, and glorifying the gangsta lifestyle, while other groups are more critical of these tendencies and advocate black independence, education and self-help, unity, and the search for genuine political solutions to the problems of blacks in the U.S.A. today.

In fact, rap is often scapegoated for the real problems of a highly divided society in which conflicts between classes, races, and the sexes are highly explosive. It is perverse to blame these divisions on rap, which simply calls attention to them. Read diagnostically, therefore, the most extreme and offensive elements of rap are symptomatic of real problems that need to be addressed and just banning rap is not going to address these problems. Most of the best rap groups are aware of the powerful effects of their form and some have tried to use rap music constructively, although there are obvious offensive expressions that should be criticized, analyzed, and debated.

But it is ridiculous to spend excessive energy attacking the fantasies of violence of an Ice Cube when real violence is being exerted against the members of his community. This is the real problem and scapegoating a rap singer for the problems is demagogic and futile. The cultural expressions will remain until the problems are addressed. Until then, one should expect violent and offensive expression from rappers who are articulating experiences of a violent and offensive society.

A diagnostic critique is thus interested in what rap means, what it is a symptom of, and what it tells us about contemporary U.S. society. Rap is a curious cultural form in that some of the more oppositional and radical tendencies have entered the mainstream, or at least the best-selling charts, and seem to be most popular. The rap effect: the more outrageous, the more widely discussed and consumed. The TV channels and many radio stations, to be sure, do not play the most radical examples of rap, but its underground popularity, the way rap music circulates and is disseminated through oppositional communities, makes it an efficacious counterhegmonic form.

Otherwise, one must often leave the mainstream to seek out the more radical and distinctive black voices. Many African-American writers and poets are not able to be published by the mainstream press and are forced to go to alternative presses. Audre Lorde in *Sister Outsider* (1984) tells of the difficulties of a black lesbian feminist getting published in the mainstream and many black writers have had to turn to alternative presses and publications. Indeed, there is quite a range of African-American publications both inside the black mainstream and outside it which cater to more marginal groups.

But not every African-American can make rap albums, films, or write books, and so therefore ordinary black people express their defiance of the white racist system in a variety of forms. Black slang and lingo provide a private language of communication and a linguistic and gestural repertoire to articulate black identity and rebellion. Black dance and modes of traversing space position black bodies in their uniqueness, as they defiantly traverse hostile space in a fashion that articulates their identities and forms of rebellion. Playing music loudly from a ghetto-blaster, or driving through urban spaces with a car radio playing rap, are other forms of black everyday cultural expression – indeed, such acts formed a key element of the plot of *Do The Right Thing* and one of the most distinctive features of Spike Lee's films is the way he is able to catch black speech patterns, humor, bodily movement, cultural style, and modes of expression and relation.

There are thus many forms of oppositional cultural expression that resist the codes, practices, and ideologies of mainstream culture. These forms are sometimes evident in the mainstream, but are found more frequently within alternative cultures and everyday lives. Such a terrain provides a goldmine for cultural studies, that is only beginning to be tapped, and that will provide important work and perspectives for cultural studies in the future. For these reasons, a critical multiculturalist agenda is an important part of educational reform and should be part of the politics of cultural studies. Our culture is deeply enriched by the contributions of groups and individuals hitherto marginal and we can only benefit from a greater diversity of voices and experiences. Cultural studies should thus listen to these voices and experiences and to bring them into its purview.

And so: what time was it in early 1991? As Ice-T completed the cutting of his album "Original Gangster," bombs were about to be dropped on Baghdad. Ice-T ends his album with sympathy for the victims of the upcoming war and for blacks taken from their communities to a fight in the deserts of the Middle East that didn't really concern them. In the next chapter, I will analyze this moment, using the resources of cultural studies to dissect the Gulf War as a media event.

In the current moment, advertising, television, films, and popular music are producing new forms of identity. It is thus obviously time to get hip to these. The future is arriving before our eyes, bringing dramatic technological change and resultant anxieties and problems. It is time, therefore, for cultural studies to address these concerns. Consequently, my studies will continue to pay attention to a multiculturalist agenda and will analyze class, race, gender, and other components of a media culture studies, paying attention to omissions and exclusions, as well as representations and discourses, in key artifacts of contemporary media culture.

In the next chapter, however, I want to enlarge the focus of a multiperspectival cultural studies to focus more intently on the production and political economy of culture, as well as analysis of text and audience, making explicit an emphasis that has so far only been implicit. The succeeding studies will illustrate such a model and will continue to probe the ways that media culture provides material for identities, transcodes existing political discourses, and forms the cultural matrix in which we live, suffer, and die.

NOTES

1   My understanding of African-American culture is deeply indebted to the works of Michael Dyson (1993a), Ed Guerrero (1993a and 1993b), bell hooks (1984, 1990, 1992), Mark Reid (1993), and Cornell West (1992a and 1992b), and to discussions with Guerrero, Reid, West, and my colleague at the University of Texas, Harvey Cormier.

2   The liberation of oppressed groups can only take place through their own struggles and in alliance with others struggling against common forces of oppression. It is from this perspective, then, that I am carrying through these studies, as a mark of solidarity and in alliance in struggle against common forms of class, race, and gender oppression. As a member of a relatively privileged social group, however, I have strongly relied in this section on the positions articulated in the writings noted in the previous note and thus consider this study as a dialogue with my African-American brothers and sisters and those interested in their voices and struggles.

3 There has been much debate concerning what terminology to use to describe black
people of African-American descent in the U.S. Following what seems to be the current
convention, I use the term "blacks" and "African-Americans" interchangeably, though
some prefer "Afro-American" and some prefer to leave out the hyphen, which to me
usefully signifies the cultural duality and tensions in the experiences of blacks in the
U.S. who have both an African origin and U.S. roots and experience.

4 Guerrero also claims that in times of a general slump, Hollywood invests in low-budget
black films to up the profit-margin, whereas it ignores African-American films when
profits are high and the industry has "no need to continue a specifically black-focused
product line" (Guerrero 1993b: 165).

5 Lee's *She's Gotta Have It* cost only $175,000 and pulled in over $8.5 million; *School
Daze* was budgeted at $5.8 million and took in over $15 million; *Do the Right Thing*
was budgeted at $6.5 million and grossed over $25 million (Patterson 1992: 55, 92, 121).
Many of Lee's films have also been profitable in the video-cassette market. Evidently,
the money made on these films persuaded the Hollywood money establishment that Lee
and other young black directors were marketable and funded a renaissance of black film
in the early 1990s (see Guerrero 1993b: 157ff. and Patterson 1992: 223f.). Reid,
however, notes that Lee's own films draw on earlier black cinema: "Lee's film journals
never recognize his debt to other black filmmakers, yet he borrows from their cinematic
portrayals of urban black life and their use of contemporary black music" (Reid 1993:
107).

6 The following study was first presented in a symposium on *Malcolm X* organized by
Mark Reid at the Society for Cinema Studies, April 17, 1993, and was then presented
in a workshop on contemporary film at the American Sociology Association in August
1993.

7 I do not know whether Brecht specifically influenced Lee, or if Lee (re)invented
something like a Brechtian cinema out of his own experiences and resources. I have not
yet found any specific references to Brecht in the book publications that Lee regularly
produces on his films, and have found only one mention of a possible Brecht/Lee
connection in the growing literature on the black director. Paul Gilroy, in a critique of
Lee in *The Washington Post* (November 17, 1991), notes that like "Brecht who has
influenced him so much," Lee's "loudly declared political commitments only end up
trivializing the political reality at stake in his work and thereby diminishing its construc-
tive political effect." But other than this (contestable) statement, Gilroy and other critics
have not yet explored Lee's appropriation of Brecht's aesthetic strategies. For a fuller
presentation of Brecht's aesthetics and politics, see Kellner 1981.

8 See Barthes (1975) on "the writerly" modernist text that requires an active reader.

9 Jameson (1990 and 1991) stresses the role of individual vision and style in modernism,
while Bürger (1984 [1974]) analyzes the "historical avant garde" that attempts to change
art and life, as opposed to more formalistically oriented modernist art.

10 This reading was suggested in conversation by Zygmunt Bauman after a series on
postmodern film at the summer 1992 10th anniversary conference of *Theory, Culture,
and Society*. In addition, Lee's *DRT* is read as a "postmodern" film in a somewhat
indeterminate sense in Denzin 1991: 125ff; likewise, Baker (1993a: 174–5) describes
Lee as a "true postmodern" with an "astute, witty, brilliant critique of postmodern, urban
hybridity" in *DRT*, but without giving the term "postmodern" any substance. I will argue
below that Lee basically grounds his politics and aesthetic strategies in modernist
positions and is not in any important sense "postmodernist."

11 Of course, there are many postmodern politics, ranging from the nihilism of the
post-1980s Baudrillard to the pragmatic reformism of Lyotard and Rorty, to the
multiculturalist identity politics of many women and minority group postmoderns; see
the survey in Best and Kellner 1991.

12 This is an homage to the Robert Mitchum character in *Night of the Hunter*, who was,

however, quite evil, thus Lee's appropriation of this symbolism perhaps inadvertently coded Raheem as more negative than Lee intended.

13 Lee indicates that he is down on Black youth exhibiting gold chains and the like ("They don't understand how worthless that shit is in the long run"), but doesn't do anything in the film to criticize this form of consumerism and in fact reproduces it in his cinematic images and capitalist ventures (see Lee and Jones 1989: 59, 110 for Lee's disclaimers).

14 Patterson (1992: 125ff.) notes some criticisms of Lee's commercial activity and I return to critical evaluation of Lee's cultural politics later in this chapter.

15 bell hooks (1990: 179) complains that a stuttering and inarticulate black youth is chosen to represent the profoundly intelligent and articulate views of Malcolm X and Martin Luther King.

16 Put differently, Lee's portrayal of racism does not take into account logical types, that there is a hierarchy of racial virulence, usually dictated by color (blacks being subject to the most extreme racism, followed by Hispanics, Asians, and ethnics like Italians). Other hierarchies are those of gender (with women below men), sexual preference (with gays subject to prejudice from straights), and so on, such that black, lesbian women would suffer significantly more oppression than, say, Hispanic men. The scene under question, however, portrays all forms of racism in terms of linguistic equivalence of cultural difference and racial hatred (I am grateful to Rhonda Hammer for this insight).

17 In interviews after the release of the film, Lee said that he was constantly amazed at how people were indignant over the destruction of property, but few of these people seemed to focus on the black youth's death. Lee was initially concerned to interrogate the conditions that could lead to wanton killings of black youth, spurred on by the Howard Beach killings in which white youth gratuitously assaulted black youth, leading to one of their deaths. Thus, Lee seems to believe that violent protest is a legitimate response to the senseless killing of blacks, as would, presumably, Malcolm X himself.

In a book on the making of *DRT* (Lee and Jones 1989), Lee remarks: "The character I play in *Do the Right Thing* is from the Malcolm X school of thought: 'An eye for an eye.' Fuck the turn-the-other-cheek shit. If we keep up that madness we'll be dead. YO, IT'S AN EYE FOR AN EYE" (ibid., 34; Lee's capitals).

18 This reading was suggested by Kelly Oliver in a comment on an earlier draft of my paper. Indeed, as indicated in note 17, Lee was angry that many viewers and reviewers seemed to be very upset by the destruction of property, but were overlooking that a black youth was killed by the police.

19 In a throw-away line, Mookie's sister Jade mentions that she'd like to see something positive happen for the community, but it isn't clear what she has in mind and in the absence of a more complete development of her political views, one can only guess.

20 It is precisely this nihilism that Cornell West warns blacks against (1992b).

21 It was generally overlooked in the reviews of the film that a good part of *Jungle Fever* was spent attacking the crack scene, portraying it as a dead end and in extremely negative terms as a major force of destruction in the black community. Lee avoided the issue of drugs, however, in his earlier films, for which he was criticized.

22 Brecht too was sympathetic to criminals and often presented them positively, as in the *Three-Penny Opera*. At times, they were figures of oppressed proletarians, though Brecht also used the gangster figure to present capitalists and fascists.

23 Although the narrative suggests that Malcolm was attracted to the white woman, Sophia, as a means of exerting sexual power and gaining racial revenge, there are both positive and negative images of the relationship, which is more favorably presented than the image of interracial relationships in *Jungle Fever*, despite the fact that Malcolm X himself came to sharply condemn black men pursuing white women; I interrogate Lee's controversial sexual politics below.

24 The Nation of Islam, for instance, preached black superiority, presented the white man as a "devil," and in general engaged in racist teachings, advocating black separatism

rather than structural social transformation. For some years, Malcolm X shared this perspective, but eventually distanced himself from such teachings and developed more revolutionary and internationalist perspectives. See such collections of Malcolm X's later writings as X 1992.

25 Obviously, the question of historical accuracy is important in evaluating a film that has the pretense of telling the truth about Malcolm X's life. Lee's book on the film (Lee and Wiley 1992) indicates that he was attempting to uncover the truth of Malcolm X's life through research and interviews, so one could validly examine the film for its historical accuracy; such a project, however, goes beyond the scope of this study. For some reflections on historical correctness and distortions of *X*, see the symposium in *Cineaste*, Vol. XIX, No. 4 (1993): 5–18 and the review by hooks 1993.

26 A curious set of images for interpreting Lee's sexual politics are found in the opening dance by Rosie Perez in *Do the Right Thing*. hooks (1989) notes how this dance replicates male behavior (male dance forms, boxing, fighting, etc). But Lee possibly intends this as a powerful image of a woman of color; the dance is accompanied by the rap song "Fight the Power" which puts positive energy into the scene. It is a striking, but ambiguous sequence, perhaps signalling the film's modernism which requires the viewers to construct their own readings.

27 For Brecht, a political learning play would impart exemplary political insights and behavior to its audience, helping to politicize them and to incite the audience to participate in social change. It is not clear that Lee's films function in this way, but rather, as I am arguing, serve instead primarily as black morality tales.

28 See, for example, Reed 1993, 18–19 and Baraka 1993, 145ff.

29 See the discussion on these issues in hooks 1992 and West 1992b.

30 Some histories and analyses of rap that I have sampled fail to cite Gil Scott-Heron and the Last Poets as a precursor of rap. I remember their work well and when I began hearing rap more and more in the 1980s, and began hearing as well a highly politicized rap, I always harked back to Gil Scott-Heron and the Last Poets, a great group worth listening and relistening to today. I was therefore gratified to read that Chuck D of Public Enemy stated:

> The thing about the Last Poets and Gil Scott-Heron is that they were into a jazz-type approach, doing poetry over a beat. When rap music came along it was poetry over a beat too, but *in time*. More important than the Last Poets and Gil-Scott Heron, to us, was James Brown. His record, 'Say it Loud, I'm Black and I'm Proud' had the most impact because it was danceable and yet you still thought about it. . . the groove was funk and soul, which was different from jazz.

(cited in Decker 1993: 63).

31 On hip hop culture, see Toop 1984; George 1988; and Dyson 1993a. Paul Gilroy (1991) points to the British and Caribbean roots of rap and hip hop. On most definitions, rap is one category of hip hop culture that includes styles of dress and expression, dancing, graffiti art, and other forms of cultural expression. Much of hip hop has disappeared, but rap has survived and rules as the music of choice of significant segments of black youth.

32 In a 1990 *New York Times* Op-Ed piece on 2 Live Crew, during the time of their obscenity trial, distinguished black scholar Henry Louis Gates defended the group, saying that its verbal excess was satire, that its songs like "Me so horny," were a carnivalesque transgression of propriety, and that they displayed "great virtuosity." One of the foremost critics of African-American culture, Houston Baker, countered that such a blanket defense fails to discriminate between various rap groups and that more discriminate evaluation would note that 2 Live Crew are distinctly inferior to the better rap groups and that their songs are offensive and mediocre (Baker 1993b: 64f.).

33 This holds true not only for the black community: rape and crimes against women are at an intolerable level in all races and socio-economic classes, thus rap articulates misogynist attitudes not only in the black community, but throughout U.S. society. Indeed, an unfortunate aspect of rap's popularity may be that it articulates negative attitudes toward women that may replicate attitudes in non-black groups who are unable to openly articulate such aggressive sexism.

34 A rap roundtable in *Essence* (September 1992: 83ff.) discusses the issue and concludes, in the words of Q-Tip: "Black men and women have both got to learn to work together" (120). So while, negatively, rap undeniably has male suprematist attitudes and blatant sexism, it has also promoted debate over these phenomena in the black community, as well as the society at large.

35 John Fiske reminds us that four months before the Rodney King affair, another black suspect, Tracy Mayberry, was beaten to death by police, but it, like so many similar cases, was practically invisible because of its failure to be documented in media culture (Fiske 1993: 227f.). Fiske has an excellent account of Black Liberation radio and other forms of resistance in contemporary Afro-American culture, but curiously ignores rap and other forms of black cultural expression like the film and novel. Indeed, Fiske's recent work marks a shift from concern with texts within cultural studies to the culture of everyday life.

36 For an illuminating discussion of the resonances of 1960s black radicalism and Afrocentric black nationalism in contemporary rap, see Decker 1993.

37 Public Enemy and other rappers are often very positive toward the Nation of Islam, and Ice Cube surprised some followers by coming out as an adherent to the movement in his 1991 album *Death Certificate* which I discuss below.

38 St. Ides is a high alcohol-content beer that Ice Cube endorsed in an ad, for which he was criticized by some.

39 Decker is strongly critical of Sister Souljah for replicating Public Enemy's patriarchal attitudes when she sang with the group, implying that she had no feminist perspective (Decker 1993: 67ff., 77), while the song cited is definitely critical of black male behavior from a feminist perspective.

40 John Singleton's *Boyz N the Hood*, in which Ice Cube plays, opens with the statistics that: "One out of every 21 black American males will be murdered in their lifetime. Most will die at the hands of another black male." Some other statistics:

> For black men between the ages of 18 and 29, suicide is the leading cause of death.... Between 1973 and 1986, the real earnings of black males between the ages of 18 and 29 fell 31 percent as the percentage of young black males in the workforce plummeted 20 percent. The number of black men who dropped out of the workforce altogether doubled from 13 to 25 percent. By 1989, almost 32 percent of black men between 16 and 19 were unemployed, compared to 16 percent of white men. And while blacks comprise only 12 percent of the nation's population, they make up 48 percent of the prison population ... Only 14 percent of the white males who live in large metropolitan areas have been arrested, but the percentage for black males is 51 percent.
> (Dyson 1993: 209)

41 Public Enemy released a 1993 collection of their "Greatest Misses," alluding to the fact that their songs were usually not played on radio, despite their great popularity. Likewise, their powerful music videos, like "Shut it Down," are rarely shown on mainstream television.

42 There is, to be sure, a postmodernism of resistance as well as a ludic or apolitical postmodernism (see Foster 1983).

43 Wife of Senator and later Vice President Al Gore, Tipper Gore was one of the founders, with Nancy Baker, wife of Republican party luminary and key player in the Reagan and

Bush administation, James Baker, of the Parents' Music Resource Center. Ms. Gore became President of the controversial group which attacked the lyrics of rock and rap music, calling for a ratings system to offer parental guidance. The group created a tremendous media stir and was widely debated (see Grossberg 1992).

Chapter 6

Reading the Gulf War
Production/text/reception

In previous chapters, I indicated some of the ways cultural studies could analyze how cultural texts transcoded political and ideological discourses on both the macro level of major political events and struggles and the micro level of everyday life. I suggested how cultural studies could also use its readings of cultural texts to illuminate the socio-political events and realities of the era and how analysis of the competing political discourses and struggles could be used as a framework to analyze cultural texts. In this chapter, I will indicate how the methods of cultural studies can be used to analyze and critique political events like the "Gulf War" and will also be concerned with expanding my conception of a multiperspectival cultural studies.

In a sense, the 1990s war against Iraq was a cultural-political event as much as a military one.[1] In retrospect, the Bush Administration and the Pentagon carried out one of the most successful public relations campaigns in the history of modern politics in its use of the media to mobilize support for the war. The mainstream media in the United States and elsewhere tended to be a compliant vehicle for the government strategy to manipulate the public, thereby imperiling democracy which requires informed citizens, checks and balances against excessive government power, and a free and vigorous critical media (see Kellner 1990a, 1992b).

And so cultural studies faces the challenge of explaining *how* the successful manipulation of the media and public took place during the "crisis in the Gulf" and the war against Iraq. A politically active cultural studies should intervene in the key social and political debates of the day and attempt to illuminate major political events and crises, as well as the popular texts of media culture and audience reception and practices. As we shall see, cultural studies is particularly well suited to undertake such tasks and practitoners who wish cultural studies to be political and to connect with the key political events of the era should not shirk such responsibilities. It is also the duty of good citizens to learn techniques of media manipulation and to see through government and commercial propaganda and disinformation, since democracy can only flourish if there are informed and active citizens.

In this chapter, I will thus apply the methods of cultural studies to the text and effects of the "Gulf War" (itself a media construct, as we shall see). I will also illustrate my model of a multiperspectival cultural studies, which combines 1) analysis of the production and political economy of texts with 2) textual analysis and interpretation, and 3) analysis of audience reception and use of media culture. I argued in Chapter 1 that, on the whole, recent work in cultural studies has tended to ignore political economy and the production of culture and has been overly textualist, or has focused narrowly and one-sidedly on ethnographic study of audience reception of texts. Thus, cultural studies has tended to focus critical attention on the analysis of media and consumer culture and its reception at the expense of context and analysis of how media culture is produced. I will accordingly demonstrate the need to focus on the production, reception, and effects of the texts of media culture in order to explain the role of the media in events like the war against Iraq.

This multiperspectival approach is necessary to overcome more limited approaches that primarily focus on text and audience. Accordingly, I first discuss the production of the text of the "crisis in the Gulf" and then "the Gulf War." This will involve analysis of disinformation and propaganda campaigns by the Bush Administration, the Pentagon, and their allies, as well as analysis of the constraints produced by the so-called pool system. I also indicate how the political economy of the media in the United States facilitated the manufacturing of consent for U.S. government policies. Then I analyze the meanings embedded in the text of the war against Iraq and the reception of the text by the audience. The latter process will involve some speculation on why the Gulf War was popular with its audiences and how the Bush Administration and the Pentagon mobilized public support for the war. My example indicates how I envisage cultural studies as a political project concerned with the key issues of the day.

DISINFORMATION AND THE PRODUCTION OF NEWS

The war against Iraq can be read as a text produced by the Bush Administration, the Pentagon, and the media which utilized images and discourse of the crisis and then the war to mobilize consent and support for the U.S. military intervention. Unpacking the text of the "crisis in the Gulf" and then the "Gulf War" requires analysis of the process of the production of news and information, including analysis of sources, gatekeeping and censorship, codes and practices of "normal" journalism, the sociology of news production, and processes of disinformation and propaganda. This dimension of cultural studies has been downplayed and I believe that this is highly unfortunate because analysis of the production of news and information, as well as entertainment, sheds important light on the origins and context of the emergence of cultural texts which contributes to understanding their meaning and effects.

Analysis of the text of the "crisis in the Gulf" indicates that from the beginning the mainstream news institutions followed the lines of the Bush Administration and Pentagon.[2] Mainstream media in the U.S. are commercial media, subject to intense competition for audiences and profits. Consequently, mainstream television,

newspapers, and news magazines do not want to alienate consumers, and thus are extremely cautious in going against public opinion and the official government line. The mainstream media also favor official government sources for their stories, especially in times of crisis. Thus, they tend to be conduits for U.S. government policies and actions, though there are significant exceptions (see Kellner 1990a).

In response to the Iraqi invasion of Kuwait in early August 1990, the U.S. government began immediately, first, to build consensus for the U.S. military intervention and, then, to promote a military solution to the crisis, and the mainstream media were compliant accomplices. When the Bush Administration sent a massive troop deployment to the region, the mainstream media applauded these actions and became a conduit for mobilizing support for U.S. policy. For weeks, few dissenting voices were heard in the mainstream media and, especially, TV reports, commentary, and discussion strongly privileged a military solution to the crisis, serving as a propaganda vehicle for the U.S. military and national security apparatus which was facing severe budget cutbacks on the very eve of the invasion. No significant TV debate took place over the dangerous consequences of the massive U.S. military response to the Iraqi invasion, or over the interests and policies which the military intervention served. Critics of U.S. policy were largely absent from the mainstream media coverage of the crisis, and little analysis was presented which departed from issues presented by the Bush Administration.

Big lies and disinformation

The Bush Administration controlled the media discourse in part through disinformation and propaganda, and in part by means of control of the press via the pool system. In the early days of "the crisis in the Gulf," for instance, the Bush Administration carried through a highly successful disinformation campaign by means of their control and manipulation of sources which legitimated the U.S. military deployment in Saudi Arabia on August 8, 1990. During the first days of the crisis, the U.S. government constantly claimed that the Iraqis were mobilizing troops on the border of Saudi Arabia, poised to invade the oil-rich kingdom. This was sheer disinformation and later studies revealed that Iraq had no intention of invading Saudi Arabia and did not have large numbers of troops on the Saudi border in a threatening posture (see the discussion below and Kellner 1992b for documentation of this claim).

The disinformation campaign that legitimated the U.S. sending troops to Saudi Arabia began working through the *Washington Post* on August 7, 1990, the same day Bush announced that he was sending U.S. troops to Saudi Arabia. In a front page story by Patrick Tyler, the *Post* claimed that in a previous day's meeting between the U.S. *chargé d'affairs*, Joseph Wilson, and Iraqi President Saddam Hussein, Hussein was highly belligerent, claiming that Kuwait was part of Iraq, that no negotiation was possible, that he would invade Saudi Arabia if they cut off the oil pipes which delivered Iraqi oil across Saudi territory to the Gulf, and that American blood would flow in the sand if the U.S. sent troops to the region.

A later transcript of the Wilson–Hussein meeting revealed, however, that Hussein was cordial, indicated a willingness to negoiate, insisted that he had no intention of invading Saudi Arabia, and opened the doors for a diplomatic solution to the crisis. The *Post* story, however, was taken up by the television networks, wire services, and press, producing an image that there was no possibility of a diplomatic solution and that decisive action was needed to protect Saudi Arabia from the aggressive Iraqis. Such a storyline legitimated the sending of U.S. troops to the Gulf and provided a perfect justification for Bush's intervention in the region.

Editorial columns in the *Washington Post* the same day supported the imminent Bush Administration deployment. Mary McGrory published a column titled "The Beast of Baghdad," which also assumed that Iraq was set to invade Saudi Arabia and which called upon Bush to bomb Baghdad! Precisely the same line appeared in an op-ed piece by the *Post*'s associate editor and chief foreign correspondent Jim Hoagland who kicked in with a column: "Force Hussein to Withdraw" (p. A19). As certain as McGrory of Iraq's imminent invasion of Saudi Arabia, Hoagland opened by proclaiming that:

> Saddam Hussein has gone to war to gain control of the oil fields of Kuwait and ultimately of Saudi Arabia. The United States must now use convincing military force against the Iraqi dictator to save the oil fields and to preserve American influence in the Middle East.
>
> (*Washington Post* August 7, 1990)

According to Hoagland, Saddam Hussein "respects only force and will respond to nothing else."

The rest of the article consisted of false analysis, questionable analogies, and bellicose banality. Hoagland claimed that the "Iraqi dictator's base of support is too narrow and too shaky to withstand a sharp, telling blow." Yet some six weeks of the most vicious bombing in history were unable to dislodge Hussein whose support, or staying power, was obviously much stronger than Hoagland could imagine. Hoagland also believed that "he [Hussein] is so hated at home that his defeat, even by foreign forces, will be greeted as deliverance by his own nation and by much of the Arab world." As it turned out, both Iraq and the Arab world were deeply divided over Hussein and the sweeping generalities that Hoagland proclaimed were totally off the mark.

Hoagland also claimed that Ronald Reagan's decision to bomb Libya was the right model for Bush to follow. This example was revealing because Muammar Qadhafi preceded Saddam Hussein as a symbolically constructed enemy upon which national hatred could be projected, and thus served as an object lesson for Third-World countries that refused to submit to domination by the neo-imperialist superpowers.[3] Moreover, it is far from certain that the terrorist incident for which Qadhafi was "punished" (i.e., the bombing of a Berlin disco) was carried out by groups affiliated with Libya. But facts have little relevance in an ideologue's brief for bombing.

In his opinion piece, Hoagland lectured George Bush on why he must take urgent and forceful action to save his presidency and, like McGrory, urged military action against Iraq. Hoagland assumed both that Iraq planned to invade Saudi Arabia and that only a military blow from George Bush could save the day. In fact, there were important Arab diplomatic initiatives underway, blocked by the United States, but these efforts were ignored by the war-mongering Hoagland.[4] Letting his reactionary beliefs slip through, Hoagland interpreted Iraq's invasion of Kuwait as a challenge to "the legitimacy of all remaining monarchies in the Arabian Peninsula, where Britain established most existing boundaries and political systems in the colonial era." Hoagland thus defined the principles at stake as the legitimacy of some of the most reactionary monarchies in the world, with borders drawn by British colonialists who deliberately deprived Iraq of a viable seaport and robbed national groups like the Palestinians and the Kurds of their homelands.

Indeed, Hoagland's whole article manifests what Edward Said (1978) described as an "Orientalist" mentality in which white Westerners establish their superiority by vacuous generalizations about people in the Arab world. Hoagland characterized Arabs as understanding only force and incapable of defending themselves and solving their own problems. For him, the Gulf crisis is thus the locus of "a rare case where the United States would be unwise not to use force." Analyzing such intellectually bankrupt pleas for a military strike against Iraq would not be worth the time and energy except that Bush Administration officials paid close attention to Hoagland's columns. Further, his poorly written, badly argued, and banal punditry was highly acclaimed in political circles; indeed, he was awarded a Pulitzer prize "for searching and prescient columns on events leading up to the Gulf War." In addition, his and McGrory's columns are significant because they were published in the *Washington Post*, supposedly a bastion of liberal enlightenment, and read by U.S. policymakers. Further, McGrory's demonization of Hussein was retooled and republished in *Newsweek* (Sept. 3, 1990), part of the Washington Post Company.

Thus, the Bush Administration and *Washington Post* disinformation and propaganda concerning the Iraqis' readiness to invade Saudi Arabia worked effectively to shape media discourse and public perception of the crisis and to legitimate Bush's sending U.S. troops to Saudi Arabia. In particular, Patrick Tyler's front-page story concerning Hussein's meeting with Joe Wilson and Iraq's alleged refusal to negotiate a solution or leave Kuwait provided the crucial media frame through which debate over the advisibility of sending U.S. troops to Saudi Arabia was conducted.[5] On August 7, PBS McNeil-Lehrer discussion of the proper U.S. response to Iraq's invasion of Kuwait, co-anchor Judy Woodruff stated: "Iraq's leader Saddam Hussein was quoted today [in the *Post* story – D.K.] as saying the invasion of Kuwait was irreversible and permanent." Later on the same show, former national security adviser (and Iran/Contra felon) Robert McFarlane quoted the story as evidence that Hussein was not going to leave Kuwait, and that therefore U.S. military intervention in Saudi Arabia was necessary. And in a discussion with Arab-American leaders as to whether a U.S. military intervention was justified, Woodruff interjected: "the U.S. *chargé* in Baghdad did have a two-hour meeting with Saddam Hussein yesterday which by all accounts was very unsatisfactory as Saddam Hussein insisted that he was going to stay in Kuwait and made what were reported to be veiled threats against other nations in the area" – all lies that Bush Administration officials fed to the *Post*, which were then disseminated by other mainstream media.

In his early morning television speech on August 8, which announced and defended sending U.S. troops to Saudi Arabia, Bush claimed that "the Saudi government requested our help, and I responded to that request by ordering U.S. air and ground forces to deploy to the kingdom of Saudi Arabia." However, accounts of the Saudi–U.S. negotiations later indicated that the United States pressured the Saudis to allow U.S. military intervention into their country (Woodward 1991: 241ff. and Salinger and Laurent 1991: 110ff.). Bush repeated the dubious claim that "Iraq has massed an enormous war machine on the Saudi border," and his administration emphasized this theme in discussion with the media, which obediently reproduced the argument. At 9:24 a.m. on August 8, for instance, Bob Zelnick, ABC's Pentagon correspondent, dutifully reported that the Pentagon informed him that Iraqi troop presence had doubled since the invasion of Kuwait, that there were now more than 200,000 Iraqi troops in Kuwait with a large force poised to invade Saudi Arabia.

Yet it is not at all certain how many troops Iraq actually deployed in Kuwait during the first weeks of the crisis. All pre-invasion reports produced by the Bush Administration indicated that Iraq had amassed about 100,000 troops on the border of Kuwait. Initial reports during the first few days after the invasion suggested that Iraq actually had between 80,000 and 100,000 troops in Kuwait, more than enough for an occupation, as the Bush Administration liked to point out and as the mainstream media diligently reported; once the U.S. forces were on their way to Saudi Arabia, the Iraqi forces suddenly doubled and reports claimed that there were at least 100,000 Iraqi troops amassed on the border of Saudi Arabia. But these figures invariably came from Bush Administration or Pentagon sources, and sources critical of the U.S. claims concerning the number of Iraqi troops deployed revealed a quite different figure.

St. Petersburg Times reporter Jean Heller published two stories (November 30 and January 6) suggesting that satellite photos indicated far fewer Iraqi troops in Saudi Arabia than the Bush Administration claimed (the January 6 story was republished in *In These Times*, February 27, 1991: 1–2). Heller's suspicions were roused when she saw a *Newsweek* "Periscope" item that ABC's "Prime Time Live" had never used several satellite photos of occupied Kuwait City and southern Kuwait taken in early September. Purchased by ABC from the Soviet commercial satellite agency Soyez-Karta, the photos were expected to reveal the presence of a massive Iraqi troop deployment in Kuwait, but failed to disclose anything near the number of troops claimed by the Bush Administration. ABC declined to use them and Heller got her newspaper to purchase the satellite photos of Kuwait from August 8 and September 13 and of Saudi Arabia from September 11. Two satellite experts who had formerly worked for the U.S. government failed to find evidence of the alleged buildup. "'The Pentagon kept saying the bad guys were there, but we don't see anything to indicate an Iraqi force in Kuwait of even 20 percent the size the administration claimed,' said Peter Zimmerman, who served with the U.S. Arms Control and Disarmament Agency during the Reagan administration" (Heller, *In These Times*, February 27, 1991: 2).

Both satellite photos taken on August 8 and September 13 showed a sand cover on the roads, suggesting that there were few Iraqi troops on the Saudi border where the Bush Administration claimed that they were massed, threatening to invade Saudi Arabia. Pictures of the main Kuwaiti airport showed no Iraqi planes in sight, though large numbers of U.S. planes were visible in Saudi Arabia. The Pentagon refused to comment on the satellite photos, but to suggestions advanced by ABC (which decided not to show the photos) that the pictures were not of high enough quality to detect the Iraqi troops, Heller responded that the photograph of the north of Saudi Arabia showed all the roads swept clean of sand and clearly depicted the U.S. troop build-up in the area. By September, the Pentagon was claiming that there were 265,000 Iraqi troops and 2,200 tanks, deployed in Kuwait, which posed a threat to Saudi Arabia. But the photographs reveal nowhere near this number and, so far, the U.S. government has refused to release its satellite photographs.

Indeed, Woodward (1991) noted that the Saudis had sent scouts across the border into Kuwait after the Iraqi invasion to see if they could detect the Iraqi troops that the United States claimed were massed for a possible invasion of their country. "The scouts had come back reporting nothing. There was no trace of the Iraqi troops heading toward the kingdom" (Woodward 1991: 258–9). Soon after, the U.S. team arrived with photos of the Iraqi troops allegedly massed on the Saudi border, and General Norman Schwarzkopf explained to the Saudis that the Iraqis had sent small command-and-control units ahead of the mass of troops, which would explain why the Saudi scouts failed to see them (ibid., 1991: 268). Former CIA officer Ralph McGehee told journalist Joel Bleifuss: "There has been no hesitation in the past to use doctored satellite photographs to support the policy position that the U.S. wants supported" (*In These Times*, September 19, 1990: 5). Indeed, Emery (1991) reported that King Hussein of Jordan was also sent pictures of tanks moving along roads near the Saudi–Kuwaiti border which had been shown to the Saudis, and that King Hussein claimed that the Saudis had "pressed the panic button" when they saw the photographs. King Hussein was skeptical and "argued that if Saddam Hussein had wanted to invade the Saudis, he would have moved immediately, when the only thing between him and the Saudi capital was a tiny and untested – if expensively equipped – Saudi army" (Emery 1991: 15).

Here is how the disinformation campaign worked to legitimate U.S. deployment of troops in Saudi Arabia: high Bush Administration officials called in journalists who would serve as conduits for stories that Iraq refused to negotiate a withdrawal from Kuwait and that they had troops stationed on the borders of Saudi Arabia, threatening to invade the oil-rich kingdom. The Pentagon and the Bush Administration also released information at press conferences concerning the Iraqi threat to Saudi Arabia and unwillingness to negotiate, and these "official" pronouncements supplemented the unofficial briefings of reporters. In turn, editorial writers and commentators on TV networks took up these claims, which they used to bolster arguments concerning why it was necessary for the U.S. to send troops to Saudi Arabia.

Hence, disinformation stories were planted and then reproduced and circulated, producing the effect desired. Indeed, as noted, there are reasons to believe that the Bush Administration may have exaggerated the number of Iraqi troops in Kuwait and the threat to Saudi Arabia to scare the Saudis into accepting the U.S. troops and to justify its own troop build-up in the region and eventual military action. The mainstream media reproduced the U.S. claims and figures as facts with newspapers like the *Washington Post* and the television networks serving as conduits for Bush Administration disinformation. Moreover, *Post* editorial writers and columnists actively promoted a military solution, urging an attack on Baghdad even before Bush announced that he was sending troops to Saudi Arabia, thus becoming doubly complicit in legitimating Bush's policies.

Moreover, the major newspapers, news magazines, and television networks did not criticize Bush's deployment or debate whether it was wise to send so many U.S. troops to Saudi Arabia in the first place. Peace activists and the alternative press argued against the deployment and for a U.N. peace-keeping force to be sent to the area, rather than a massive U.S. military force, but this position got no hearing in the mainstream media (FAIR, Press Release, January 1991). Furthermore, the leaders of the Democratic party also failed to criticize the U.S. military deployment and the press tended to neglect those congressional and other voices that opposed the deployment, especially during its first weeks. Indeed, there were many opposi-tional voices to the Bush Administration's policies that were simply excluded from the mainstream media, thus precluding serious debate over the proper U.S. response to Iraq's invasion of Kuwait. But the mainstream media only draw on an extremely limited repertoire of voices and privilege the same administration officials and top Democratic party leaders, thus freezing significant views out of public policy debates and contributing to the crisis of democracy which is now a central aspect of political life in the United States (Kellner 1990a).

The Hill and Knowlton propaganda campaign

And so we see that a successful disinformation campaign was undertaken by the Bush Administration and the Pentagon in order to legitimate sending U.S. troops to Saudi Arabia. Beginning in early October, a sustained propaganda campaign was underway that legitimated the U.S. use of military power to force Iraq out of Kuwait. This campaign involved demonization of the Iraqis for their "rape of Kuwait" and the demonization of Saddam Hussein as "another Hitler" and the incarnation of evil.[6] This campaign was inspired by a British campaign during World War I, repeated by the U.S. when it entered the war, on the "rape of Belgium" which demonized the Germans as rapists and murderers of innocent children – charges later proven to be false.

The demonization of Hussein and the Iraqis was important because if they were absolutely evil and a threat on a par with Hitler and the Nazis, no negotiation could be possible and a diplomatic solution to the crisis was excluded. To help demonize the Iraqis, a Kuwaiti government group financed a propaganda campaign, undertaken by the U.S. public relations firm Hill & Knowlton, which invented Iraqi atrocities in Kuwait, such as the killing of premature babies who were allegedly taken out of incubators and left to die on the floor. In October 1990 a tearful teenage girl testified to the House of Representatives Human Rights Caucus that she had seen Iraqi soldiers remove fifteen babies from incubators and leave them to die on the floor of the hospital. The girl's identity was not revealed, supposedly to protect her family from reprisals. This story helped mobilize support for U.S. military action, much as Bush's Willie Horton ads had helped him win the presidency by playing on primal emotions. Bush mentioned the story six times in one month and eight times in forty-four days; Vice-President Dan Quayle referred to it frequently, as did Norman Schwarzkopf and other military spokespersons. Seven U.S. senators cited the story in speeches supporting the January 12 resolution authorizing war.

In a January 6, 1992 op-ed piece in the *New York Times*, John MacArthur, the publisher of *Harper's* magazine, revealed that the unidentified congressional witness was the daughter of the Kuwaiti ambassador to the U.S. The girl had been brought to Congress by Hill & Knowlton, who had coached her and helped organize the congressional human rights hearings. In addition, Craig Fuller, Bush's former chief of staff when he was vice-president and a Bush loyalist, was president of Hill & Knowlton and was involved with the PR campaign, as were several other former officials for the Reagan administration, who had close relations with the Bush Administration.

Thus, the Kuwaiti government developed a propaganda campaign to manipulate the American people into accepting the Gulf War and the Bush Administration used this campaign to promote their goals. Hill & Knowlton organized a photo exhibition of Iraqi atrocities displayed at the United Nations and the U.S. Congress and widely shown on television. They also assisted Kuwaiti refugees in telling stories of torture, lobbied Congress, and prepared video and print material for the media.

On January 17, 1992, ABC's "20/20" disclosed that a "doctor" who testified that he had "buried fourteen newborn babies that had been taken from their incubators by the soldiers" was also lying. The "doctor" was actually a dentist and later admitted to ABC that he had never examined the babies and had no way of knowing how they had died. The same was true of Amnesty International, which published a report based on this testimony. (Amnesty International later retracted the report, which had been cited frequently by Bush and other members of his administration). ABC also disclosed that Hill & Knowlton had commissioned a "focus group" survey, which brings groups of people together to find out what stirs or angers them. The focus group responded strongly to the Iraqi baby atrocity stories, and so Hill & Knowlton featured them in its PR campaigns for the Free Kuwait group.

The effect of the demonization of Saddam Hussein was to promote a climate in which the necessity to take decisive military action to eliminate him was privileged. Countless stories were endlessly repeated throughout the mainstream media of his brutality, often reproducing uncritically the Hill & Knowlton stories. Moreover, there was report after report on Iraqi chemical weapons, its potential nuclear capacity, and its ability to mobilize terrorist attacks on the U.S. and its allies – stories promoted by Bush Administration officials to demonize the Iraqis. TV broadcast stories about radio stations playing records that simulated rock classics with new lyrics vilifying Saddam. T-shirts appeared with vicious images of Saddam Hussein and the Iraqis. Tabloid magazines published sensational stories detailing his alleged sexual crimes and perversions (Rifas 1994) It is as if U.S. popular and political culture needs evil demons to assure its sense of its own goodness and the media responded with the demonology of the Iraqi dictator.

Thus, the extremely negative framing of Hussein and the Iraqis ruled out a diplomatic solution to the crisis. In addition, the constant war talk created a climate in which only military action could resolve the crisis. The media presentation of the confrontation as a struggle between good and evil, with the evil Hussein unwilling to negotiate and threatening the allies, produced tension and the need for a resolution that war could best provide. The rhetoric of Iraqi "rape" and "penetration" was deployed from the beginning of the crisis throughout the war. The media demonized Saddam's Big Gun and chemical weapons, as well as his missiles that could hit Cairo and Tel Aviv. His very name was mispronounced as Sad-dam, evoking sadism and damnation, and Sod-dom, evoking sodomy. Deploying both racist and sexual rhetoric, Bush claimed that the U.S. went to war against the "dark chaos" of a "brutal dictator" who followed the "law of the jungle" and "systematically raped" a "peaceful neighbor" (quoted in Joel Bleifuss, "The First Stone," *In These Times*, March 20–6, 1991: 4). Undersecretary of Defense Paul Wolfowitz was cited in the same article, rhetorically asking if you would "let a man like that [Hussein] get his hands on what are essentially the world's vital organs?"

Throughout American history, vengeance for rape – especially the rape of white women by people of color – has been used to legitimate political and military action against colored people. Captivity drama narratives of white women captured and raped by Native Americans were a standard genre of colonial literature and during the Spanish–American war, the Hearst newspapers popularized the story of the Spanish kidnapping of an upper-class and light-skinned Cuban woman as a pretext for U.S. intervention. John Gottlieb wrote in *The Progressive* that:

> Bush not only used rape as a justification for the war against Iraq, but also . . . cited the sexual assault of an American officer's wife by a Panamanian soldier as a reason for invading that country, and . . . used the rape of a white woman by black convict Willie Horton to attack Michael Dukakis in 1988.
>
> (April 1991: 39)

In addition to carrying out a massive propaganda campaign, the U.S. government also instituted a sustained effort to control information and images. A military pool system was set up which restricted the access of the press to soldiers and the battlefield; the press was taken to chosen sites in limited "pools" and were accompanied at all times by military personnel who restricted their access and who even censored their reports. This was the tightest control over the press in any war in U.S. history and assured that primarily positive pictures and reporting of the war would take place. The pool system was established after the Grenada invasion, in which the press was not allowed on the island until after the significant military activity. A commission was set up which outlined rules through which the press would be allowed to report on military action in pools, supervised by the military, which would also have censorship power. This system was used in both the Panama invasion and war against Iraq, with highly controversial results.[7]

In addition, few significant antiwar voices were heard in the mainstream media during the first months of the troop build-up in Saudi Arabia. A study by the media watchdog group FAIR reported that during the first five months of TV coverage of the crisis, ABC devoted only 0.7 percent of its Gulf coverage to opposition to the military buildup. CBS allowed 0.8 percent, while NBC devoted 1.5 percent, or 13.3 minutes for all stories about protests, antiwar organizations, conscientious objectors, and religious dissenters. Consequently, of the 2,855 minutes of TV coverage of the crisis from August 8 to January 3, FAIR found that only 29 minutes, or roughly 1 percent, dealt with popular opposition to the U.S. military intervention in the Gulf (FAIR, Press Release, January 1991).

The few images of antiwar demonstrators in the U.S. that appeared during the crisis in the Gulf often juxtaposed anti-American Arab demonstrations that frequently burned U.S. flags with images of U.S. demonstrations. Such a juxtaposition coded antiwar demonstrators as Arabs, as irrational opponents of U.S. policies. U.S. demonstrators were portrayed as an unruly mob, as long-haired outsiders; their discourse was rarely cited and coverage focused instead on the chanting of slogans, or images of marching crowds, with media voice-overs supplying the context and interpretation. Major newspapers and newsmagazines also failed to cover the burgeoning new antiwar movement. Thus, just as the media symbolically constructed a negative image in the 1960s of antiwar protestors as irrational, anti-American, and unruly, so too did the networks present the emerging antiwar movement of the 1990s in predominantly negative frames.

Not only was the discourse of the antiwar movement ignored, but "none of the foreign policy experts associated with the peace movement – such as Edward Said, Noam Chomsky or the scholars of the Institute for Policy Studies – appeared on any nightly news program" (FAIR Press Release, January 1991). A Times-Mirror Poll, however, that was recorded in September 1990 and January 1991 discovered "pluralities of the public saying they wished to hear more about the views of Americans who oppose sending forces to the Gulf" (Special Times-Mirror News Interest Index, January 31, 1991). Furthermore, soldiers who were alarmed at their deployment in the Saudi desert and objected to the primitive living conditions there were silenced, in part by Pentagon restrictions on press coverage and in part by a press corps unwilling to search for dissenting opinions.

And yet on the eve of the war, more than 50 percent of the American public opposed a military solution to the crisis. Perhaps images of families being separated and young troops being sent to the Saudi desert produced a negative response to the possibility of a war in the region that could take many U.S. lives. Perhaps, despite the lack of critical discourse on the media, many individuals could still think for themselves and produce antiwar opinions against the grain of the dominant promilitary solution government and media discourse. Perhaps the memory of Vietnam and U.S. military misadventures produced apprehensions over a war in the Persian Gulf. But the disinformation and propaganda campaigns were successful in that they persuaded the majority of nations in the U.N. and the U.S. Congress to support a declaration legitimating the use of force to expell Iraq from Kuwait. And once the war began, the Bush Administration was quickly able to mobilize support for its positions. How was this possible and how can cultural studies contribute to explaining the public support for a nasty and vicious military adventure?

THE MEDIA PROPAGANDA WAR

When the U.S. began military action against Iraq on January 16, 1991, the mainstream media became a conduit for Bush Administration and Pentagon policies and rarely allowed criticism of its positions, disinformation, and atrocities during the war. Television served primarily as a propaganda apparatus for the multinational forces arrayed against the Iraqis and as a cheerleader for their every victory. Anchors like Dan Rather of CBS and Tom Brokaw of NBC went to Saudi Arabia and, along with the network correspondents there, seemed to totally identify with the military point of view. Whenever peace proposals were floated by the Iraqis or the Soviet Union, the networks quickly shot them down and presented the Bush Administration and Pentagon positions on every aspect of the war (for systematic analysis and critique, see Kellner 1992b).

The media framed the war as an exciting narrative, as a nightly miniseries with dramatic conflict, action and adventure, danger to allied troops and civilians, evil perpetuated by villainous Iraqis, and heroics performed by American military planners, technology, and troops. Both CBS and ABC used the logo "Showdown in the Gulf" during the opening hours of the war, and CBS continued to utilize the logo throughout the war, coding the event as a battle between good and evil. Indeed, the Gulf War was presented as a war movie with beginning, middle, and end. The dramatic bombing of Baghdad during the opening night and exciting Scud wars of the next days enthralled a large TV audience and the following weeks provided plenty of excitement, ups and downs, surprises, and complex plot devices. The threats of chemical weapons, terrorism, and a bloody Iraqi ground offensive seemed to produce great fear in the TV audiences and helped to mobilize support against the villainous Iraqis (see discussion below for documentation). The ground war in particular produced a surge of dramatic action and a quick resolution and happy ending to the war (at least for those rooting for the U.S.-led coalition).

Television also presented the war visually with dramatic techno-images, playing repeatedly the videos of high-tech precision bombing and the aerial war over Baghdad and the Patriot/Scud wars over Saudi Arabia and Israel. The effects of the war on American families was a constant theme, and patriotism and support for the troops was a constant refrain of the commentators. The military released video-tapes of high-tech precision bombing which were replayed repeatedly, similar to replays of heroics in a sports event. Indeed, sports metaphors were constantly used and the pro-war demonstrators who chanted "USA! USA!" rooted for the American side as sports fans, as if the Gulf War were the Super Bowl of wars. The military and media kept daily tally of the score of Iraqi tanks and equipment eliminated, though the sanitized war coverage contained no "body count"; figures and images of wounded or dead soldiers were strictly forbidden. The "winnability" and justification for the war were stressed and the narrative was oriented toward a successful conclusion which was presented as a stunning victory.

It was obviously in the TV networks' interests to attract the audience to their programming and competition revolved around presenting the most patriotic, exciting, and comprehensive coverage. To properly explicate this dimension of the text of the Gulf War, one needs to focus on the production of the text within the framework of the political economy of commercial television. First, the sources of the news on the mainstream media were severely limited to the Bush Administration and the military. This was partly the result of the pool system that restricted media access to the theater of battle and that exercized censorship over every image and report filed. Yet the networks themselves also restricted the range of voices that appeared. A survey by FAIR of the TV coverage of the first two weeks of the war revealed that of the 878 news sources used by the three major commercial networks, only 1.5 percent were identified as antiwar protestors – roughly equivalent to the amount of people asked to comment on how the Gulf War disrupted their travel plans. In the forty-two nightly news broadcasts, only one leader of a peace organization was interviewed, while seven Super Bowl players were asked their views of the war (cited in Joel Bleifuss, *In These Times*, March 20, 1991: 5).

On the other hand, in report after report, television portrayed prowar rallies, yellow ribbons, and the wave of patriotism apparently sweeping the country. The networks also personalized the U.S. troops and their families, thus bonding the public to the troops in the desert, helping manufacture support for the U.S. military policies. In these ways, the audience was mobilized to support every move of the Bush Administration and the Pentagon and as the war went well and relatively fast, the country was swept along in a victory euphoria, as if it was winning the Super Bowl of wars and was thus number one in the world. Such imagery and discourse helped create support for a war that barely 50 percent of the public and Congress desired on the eve of Bush's bombing of Baghdad.

Furthermore, the audience was terrorized into support for the U.S. troops by a series of propaganda campaigns, masterfully orchestrated by the Bush Administration and the Pentagon. Early in the crisis, reports were leaked that Iraqi chemical weapons were being brought to the field of battle, and throughout the war there were many reports of the threat of Iraqi chemical weapons. In addition, there were almost daily reports on the threats of terrorism manipulated by the Iraqis. When the Iraqis paraded U.S. POWs on TV, there were claims that they were torturing coalition troops. Such reports created a mass hysteria in sectors of the audience, who were positively bonding with the troops. Moreover, after the Iraqi Scud attacks on Israel and Saudi Arabia, there were reports of thousands of people buying gas masks and vignettes of families producing sealed rooms in their home in the case of chemical attack. Obviously, such hysteria helped mobilize people against the Iraqis and desire their military defeat and punishment.

Analyzing the war discourse from the perspective of the production and effects of the media representation of the war, television and the mainstream media arguably served as propaganda arms for U.S. government policy. The media endlessly repeated Bush Administration "big lies," such as its alleged efforts to negotiate a settlement with the Iraqis when it was actively undermining the possibility of a diplomatic settlement. The mainstream media repeated that the goal of the U.S. war policy was the liberation of Kuwait until the very end when it was obvious that the destruction of the Iraqi military and Iraq's economic and military infrastructure was the goal. And the media repeated every propaganda line of the day, amplifying Bush Administration claims concerning alleged torture and mis-treatment of U.S. POWs (later revealed to be highly exaggerated), that an Iraqi infant formula milk factory destroyed by U.S. bombing was really a military installation producing chemical/biological weapons, that a civilian sleeping shelter was really a military command and control center, or that Iraqi "environmental terrorism" was responsible for the Persian Gulf oil spill and other ecological devastation (whereas allied bombing was also responsible; see the documentation of all these claims in Kellner 1992b).

The mainstream media projected the image of the war most desired by the Pentagon and the Bush Administration; i.e. that it was fighting an eminently clean and successful high-tech war. From the beginning, the bombing of Iraq was portrayed as efficient and humane, targeting only military facilities. Over and over, despite pictures from Iraq which revealed the contrary, the Pentagon and Bush Administration stressed the accuracy of their bombing strategies and the oft-re-peated images of the precision bombs, with video cameras built into their heads, presented an image of such accurate bombing. Likewise, the frequent pictures of Patriot missiles apparently knocking out Iraqi Scud missiles created the impressions of a clean high-tech war. Later, the Pentagon itself admitted that only 7 percent of the bombs used were so-called "smart bombs" and admitted that over 70 percent of its bombs missed their targets, but the dominant images of a high-tech war presented an impression of a highly efficient techno-war. It was also revealed that a large percentage of U.S. casualties resulted from "friendly fire," from the bombing of one's own troops.

Although the mainstream media served as propaganda conduits for the U.S. government and military, in my interpretation, the media are not propaganda instruments *per se* for the state as some argue (Herman and Chomsky 1988; Chomsky 1989). Rather, one should see the major commercial networks primarily as money machines seeking ratings and profits. If the war is popular, then in pursuit of ratings the networks will provide a positive picture of the war, eliminating discordant voices, as happened in the Persian Gulf War. Moreover, General Electric and RCA, which own NBC, are major military contractors who will benefit tremendously from a successful war, and NBC dutifully served as a Pentagon propaganda organ from beginning to end of the war (for evidence, see Kellner 1992b). It was claimed that GE produced parts of every major weapon system used in the war, so that the file footage of U.S. weapons and the gushingly positive reports of their technological wonder were in effect free advertisements for products produced by GE/NBC – indeed, desire to promote U.S. weapons for sale was one of the major purposes of the war in the first place.

But it was "liberal" Dan Rather of "liberal" CBS who served as the biggest booster and cheerleader of the military. During the first days of the war, Rather was the most skeptical and critical network reporter. But Rather's ratings were falling and so he went to Saudi Arabia to report the war directly. Henceforth, he celebrated the military and became the most fervent supporter of the ground war, exulting in the "blow out" and "magnificent" and "brilliant" military action which slaughtered the hapless Iraqis, totally demoralized after forty days of bombing and without the technology to fight a high-tech, U.S.-led, multinational coalition military machine.

The lack of significant critical voices in the mainstream media during the crisis in the Gulf and then the Gulf War also can be explained by reflection on the political economy of the media and the system of media production in the United States. The broadcast media are afraid to go against a perceived popular consensus, to alienate people, and to take unpopular stands because they are afraid of losing audience shares and thus profits. Because U.S. military actions have characteristically been supported by the majority of the people, at least in their early stages, television is extremely reluctant to criticize what might turn out to be popular military actions.

The broadcast media also characteristically rely on a narrow range of established and safe commentators and are not likely to reach out to new and controversial voices in a period of national crisis. The media generally wait until a major political figure or established "expert" speaks against a specific policy and that view gains certain credibility as marked by opinion polls or publication in "respected" newspapers or journals. Unfortunately, the crisis of democracy in the United States is such that the Democratic Party has largely supported the conservative policies of the past decade and the party leaders are extremely cautious and slow to criticize foreign policy actions, especially potentially popular military actions. The crisis of liberalism is so deep in the U.S. that establishment liberals are afraid of being called "wimps" or "soft" on foreign aggression, and thus often support policies that their better instincts should lead them to oppose.

Consequently, the only criticisms of a major U.S. military intervention that appeared in the mainstream media during the first weeks of the U.S. intervention came from hawks like Zbigniev Brzezinski, and even some far right conservatives like Pat Buchanan, while Democrats and liberals tended to go along with the initial military build-up, until Bush doubled the U.S. forces after the November 1990 election. Then the Democrats supported the policy of sanctions (rather than calling for a negotiated settlement) and once the war began, for the most part supported the Bush Administration policies, pointing again to the crisis of liberalism in the U.S.

In addition, the commercial nature of the broadcast media also intensified the propagandistic effects of Gulf War coverage. The big advertising agencies were extremely nervous concerning the perceived negative impact of having their products associated with controversial and perhaps depressing events like war.[8] Yet as the war proceeded, many corporations tailored their advertisements to the growing patriotism, sprinkling their ads with flags, praises of troops, and patriotic slogans. Red, white and blue merchandise boutiques appeared in Bloomingdale's and Neiman Marcus's department stores and in their advertising. Ralph Lauren robes, bathing trunks, and other objects appeared embroidered with the flag. Britches ads spouted "Rugged Patriotism" fashion, while Ross-Simon ads displayed "Fashionable Patriotism" (McAllister 1993: 224). Advertising discourse shifted from "you" to "our" appeals, binding together the product and nation with "our troops." Golf balls apppeared with Saddam Hussein's face on them, a T-shirt was marked with a drawing of Hussein fleeing a missile with the caption: "You can run but you can't hide." Another ad featured a Saddam Condom with "Directions: use this condom to help prevent unwanted mistakes like Saddam Hussein", and a mass of other Desert Storm paraphernelia was marketed (ibid., 1993).

The result of the propaganda blitz and war hysteria was a warrior nation that turned many in the TV audience into fanatic supporters of the Bush Administration war policy.

WARRIOR NATION

Part of the reason why people supported the Gulf War has to do with what might be called "territorial herd instincts." When a country is at war and in danger people tend to support their government and pull together.[9] It could be argued, however, that during the Gulf War the country was not really in danger, that a diplomatic rather than a military solution could best serve the national interests, and that support of the troops required bringing them home as soon as possible. Moreover, the country was genuinely divided at the start of the war and there was a large antiwar movement in place before Bush began the military hostilities with Iraq. Furthermore, Kolko (1991: 25) points out that public opinion since 1969 has been increasingly anti-interventionist and that every Rand Corporation poll had indicated that U.S. military intervention would not receive adequate public support. Yet during the Gulf War, the public was mobilized to support Bush's interventionist policies, in part at least, because of the media support for the war.

To begin, the prowar consensus was mobilized through a variety of ways in which the public identified with the troops. TV presented direct images of the troops to the public through "desert dispatches" which produced very sympathetic images of young American men and women, "in harm's way" and serving their country. TV news segments on families of the troops also provided mechanisms of identification, especially because many of the troops were reservists, forced to leave their jobs and families, making them sympathetic objects of empathy and identification for those able to envisage themselves in a similar situation. There were also frequent TV news stories on how church groups, schools, and others adopted U.S. troops in Saudi Arabia as pen pals, thus more intimately binding those at home to the soldiers abroad. As we shall see in this section, people were also bound to troops through rituals of display of yellow ribbons, chanting and waving flags in prowar demonstrations, and entering into various prowar support groups.

The media also generated support for the war, first, by upbeat appraisals of U.S. successes and then by demonizing the Iraqis that made people fervently want a coalition victory. Initial support was won for the war effort through the media-generated euphoria that the war would be over quickly, with a decisive and easy victory for the U.S.-led coalition. Then, the audience got into the drama of the war through experiencing the excitement of the Scud wars and the thrills of techno-war with its laser-guided bombs and missiles and videotapes of its successes. The POW issue, the oil spills and fires, and intense propaganda campaigns by both sides also involved the audience in the highly emotional experience of a TV war. The drama of the war was genuinely exciting and the public immersed itself in the sights, sounds, and language of war.

The media images of the high-tech precision bombing, (seeming) victories of Patriot over Scud missiles, bombing of Iraq, and military hardware and troops helped to mobilize positive feelings for the U.S. military effort in much of the audience. Military language helped normalize the war, propaganda and disinformation campaigns mobilized prowar discourse, and the negative images and discourses against the Iraqis helped mobilize hatred against Iraq and Saddam Hussein. Polls during the first weeks of the war revealed growing support for the war effort, revealing a wide-spread propensity to believe whatever the media and military were saying. A Times-Mirror survey of January 31, 1991, revealed that 78 percent of the public believed that the military was basically telling the truth, not hiding anything embarrassing about its conduct of the war, and providing all of the information it prudently could. Also in the survey 72 percent called the press coverage objective and 61 percent called it for the most part accurate. Eight out of ten said the press did an excellent job and 50 percent claimed to be addicted to TV watching and said that they could not stop watching coverage of the war. Of adults under 30, 58 percent called themselves "war news addicts" and 21 percent of these "addicts" claimed that they were having trouble concentrating on their jobs or normal activities, while 18 percent said that they were suffering from insomnia.

It was, I would argue, the total media and social environment that was responsible for mobilizing support for the U.S. war policies. From morning to evening, the nation was bombarded with images of military experts, vignettes of soldiers at home and abroad, military families, former POWs, and others associated with the military. Military figures, images, and discourse dominated the morning talk shows, the network news, discussion programs, and the 24-hours-a-day CNN war coverage, as well as saturation coverage on C-Span and many other cable networks. On home satellite dishes, the channels were saturated with live transmissions concerning the war, as the networks prepared or presented their reports from the field, and one satellite transponder provided hours per day of live military pool footage from Saudi Arabia for use by the networks – propaganda provided by the military free of charge. TV news preempted regular programs for weeks. The result was a militarization of consciousness and an environment dominated by military images and discourses.

I have already noted how the audience was terrorized into identification with the U.S. war policy and there is much evidence that war hysteria indeed swept through the nation. TV news featured frequent reports on the tremendous increase in sales of army-surplus war merchandise. Segments showed stockbrokers buying gas masks to take to work because they feared a terrorist attack on the New York subways. Stores all over the country sold out of gas masks after the dramatization of the Scud attacks on Israel and an announcement that President Bush's bodyguards were carrying gas masks at all times. One TV news episode featured a saleswoman who told of how a frantic mother came in the store that day to buy a plastic covering for her child's crib "like they have in Israel." On January 29, NBC featured a woman buying a gas mask, telling how her child had been waking up in terror at night, fearing an attack, and that she is buying a gas mask for the child to comfort her. On February 3, CNN broadcast a segment that showed an Atlanta family buying gas masks and constructing "safe rooms" in their house in case of a terrorist attack.

It is difficult to determine the degree of fear, and, in particular, fear of terrorism, evident in the American public during the Gulf War. In his analysis of the symbolic culture of violence in the United States, George Gerbner and his colleagues in the Annenberg School of Communication argued for years that the culture of TV violence produced a "mean world" syndrome whereby people who watched heavy doses of TV violence were highly fearful and tended to submit to conservative leaders who offered to alleviate their fear (Gerbner and Gross 1976). During the crisis in the Gulf, Gerbner and his associates (1992) did research that indicated that the amount of violence in film culture was accelerating significantly; the number of episodes of violence in sequels to popular films like *Robocop*, *Die Hard*, and *Young Guns* doubled or tripled in comparison to the original, showing that a culture nurtured on violence needed ever heavier doses to get their fix. Such heavy doses of violence from popular culture, however, created dispositions toward fear that led the public to seek refuge in authoritarian leaders like George Bush or Norman Schwarzkopf.

The war hysteria in the United States produced an infantilization of U.S. society, which was especially evident in the fetishism of yellow ribbons and the prowar demonstrations. Yellow ribbons had been broadly displayed during the Iranian hostage crisis in which U.S. hostages were held in the late 1970s by militant Iranians. The yellow ribbons go back to the Civil War and Indian wars in which the families of soldiers displayed yellow ribbons when their loved ones were away at war and held in captivity (recall John Ford's John Wayne vehicle *She Wore a Yellow Ribbon* and the popular song "Tie a yellow ribbon 'round the old oak tree"). The ribbons reappeared when U.S. citizens were held captive by the Iraqis in Iraq and Kuwait during the crisis in the Gulf.

The yellow ribbon symbolism in the Gulf War combined the hostage and soldiers-in-harm's-way connotation, with a popular discourse portraying the U.S. troops as the hostages of "Sad-dam In-sane." Curiously, the symbolism of the ribbons was transferred from hostages to soldiers; previously, the ribbons were displayed to commemorate the situation of U.S. hostages in Iraq but were soon transferred to the soldiers. This symbolic transference suggested that the U.S. troops in Saudi Arabia were hostages, held against their will in the desert because of the presence of an evil which had to be surgically removed (actually the troops and the entire world were the hostages of the respective Iraqi and U.S. political and military establishments which produced the war). The symbolism implied that innocent Americans abroad were victims of foreign aggression and linked the soldiers with their supporters on the domestic front.

Displaying yellow ribbons provided talismans, good luck charms, and signs of social conformity all at once. It enlisted those who displayed yellow ribbons in the war effort, making them part of the adventure. Drawing on mythological resonances, tying ribbons to trees connected culture with nature, naturalizing the solidarity and community of Gulf War supporters. The ribbons symbolically tied together the community into a unified whole, bound together by its support for the troops.[10] The ribbons thus signified that one supported the troops, that one was a loyal member of the patriotic community, that one was a team player, and a good American. They also signified, however, that one was ready to give up one's faculties of critical thought and to submit to whatever policies and adventures the Bush Administration might attempt.

Indeed, the sight of yellow ribbons mesmerized the media, scared Congress, and demoralized antiwar protestors. Yellow ribbons appeared everywhere in some neighborhoods and regions of the country and some individuals who refused to put yellow ribbons on their homes were threatened by their neighbors. This mode of forced conformity reveals a quasi-fascist hysteria unleashed by the Gulf War and a disturbing massification of the public. There were indeed many examples of protofascist behavior among the U.S. population during the Gulf War. An Italian basketball player at Seton Hall University was thrown off the team when he refused to wear a U.S. flag on his uniform and eventually returned to Italy after harassment by "patriots." After Professor Barbara Scott, at a campus rally at the State University of New York, New Paltz, urged U.S. military personnel not to kill innocent people, she was dubbed "Baghdad Barbara," accused of treason by a state senator, and subjected to hate mail and a letter campaign aimed at the university president and Governor Mario Cuomo, urging them to fire her. In Kutztown Pennsylvania, a newspaper editor was fired for his editorial titled "How about a little peace?" and an editor was fired from a Round Rock, Texas paper for publishing an interview with a Palestinian-American expressing antiwar views.[11]

Arab-Americans were victims of government harassment and intimidation since the beginning of the crisis. Neal Saad described how Arab-Americans were visited by the FBI in their homes, places of business, and neighborhoods and were questioned concerning attitudes to U.S. policy in the Middle East, the PLO, Arab-American political activities, and terrorism (in Clark 1992: 188ff.). During the war, harassment intensified and Pan American Airlines actually decided not to allow Arab passengers on their planes! Identifying ethnic members of a country with "the enemy" itself promotes oppression of minorities who belong to these groups. This identification happened in World War II with Japanese-Americans who were interned in concentration camps and began in the crisis in the Gulf with FBI investigations of Arab-Americans. The result was a resurgence of racism against Arabs and acts of violence against them.

Anti-Arab racism proliferated within U.S. popular culture. For years, Arabs had regularly been villainized in Hollywood films and American television entertainment (see Kellner and Ryan 1988 and my study in Chapter 2), and during the Gulf War anti-Arab sentiments were mobilized against Iraqis. The words "Bomb Iraq" were superimposed on the lyrics of the Beach Boys' song "Barbara Ann." A radio show in Georgia proclaimed, "towelhead weekend," telling callers to phone in when they heard the traditional Islamic call to prayer; a disk jockey in Toledo, Ohio solicited funds from listeners to buy a ticket to Iraq for an Iraqi-American professor who was critical of the war. Jennie Anderson wrote:

> In the United States, anti-Arab propaganda is a hot commercial item. A widely disseminated T-shirt pictures a U.S. Marine pointing a rifle at an Arab on the ground, with the caption, HOW MUCH IS OIL NOW? Another briskly selling T-shirt shows military planes attacking an Arab on a camel, with the caption, I'D FLY 10,000 MILES TO SMOKE A CAMEL,
>
> (*The Progressive*, February 1991: 28–9).

Another T-Shirt read: "Join the army, see interesting places, meet new people, and kill them."

In addition, there was much violence against Arab-Americans in the United States during the Gulf War.[12] Even before the war began, businesses owned by Arab-Americans were bombed, an Arab-American businessman was beaten by a white supremacist mob in Toledo, a Palestinian family riding in a car was shot at in Kansas City, and an Arab-American who appeared on a Pennsylvania television program received seven death threats. Later, Edward Said and other Arab-American activists received death threats, and during the Gulf War itself violence against Arab-Americans accelerated. The United States had demonized Arabs for years in the figures of the Yasar Arafat, Muammar Qadhafi, and images of Arab terrorists. The demonization of Saddam Hussein and the Iraqis heated up racist passions that exploded into violence against Arab-Americans.

Yet wars also divide countries between those who do and do not support the official war policies and the Gulf War produced such division and conflict in the country. It polarized individuals into pro- and anti-war groups, it alienated people from those who did not share their views, it ruptured families, friendships, and the vestiges of communities that have survived the onslaught of television and the consumer society. Although TV portrayed the division clearly in the case of Arcata, California, a town torn between pro- and anti-war citizens (i.e. on a CBS news segment on January 24 and an NBC segment on February 3), one rarely saw the genuine divisions in the country over the Gulf War, or the anti-war voices as the war ground on.

During the Gulf War individuals were not merely passive spectators of the media war, but there were active pro- and anti-war demonstrations and organizing. Indeed, the Bush Administration promoted the line that one was either pro-war and a good citizen, or anti-war and thus not a good citizen, not a patriotic American. Call-in radio and television shows featured rabid and aggressive attacks on the anti-war demonstrators, and more and more pro-war demonstrations and violent opposition to the antiwar demonstrators appeared on television. On January 17 at a basketball game in Missoula, Montana, as anti-war protesters were being dragged off the courts by police, the crowd pelted the protestors with potatoes and began chanting "USA USA" In fact, one began seeing pro-war demonstrations almost every day on television, with crowds waving the flag and chanting. Revealingly, these usually small demonstrations got increasingly more coverage than the larger anti-war demonstrations. The networks quickly shifted, on cue from the Bush Administration, to segments covering the "new patriotism" and love of the flag. News reports featured yellow ribbons and flags with many stories on flag factories where the managers indicated that they could barely keep up with the demand.

Divisions in the country and the quasihysteria involved in those who supported the war was evident on talk radio. The talk radio shows overwhelmingly supported the war and most callers supported the lines of the mostly pro-war talk show hosts (Nimmo and Hovind in Denton 1993). Callers frequently wanted to "nuke" Iraq and attacked anti-war protestors, calling them "looney tunes," traitors and worse. Many callers attacked CNN's Peter Arnett, the sole Western correpondent remaining in Baghdad, as supportive of Saddam Hussein and many talk show hosts and callers claimed that CNN owner Ted Turner was sympathetic to Iraq (Nimmo and Hovind 1993: 95). One caller labeled ABC anchor Peter Jennings "a jerk" for an ABC report on the bombing of the Iraqi sleeping shelter that the U.S. was claiming was a command and control center; the talk show host agreed, noting that "Jennings isn't an American anyway" (he is, in fact, a Canadian; cited in Nimmo and Hovind 1993: 95).[13]

Carl Boggs (1991) argued that the intense nationalism, racism, glorification of violence, and militarism evident during the Gulf War was a response to growing powerlessness and insecurity, and was similar to the situation in Nazi Germany analyzed by Erich Fromm in *Escape From Freedom* (1941). The pro-war demonstrations seemed to offer mechanisms through which individuals could escape their powerlessness and overcome (temporarily) their insecurities. The flag-waving and chanting pointed to individuals immersing themselves in masses and exhibiting collectivist, conformist behavior. It appeared that powerless individuals felt themselves part of something greater than themselves when they chanted and waved flags. "Human flag" phenomena began to appear: in San Diego, 30,000 people appeared in red, white, and blue T-shirts on January 25 to form the world's largest human flag, photographed from a blimp and dutifully broadcast by the television networks. On February 2, an even larger human flag was formed in Virginia Beach, Virginia, with 40,000 people chanting "USA, USA" as they became one with their country and flag. On February 15, CNN featured a story on the new patriotism in which flags were shown flying en masse throughout the country and TV images linked the flags to portraits of George Bush, accompanied by the 1988 Republican campaign song as background music.

All over the country, whenever there was a pro-war demonstration, crowds chanted "USA USA!" The lack of specific content in the chant in favor of empty patriotism contrasted with the anti-war chants and slogans that always had a specific content–attacking the war, calling for the troops to come home now, or affirming specific values like peace. Yet the masses of pro-war demonstrators who chanted "USA!" every time they were given the occasion were not articulating any particular values or reasons for their pro-war and pro-America stance. Rather, they were simply immersing themselves in a crowd and expressing primal patriotism, national narcissism, and aggressive threats against anyone who was different. The "USA!" chant thus expressed loyalty to the home team in the Super Bowl championship of contemporary war and bound together the prowar constituency into a national community of those identifying with the U.S. war policy, becoming part of something bigger than themselves through participation.

In addition, the pro-war demonstrations seemed to make people feel good through providing experiences of community and empowerment denied them in everyday life. Those who were usually powerless were able to feel powerful, identifying themselves as part of the nation proudly asserting itself in the war. Losers in everyday life, the pro-war demonstrators could experience themselves as part of the winning team in the Gulf War. Participating in the prowar rituals thus gave individuals new and attractive identities that gave them a renewed sense of participation in a great national adventure. Like sports events and rock concerts, the prowar demonstrations thus provided the participants with at least a fleeting sense of community, denied them in the privatized temples of consumption, serialized media watching, and isolated "life styles." For almost 100 years, sociologists have studied crowd behavior and analyzed the mechanisms through which individuals dissolve themselves in mass behavior. During the Gulf War the phenomenon of individuals immersing themselves in mass behavior was a daily feature of the TV war. Usually, American community in the Age of Media Culture is a simulated TV community, whereby one becomes one with the others by watching the same images and participating in the same ritualized experience of events like the Super Bowl or Gulf War. Yet one could participate in the ritual of the Gulf War more fully by leaving one's home and joining into pro-war demonstrations, in which one could become more vitally integrated into the patriotic community.

The flag-waving and chanting also provided a new form of participatory experience that enabled individuals to be part of an aesthetic spectacle. The pro-war flag-wavers and chanters had been immersed for years in the aesthetic of consumer culture: viewing seductive commodities in advertisements; fascinated by images of luxury, eroticism, and power in the images of popular entertainment; tempted by the dazzling display of the commodity world in malls and stores; and gratified by whatever items they could afford to buy in their everyday lives (i.e., cars, clothes, electronics, etc.). The Gulf War was packaged as an aesthetic spectacle, with CNN utilizing powerful drum music to introduce their news segments, superimposing images of the U.S. flag over American troops, and employing upbeat martial music between breaks. The audience was thus invited to participate in a dazzling war spectacle by its media presentation.

Moreover, pro-war demonstrators were able to overcome the usual privatization and passivity of TV culture by more actively participating in the public celebrations of the war. Many individuals of the TV war audience were normally isolated, disempowered, and able to feel that they belonged in the consumer society only if they could afford to buy the icons and totems of social prestige. A pro-war demonstration and flag-waving, however, is a cheap thrill, offering anyone the opportunity to become part of an aesthetic spectacle of a sea of flags, rousing music, and enthusiastic chanting. Although individuals at home watching television are passive and isolated, in pro-war demonstrations the participants were active and socially bonded.

Indeed, the pro-war constituency rooted for the U.S. team as if it were a sports event and from the beginning there was a close relation between war and football. During a break in a nationally televised football game from El Paso shown on New Years Eve 1990, an announcer greeted U.S. soldiers in the stands who were there courtesy of the John Hancock insurance company. Then, as Haynes Johnson put it:

> while the cameras panned rows of cheering, waving soldiers, the sportscaster pointed to a mural painted across the stadium wall. Depicted was an eagle swooping down on prey. Helpful as ever, while the cameras slowly played across the mural, the sportscaster read aloud the message spelled out there: 'Go Desert Shield, Beat Iraq'.
>
> (*Washington Post*, January 4, 1991: A2)

There are, in fact, interesting connections between war and football, patriotism and sports in the American imagination. Both activities involve teamwork, coordination, and game plans, and both activities are highly competitive and violent. In both, squadrons of helmeted men seek to gain territory and try to drive their enemy back, while throwing balls, bombs, or bullets downfield. Both stress the values of discipline, training, hitting the opposition hard, and, above all, winning. On December 19, Lt. Gen. Calvin Waller told the press, "I'm like a football coach. I want everything I can possibly get and have at my side of the field when I get ready to go into the Super Bowl" (United Press International, December 20, 1990). On a news segment on the CBS morning show on January 25, a sports fan stated that he liked Buffalo in the bowl because "it's an impressive unit with powerful weapons." A U.S. soldier in a January 23 report on CNN said that "Saddam Hussein doesn't have much of a team; in comparison with football he'd be the Cleveland Browns." Army Chief Warrant Officer Ron Moring stated on the eve of the war: "It's time to quit the pregame show. We're a lot more serious about what we're doing. There's a lot more excitement in the air."[14]

Football metaphors were also employed in war rhetoric when Bush said that Tariq Aziz gave them a "stiff arm" after the unsuccessful Geneva meeting at the eve of the war. A U.S. pilot returning from the first night's bombing raid said that "it was just like a football game where the other team didn't show up." Helen Thomas asked Bush in a January 18 press briefing if the Gorbachev peace initiative was perceived as an "end run" [around Bush's desire to start and win the war]. A Canadian Broadcasting Corporation (CBC) Radio headline indicated that the Canadian armed forces in the Gulf were given "the green light to tackle the Iraqis." ABC's "Nightline" (January 17, 1991), quoted fliers just back from the first missions of the war, enthusing: "It's just like a football game once you get airborne and you get the jet under you and you start feeling good, then you just start working – working your game plan." Another pilot exclaimed:

It's like being a professional athlete and never playing a game. Today was the first game and the enemy didn't show up, the opponent didn't show up. We went out there and ran our first play and it worked great, scored a touchdown, there was nobody home.

(ABC's "Nightline", January 17, 1991)

In addition, the military planners talked of making an "end run" around the Iraqi troops massed on the Kuwaiti border. Scud missiles were "intercepted" by Patriots and Col. Ray Davies described the U.S. air team as "like the Dallas Cowboys football team. They weren't a real emotional team. That's exactly what it's like with these pilots out here. They know exactly what they've got to do" *(Washington Post,* January 19: C1). Furthermore, the audience processed the Gulf War as a football game. A Jesuit professor wrote in the *National Catholic Reporter*:

A resident adviser in one of our college dorms tells me his students watched the CNN live war and cheered and took bets as if they were watching a football game. Small wonder. A sports mind-set has revved us up for the war. Some weeks ago, TV's most disconcerting image was of Defense Secretary Dick Cheney whipping the cheering troops into a fighting frenzy as if he were a coach at halftime in a locker room.

(National Catholic Reporter February 1, 1991: 1)

And so the Gulf War became a game in which the U.S. emerged victorious in the Super Bowl of wars.

SOME CONCLUDING REFLECTIONS

The analysis in the last sections suggested how the media helped mobilize support for the Gulf War. The examples that I gave of Gulf War hysteria and the warrior nation were all derived from the media which in their polls, nightly news reports, and discussion shows presented the appearence that the Gulf War was wildly popular and that the nation was undergoing orgies of patriotism, as well as the irrational hysteria that I noted. But this picture might be highly misleading, replicating the very picture produced by the media themselves. Most of the people that I spoke to, ranging from my Texas neighbors and colleagues to students, were against the war and we had well-attended teach-ins every day at the University of Texas, so there was certainly an anti-war public in the United States. In the months after the war, I talked to many people who said that in their travels and work in rural Kentucky, south Texas, Michigan, West Virginia, and other parts of the country there was significant opposition to the war – much more than the polls and media let on. Before the war began, polls and media discourse revealed a divided nation, but once the war began these divisions became invisible.

Thus, the media might have produced a false picture of the degree of support for Bush Administration Gulf War policy. A study in Britain revealed that support for the Gulf War was much softer and more ambivalent than the polls indicated. Martin Shaw and Roy Carr-Hill argued:

> two surveys of a local population in Northern England, based on random samples of the electorate . . . {reveal} that while perceptions of the war closely reflected the pictures of the war provided by the media, there was a great deal of anxiety not reflected in national poll findings, and 'resistance' to media coverage – reflected particularly in the finding that large minorities agreed that television and the popular press 'glorified the war too much'.
>
> (Shaw and Carr-Hill 1991)

The authors also claim that their surveys indicated that people's attitude toward the war often varied according to what newspaper they read.

A study in the U.S. noted a distinct bias in the very mode of questioning concerning audience support for the war. Eveland, McLeod and Signorielli (forthcoming) noted that poll questions tended to focus on presidential job approval, or confidence in the military, rather than whether people really supported the war and wanted it to continue. A January 17 Gallup poll indicated that when asked if respondents approved of the way Bush was handling the crisis in the Gulf, 81 percent said that they approved; by January 27th, Bush's approval rating (for handling the Gulf situation) went up to 84 percent; by February 3, approval of the way the president was handling the situation inched up to 85 percent, though it decreased to 79 percent by February 13 (Eveland *et al.* forthcoming).

After the successful ground war, Bush's approval ratings shot up to a high of 90 percent. But more detailed analysis of poll data indicated that there was not the seemingly overwhelming bipartisan support. Solop and Wonders' (1991) review of published poll date indicated that those most supportive of President Bush and his war policies were republican white males who had conservative attitudes. Females, blacks, liberals, and Democrats were less supportive. Moreover, the study by Eveland, McLeod, and Signorielli based on interviews during and after the war:

> revealed that there was less overall support for the war than would be expected given the degree and type of media coverage relating to public opinion about the war . . . . Both during and after the war, more than 50 percent of the respondents said they were 'neutral' or disagreed with the statements in the 'I support the war' scale. In addition, during the war only 6.6% of the respondents said that they strongly agreed with statements describing support for the war; this figure fell to 2.8% in the survey conducted one year later.
>
> (Eveland *et al.* forthcoming)

Moreover, further focus on audience reception and how audiences might process the propagandistic and jingoist images of the military and the U.S. intervention suggests that television images and discourse may have contradictory effects and that audiences may resist media manipulation. Utilizing a deconstructive perspective, one might argue that the extremely ideological and propagandistic nature of the TV coverage could be read as evidence that the population did not swallow the Bush Administration rationale for the war and needed to be constantly indoctrinated to assure that they accepted the official war policy. For, as noted, further research and more in-depth interviews indicated that support for the U.S. policy was "soft," and the one-sidedness, limited range of voices, and blatant propaganda could be read as signs that government and media elites knew that they needed to maintain a hard-sell propaganda campaign to manage and maintain a prowar consensus in a public that had serious (and legitimate) doubts concerning the war.

Furthermore, although saturation television coverage was strongly propagandistic and seemed to help mobilize audience support for the war, continued coverage of turmoil in the region, especially images of the suffering of the Kurds and other Iraqis at the end of the war, soured much of the audience on the war and perhaps on military intervention, which didn't seem to have achieved promised positive results. Thus, ultimately, the media may have contributed to turning large segments of the public against military solutions to the problems of the Middle East and elsewhere and to the commitment of U.S. forces to resolve the problems of the world. It may be that the nightly images of the soldiers in the desert and then the images after the war of continued suffering and turmoil might have raised questions concerning the wisdom of U.S. military intervention.

Moreover, the fact that the war was experienced by much of the audience as a dramatic spectacle meant that it could be soon forgotten, overwhelmed by Hollywood, TV, and other subsequent spectacles of the culture industry. By the summer of 1992, Bush's presidency was in serious trouble and, as it turned out, patriotic images and discourse from the war were unable to save him in the 1992 election. Revelations of the positive and supportive Reagan/Bush policies before the war toward Iraq suggested that Bush and his cohorts had constantly miscalculated in providing aid and diplomatic support to the Iraqi regime from the early 1980s to the eve of the invasion of Kuwait (see Friedman 1993). The fact that Saddam Hussein continued to rule with an iron fist in Iraq and that his neighbors continued to feel threatened, fueling a further and potentially catastrophic arms race in the region, raised questions as to the success of Bush's Gulf War policy and whether the war really accomplished any significant long-term goals, other than temporarily boosting Bush's ratings in the polls and producing a positive image of the U.S. military after the shame of defeat in Vietnam.

Thus, in the chaotic aftermath of the U.S. intervention, the extreme hyperbole of the construction of Saddam Hussein and his regime as absolute evil to some extent backfired because Hussein was not removed from power in the aftermath of the war. Although Bush urged the Iraqis to overthrow Hussein, once the U.S. declared an end to the fighting and Iraqi rebels rebelled against Hussein's regime, the U.S. remained on the sidelines. General Schwarzkopf himself stated in a PBS TV interview on March 27, 1991, that he had preferred to continue fighting to "annihilate" completely the Iraqi military which was violently suppressing the insurgent forces against Hussein as Schwarzkopf spoke. The continuation of Saddam Hussein in power, the destructive environmental effects of the war that may continue for years, and instability of the region may reveal the Persian Gulf War to be a Pandora's box of evils that produced a brief euphoric high with a long hangover.

Consequently, saturation television coverage of dramatic political events is a two-edged sword: it might shape public opinion into supporting the U.S. intervention, as it obviously did during the Gulf War, but repeated images of a drawn-out stalemate, or images of death and destruction in a fighting war, or images of protracted suffering as long-term effects of the war, could be turned against the system and its leaders who produced such destruction. The very ubiquitousness of television and the central role that television is playing in contemporary politics renders it a complex and unpredictable political force. Lust for pictures to attract audiences led the networks into a race to get into Iraq and to interview its leaders and to show its people. Although Saddam Hussein proved to be a total media flop, the images of the Iraqi people going about their daily lives were the only humane images of Arabs that appeared during the period leading up to the war. Images of continual and increased suffering of the Iraqi people and others in the area as a result of U.S. military intervention might ultimately lead people to see that war is no way to solve political conflict, and that it produces overwhelming destruction, suffering, and death.

Hence, a multiperspectival approach that captures different aspects of a complex phenomenon like mainstream media coverage of U.S. interventions in the Middle East should also analyze the contradictions of audience reception of the media texts and television's potentially contradictory images and effects, as well as analyzing the media text and its conservative, systems-maintenance effects. Although my analysis has focused primarily on the ways that television coverage of the U.S.-led war against Iraq supported the policies of the Bush Administration and Pentagon, analysis of the reception by audiences of the Middle East Crisis, the war, and its aftermath might have ultimately helped undermine Bush and the conservative hegemony, contributing to his defeat. Perhaps Bush went overboard in demonizing Hussein and his continued rule of Iraq served to rob Bush of claims of genuine victory.

In any case, the effects of television and the mainstream media, as always (see Kellner 1990a), are contradictory and may have unintended consequences. While in the spring of 1991, the Gulf crisis and War constituted a tremendous victory for the Bush Administration and Pentagon, the event did not save his presidency and eventually raised questions concerning whether he was really an effective President. It's short-term positive effects also point to the fickleness of audiences in a media-saturated society, who soon forget the big events of the previous year.

And yet the woefully one-sided coverage of the Gulf crisis and War by the mainstream media calls attention once again to the need for alternative media to provide essential information on complex events like the Gulf War. During the War, those of us who opposed it got information from computer data-bases, such as PeaceNet, or progressive publications like *The Nation*, *In These Times*, and *Z Magazine*. Locally, in addition to holding daily teach-ins at universities, critics of the war attempted to make use of public access television and radio to criticize the Bush Administration's war policy and refusal to negotiate a diplomatic solution. Democratizing our media system will require a revitalization of public television, an increased role for public access television, the eventual development of a public satellite system, and the production of progressive computer data-bases (Kellner 1990a). Because politics are more and more acted out on media screens and texts, without the reconstruction of television and the mass media, the prospects for democratization of the American political system are dim.

NOTES

This study was presented in lectures at the University of Michigan, at the Popular Culture Association conference in San Antonio, at the Marxist Literary Group summer conference in Delaware, at York University and Trent University in Canada, at an international cultural studies conference in Taiwan, and at several other colleges and Universities. For critical comments and useful discussion, I would like to thank members of audiences at these venues, and Richard Keeble, who has constructively criticized the text. Different versions of this study were published in the *Centennial Review*, Vol. XXXVI, No. 1 (Winter 1992) pp. 5–42 and *Styles of Cultural Activism*, edited by Philip Goldstein and published by the University of Delaware Press (1994). In this study, I draw on my book *The Persian Gulf TV War* (Kellner 1992b).

1 I am using the term "war against Iraq" for reasons that will be spelled out below. As of this writing (spring 1994), the war is still going on so it would be a mistake to limit the event under scrutiny to the events described as "the Gulf War" from January through March of 1991.

2 By the mainstream media in the United States, I mean the major national television networks, including ABC, CBS, CNN and NBC; the national weekly news magazines *Time*, *Newsweek*, and *U.S. News and World Report*; and national newspapers such as the *New York Times*, *The Wall Street Journal*, *USA Today*, and the *Washington Post*.

See the contrast between mainstream and alternative media that I develop in Kellner 1990a.

3 On August 6, 1954, the *New York Times* published an editorial celebrating the overthrow of the Mossadegh Government in Iran and the restoration of the Shah, accompanied by a takeover of 40 percent of the Iranian oil by U.S. corporations, breaking a British monopoly. The editors wrote:

> Underdeveloped countries with rich resources now have an object lesson in the heavy cost that must be paid by one of their number which goes berserk with fanatical nationalism. It is perhaps too much to hope that Iran's experience will prevent the rise of Mossadeghs in other countries, but that experience may at least strengthen the hands of more reasonable and more far-seeing leaders.

Namely, those who will have a clear-eyed understanding of the U.S.'s overriding priorities (thanks to Noam Chomsky for this reference). In this context, the U.S. military intervention and Gulf War was an object lesson to Third-World leaders who do not follow U.S. priorities and policies.

4 From the beginning, Iraq was feverishly trying to negotiate a solution to the crisis and was cooperating with Arab efforts to mediate the crisis; there were over eight Iraqi secret missions which attempted to reach a diplomatic solution, all of which were rebuffed by the Bush Administration, which obviously wanted a war; see the discussion in Kellner 1992b.

5 Through data-base searches, I discovered how this story was taken up by the television networks, most major newspapers, and was used in many later summaries of the story to explain why Bush *had* to send U.S. troops to Saudi Arabia; see the documentation in Kellner 1992b.

6 A study undertaken by the Gannett Foundation indicated that there were over 1,170 articles linking Hussein with Hitler (La May, *et al.* 1991: 42). This comparison obviously presupposes a false analogy in terms of the military threat to the region and the world from the Iraqi army – whose threat was hyped up from the beginning. Iraq's 17 million population can hardly compare with Germany's 70 million and its military was significantly less threatening than Hitler's military machine, which was the most powerful in the world in the 1930s. Nor could Iraq, which depends on oil for over 95 percent of its exports, be compared with an industrial powerhouse like Germany. It is also inappropriate to compare a major imperialist superpower with a regional power, Iraq, that itself is the product of colonialization.

It might also be noted how the Bush Administration and media personalized the crisis, equating Iraq with its leader. Whereas in coverage during the 8-year war between Iran and Iraq, in which the U.S. covertly supported Iraq, references were to "Baghdad" and "Iraq," during the Gulf crisis and war it was usually "Saddam Hussein" who was referred to as the actor and source of all evil (I am grateful to Richard Keeble for this insight).

7 See the critical discussions of the pool system in the *New York Times* Sunday Magazine, March 3, 1991; the *Washington Journalism Review* (March 1991); the *Columbia Journalism Review*, March/April 1991, pp. 23–9; *Index on Censorship*, April/May 1991; *Le monde diplomatique*, May 1991, pp. 11–18; and the articles in the *New York Times* May 5 and 6, 1991 and the discussion in Kellner 1992b.

8 In an otherwise illuminating article, that I draw upon in this discussion, McAllister (in Denton 1993: 212) claims that: "During the Persian Gulf War, government-produced propaganda was less prevalent than during the world wars." But McAllister apparently failed to see the propaganda campaigns that I am analysing here and that the very advertising he discusses contributed to the propaganda effects of TV war coverage.

9 In his book *The Territorial Imperative* (London: Fontana, 1967), Robert Ardrey tells how he was a young playwright in New York at the time of the Pearl Harbor bombing,

thinking only of his career and personal life, when he was transformed overnight into a patriot when he perceived that his country was under attack.

10 As Elissa Marder argued in an unpublished paper, "Arbologies of Roland Barthes," the tying of ribbons to trees played on mythological resonances of the sort analyzed by Barthes in *Mythologies* (1972). The very concept of "Operation Desert Storm" is a mythology in Barthes' sense of naturalizing unnatural events, making a phenomenon of ugly history appear to be an event of nature, an inevitable desert storm bringing just retribution on the evils of Saddam Hussein.

11 The first three examples are from winter 1991, while the last examples are documented in *The Texas Observer*, (February 8, 1991: 8–9 and April 19, 1991: 22.

12 The Anti-Discrimination League reported that incidences of violence against Arab-Americans reached an all-time high during 1991, with 119 hate crimes compared with 39 in 1990 (the *New York Times*, February 22, 1991).

13 ABC Baghdad correspondent Bill Blakemore reported directly from the bombed sleeping shelter, poking holes in the U.S. account that it was a military command and control center; later, it turned out that the U.S. was lying, or had faulty information (see the account in Kellner 1992b).

14 Some of these football examples are from the Greenpeace "Gulf Report" on January 18, 1991, "Situation Report No. 2" from the PeaceNet mideast.gulf bulletin board. During the ground war, General Schwarzkopf and media reporters regularly used football metaphors to describe U.S. tactics.

Part III

Media
culture/identities/politics

Chapter 7

Television, advertising, and the construction of postmodern identities

According to anthropological and sociological folklore, in traditional societies, one's identity was fixed, solid, and stable. Identity was a function of predefined social roles and a traditional system of myths which provided orientation and religious sanctions to define one's place in the world, while rigorously circumscribing the realm of thought and behavior. One was born and died a member of one's clan, of a fixed kinship system, and of one's tribe or group with one's life trajectory fixed in advance. In premodern societies, identity was unproblematical and not subject to reflection or discussion. Individuals did not undergo identity crises, or radically modify their identity. One was a hunter and a member of the tribe and gained one's identity through these roles and functions.

In modernity, identity becomes more mobile, multiple, personal, self-reflexive, and subject to change and innovation.[1] Yet identity in modernity is also social and other-related. Theorists of identity from Hegel through G.H. Mead have often characterized personal identity in terms of mutual recognition, as if one's identity depended on recognition from others combined with self-validation of this recognition. Yet the forms of identity in modernity are also relatively substantial and fixed; identity still comes from a circumscribed set of roles and norms: one is a mother, a son, a Texan, a Scot, a professor, a socialist, a Catholic, a lesbian – or rather a combination of these social roles and possibilities. Identities are thus still relatively fixed and limited, though the boundaries of possible identities, of new identities, are continually expanding.

Indeed, in modernity, self-consciousness comes into its own; it becomes possible to continually engage in reflection on available social roles and possibilities and gains a distance from tradition (Kolb 1986). One can choose and make – and then remake – one's identity as one's life-possibilities change and expand or contract. Modernity also increases other-directedness, however, for as the number of possible identities increases, one must gain recognition to assume a socially validated, recognized identity. In modernity, there is still a structure of interaction with socially defined and available roles, norms, customs, and expectations, among which one must choose and reproduce to gain identity in a complex process of mutual recognition. In this way, the other is a constituent of identity in modernity and, consequently, the other-directed character is a familiar type in late modernity, dependent upon others for recognition and thus for the establishment of personal identity (Riesman *et al.* 1950).

In modernity, identity therefore becomes both a personal and a theoretical problem. Certain tensions appear within and between theories of identity, as well as within the modern individual. On one hand, some theorists of identity define personal identity in terms of a substantial self, an innate and self-identical essence which constitutes the person. From Descartes' cogito, to Kant's and Husserl's transcendental ego, to the Enlightenment concept of reason, to some contemporary concepts of the subject, identity is conceived as something essential, substantial, unitary, fixed, and fundamentally unchanging. Yet other modern theorists of identity postulate a non-substantiality of the self (Hume), or conceive of the self and identity as an existential project, as the creation of the authentic individual (Kierkegaard, Marx, Nietzsche, Heidegger, Sartre). The existential self is always fragile and requires commitment, resolve, and action to sustain, thus making the creation of identity an existential project for each individual.

Anxiety also becomes a constituent experience for the modern self. For one is never certain that one has made the right choice, that one has chosen one's "true" identity, or even constituted an identity at all. The modern self is aware of the constructed nature of identity and that one can always change and modify one's identity at will. One is also anxious concerning recognition and validation of one's identity by others. Further, modernity also involves a process of innovation, of constant turnover and novelty. In some formulations, modernity signifies the destruction of past forms of life, values, and identities, combined with the production of ever new ones (Berman 1982). The experience of *modernité* is one of novelty, of the ever-changing new, of innovation and transitoriness (Frisby 1985). One's identity may become out of date, or superfluous, or no longer socially validated. One may thus experience anomie, a condition of extreme alienation in which one is no longer at home in the world.

By contrast, one's identity may crystallize and harden such that ennui and boredom may ensue. One is tired of one's life, of who one has become. One is trapped in a web of social roles, expectations, and relations. There appears to be no exit and no possibility of change. Or, one is caught up in so many different, sometimes conflicting, roles that one no longer knows who one is. In these ways, identity in modernity becomes increasingly problematic and the issue of identity itself becomes a problem. Indeed, only in a society anxious about identity could the problems of personal identity, or self-identity, or identity crises, arise and be subject to worry and debate. Theorists of self-identity are often anxious (Kierkegaard, Heidegger, Sartre) concerning the fragility of identity and analyze in detail those experiences and social forces which undermine and threaten personal identity.

Identity in modernity was also linked to individuality, to developing a uniquely individual self. Whereas traditionally, identity was a function of the tribe, the group, or a collective, in modernity identity was a function of creating a particularized individuality. In the consumer and media societies that emerged after World War II, identity has been increasingly linked to style, to producing an image, to how one looks. It is as if everyone has to have their own look, style, and image to have their own identity, though, paradoxically, many of the models of style and look come from consumer culture, thus individuality is highly mediated in the consumer society of the present.

Thus, in modernity, the problem of identity consisted in how we constitute, perceive, interpret, and present ourself to ourselves and others. As noted, for some theorists, identity is a discovery and affirmation of an innate essence which determines what I am, while for others identity is a construct and a creation from available social roles and material. Contemporary postmodern thought has by and large rejected the essentialist and rationalist notion of identity and builds on the constructivist notion which it in turn problematizes. Consequently, one of the goals of this chapter will be to explicate how identity is formulated in postmodern theory and is constructed in contemporary cultural forms. At stake is whether identity is fundamentally different in so-called postmodernity and whether a distinction between modernity and postmodernity, and modern and postmodern identities, can be sustained.

IDENTITY IN POSTMODERN THEORY

From the postmodern perspective, as the pace, extension, and complexity of modern societies accelerate, identity becomes more and more unstable, more and more fragile. Within this situation, the discourses of postmodernity problematize the very notion of identity, claiming that it is a myth and an illusion. One reads both in modern theorists like the Frankfurt School, and in Baudrillard and other postmodern theorists that the autonomous, self-constituting subject that was the achievement of modern individuals, of a culture of individualism, is fragmenting and disappearing, due to social processes which produce the levelling of individuality in a rationalized, bureaucratized and consumerized mass society and media culture.[2] Post-structuralists in turn have launched an attack on the very notions of the subject and identity, claiming that subjective identity is itself a myth, a construct of language and society, an overdetermined illusion that one is really a substantial subject, that one really has a fixed identity (Coward and Ellis 1977; Jameson 1983, 1991).

It is thus claimed that in postmodern culture, the subject has disintegrated into a flux of euphoric intensifies, fragmented and disconnected, and that the decentered postmodern self no longer experiences anxiety (with hysteria becoming the typical postmodern psychic malady) and no longer possesses the depth, substantiality, and coherency that was the ideal and sometimes achievement of the modern self (Baudrillard 1983c; Jameson 1983, 1991). Postmodern theorists claim that subjects have imploded into masses (Baudrillard 1983b), that a fragmented, disjointed, and discontinuous mode of experience is a fundamental characteristic of postmodern culture, of both its subjective experiences and texts (Jameson 1983, 1991). It is argued that in a postmodern media and information society one is at most a "term in the terminal" (Baudrillard 1983c), or a cyberneticized effect of "fantastic systems of control" (Kroker and Cook 1986). Deleuze and Guattari (1977) celebrate schizoid, nomadic dispersions of desire and subjectivity, valorizing precisely the breaking up and dispersion of the subject of modernity. In these theories, identity is highly unstable and has in some postmodern theories disappeared altogether in the "postmodern scene" where:

> The TV self is the electronic individual *par excellence* who gets everything there is to get from the simulacrum of the media: a market-identity as a consumer in the society of the spectacle; a galaxy of hyperfibrillated moods. . . traumatized serial being.
>
> (Kroker and Cook 1986: 274)

Many of the postmodern theories privilege media culture as the site of the implosion of identity and fragmentation of the subject, yet there have been few in-depth studies of media texts and their effects from this perspective. With the exception of the work of Jameson (see Kellner 1989c), few of the major postmodern theorists have carried out systematic and sustained examination of the actual texts and practices of popular media culture. For instance, Baudrillard's few references to the actual artifacts of media culture are extremely sketchy and fragmentary, as are those of Deleuze and Guattari (while Deleuze has written extensively on film, he does not theorize it as postmodern). Foucault and Lyotard have ignored media culture almost completely. And while Kroker and Cook (1986) carry out detailed readings of contemporary painting, they too neglect to carry out concrete studies of media culture in their explorations of the postmodern scene (though, *à la* Baudrillard, they ascribe tremendous power to the media in the constitution of "the postmodern scene").[3]

For instance, the film *Pretty Woman* puts on display the key role of image in the construction of identity in contemporary societies. A working-class prostitute (played by Julia Roberts) meets a corporate Prince Charming (played by Richard Gere) and transforms herself from fashionless street girl to high-fashion beauty. The film illustrates the process of self-transformation through fashion, cosmetics, diction, and style, and the extent to which identity is mediated through image and look in contemporary culture. The result of the Roberts character's transformation was thus a new personality, a new identity, enabling her to get her man and become a success in the image identity market. The message of the film is thus that if you want to become a new you, to transform your identity, to become successful, you need to focus on image, style, and fashion.

In this and the following chapter, I examine, in somewhat more detail than is usual in rapid postmodern raids into media culture, some popular artifacts to see what they tell us about identity in contemporary societies. My selections are hardly innocent although they are symptomatic of what are generally taken to be salient features of postmodern culture: proliferation and dissemination of images without depth; glitzy, high-tech produced intensities; pastiche and implosion of forms; and quotation and repetition of past images and forms. My focus will be on images of identity in a popular television series *Miami Vice*, which is often taken as a symptomatic postmodern media text, and cigarette advertisements which so far have been relatively unexplored by postmodern theory, but which reveal some interesting changes in contemporary image production. Together these studies should illuminate some of the dynamics of identity in so-called postmodern societies.

My take on identity in contemporary society and culture will, however, be critical of several central claims of postmodern theory. I criticize what I consider to be one-sided and inadequate postmodern positions on contemporary culture and what I take to be the limitations of excessively formalistic postmodern analysis. I also put in question claims concerning postmodernism as a concept that interprets contemporary culture as a whole, and conclude with some critical reflections on the very concept of postmodernity as a new epoch in history and the concept of postmodernism as a cultural dominant.

Television and postmodernity

While the postmodern intervention in the arts is often interpreted as a reaction against modernism,[4] against the stifling elitist canonization of the works of high modernism, the postmodern intervention within television is a reaction against realism and the system of coded genres (sitcom, soaps, action/adventure, and so on) that define the system of commercial television in the United States. In this sense, postmodern interventions within television replicate the assault on realism and genre which modernism itself had earlier attacked. Modernism never took hold in television, especially in the commercial variety produced in the United States – which is culturally hegemonic in many sites throughout the world. Instead, commercial television is predominantly governed by the aesthetic of representational realism, of images and stories which fabricate the real and attempt to produce a reality effect (Kellner 1980). Television's relentless representational realism has also been subordinate to narrative codes, to story-telling, and to the conventions of highly coded genres. Commercial television has been constituted as an entertainment medium and it appears that its producers believe that audiences are most entertained by stories, by narratives with familiar and recognizable characters, plot-lines, conventions, and messages, as well as by familiar genres. This aesthetic poverty of the medium has probably been responsible for its contempt by high cultural theorists and its designation as a "vast wasteland" by those who have other aesthetic tastes and values.

If for most of the history of television, narrative story-telling has been the name of the game, on a postmodern account of television *image* often decenters the importance of narrative. It is claimed that in those programs usually designated "postmodern" – MTV music videos, *Miami Vice*, *Max Headroom*, high-tech ads, and so on – there is a new look and feel: the signifier has been liberated and image takes precedence over narrative, as compelling and highly artificial aesthetic images detach themselves from the television diegesis and become the center of fascination, of a seductive pleasure, of an intense but fragmentary and transitory aesthetic experience.

While there is some truth in this conventional postmodern position, such descriptions are also in some ways misleading. In particular, I reject the familiar account that postmodern image culture is fundamentally flat and one-dimensional. For Jameson, postmodernism manifests "the emergence of a new kind of flatness or depthlessness, a new kind of superficiality in the most literal sense – perhaps the supreme formal feature of all the postmodernisms" (1984: 60). According to Jameson, the "waning of affect" in postmodern image culture is replicated in postmodern selves who are allegedly devoid of the expressive energies and individualities characteristic of modernism and the modern self. Both postmodern texts and selves are said to be without depth and to be flat, superficial, and lost in the intensities and vacuities of the moment, without substance and meaning, or connection to the past.

Such one-dimensional postmodern texts and selves put in question the continued relevance of hermeneutic depth models such as the Marxian model of essence and appearance, true and false consciousness, and ideology and truth; the Freudian model of latent and manifest meanings; the existentialist model of authentic and inauthentic existence; and the semiotic model of signifier and signified. Cumulatively, postmodernism thus signifies the death of hermeneutics; in place of what Ricoeur (1970) has termed a "hermeneutics of suspicion" and the polysemic modernist reading of cultural symbols and texts, there emerges the postmodern view that there is nothing behind the surface of texts, no depth or multiplicity of meanings for critical inquiry to discover and explicate.

From this postmodern view of texts and selves, it follows that a postmodern cultural theory should rest content to describe the surface or forms of cultural texts, rather than seeking meanings or significance.[5] Against such a formalist and anti-hermeneutical postmodern type of analysis connected with the postulation of a flat, postmodern image culture, I would advocate a cultural studies which draws on both postmodern and other critical theories in order to analyze both image *and* meaning, surface *and* depth, as well as the politics *and* erotics of cultural artifacts. Thus, I argue here that interpretive analysis of image, narrative, ideologies, and meanings continues to be of importance in analyzing even those texts taken to be paradigmatic of postmodern culture – though analysis of form, surface, and look is also important. I argue in the following pages that the images, fragments, and narratives of media culture are saturated with ideology and polysemic meanings, and that therefore – against certain postmodern positions (Foucault 1977; Baudrillard 1981; and Deleuze and Guattari 1977) – ideology critique continues to be an important and indispensable weapon in our critical arsenal (see Chapter 2 for discussion of the issues at stake here).

In addition, there is another familiar postmodern position which I would also like to distance myself from: the view, associated with Baudrillard (1983b, 1983c), that television is pure noise in the postmodern ecstasy, a pure implosion, a black hole where all meaning and messages are absorbed in the whirlpool and kaleidoscope of radical semiurgy, of the incessant dissemination of images and information to the point of total saturation, of inertia and apathy where meaning is dissolved, where only the fascination of discrete images glow and flicker in a mediascape within which no image any longer has any discernible effects, where the proliferating velocity and quantity of images produces a postmodern mindscreen where images fly by with such rapidity that they lose any signifying function, referring only to other images ad infinitum, and where eventually the multiplication of images produces such saturation, apathy, and indifference that the tele-spectator is lost forever in a fragmentary fun house of mirrors in the infinite play of superfluous, meaningless images.

Now, no doubt, television can be experienced as a flat, one-dimensional wasteland of superficial images, and can function as well as pure noise without referent and meaning. One can also become overwhelmed by – or indifferent to – the flow, velocity, and intensity of images, so that television's signifying function can be decentered and can collapse altogether. Yet there is something wrong with this account. People regularly watch certain shows and events; there are fans for various series and stars who possess an often incredible expertise and knowledge of the subjects of their fascination; people do model their behavior, style, and attitudes on television images; television ads do play a role in managing consumer demand; and, most recently, many analysts have concluded that television is playing the central role in political elections, that elections have become a battle of images played out on the television screen, and that television is playing an essential role in the new art of governing (Kellner 1990a).

Now, obviously, different audiences watch television in different ways. For some, television is nothing more than a fragmented collage of images that people only fitfully watch or connect with what goes before or comes after. Many individuals today use devices to "zap" from one program to another, channel hopping or "grazing" to merely "see what's happening," to go with the disconnected flow of images. Many individuals who watch entire programs merely focus on the surface of images, with programs, ads, station breaks, and so on flowing into each other, collapsing meaning in a play of disconnected signifiers. Many people cannot remember what they watched the night before, or cannot provide coherent accounts of the previous night's programming.

And yet it is an exaggeration to claim that the apparatus of television itself relentlessly undermines meaning and collapses signifiers without signifieds into a flat, one-dimensional hyperspace without depth, effects, or meanings. Thus, against the postmodern notion of culture disintegrating into pure image without referent or content or effects – becoming at its limit pure noise – I argue by contrast that television and other forms of media culture play key roles in the structuring of contemporary identity and shaping thought and behavior. I have argued elsewhere that television today assumes some of the functions traditionally ascribed to myth and ritual (i.e. integrating individuals into the social order, celebrating dominant values, offering models of thought, behavior, and gender for imitation, and so on). I also argued that TV myth resolved social contradictions in the way that Levi-

Strauss described the function of traditional myth and provided mythologies of the sort described by Barthes which idealize contemporary values and institutions, and thus exalt the established way of life (Kellner 1982). I illustrate these points in the following sections where I discuss how popular television programs, and more generally advertising, function to provide models of identity in the contemporary world.

Consequently, I argue that much postmodern cultural analysis is too one-sided and limited, in either restricting its focus on form, on image alone, or in abandoning media culture analysis altogether in favor of grandiose totalizing metaphors (black holes, implosion, excremental culture, and so on). Instead, it is preferable to analyze both form and content, image and narrative, and postmodern surface and the deeper ideological problematics within the context of specific exercises which explicate the polysemic nature of images and texts, and which endorse the possibility of multiple encodings and decodings. With these qualifications in mind, let us then examine *Miami Vice* to discover what we might learn concerning television, postmodernity, and identity.

Miami Vice and the politics of image and identity

Miami Vice, along with MTV, was many critics' favorite example of postmodern television (Gitlin 1987; Fiske 1987b; Grossberg 1987). The program originated in 1984 as a product of "Hill Street Blues" producer Anthony Yerkovich and film director Michael Mann; Mann became the controlling figure and remained with the program until its end in 1989. The series took the form of a crime drama centered around two undercover officers, Sonny Crockett, a Miami native and former University of Florida football player (Don Johnson) and Ricardo Tubbs (Paul Michael Thomas), a Puerto Rican detective who migrated south from New York City. Their superior, Castillo (Edward James Olmos), was a Cuban-American and they had a variety of police co-workers and street informants who were series regulars. Action focused on Miami drug and crime scenes, and was shot at actual Florida locations around Miami.

In *Miami Vice*, images are detached from the narrative and seem to take on a life of their own. Its producers rejected familiar earth tones and offered instead a wealth of artificial images, emphasizing South Florida colors of flamingo pink, lime green, Caribbean blue, subdued pastels, and flashing neon. On the cutting edge of image and sound production from the beginning, the series deployed four-track stereo and used popular rock music to establish ambience, often playing entire songs as background to the action, replicating the music video form of MTV.[6] Their use of lighting, camera angles, cutting, sound, and the exotic terrain of Miami's high-tech, high-rise, high-crime, and multiracial culture makes for a wealth of resonant images which its producers sometimes successfully turned into aesthetic spectacles that are highly intense, fascinating, and seductive. The sometimes meandering narratives replicate experiences of fragmentation and of slow ennui, punctuated with hallucinogenic intensity. Image frequently takes precedence over narrative and the look and feel become primary, often relegating story-line and narrative meanings to the background.

No doubt, this arguably postmodern style is a fundamental aspect of *Miami Vice* and yet I would submit that most analyses of the series as "postmodern" get it wrong, or miss key aspects of the phenomenon. Privileging Jameson's category of the waning of affect, Gitlin (1987), for example, claims that *Miami Vice* is the ultimate in postmodern blankness, emptiness, and world-weariness. Yet, against this reading, one could argue that it pulsates as well with intense emotion, a clash of values, and highly specific political messages and positions (see Best and Kellner 1987 and the following analysis). Grossberg (1987) also argues that *Miami Vice* and other postmodern culture obliterates meaning and depth, claiming:

> *Miami Vice* is, as its critics have said, all on the surface. And the surface is nothing but a collection of quotations from our own collective historical debris, a mobile game of Trivia. It is, in some ways, the perfect televisual image, minimalist (the sparse scenes, the constant long shots, etc) yet concrete.
>
> (Grossberg 1987: 28)

Grossberg goes on to argue that "indifference" (to meanings, ideology, politics, and so on) is the key distinguishing feature of *Miami Vice* and other postmodern texts which he suggests are more akin to billboards to be scanned for what they tell us about our cultural terrain rather than texts to be read and interrogated.

Against Grossberg, I would argue that *Miami Vice* is highly polysemic and is saturated with ideologies, messages, and quite specific meanings and values. Behind the high-tech glitz are multiple sites of meaning, multiple subject positions, and highly contradictory ideological problematics. The show had a passionately loyal audience which was obviously not indifferent to the series which had, as I attempt to show, its own intense, affective investments and passions. In the following discussion, I thus argue that *reading* the text of *Miami Vice* hermeneutically and critically provides access to its polysemic wealth and that therefore it is a mistake to rapidly speed by such artifacts, however some audiences may relate to them.

By contrast, for a one-dimensional postmodern reading, an artifact like *Miami Vice* is all surface without any depth or layered meanings. On my reading, however, the form, narrative, and images constitute a polysemic text with a multiplicity of possible meanings which require multivalent readings that probe the various layers of the text. For my political hermeneutic, the show is read as a social text which tells us some things about contemporary society. In particular, I wish to suggest that *Miami Vice* provides many insights into the fragmentation, reconstruction, and fragility of identity in contemporary culture and that it also provides insight into how identities are constructed through the incorporation of subject positions offered for emulation by media culture. Against the Althusserian position, taken at one time by *Screen*, which claims that ideological texts interpolate individuals into subject positions that are homogenous, unified, and untroubled, I shall suggest that on the contrary the "subject positions" of media culture are highly specific, contradictory, fragile, and subject to rapid reconstruction and transformation.[7]

To begin, media culture provides images and figures with which its audiences can identity and emulate. It thus possesses important socializing and enculturating effects via its role models, gender models, and variety of subject positions which valorize certain forms of behavior and style while denigrating and villainizing other types. For example, it is well-documented that *Miami Vice*'s detectives Crockett (Don Johnson) and Tubbs (Paul Michael Thomas) have become fashion icons, arbiters of taste. Crockett's unconstructed Italian jackets, his tennis shoes without socks, his T-shirts and loose pants, his frequently stubbled beard, his changing hairstyle, and so on produced a model for a new male look, a new hip alternative to straight fashion, a legitimation for "loose and causal." Tubbs, by contrast, provides an icon of the hip and meticulously fashionable with his Vern Uomo double-breasted suits and thin Italian ties, fashionable shoes, trendy earring, and nouveau-cool demeanor. Their male associates, Zito and Switek, with their Hawaiian shirts, loose, colorful pants, and very lack of high fashion provide models of more informal clothing and looks, while the women detectives Gina and Trudy are constantly changing their clothes, hairstyles, and looks, validating a constant turn-over and reconstruction of image and look.

The social horizon of *Miami Vice* is the materialist consumer society of the 1980s and the Reaganist emphasis on wealth, affluence, fashion, style, and image. During this time, a new image culture defined identity in terms of image. *Miami Vice*, in its images and stories, transcoded these fashion and identity discourses and in turn influenced the fashion, style, and look of its era. The *Miami Vice* effect: it was now cool to engage in more casual fashion styles and to constantly change one's look and image. Don Johnson and other actors on the show became fashion icons and role models, and the show promoted a glitzy high-tech look which synthesized advertising and TV techniques, combining dazzling images with fast editing and intense musical soundtracks and background.

Crockett and Tubbs and their colleagues are arguably role models for macho white males, blacks, Hispanics, women, and teenagers, while the criminal under-class portrayed provides criminal identities. Thus, quite specific gender and role models and subject positions are projected, as are quite different images of sex, race, and class than are usual in the typical mediascapes of television world. In general, *Miami Vice* positions its viewers to identify with and desire an affluent, up-scale lifestyle via its projection of images of a high-tech, high-consumption affluent society. Its iconic images of high-rise buildings, luxury houses, fast and expensive cars and women, and, of course, the pricey and ambiguous commodities of drugs and prostitution produce images of affluence and high-level consumption which position viewers to envy the wealth and power of the villains while identifying as well with the lifestyles, personality traits, and behavior of the heroes. The challenge of *Miami Vice* is to present the "good" cops as more appropriate and desirable role models than the "bad" drug dealers and affluent criminal underworld who in a sense live out the fantasy of unbridled capitalism.

The program also invites viewers to identify with a fast, mobile lifestyle focusing on exciting consumerist leisure. The opening iconic images of the show present a speedboat racing across the ocean with blue waves and white foam pulsating to an intense musical beat; the images cut to exotic birds, sensual women, sports competition, horse and dog racing, and other leisure images with affluent Miami as the backdrop. These opening images are packed together with quick editing which provide a sensation of speed and mobility, iconic invitations to get into the fast lane and join the high life. The show itself will then demonstrate how individuals enter into this leisure utopia and find the good life within its spectacles and enticements.

As its narratives unfold, *Miami Vice* presents some revealing insights into the problematics of identity in contemporary techno-capitalist societies. The chief characters (Crockett, Tubbs and their boss Castillo) all have multiple identities and multiple pasts which intersect in unstable ways with the present. In each case, their identity is fragmented and unstable, different and distinctive in each character, yet always subject to dramatic change. Crockett is presented as an ex-football star, a Vietnam veteran, and a young man familiar with the criminal underworld, with the players in the drug and crime scene. His nickname "Sonny" codes him as an icon of youth while his last name "Crockett," evokes the hero image derived from the name of one of the heroes of the Alamo, Davy Crockett, who was subject of a successful Disney TV miniseries in the 1950s and the hero of John Wayne's *The Alamo* in 1960. Unlike the stolid bourgeois Davy, however, Sonny is presented as having been married and divorced with several episodes depicting him with his former wife and son, yet these encounters are infrequent and he gains no real lasting identity as a father or husband in the series.

Instead, Crockett is portrayed in multiple relationships, relatively unstructured and subject to quick change. In early seasons, he is shown involved with his colleague Gina and is also involved with a fashionable architect, a stewardess who dies of a drug overdose, and a woman doctor who is also a drug addict. These relationships were featured in single episodes within which the relationship disintegrated, never to reappear (his two lovers involved with drugs died). In the 1987/8 season, Crockett marries a successful rock singer who he was assigned to protect (played by Scottish rock star Sheena Easton), yet she soon disappears on a seemingly interminable rock tour and when he is shot and almost dies ("A Bullet for Crockett," 1988), she cannot be reached and only his colleagues are there for the death watch – a substitute family of a type increasingly familiar in TV world as the divorce rate soars in the real world.

Tubbs, by contrast, is presented as a street-wise black cop who leaves New York after his brother is shot and comes to Miami to seek his brother's killer; he decides to stay and teams up with Crockett. His name Ricardo Tubbs, his nickname Rico, and his dark, multiple-hued skin codes him as of mixed racial descent. Tubbs rarely talks about his past and lives a perpetual present, closely connected only to his partner Crockett. Their boss Castillo was also, like Crockett, a Vietnam veteran who worked as well for the Drug Enforcement Agency in Thailand where he married and lost his wife in a battle with a drugs baron. Presumed dead, she and the drugs baron arrive in Miami ("Golden Triangle," 1985); Castillo learns that she is now happily married, but was kidnapped and is in effect the hostage of the drug dealer, who threatens to kill her husband if she leaves or betrays him. After Castillo rescues the woman, in a *Casablanca*-inspired ending, he bids her and her husband farewell at the end of the episode.

Castillo appears as the brooding patriarch, the self-contained and self-enclosed autonomous subject who defines himself by his morality and actions. His is the most stable identity in *Miami Vice* and he presents a figure of an autonomous self with a strongly fixed personal identity. Yet Castillo too is presented as a man of great passion and intensity which he constantly suppresses, producing the image of a smoldering figure who could explode any moment into violence and chaos, whose carefully constructed moral boundaries might at any moment dissolve – a quiet, tragic figure who could easily fall into the more chaotic world of violence and nihilism which threatens all boundaries and identities in the fragile and unstable world of *Miami Vice*.

Crockett and Tubbs in contrast to Castillo are constantly changing their looks, styles, and behavior. At the beginning of the 1988/9 season, Crockett appeared with shoulder-length hair, sometimes held back in a ponytail, while Tubbs appeared with a thick beard – which disappeared later in the season. The instability of the cops' identity in *Miami Vice* is exploited in a plot device which utilizes their multiple identities as cops and undercover players in the underworld. Both assume under-cover roles with Crockett living on an expensive boat, masquerading as drug runner Sonny Burnett, while Tubbs assumes the role of buyer/dealer Ricardo Cooper who sometimes assumes a Jamaican, Caribbean persona, while other times he appears as a hip, black urban hood. One would think that the word would soon get around that "Burnett" is "really" the vice cop "Crockett" and that the various criminals who Tubbs "plays" are "really" masks for the vice cop "Tubbs." Yet in show after show, Crockett and Tubbs assume their criminal identities and slide from good guy to bad guy as easily as one would change one's undershirt.[8] Such doubled-coded identities signals the artificiality of identity, that identity is constructed not given, that it is a matter of choice, style, and behavior rather than intrinsic moral or psychological qualities. It also suggests that identity is a game that one plays, that one can easily shift from one identity to another.

Postmodern identity, then, is constituted theatrically through role playing and image construction. While the locus of modern identity revolved around one's occupation, one's function in the public sphere (or family), postmodern identity revolves around leisure, centered on looks, images, and consumption. Modern identity was a serious affair involving fundamental choices that defined who one was (profession, family, political identifications, and so on), while postmodern identity is a function of leisure and is grounded in play, in gamesmanship, in producing an image. The notion of a "player" – central to identity construction in *Miami Vice* – provides clues to the nature of postmodern identity. A "player" knows the rules and the score and acts accordingly. The player plays with and often flouts social conventions and attempts to distinguish herself through ritualized activities, through gambling, sports, drug-dealing and use, sexual activity, or other leisure and social concerns. The player "becomes someone" if she succeeds and gains identity through admiration and respect of other players.

One of the structuring principles of *Miami Vice* points to a schizoid dichotomy within the identity construction of the two main characters which I believe points to tensions within contemporary identity construction. As noted, Crockett and Tubbs are both cops and players in many episodes, acting as criminals to entrap the "real" players. In the 1988/9 season, the plot lines played on this double identity, as Crockett schizophrenically slid from Burnett back to Crockett. The story suggests that it is easy to fall into, to become, the roles that one plays and that identity construction today is highly tenuous and fragile. Suspense was built around whether "Crockett" could continue to be "Crockett," or whether he would suddenly become "Burnett." The moral seems to be that when one radically shifts identity at will, one might lose control, one might become pathologically conflicted and divided, disabled from autonomous thought and action.

Thus it appears that postmodern identity tends more to be constructed from the images of leisure and consumption than modern identities and tends to be more unstable and subject to change. Both modern and postmodern identity contain a level of reflexivity, an awareness that identity is chosen and constructed, though, in contemporary society, it may be more "natural" to change identities, to switch with the changing winds of fashion. While this produces an erosion of individuality and increased social conformity (to contemporary models of identity), there are, however, some positive potentials of this postmodern portrayal of identity as an artificial construct. For such a notion of identity suggests that one can always change one's life, that identity can always be reconstructed, that one is free to change and produce oneself as one chooses.

This notion of multiple, freely chosen, and easily disposed of postmodern identities can be interestingly contrasted to more traditional images of police who had quite different "modern" identities and who offered quite different subject positions. In *Dragnet* (1951–9 and 1967–70) Jack Webb's Sgt. Friday was the model of the tight, moralistic, and ascetic authoritarian personality, while Robert Stack's Elliot Ness in "The Untouchables" (1959–63) was literally untouchable and incorruptible by women or criminals. Both were extremely rigid, authoritarian figures without apparent personal lives or any individuality or complex personality traits. The chief cop in *The F.B.I.* (1965–74) was also highly impersonal, with no distinctive personal identity, as were the cops in 1950s police dramas like *Highway Patrol*, *M Squad*, and *The Naked City*.

In the 1960s and 1970s more "personable" cops began to appear with *Columbo*, *Kojak*, *Baretta*, *Starsky and Hutch*, and so on. Yet these TV cops too had relatively fixed identities which were readily identifiable by their personality quirks, by their marks of individuality. Columbo's shuffling, modest, and sly methods of interrogation, Kojak's bully-boy masculist tactics, Baretta's identification with the little guy and rage at criminals who hurt "his" people, and Starsky and Hutch's explosions of moral rage provided these TV cops with stable, familiar identities – more highly individualized than previous ones, but equally substantial and fixed. Such stability is no longer visible in *Miami Vice* where Crockett and Tubbs assume different hairstyles, looks, roles, and behavior, from show to show, season to season.

Although identity in *Miami Vice* in the figures of Crockett and Tubbs is unstable, fluid, fragmentary, disconnected, multiple, open, and subject to dramatic transformation, it nonetheless privileges certain male subject positions. In particular, macho male identity is positively valorized throughout; Crockett, Tubbs, and Castillo are all highly macho figures and their male and female subordinates emulate their behavior. The viewer is thus positioned to view highly aggressive, highly masculist, and, fairly often, highly sexist behavior as desirable, and a macho male subject is thus privileged as the most desirable role model. The two women vice cops – Trudy and Gina – are often assigned to play prostitutes, or to seduce criminals and are thus presented in negative stereotypes of sluts and seducers; they often fall into situations of danger and must be rescued by the male cops. When they are allowed subjectivity of their own, they fall for criminals, as when Gina falls in love with an unscrupulous IRA thug in the episode entitled "When Irish Eyes are Shining" (1985). The women cops are presented most positively when they engage in aggressive male behavior, as when Gina shoots the IRA gunmen, or Trudy shoots an especially sleazy criminal who she was forced to sleep with in her undercover work. Such macho behavior replicates the images of women warriors which became an increasingly central image in the late 1970s and 1980s (*Alien, Aliens, Superwoman, Sheena*, and so on). Equality in this ideological scenario thus becomes equal opportunities to kill, to become women warriors equal to the macho males in the realm of primal aggressivity.

The show is also arguably racist, privileging the white male Crockett as the subject of power and desire, as the center around which most of the narratives revolve. In January of 1989, NBC devoted its Friday night primetime schedule to "Three for Crockett," broadcasting three straight episodes that centered on the central white male figure. In terms of image construction, white is also the privileged color: Crockett often wears white jackets, drives a white car, carouses on white sand beaches, and pursues beautiful white women. Black – as in the traditional melodrama genre – is coded as the site of danger, mystery, uncertainty, and evil. Few shows have used as many and as menacing black, nighttime backdrops, in which the light forms and figures are privileged as the positive index against the negatively valorized black background.

And yet the black/white friendship of Crockett and Tubbs – interpreted by some critics as blatantly homoerotic (Butler 1985) – presents one of the most striking images of interracial friendship in the history of television, and Tubbs and Castillo are two of the most positive images of people of color yet to appear. On the other hand, while Tubbs and Castillo arguably provide positive role models for young black and Hispanic males, most of the images of blacks, Hispanics and Third-World people of color in the series are strongly negative. Two informers featured on many episodes – the Cuban Izzie and the black Noogie – are stereotypes of Hispanic and black street hustlers, the improper role models against which Tubbs and Castillo are defined. Two black policeman have been featured in supporting roles – an obnoxious New York officer and an overly aggressive and incompetent federal drug enforcer – who also present the negative antithesis of the ideal black professional. The criminals are also stereotyped people of color who play the usual conventional roles: drug dealers, war lords, prostitutes, gun runners, and so on, who are predominantly vicious, unprincipled, dangerous, and violent.

Third-World scenes are likewise presented negatively as places of corruption, violence, and multiple forms of evil and these negative emanations from the site of otherness, the hearts of darkness, are shown as threatening the utopia of Miami with its easy affluence and upscale lifestyles. The underclass of the United States by contrast is rarely portrayed, though some episodes have shown quite striking images of ghetto life and one 1986 episode realistically depicts the problems of ghetto blacks in a story of a young black athlete, unable to escape from the violence and degradation of the ghetto.

In fact, there are some socially critical and progressive aspects to the series. In a sense, the "vice" portrayed is as much capitalism's vice as Miami's. While Miami is the site of unbridled crime, it is also the site of unbridled "free enterprise" and drug dealing is the ultimate in high-profit capital accumulation, while drugs represent the ultracapitalist dream of a commodity that is cheap to produce and that can provide tremendous profits in its selling. A Thai drugs baron in a 1985 episode "The Golden Triangle" states that drugs are "no different from tapioca or tin ore from Malaysia. It is simply a commodity for which there is a demand." Indeed, the series is one of the few to present critical images of capitalism. One episode, "The Prodigal Son" (1985), featured *Living Theater* impresario Julien Beck as a New York banker. In a meeting with drugs barons, the banker stated that the financial establishment favored continued drug trade to help them recoup their loans to Third-World countries, for whom drugs was one of the few high yield exports. In this and other episodes *Miami Vice* thus practices mild social critique.[9]

Like Balzac and Brecht, *Miami Vice* associates wealth with crime, capitalist enterprise with criminality. On the other hand, the very glamorizing of crime also celebrates high-powered capitalism, so the equation of crime and business is highly ambiguous – an ambiguity that runs through the series and which constitutes postmodern identity as ambivalent and beyond traditional "good" and "bad" role models. For identity is often constructed in media culture and society *against* dominant conventions and morality; thus there is something amoral or morally threatening about postmodern selves which are fluid, multiple, and subject to rapid change. From this perspective, Crockett is a highly ambivalent hero for American culture: he is frequently unshaven, never wears a tie and often goes without socks, is sexually promiscuous, and often reverts into his undercover "Burnett" role in which he plays with gusto the hip "player," ready to do anything for some bucks.

Yet *Miami Vice* is really neither nihilistic nor celebratory of crime. Like the traditional gangster genre in Hollywood film (see Warshow 1962), the series can be read as a cautionary morality tale which shows that those who go beyond acceptable boundaries in the pursuit of wealth and power are bound to fall. Like the gangster genre, *Miami Vice* is deeply attracted to its criminal underworld and plays out the primal passion play of capitalist free enterprise: devotion at all costs to maximizing capital accumulation. *Miami Vice* thus identifies the ultra-capitalist subject position as one of greed, uncontrolled appetite, and violent aggression which inevitably leads to death and destruction.

And yet the images of the affluent lifestyles of the criminals are so attractive and appealing that the series itself is morally ambivalent, investing both the professional identity of the cops and the outlaw identity of the criminals with positive value – an ambivalence intensified by the dual identities of Crockett and Tubbs who play out both affluent criminal roles and professional cop roles, within the same episode. Such ambivalence perhaps intensifies the sort of relativism that certain postmodern theorists claim is symptomatic of the contemporary condition. The series also puts on display and reinforces tendencies in contemporary society to adopt multiple identities, to change one's identity and look as one changes one's clothes, job, or habitat. This analysis of *Miami Vice* suggests, in fact, that *image*, *look*, and *style* are key constituents of a postmodern image culture and key constituents of postmodern identity.

Consequently, *Miami Vice* puts on display the way that identity is constituted in contemporary society through image and style, and suggests that such a mode of identity is highly fluid, multiple, mobile, and transitory. Yet I have attempted to show that certain images of fashion, gender, and style are connected to specific content and values, thus constituting specific modes and forms of identity. Likewise, the images and narratives of media culture are also saturated with ideology and value, so that identity in contemporary societies can (still) be interpreted as an ideological construct, as a means whereby enculturation produces subject positions which reproduce dominant capitalist and masculist values and modes of life.

Throughout this book, I have attempted to redeem Marxist, feminist, and multiculturalist modes of ideology critique against postmodern formalism which abstracts ideological content from image and spectacle and which affirms theses concerning the collapse of meaning and identity in a postmodern mediascape. Against this operation, I have suggested that rather than identity disappearing in contemporary society, it is rather reconstructed and redefined and I have attempted to show the relevance and importance of theories which focus on specific ideological subject positions and modes of identity formation to help illuminate these processes. Thus, whereas the modern self often assumed multiple identities, the necessity of choice and instability of a constructed identity often produced anxiety. Moreover, a stable, substantial identity – albeit self-reflexive and freely chosen – was at least a normative goal for the modern self – a type of stable identity clearly observable in the television heroes of the 1950s through the 1970s. The rapid shifts of identity in *Miami Vice*, by contrast, suggest that the postmodern self accepts and affirms multiple and shifting identities. Identity today thus becomes a freely chosen game, a theatrical presentation of the self, in which one is able to present oneself in a variety of roles, images, and activities, relatively unconcerned about shifts, transformations, and dramatic changes.

This analysis would suggest that what might be called postmodern identity is an extension of the freely chosen and multiple identities of the modern self which accepts and affirms an unstable and rapidly mutating condition. Yet precisely this condition of a multiplicity of choices was a problem for the modern self, producing anxiety and identity crisis. For the postmodern self, however, anxiety allegedly disappears for immersion in euphoric fragments of experience and frequent change of image and identity. I would not, however, want to go as far as Jameson (1984: 62f.) who claims that anxiety disappears in postmodern culture, nor would I want to deny that identity crises still occur and are often acute (a psychiatrist friend told me that gender confusion is especially acute among teenagers today, who are deeply attracted to androgynous figures like Boy George and Michael Jackson, as well as to feminine males like Prince, or "macho" women like Madonna). Indeed, when one changes one's images and style frequently, there is always anxiety concerning whether others will accept one's changes and validate through positive recognition one's new identity.

Yet one surmises that there is a shift in identity formation and that postmodern selves are becoming more multiple, transitory, and open. For Jameson (1984: 76), the figure of David Bowie gazing in fascination at a stack of television sets was a privileged figure of the postmodern self – an image to which we might add figures of the TV channel-switcher, rapidly changing channels and mediascapes, or the modem-connected computer freak, rapidly switching from computer games, to data-bases and bulletin boards, to one's own personal word-processing system and files, which figure the new postmodern terminal self. Moreover, there are emancipatory possibilities in the perpetual possibility of being able to change one's self and identity, to move from one identity to another, to revel in the play of multiple and plural identities.

In any case, whatever its nature – modern or postmodern – identity in contemporary society is increasingly mediated by media images which provide the models and ideals for modelling personal identity. Media stars like the cops on *Miami Vice*, or pop superstars like Michael Jackson or Madonna, also provide models of identity through the construction of looks, image, and style. Advertising too provides such models of identity and in the following discussion I want to show how some cigarette ads provide figures of the dramatic shift in the nature and substance of personal identity in contemporary society. After an examination of these artifacts, I'll draw some provisional conclusions concerning identity and postmodernity.

ADVERTISING IMAGES

Like television narratives, advertising too can be seen as providing some functional equivalents of myth. Like myths, ads frequently resolve social contradictions, provide models of identity, and celebrate the existing social order. Barthes (1972 [1957]) saw that advertising provided a repertoire of contemporary mythologies, and in the following discussion I depict how cigarette ads contribute to identity formation in contemporary society. The following analysis is intended to show that even the static images of advertising contain subject positions and models for identification that are heavily coded ideologically. As in the previous discussion, I argue here – against a certain type of postmodern formal analysis – that the images of media culture are important both in the mode of their formal image construction and address, as well as in terms of the meanings and values which they communicate. Accordingly, I discuss some print ads which are familiar, are readily available for scrutiny, and lend themselves to critical analysis.

Print ads are an important sector of the advertising world with about 50 percent of advertising revenues going to various print media while 22 percent is expended on television advertising. Let us look first, then, at some cigarette ads, including Marlboro ads aimed primarily at male smokers and Virginia Slims ads which try to convince women that it is cool to smoke and that the product being advertised is perfect for the "modern" woman (see the illustration following).[10] Corporations such as those in the tobacco industry undertake campaigns to associate their product with positive and desirable images and gender models. Thus, in the 1950s, Marlboro undertook a campaign to associate its cigarette with masculinity, associating smoking its product with being a "real man." Marlboro had been previously packaged as a milder women's cigarette, and the "Marlboro man" campaign was an attempt to capture the male cigarette market with images of archetypically masculine characters. Since the cowboy, Western image provided a familiar icon of masculinity, independence, and ruggedness, it was the preferred symbol for the campaign. Subsequently, the "Marlboro man" became a part of American folklore and a readily identifiable cultural symbol.

Such symbolic images in advertising attempt to create an association between the products offered and socially desirable and meaningful traits in order to produce the impression that if one wants to be a certain type of person, – for instance, to be a "real man" – then one should buy Marlboro cigarettes. Consequently, for decades, Marlboro used the cowboy figure as the symbol of masculinity and the center of their ads. In a postmodern image culture, individuals get their very identity from these figures, thus advertising becomes an important and overlooked mechanism of socialization, as well as manager of consumer demand.

Ads form textual systems with basic components which are interrelated in ways that positively position the product. The main components of the classical Marlboro ads are the conjunction of nature, the cowboy, horses, and the cigarette (see Figure 1). This system associates the Marlboro cigarette with masculinity, power, and nature. Note, however, in the Marlboro ad in Figure 2, how the cowboys decline in size, dwarfed by the images of desert and sky. Whereas in earlier Marlboro ads, the Marlboro man loomed largely in the center of the frame, now images of nature are highlighted. Why this shift?

All ads are social texts which respond to key developments during the period in which they appear. During the 1980s, media reports concerning the health hazard of cigarettes became widespread – a message highlighted in the mandatory box at

the bottom of the ad that "The Surgeon General Has Determined That Cigarette Smoking is Dangerous to Your Health." As a response to this attack, the Marlboro ads now feature images of clean, pure, wholesome nature, as if it were "natural" to smoke cigarettes, as if cigarettes were a healthy "natural" product, an emanation of benign and healthy nature. The ad, in fact, hawks *Marlboro Lights* and one of the captions describes it as a "low tar cigarette." Many 1980s Marlboro ads deployed imagery that was itself "light," white, green, snowy, and airy. Through the process of metonomy, or contiguous association, the ads tries to associate the cigarettes with "light," "natural," healthy deserts, clean snow, horses, cowboys, trees, and sky, as if they were all related "natural" artifacts, sharing the traits of "nature," thus covering over the fact that cigarettes are an artificial, synthetic product, full of dangerous pesticides, preservatives, and other chemicals.[11]

Thus, the images of healthy nature are a Barthesian mythology (1972) which attempt to cover over the image of the dangers to health from cigarette smoking. The Marlboro ad also draws on images of tradition (the cowboy), hard work, caring for animals, and other desirable traits, as if smoking were a noble activity, metonomically equivalent to these other positive social activities. The images, texts, and product shown in the ad thus provide a symbolic construct which tries to cover over and camouflage contradictions between the "heavy" work and the "light" cigarette, between the "natural" scene and the "artificial" product, between the cool and healthy outdoors scene and between the hot and unhealthy activity of smoking, and the rugged masculinity of the Marlboro man and the Light cigarette, originally targeted at women. In fact, this latter contradiction can be explained by the marketing ploy of suggesting to men that they can both be highly masculine, like the Marlboro man, and smoke a (supposedly) "healthier" cigarette, while also appealing to macho women who might enjoy smoking a "man's" cigarette which is also "lighter" and "healthier," as women's cigarettes are supposed to be.

The 1983 Virginia Slims ad pictured in Figure 3 attempts in a similar fashion to associate its product with socially desired traits and offers subject positions with which women can identify. The Virginia Slims textual system classically includes a vignette at the top of the ad with a picture underneath of the Virginia Slims woman next to the prominently displayed package of cigarettes. In the example pictured, the top of the ad features a framed box that contains the narrative images and message, which is linked to the changes in the situation of women portrayed through a contrast with the "modern" woman below. The caption under the boxed image of segregated male and female exercise classes in 1903 contains the familiar Virginia Slims slogan "You've come a long way, baby." The caption, linked to the Virginia Slims woman, next to the package of cigarettes, connotes a message of progress, metonomically linking Virginia Slims to the "progressive woman" and "modern" living. In this ad, it is the linkages and connections between the parts that establish the message which associates Virginia Slims with progress. The ad tells women that it is progressive and socially acceptable to smoke, and it associates Virginia Slims with modernity, social progress, and the desired social trait of slimness.

In fact, Lucky Strike carried out a successful advertising campaign in the 1930s which associated smoking with weight reduction ("Reach for a Lucky instead of a sweet!"), and Virginia Slims plays on this tradition, encapsulated in the very brand name of the product. Note too that the cigarette is a "Lights" variety and that, like the Marlboro ad, it tries to associate its product with health and well-being. The pronounced smile on the woman's face also tries to associate the product with happiness and self-contentment, struggling against the association of smoking with guilt and dangers to one's health. The image of the slender woman, in turn, associated with slimness and lightness, not only associates the product with socially desirable traits, but in turn promotes the ideal of slimness as the ideal type of femininity.

Later in the 1980s, Capri cigarettes advertised its product as "the slimmest slim!", building on the continued and intensified association of slimness with femininity. The promotion of smoking and slimness is far from innocent, however, and has contributed to eating disorders, faddish diets and exercise programs, and a dramatic increase in anoxeria among young women, as well as rising cancer rates. As Judith Williamson points out (1978), advertising "addresses" individuals and invites them to identify with certain products, images, and behavior. Advertising provides a utopian image of a new, more attractive, more successful, more prestigious "you" through purchase of certain goods. Advertising magically offers self-transformation and a new identity, associating changes in consumer behavior, fashion, and appearance with metamorphosis into a new person. Consequently, individuals are taught to identify with values, role models, and social behavior through advertising which is thus an important instrument of socialization as well as a manager of consumer demand.

Advertising sells its products and view of the world through images, rhetoric, slogans, and their juxtaposition in ads to which tremendous artistic resources, psychological research, and marketing strategies are devoted. These ads express and reinforce dominant images of gender and position men and women to assume highly specific subject positions. A 1988 Virginia Slims ad (shown in Figure 4), in fact, reveals a considerable transformation in its image of women during the 1980s and a new strategy to persuade women that it is all right and even "progressive" and ultramodern to smoke. This move points to shifts in the relative power between men and women and discloses new subject positions for women validated by the culture industries.

Once again the sepia-colored framed box at the top of the ad contains an image of a woman serving her man in 1902; the comic pose and irritated look of the woman suggests that such servitude is highly undesirable and its contrast with the Virginia Slims woman (who herself now wears the leather boots and leather gloves and jacket as well) suggests that women have come a long way while the ever-present cigarette associates woman's right to smoke in public with social progress. This time the familiar "You've come a long way, baby" is absent, perhaps because the woman pictured would hardly tolerate being described as "baby" and because women's groups had been protesting the sexist and demeaning label in the slogan. Note, too, the transformation of the image of the woman in the Virginia Slims ad.

No longer the smiling, cute, and wholesome potential wife of the earlier ad, she is now more threatening, more sexual, less wifely, and more masculine. The sunglasses connote the distance from the male gaze which she wants to preserve and the leather jacket with the military insignia connotes that she is equal to men, able to carry on a masculine role, and is stronger and more autonomous than women of the past.

The 1988 ad is highly antipatriarchal and even expresses hostility toward men with the overweight man with glasses and handlebar mustache looking slightly ridiculous while it is clear that the woman is being held back by ridiculous fashion and intolerable social roles. The "new" Virginia Slims woman, however, who completely dominates the scene, is the epitome of style and power. This strong woman can easily take in hand and enjoy the phallus (i.e. the cigarette as the sign of male power accompanied by the male dress and military insignia) and serve as an icon of female glamour as well. This ad links power, glamour, and sexuality and offers a model of female power, associated with the cigarette and smoking. Ads work in part by generating dissatisfaction and by offering images of transformation, of a new personal identity. This particular ad promotes dissatisfaction with traditional images and presents a new image of a more powerful woman, a new lifestyle and identity for the Virginia Slims smoker. In these ways, the images associate the products advertised with certain socially desirable traits and convey messages concerning the symbolic benefits accrued to those who consume the product.

Although Lights and Ultra Lights continue to be the dominant Virginia Slims types, the phrase does not appear as a highlighted caption in the 1988 ad as it used to and the package does not appear either. No doubt this "heavy" woman contradicts the "light" image and the ad connotes instead power and (a dubious) progress for women rather than slimness or lightness. Yet the woman's teased and flowing blonde hair, her perfect teeth which form an obliging smile, and, especially her crotch positioned in the ad in a highly suggestive and inviting fashion code her as a symbol of beauty and sexuality, albeit more autonomous and powerful.

The point I am trying to make is that it is precisely the images which are the vehicles of the subject positions and that therefore critical literacy in a postmodern image culture requires learning how to read images critically and to unpack the relations between images, texts, social trends, and products in commercial culture (Kellner 1989d). My reading of these ads suggests that advertising is as concerned with selling lifestyles and socially desirable identities, which are associated with their products, as with selling the product themselves – or rather, that advertisers use the symbolic constructs with which the consumer is invited to identify to try to induce her to use their product. Thus, the Marlboro man (i.e. the consumer who smokes the cigarette) is smoking masculinity or natural vigor as much as a cigarette, while the Virginia Slims woman is exhibiting modernity, thinness, or female power when she lights up her "slim."

This sort of reading of advertising not only helps individuals to resist manipulation, but it also depicts how something as seemingly innocuous as advertising can depict significant shifts in modes and models of identity. For example, the two

Virginia Slims ads suggest that at least a certain class of women (white, upper-middle and upper class) were gaining more power in society and that women were being attracted by stronger, more autonomous, and more masculine images. Advertising campaigns attempt to incorporate such images to associate their products with the socially desired traits which are then further promoted with the ads' attempts to promote their products.[12]

A comparison of late 1980s Marlboro ads with their earlier ads also yields some interesting results. While the Marlboro ads once centered on the "Marlboro man," and in the early 1980s continue to feature this figure, curiously, by the late 1980s, human beings disappeared altogether from some Marlboro ads which projected pure images of wholesome nature associated with the product. The caption "Made especially for menthol smokers," the green menthol insignia on the cigarette package, and the blue and green backdrops of the trees, grass, and water in the ad all attempt to incorporate icons of health and nature into the ads, as if these menthol Lights would protect the buyer from cigarette health hazards. Undoubtedly this transformation in the Marlboro ads points to growing concern about the health hazards of cigarettes which required even purer emphasis on nature. Yet the absence of the Marlboro cowboy might also point to the obsolescence of the manual worker in a new postmodern information and service society where significant sectors of the so-called "new middle class" work in the industries of symbol and image production and manipulation.

The prominent images of the powerful horses in the late 1980s ad, however, point to a continued desire for power and fantasies of virility and masculinity. The actual powerlessness of workers in contemporary capitalist society makes it in turn difficult to present concrete contemporary images of male power that would appeal to a variety of male (and female) smokers. Eliminating the male figure also allows appeal over a wider range of social classes and occupational types, including both men and women who could perhaps respond more positively to images of nature and power than to the rather obsolete cowboy figure. Further – and these images are clearly polysemic, subject to multiple readings, – the new emphasis on "Great refreshment in the flip-top box" not only harmonizes with the "refreshing" images of green and nature, but points to the new hedonist, leisure culture in postmodern society with its emphasis on the pleasures of consumption, spectacle, and refreshment. The refreshment tag also provides a new legitimation for cigarette smoking as a refreshing activity (building on the famous Pepsi "pause that refreshes"?) which codes an obviously dangerous activity as "refreshing" and thus as health-promoting.

Moreover, the absence of human figures in the late 1980s Marlboro ads could be read as signs of the erasure of the human in postmodern society, giving credence to Foucault's claim that in a new episteme the human itself could be washed away like a face drawn on sand at the edge of the sea (1970: 387). Yet the human cannot so easily be washed away and lo and behold in 1989, not only human figures, but the Marlboro man himself returned in a new ad campaign. One ad provides an example of a new advertising strategy which requires the consumer to produce the meaning herself, much like a modernist text. This fully two-page ad portrays giant hands (presumably those of the Marlboro man himself) holding a pair of gloves, with a cigarette held between two gnarled and weatherbeaten fingers. The only caption – besides the federally mandated list of ingredients and warnings to one's health -says: "Come to where the flavor is." There is no Marlboro cigarette box, portrayed nor any caption stating the brand name. Instead one has to look quite closely at the small brand name inscribed on the cigarette itself to discern precisely what brand is being advertised.

Half of the two-page ad is buried in darkness with only the caption and difficult to decipher fragments of images emerging. The other half of the ad centers on the gnarled hands, perhaps projecting the subliminal message to those concerned with the health risks of smoking that it is possible to smoke and survive. For the heavily lined hands are obviously those of someone who has lived life to the full, whose vicissitudes and experience are etched into the very skin of his hands, whose deeply textured skin attests to a long-lived life. In this way, the cigarette is associated with survival and a full life, thus assuaging worries that smoking constitutes a serious risk of cancer and other dread diseases and providing subliminal functions of anxiety reduction – a typical task of contemporary advertising.

This Marlboro ad is one of a genre of contemporary ads which forces the consumer to work at discerning the brand being sold and at deciphering the text to construct meaning. The minimalism of product signifiers appeals to readers jaded with traditional advertising, tired of the same old stale images, and bored with and cynical toward advertising manipulation. To the cool postmodern reader, the association of masculinity with smoking Marlboros might be laughable, yet even such minimalist ads utilize product differentiation and use new images while building on old cues. In addition to appealing to a survivalist urge in the contemporary smoker, the 1989 ad invites her to "Come to where the flavor is." The emphasis on flavor appeals to hedonist tastes, to enjoy the flavor, to light up for pleasure. Such appeals interpellate contemporary individualist-hedonist impulses to have fun, to do what one wants and pleases at all costs – even the destruction of one's health.

The textual system of this 1989 Marlboro ad as a whole thus addresses its reader as an individual, as someone able to read the complex ad and to choose their own pleasures as they will. There is thus a subliminal appeal to the individual's freedom and creativity which invites the reader to interpret the ad as one chooses and to light up the cigarette when one pleases in disregard of the obligatory government warnings linking cigarettes to health risks. The gnarled hands as well are those of an individual who is charge of his life and who makes his own decisions, so the text as a whole is structured to associate smoking Marlboro with individuality and power. Interestingly, this ad and the other Marlboro ads which erase human subjects play down gender identity and one might read this as a decentering of gender identity in contemporary society, as a disassociation between the product and gender, as a bracketing of the centrality of gender in the constitution of identity.

The appeal here is directly to use-value, to the pleasure and flavor that the cigarette produces rather than the sign value of masculinity, or the appeal to power.

Moreover, this text works to get the reader to identify with the product and to produce a pleasurable feeling from the feat of producing meaning, from reading the ambiguous text, that is presumably then transferred to and associated with the product, so that the image of Marlboro is associated with free choice and creativity. And yet the highly paid cultural interpreters who work for advertising agencies are hedging their bets concerning the Marlboro ads of recent years. For the 1990s has seen a return of the previous realist ads which center on the old Marlboro cowboy, along with production of a new type of ad just analyzed, as well as a new series of pure nature imagery.

In the 1990s, Marlboro has returned to recycling old images, especially of the famous cowboy and nature. The December 11–17, 1993 *TV Guide* back-cover ad, for instance, features the cowboy riding a horse, followed by another horse which he has roped and is leading through a snowy field. The white snow is blowing behind the cowboy deploying the images of nature. Thus, the image combines power and control with images of nature, implying that if you want to be a natural man and in control, smoke a Marlboro. Curiously, however, although the corporate insignia "Marlboro" is featured in bright red script there is no pack of cigarettes, or even a single cigarette, shown, nor is the cowboy, pictured hard at work, smoking. It is if Marlboro is embarrassed by their product and can only sell the qualities of nature and masculinity – and death, as the Surgeon General's warning, boldly emblazoned in a letter box in the bottom right-hand corner notes.

The multiplicity of strategies in cigarette ads show that the advertising agencies of contemporary capitalism are not at all sure as to what will attract consumers to their products, or with what images consumers identify. For, as I have been arguing, one of the features of contemporary culture is precisely the fragmentation, transitoriness, and multiplicity of images, which refuse to crystalize into a stable image culture. Thus, the advertising and cultural industries draw on modern and postmodern strategies, and on traditional, modern, and postmodern themes and iconography.

SITUATING THE POSTMODERN

In a sense, it is undecidable whether contemporary image culture and forms of identity should be described as modern or postmodern. The multiplicity of types of Marlboro ads currently circulating helps put into question claims concerning a radical postmodern rupture with modern culture and that postmodernism is a new cultural dominant. For the current Marlboro ads draw on traditional, modernist, and postmodern image production and aesthetic strategies, while deploying a variety of traditional and contemporary ideological appeals as well. Rather than taking postmodernity as a new cultural totality, I would thus argue that it makes more sense to interpret the many facets of the postmodern as an emergent cultural trend in contrast to residual traditional values and practices still operative and a dominant capitalist modernity defined as the project of the hegemony of capital whereby commodification, individualism, fragmentation, reification, and consumer culture are still key constituents of the modern age.[13]

On the other hand, one could describe precisely this co-existence of styles, this mixture of traditional, modern, and postmodern cultural forms, as "postmodern." Perhaps the very lack of a cultural dominant and the mixing of a variety of aesthetic styles and strategies, such as one sees in advertising, is postmodern. Yet contemporary Marlboro advertising campaigns suggest that the highly paid and often sharp interpreters of the contemporary scene in the employment of corporate capital see the continuing existence of traditional identities, where masculinity is still important, combined with a modern concern for power and enjoyment as a continuing social force and matrix of contemporary values and identity. These ads show that traditional and modern culture co-exists with a postmodern culture whereby new forms of images are needed to catch the attention of a jaded and cynical consumer. If postmodernity were the cultural totality that some of its celebrants claim, one imagines that the most highly paid and sophisticated image producers would inundate its denizens with postmodern imagery, but no, contemporary advertising and media culture suggests that instead the contemporary culture is highly fragmented into different taste cultures which respond by producing quite different images and values.

A megacorporation like Marlboro goes after all of these audiences, thus one sees a certain heterogeneity in its image productions with different appeals sent out to different audiences according to market segmentation: the old Marlboro man for readers of *TV Guide*; horses and nature for the health and vitality conscious readers of fashion magazines like *Elle* and *M*; and more complex aesthetic spectacles for the gourmet hedonists who read *Vanity Fair* and the like. The multiplicity of advertising strategies pursued by the Marlboro folks also points to the immanent contradictions of commodity culture. For advertising attempts to produce identities by offering products associated with certain traits and values. And yet the inexorable trends of fashion and the new advertising campaigns undermine previously forged identities and associations to circulate new products, new images, new values.

To be sure, there have been ad campaigns that adopt postmodern strategies of image construction to sell their goods. Robert Goldman describes one Reebok campaign that failed (1992) and in 1993/4, Levi's ran an ad campaign that showed disconnected fragments of images and words of the contemporary scene with the product logo submerged in the text as just another fragment, forcing the viewer to figure out what was being advertised – which is, one supposes, an effective way to get the brand name in the viewer's mind which is a major function of the advertisement, though as failed postmodern ad campaigns indicate, the strategy of deploying postmodernism in the aesthetics of advertising is risky.

And so it is that advertising, fashion, consumption, television, and media culture constantly destabilize identity and contribute to producing more unstable, fluid, shifting, and changing identities in the contemporary scene. And yet one also sees the inexorable processes of commodification at work in this process. The market segmentation of multiple ad campaigns and appeals reproduces and intensifies fragmentation and destablizes identity which new products and identifications are attempting to restabilize. Thus, it is capital itself which is the demiurge of allegedly postmodern fragmentation, dispersal of identity, change, and mobility. Rather than postmodernity constituting a break with capital and political economy as Baudrillard (1976) and others would have it, wherever one observes phenomena of postmodern culture one can detect the logic of capital behind them.

This argument suggests that much postmodern theory is excessively abstract in bracketing political economy and capitalism from the phenomena which it describes and thus occludes their economic underpinnings. Furthermore, such theory tends to overgeneralize, taking examples from new emergent trends which it conflates into a new cultural dominant. Some postmodern cultural theory also abstracts from ideological content and effects, focusing merely on formal structures or image construction. Against such positions, I have argued that rather than advertising and the other images of media culture being flat, one-dimensional and without ideological coding, as some postmodern theory would have it, many ads are multi-dimensional, polysemic, ideologically coded, open to a variety of readings, and expressive of the commodification of culture and attempts of capital to colonialize the totality of life, from desire to satisfaction.

My analyses thus suggest that in a postmodern image culture, the images, scenes, stories, and cultural texts of media culture offer a wealth of subject positions which in turn help structure individual identity. These images project role and gender models, appropriate and inappropriate forms of behavior, style and fashion, and subtle enticements to emulate and identify with certain identities while avoiding others. Rather than identity disappearing in a postmodern society, it is merely subject to new determinations and new forces while offering as well new possibilities, styles, models, and forms. Yet the overwhelming variety of possibilities for identity in an affluent image culture no doubt creates highly unstable identities while constantly providing new openings to restructure one's identity.

It is difficult to say whether on the whole this is a "good" or "bad" thing and it is probably safer to conclude with Jameson that the phenomena associated with postmodernity are highly ambivalent and exhibit both progressive and regressive features. There does seem to be more of an acceptance of multiple and unstable identities in the contemporary cultural mileux than was the case previously. Modern identities – however multiple and subject to change – appeared to be more stable, whereas there currently seems to be more acceptance of change, fragmentation, and theatrical play with identity than was the case in the earlier, heavier, and more serious epoch of modernity.

On one hand, this increases one's freedom to play with one's identity and to dramatically change one's life (which may be good for some individuals), while, on the other hand, it can lead to a totally fragmented, disjointed life, subject to the whims of fashion and the subtle indoctrinations of advertising and popular culture. Against a totally dispersed, fragmented, and disconnected identity, one might want to valorize certain features central to modern identity, like autonomy, rationality, commitment, responsibility, and so on, or one might want to reconstruct these concepts, as, for instance, Habermas has attempted to do with rationality. In any case, identity continues to be the problem it was throughout modernity, though it has been problematized anew in the current orgy of commodification, fragmentation, image production, and societal, political, and cultural transformation that is the work of consumer capitalism.

Indeed, the quest for identity is arguably more intense than ever in the present moment. There has been something of a rebellion against producing identity solely as an individual achievement in the contemporary era, with increased emphasis on tribal, national, group, and other forms of collective identity. In many parts of the world, there has been a return to tribalism, to past forms of collective identities – national, religious, or ethnic – and one finds parallel projects in so-called identity politics whereby individuals gain identity through membership in groups and affirmation of a collective identity (i.e. as a woman, a black, a gay, or some combination thereof).

Yet the quest for individuality and particularity in one's look, image, style, and life continues apace. Media figures like Michael Jackson and Madonna show that identity is a construct, that it can be constantly changed and refined and fine-tuned, that identity is a question of image, style, and looks. Michael Jackson, for instance, erases the boundary between black and white, male and female, adult and youth in his image constructions. In some of his music videos, he appears black, in others white and in yet others indeterminate; sometimes he appears highly masculine, sometimes more feminine, sometimes androgenous. At times, he appears as an adult, firmly in control of his career as King of Pop, and other times he appears as a youth, as a lover of children who is more comfortable with kids and being a kid than with adults.[14]

The point is that many icons of media culture suggest that identity is a matter of individual choice and action and that each individual can produce their own unique identity. In any case, the issue of identity is more pressing and contested than ever before in contemporary societies. Against the globalization of culture, there are intense struggles to preserve and enhance national identities; against the forced identities of modern nationhood (often a product of imperialism), individuals and groups are constructing identities in terms of religion, ethnicity, and region against former national identities; against all collective identities, other individuals are attempting to construct their own personal identities, which often are, however, highly mediated by collective forces.

Personal identity is thus fraught with contradictions and tensions. Many individuals, for often different reasons, are indifferent to national or other collective identities and wish to construct their identities through their own lifestyles, looks, and image. Others fervently embrace identity politics and construct their identities, their deepest sense of who they are, by affirming their membership in various groups or collectivities (i.e. women, blacks, gays, or whatever). Some have labelled this form of identity politics "postmodern," but interest group politics and even gaining identity through political and group affiliation is also a modern phenomenon.

And so we are left with the question: Is the current construction of identity distinctly postmodern, and has a fundamental shift in the construction of identity taken place? If so, are we living in a completely new epoch, a postmodernity? I would argue that it is equally arbitrary and open to debate as to whether one posits that we are in a situation of late modernity or a new postmodernity, or whether one posits identity as primarily modern or postmodern. Either could be argued. The features that I have ascribed to postmodern identity could be read as an intensification of features already present in modernity, or as a new configuration with new emphases that one could describe as "postmodern." In fact, concepts and terms, like identity itself, are social constructs, arbitrary notions which serve to mark and call attention to certain phenomena and which fulfill certain analytical or classifactory tasks. So the debate over the postmodern is largely a debate over what terminology we should use to describe the contemporary socio-cultural matrix. If the terminology illuminates shifts in contemporary culture, it is useful. If it covers over phenomena like the continuing role of capitalism in constructing contemporary societies and identities, then it is harmful.

Likewise, it is an open question as to whether one wants to keep using the category of the subject in cultural theory and elsewhere. The concept of the subject has been shown to be socially constructed and the notion of an unified, coherent, and essential subject illusory.[15] Rather than constructing something like a subject, or interpellating individuals to identify themselves as subjects, media culture tends to construct identities and subject positions, inviting individuals to identify with very specific figures, images, or positions, such as the Marlboro man, the Virginia Slims woman, a soap opera mother, or a Madonna.

Yet postmodern claims concerning the complete dissolution of the subject in contemporary culture seem exaggerated. Rather, it seems that media culture continues to provide images, discourses, narratives, and spectacles that produce pleasures, identities, and subject positions that people appropriate. Media culture provides images of proper role models, proper gender behavior, and images of appropriate style, look, and image for contemporary individuals. Media culture thus provides resources for identity and new modes of identity in which look, style, and image replaces such things as action and commitment as constituitives of identity, of who one is. Once upon a time, it was who you were, what you did, what kind of a person you were – your moral, political, and existential choices and commitments, which constituted individual identity. But today it is how you look, your image, your style, and how you appear that constitutes identity. And it is media culture that more and more provides the materials and resources to constitute identities.

And so "Strike a pose! Vogue!" as Madonna orders. The advantage of this shift in the constitution of identity is that postmodern identities suggest that one can change, that one can remake oneself, that one can free oneself from whatever traps and restrictions one finds oneself ensconced in. The disadvantage is that identity becomes flattened out and trivialized in terms of style, look, and consumption in which one is defined by one's image, possessions, and lifestyle. One's identity is a construct, constituted out of the materials of one's life-situation and one can change and transform one's life according to one's projects, as Sartre, Foucault, and others remind us. But constituting a substantial identity is work which requires will, action, commitment, intelligence, and creativity, and many of the postmodern identities constructed out of media and consumer culture lack these features, being little more than a game someone plays, a pose, a style and look that one can dispose of tomorrow for a new look and image: disposable and easily replaceable identities for the postmodern carnival.

Even weirder are some of the mutations of identity in computer culture. Many people who join MUDS – Multi-User Dimension real-time discussion sites on computers – take on identities of members of the opposite sex – or of different races, classes, professions, or whatever. Some players in MUD games take on multiple personalities and play out different roles and identities in their computer interactions. In MUDs, Sherry Turkle notes, "the self is not only decentered but multiplied without limit" (cited in David 1994: 44). Turkle also noted in a 1994 conference that the drastic rise in the number of patients diagnosed with multiple-personality disorders might be correlated with computer and other role-playing games, though she also defined health as "a fluidity of access to different selves" and suggested that computer role-playing might also serve as a form of self-therapy (David 1994: 44).

We will explore further transmutations of identity in contemporary society in the theories of Jean Baudrillard and cyberpunk fiction in Chapter 9. But first let us examine Madonna as a celebrity and identity-machine for the end of the millenium. Continuing our probing of contemporary culture, politics, and identity, and the proper terminology to describe our present moment, we shall accordingly turn next to interrogation of the Madonna phenomenon which is deeply connected with the problematics sketched out in this chapter.

NOTES

1 On identity in modernity, see Berman 1982 and the essays collected in Lash and Friedman 1992. On the discourses of modernity, see Antonio and Kellner, forthcoming. I am interpreting modernity here as an epoch of rapid change, innovation, and negation of the old and creation of the new, a process bound up with industrial capitalism, the democratic revolutions, urbanization, and social and cultural differentiation. Following the conventions of modern social theory, I am assuming a distinction between modern and premodern societies, but it should be kept in mind that such distinctions are ideal types that highlight certain features of a social order, while sometimes covering over similarities and continuities.

2 On the Frankfurt School analysis of the decline of individuality, see Kellner 1989a. On the dissolution of identity in postmodernity, see Baudrillard 1983a, 1983b, 1983c; Jameson 1983, 1984, 1991; and other texts that I discuss below.

3 For some other attempts to analyze postmodernism and popular culture, see the articles in *Journal of Communication Inquiry*, Vol. 10, No. 1 (1986) and Vol. 10, No. 2 (1986);

Screen Vol. 28, No. 2 (1987); Kaplan 1987; Ross 1988; Connor 1989, with bibliography: 263ff.; and Hutcheon 1989: 107f.

4 On modernism in the arts, see the discussion in Chapter 4. I am using the term "modernism" here to denote a series of artistic practices that attempt to produce innovation in the arts in form, style, and content, which begin with Baudelaire in the mid-nineteenth century and continue through Madonna.

5 This antihermeneutical position was argued earlier by Sontag 1969 and Barthes 1975.

6 Audiences and critics immediately took to the series use of rock music soundtrack. One early review noted:

> Throbbing with rock-and-rhythmic camera work, the weekly drama is in the vanguard of network series that have begun to move to a name-brand beat. Its detective heroes dress to Devo, cruise to Phil Collins and fight crime to the Rolling Stones. As executive producer Michael Mann observes, 'Miami Vice and MTV are really first cousins.' Adds composer James Di Pasquale: 'There is no question that the marriage of television and rock is getting more romantic'.
>
> (*People*, October 29, 1984)

And:

> The most striking aspect of 'Miami Vice' is its use of music. In most television programs music is employed to emphasize the action on the screen, to highlight tension, for example, or underscore sadness. But 'Miami Vice' takes rock-and-roll selections by popular performers, such as the Rolling Stones and Phil Collins, as well as more obscure works by Jamaican Rastafarian reggae groups, and combines them with closely edited film montages to create music videos similar to those shown on MTV Music Television, the round-the-clock rock-music cable channel.
>
> (*The New York Times*, January 3, 1985)

7 I hesitate to use the term "subject positions" since I do not believe that things like "subjects" exist, that the notion of the subject is purely ideological and a socially constructed fiction. Yet media culture does produce positions through which audiences are invited or induced to identify with, thus I use the term "subject positions" in this sense to describe identities, roles, looks, or images established by media models and discourse.

8 This double-coded identity for the vice cops fooled Gitlin (1987) who claims that "the viewer has to take for granted that two Miami cops (1985 take-home pay: $429 a week) can blithely afford the latest and flashiest in cars and clothes" (1987: 152) and that the cops exhibit "traces of outlawry" (ibid.,: 153). He misses here the recurrent plot line that they have been assigned undercover identities as "players" in the drug scene – a plot device made explicit in the pilot (available for video-cassette rental) and in many episodes of the series.

9 For further examples of some progressive political messages on the series, see Best and Kellner 1987.

10 The method of reading ads and the interpretation of advertising which follows is indebted to the work of Robert Goldman (1992) and his collaborative work with Steve Papson (forthcoming).

11 The tobacco leaf is (for insects) one of the most sweet and tasty of all plants – which requires a large amount of pesticides to keep insects from devouring it. Cigarette makers use chemicals to produce a distinctive smell and taste to the product and use preservatives to keep it from spoiling. Other chemicals are used to regulate the burning process and to filter out tars and nicotine. While these latter products are the most publicized dangers in cigarette smoking, actually the pesticides, chemicals and preservatives may well be more deadly. Scandalously, cigarettes are one of the most unregulated products

in the U.S. consumer economy (European countries, for example, carefully regulate the pesticides used in tobacco growing and the synthetics used in cigarette production).

Government sponsored experiments on the effects of cigarette smoking use generic cigarettes which may not have the chemicals and preservatives of name brands, thus no really scientifically accurate major survey on the dangers of cigarette smoking has ever been done by the U.S. government. The mainstream media, many of whom are part of conglomerates who have heavy interests in the tobacco industry, or who depend on cigarette advertising for revenue, have never really undertaken to expose to the public the real dangers concerned with cigarette smoking and the scandalous neglect of this issue by government and media in the United States. Cigarette addiction is thus a useful object lesson in the unperceived dangers and destructive elements of the consumer society and the ways these dangers are covered over. (My own information on the cigarette industry derives from an "Alternative Views" television interview which Frank Morrow and I did with Bill Drake on the research which will constitute his forthcoming book on the dangers of tobacco.)

12 Michael Schudson (1984) summarizes the literature and studies which put in question the effectiveness of advertising campaigns in actually getting consumers to buy their products; in fact, advertising's functions in promoting style, models and images of identification, and various ideologies is more interesting to cultural studies which should see advertising as an important and powerful legislator of style, fashion, and identity.

13 The distinction between residual, emergent, and dominant culture comes from Raymond Williams (1977).

14 In 1993, there were widespread accusations that Jackson regularly sexually molested young boys, that he was a pedophile whose house was a lure for young boys, whose parents he often paid to let them "visit" him and spend the night. Interpreting some of Jackson's music videos in this context suggests that the lyrics of many of his most popular songs can be read as legitimations of pedophilia which are addressed to young boy lovers. I do not know if Jackson is guilty of child molestation, but it is clear that the extensive media coverage of the charges, supported by former employees in his mansion and one of his own sisters, has produced an image of Jackson as pedophile, as child molester. He who lives by the media and its images dies by it as well. And yet media resurrection is also possible. In the summer of 1994, Jackson married Elvis Presley's daughter, positioning himself as responsible adult, as husband, and as part of the lineage of the King of Pop, a role that he has long sought. Media culture is thus a question of image, of the production and fine-tuning of images and of the attempt to erase negative images when they appear.

15 During the 1970s, contributors to *Screen* magazine polemicized against essentialist conceptions of an unified subject, following French post-structuralism, and argued – following Althusser's theory of ideology – that the cinema constructed illusory individual subjects, "interpellating" individuals to see themselves as subjects. This too is probably an illusion, for it makes more sense to see media culture as "interpellating" individuals to construct specific identities, to identify with specific subject positions, rather than with some occult "subject." In fact, the concept of the subject is highly abstract and can often be usefully replaced by cognate terms such as identities, subject-positions, ways of seeing, discourse positions, and the like.

Chapter 8

Madonna, fashion, and image

For the past decade, Madonna Louise Ciccone has been a highly influential pop culture icon and the center of a storm of controversy. She is the best-selling and most discussed female singer in popular music, one of the most prominent stars of music video, an aspiring movie actress, and, most of all, a superstar of pop culture. For her fans, she is the ultimate pop icon, the image of fashion and identity, who produced legions of Madonna wannabees who slavishly imitated her fashion statements. For her detractors, she is the ultimate in crass commercialism and media manipulation, the epitome of banal consumerism run rampant in media culture.

Madonna has thus become a site of contestation and controversy, adored and abhorred by audiences, critics, and academics alike. Most of the polemics, however, are contentious, of an either/or and pro or con nature, and they fail to grasp the many sides of the Madonna phenomenon. While some celebrate her as a subversive cultural revolutionary, others attack her as antifeminist, or as irredeemably trashy and vulgar. Against such one-sided interpretations, however, I argue that "Madonna" is a site of genuine contradiction that must be articulated and appraised to adequately interpret her images, works, and their effects.

My argument is that Madonna's images and reception highlights the social constructedness of identity, fashion, and sexuality. By exploding boundaries established by dominant gender, sexual, and fashion codes, she encourages experimentation, change, and production of one's individual identity. Yet by privileging the creation of image, looks, fashion, and style in the production of identity, Madonna reinforces the norms of the consumer society which offers the possibilities of a new commodity "self" through consumption and the products of the fashion industry. I argue that grasping this contradiction is the key to Madonna's effects and to interrogating the conditions under which the multiplicity of discourses on Madonna, and contradictory readings and evaluations, are produced. Madonna pushes the most sensitive buttons of sexuality, gender, race, and class, offering challenging and provocative images and cultural artifacts, as well as ones that reinforce dominant conventions. The Madonna construct *is* a set of contradictions and in the following pages I'll explore the images, codes, and effects that constitute the Madonna phenomenon.

FASHION AND IDENTITY

Madonna is interesting for cultural studies because her work, popularity, and influence reveal important features of the nature and function of fashion and identity in the contemporary world. Fashion offers models and material for constructing identity. Traditional societies had relatively fixed social roles and sumptuary codes, so that clothes and one's appearance instantly denoted one's social class, profession, and status.[1] Identity in traditional societies was usually fixed by birth, marriage, and accomplishment, and the available repertoire of roles was tightly constricted. Gender roles were especially rigid, while work and status were tightly circumscribed by established social codes and an obdurate system of status ascription.

During the medieval period, identities in Western Europe were especially circumscribed and rules even dictated what members of different classes could or could not wear. Modern societies eliminated rigid codes of dress and fashion, and beginning around 1700 changing fashions of apparel and appearance began proliferating (Wilson 1985). Although a capitalist market dictated that only certain classes could afford the most expensive attire, which signified social privilege and power, in the aftermath of the French Revolution, fashion was democratized in countries which carried through a democratic revolution, so that anyone who could afford certain clothes and make-up could wear and display what they wished (whereas previously, sumptuary laws forbade members of certain classes from dressing and appearing like the ruling elites; Ewen and Ewen 1982; Ewen 1988).

Modernity also offered new possibilities for constructing personal identities. Modern societies made it possible for individuals to produce – within certain limits – their own identities and to experience identity crises. Already in the eighteenth century, the philosopher David Hume formulated the problem of personal identity, of what constituted one's true selfhood, even suggesting that there was no substantial or transcendental self. The issue became an obsession with Rousseau, Kierkegaard, and many other Europeans who experienced rapid change, the breakdown of traditional societies, and the emergence of modernity (see Chapter 7).

In modernity, fashion is an important constituent of one's identity, helping to determine how one is perceived and accepted (see Wilson 1985; Ewen 1988). Fashion offers choices of clothes, style, and image through which one could produce an individual identity. In a sense, fashion is a constituent feature of modernity, interpreted as an era of history marked by perpetual innovation, by the destruction of the old and the creation of the new (Berman 1982). Fashion itself is predicated on producing ever new tastes, styles, dress, and practices. Fashion perpetuates a restless, modern personality, always seeking what is new and admired, while avoiding what is old and passé. Fashion and modernity go hand in hand to produce modern personalities who seek their identities in constantly new and trendy clothes, looks, attitudes, and style, and who are fearful of being out-of-date or unfashionable.

Of course, fashion in modern societies was limited by gender codes, economic realities, and the force of social conformity which continued to dictate what one could or could not wear, and what one could or could not be. Fashion in modernity itself underwent complex stages of historical development, though by the beginning of the twentieth century, modern fashion rationalized clothing and cosmetics, and mass markets began to make changes in fashion open to mass consumption (Ewen and Ewen 1982; Ewen 1988). Yet fashion codes continued to be relatively fixed for some classes and regions. Documentary footage from the U.S. in the 1950s, shown in the 1982 ABC documentary *Heroes of Rock* and other sources, depicted parents, teachers, and other arbiters of good taste attempting to dictate proper and improper fashion, thus policing the codes of fashion and identity. Crossing gender codes in fashion was for centuries a good way to mark oneself as a social outcast or even to land in jail or a mental institution.

The 1960s exhibited a massive attempt to overthrow the cultural codes of the past and fashion became an important element of the construction of new identities, along with sex, drugs, and rock and roll, phenomena also involved in the changing fashions of the day. In the 1960s, "antifashion" in clothes and attire became fashionable and the subversion and overthrowing of cultural codes became a norm. So-called fashion subversion continued to be in vogue during the following decades, and the fashion industry allowed new flexibility and marketed an ever-changing array of new styles and looks. By means of such fashion moves, individuals could quickly produce their own identities through resisting dominant fashion codes and producing their own fashion statements, or using dominant styles in their own ways. One of Stuart Ewen's students provides interesting testimony concerning how it was possible to produce one's own style against dominant fashion codes:

> I went to Catholic school for twelve years. In grammar school, I wore a uniform for eight years. I used to try to rebel against this in little ways, such as not wearing the tie I was supposed to, or by wearing the wrong type of collar. . . . It was a way of finding myself a little freedom, a way of fighting the system in a small way.
>
> (cited in Ewen 1988: 5)

Indeed, Madonna herself tells in an early interview how she expressed adolescent rebellion through fashion from the time she was a young girl, indicating she and her girlfriend dressed extravagantly:

> Only because we knew that our parents didn't like it. We thought it was fun. We got dressed to the nines. We got bras and stuffed them so our breasts were over-large and wore really tight sweaters – we were sweater-girl floozies. We wore tons of lipstick and really badly applied makeup and huge beauty marks and did our hair up like Tammy Wynette.
>
> (Madonna, cited in Lewis 1993: 142)

During this period, media culture became a particularly potent source of cultural fashions, providing models for appearance, behavior, and style. The long-haired and unconventionally dressed rock stars of the 1960s and the 1970s influenced changes in styles of hair, dress, and behavior, while their sometimes rebellious attitudes sanctioned social revolt, as when Bob Dylan proclaimed that "The Times They are A'Changing," or that change was "Blowing in the Wind." Groups like The Beatles, The Rolling Stones, Jefferson Airplane, and performers like Janis Joplin or Jimi Hendrix sanctioned countercultural revolt and the appropriation of new styles of dress, behavior, and attitudes. The association of rock culture with long hair, social rebellion, and nonconformity in fashion continued through the 1970s with successive waves of heavy metal rock, punk, and new wave attaining popularity.

More conservative television programming, films, and pop music by contrast provided mainstream models for youth. During the past two decades, cultural conservatives have been reacting strongly against 1960s radicalism and fashion, and youth culture and fashion have become battlefields between traditionalist conservatives and cultural radicals, attempting to overturn traditional gender roles, fashion codes, and values and behavior. Thus, fashion and social identities are themselves part of a process of social struggle and conflict between opposing models and ideologies. Conservatives have their fashion models and style, as do subcultural rebels. Political struggles thus are partly played out in fashion wars as well as elections and political debate.

High school in particular is a period in which young people construct their identities, attempting to "become someone" (Wexler 1992). High school has been a terrain of contradiction and struggle for the past decades. While some parents and teachers attempt to instill traditional values and ideas, youth culture is often in opposition to conservative culture. Although the 1980s was a predominantly conservative period with the election of Ronald Reagan and a "right turn" in U.S. culture (see Ferguson and Rogers 1986; Kellner and Ryan 1988; Kellner 1990a), the images from popular music figures sometimes cut across the conservative grain. Michael Jackson, Prince, Boy George, and other rock groups undermined traditional gender divisions and promoted polymorphic sexuality. Cyndi Lauper revelled in offbeat kookiness, while Pee Wee Herman engaged in silly and infantile behavior to the delight of his young (and older) audiences. Throwing off decades of cool sophistication, maturity, respectability, and taste, Pee Wee made it OK to be silly and weird, or at least different.

THE MADONNA PHENOMENON

It was in this period during the 1980s, in which youth identities were being renegotiated in a conservative era, that Madonna first came to prominence. Her early music videos and concert performances transgressed traditional fashion boundaries and she engaged in overt sexual behavior and titillation, subverting the boundaries of "proper" female behavior. Thus, from the beginning Madonna was one of the most outrageous female icons among the repertoire of circulating images sanctioned by the culture industries. Although there were no doubt many more far

out and subversive figures than Madonna, their images and messages did not circulate through mainstream culture and thus did not have the efficacy of the popular. The early Madonna sanctioned rebellion, nonconformity, individuality, and experimentation with fashion and lifestyles. Madonna's constant change of image and identity promoted experimentation and the creation of one's own fashion and style. Her sometimes dramatic shifts in image and style suggested that identity was a construct, that it was something that one produced, and that it could be modified at will. The way that Madonna deployed fashion in the construction of her identity made it clear that one's appearance and image helps produce what one is, or at least how one is perceived and related to.

Thus, Madonna problematized identity and revealed its constructedness and alterability. Madonna was successively a dancer, musician, model, singer, music video star, movie and stage actress, "America's most successful businesswoman," and a pop superstar who excelled in marketing her image and selling her goods. Consciously crafting her own image, she moved from being a boy toy, material girl, and ambitious blonde, to artiste of music videos, films, and concerts. Her music shifted from disco and bubblegum rock, to personal statements and melodic torch singing, to (with the aid of her music videos) pop modernism. Madonna's hair changed from dirty blonde to platinum blonde, to black, brunette, redhead, and multifarious variations thereof. Her body changed from soft and sensuous to glamorous and svelte to hard and muscular sex machine to futuristic technobody. Her clothes and fashion changed from flashy trash, to haute couture, to far-out techno-couture, to lesbian S. & M. fashion, to postmodern pastiche of all and every fashion style. New images and a new identity for all occasions and epochs. As it turns out, Madonna's fashion moves generally caught shifts in cultural style and taste, and thus achieved the status of the popular, providing fashion models and material for appropriation by her vast and varied audiences.

Consequently, to properly grasp the Madonna phenomenon, one must perceive her marketing strategies, the ways that she sold successive images and incorporated various audiences, and the mechanisms through which she herself became a pop superstar. Madonna is one of the greatest PR machines in history and she has hired top agents, publicists, and "creative" personnel to market her and produce her images. From the beginning her every move was surrounded by publicity and year after year Madonna references in media culture have proliferated. Indeed, a Nexis data-base search for "Madonna and pop" references from the decade from 1984 to 1993 indicated over 20,000 citations! "Madonna" is her publicity and image and the "Madonna phenomenon" is thus importantly a successful marketing and pub-licity story.

While there are certain continuities in Madonna's development which I will explicate, there are also at least three distinct periods that can be (roughly) equated to shifts in her music production, her deployment of fashion and sexuality, and the construction of her image. I will accordingly delineate these periods to articulate the contours of what has become known as the "Madonna phenomenon." My focus will be on Madonna's images and cultural production, their impact on their audiences, and her cultural effects over the past decade. Although I deploy the standard methods of cultural studies featuring textual analysis and reception of texts by audiences, I argue that a generally neglected component of cultural studies – political economy and the production of culture – is an important key to the Madonna phenomenon.[2] For Madonna's success is largely a marketing success and her music, videos, other products, and image are triumphs of extremely successful production and marketing strategies – though she has had her marketing and critical failures, mainly her films. Madonna has made the right connections, has worked with talented music and video producers, has a phalanx of professional business managers and publicists, and has for the most part brilliantly produced her own image and sold it successfully to her audiences.

Madonna I: the boy toy

In 1983, Madonna released her first album, *Madonna,* and two of the songs ("Lucky Star" and "Holiday") became major hits. Her early music and songs are rather conventional popular dance music aimed at a teenage market. But Madonna was an especially flashy performer and began to attract notice at this point with music videos of her top hits which were featured on MTV, a relatively new channel which was to play a key role in her career.[3] Indeed, Madonna emerged as one of the first MTV superstars, whose music videos quickly sold her image to a vast national audience. From the beginning, Madonna crafted music videos that produced a distinct image which marketed her to various audiences.

One of her early music videos, "Lucky Star," features Madonna as an especially voluptuous sex object, energetic dancer, and innovative fashion trend-setter. The video opens with a black and white sequence with Madonna wearing black sunglasses which she slowly pulls down revealing sultry eyes, intensely focusing on the camera (and viewer). The sunglasses, of course, were symbols of the punk generation, which influenced Madonna during her early 1980s days in New York, and would later become a symbol of the cyberpunk movement as well (as Bruce Sterling claims in the introduction to his anthology *Mirrorshades* 1986: vii). Their deployment suggested that Madonna would reveal something of herself in the video, but that she knew that her performance was an act and that she would maintain her control and subjectivity. The final sequence returns to black and white, depicting Madonna pulling the shades over her eyes as the screen fades to black.

At the end of the brief opening sequence, the screen dissolves to white and a color sequence shows Madonna dressed totally in black. As the music slowly begins, she writhes in an erotic pose, the camera cuts to a freeze frame of her face, she winks, and the video cuts to Madonna dancing and cavorting with two dancers. The wink, like the opening frame, tells the viewer not to take this too seriously and perhaps to say to women and feminists that although she is presenting herself as the object of the male gaze, as an objectified sexual object, she knows what she is doing, that she is controlling *her* image. This opens the possibility that Madonna will subvert the very images and frames that she is now exploiting to make herself a lucky star.

Eschewing the narrative frame of most music videos of the day, "Lucky Star" presents a collage of images of Madonna's body. The video shows her energetically dancing, alone or with the two dancers, striking erotic poses, and showing off her body and clothes. It is important to note that the emerging Madonna phenomenon, Madonna as pop megasuperstar, is related to her deployment of music, dance, and image. The music is conventional dance music, but it is good dance music that empowers the audience to dance and exhibit themselves à la Madonna. Indeed, she distinguished herself early on as a dancer in the New York club scene and emerged in her music videos as a spirited performer of her own songs in the form of dance.

Now Madonna might not be a great dancer, but the edits, framing, and movement of her music videos allow her to appear as an attractive image and her dance movements presented her as a free, lively, expressive young woman, using dance to present her as a moving, attractive, and seductive image. In "Lucky Star," Madonna is dressed in a tight and short black skirt with a black leotard underneath. She wears a loose black blouse which lightly covers a black veiled lace body shirt underneath. Around her waist, one sees the famous "unchastity belt" – later marketed by her Boy Toy line of fashion – with a large buckle and chains around the waist. Madonna has a black bow in her hair and a distinctive star earring with smaller crucifix earrings as well. Completing the outfit are black bobby socks and short black boots.

Madonna's fashion at this stage constitutes a subversion of conventional codes and justified wearing any combination of clothes and ornaments that one wished. Of course, Madonna herself became a model of teen fashion and the infamous Madonna "wannabes" slavishly imitated every aspect of her early "flashy trash" clothing and ornamentation. She linked fashion to exhibitionism and aggressive sexuality, connecting fashion revolt with sexual rebellion and the unconventional use of religious symbols like crucifixes. Thus, Madonna legitimated unconventional fashion and sexual behavior, endearing her to an audience that felt empowered by Madonna's flaunting of traditional standards and codes.

Her other early rock video hit, "Borderline," depicts motifs and strategies that would make Madonna a lucky star. The video narrative images weave two sequences together to illustrate the love song. In color sequences, Madonna sings, flirts, and seduces a Hispanic youth, while in a black and white sequence an Anglo photographer snaps pictures of her and courts her. In one black and white sequence, she sprays graffiti over lifeless classical sculptures, a modernist gesture of the sort that codes her music videos as transgressors of the codes of high culture, establishing her as a practitioner of pop modernist subversion which breaks rules and attempts innovation, though within the limits of the popular.

In "Borderline," she breaks the taboo of interracial relationships, by depicting her character with a Hispanic youth. While she seems to reject him for the fashion photographer who will make her a star, she rejects the photographer in turn, implying, perhaps, a desire to control her own image, or to pursue her own sexual pleasures. Madonna is already pushing the buttons of sexuality, and going over established pop borderlines, with the lyrics promising a utopia of sexual ecstasy ("You keep on pushing my love over the borderline") and the music has upbeat dancing rhythms which enables Madonna to exhibit her energy and talent as a dancer.

In the video of "Borderline," Madonna wears several different outfits and her hair ranges from dirty and messy blonde in the Hispanic color sequences to beautifully fashioned glamorous blonde in the black and white sequences. The contrasting video images of the two Madonnas suggests that one's identity is a construct that one can modify or change at will, and indeed Madonna herself was to precisely do this. In addition, Madonna's offering herself to males of various colors in her music videos (and in reality, if the gossip is true) breaks down racial barriers to sexuality, but is also a clever marketing strategy inviting white, Hispanic, and black youths to fantasize that they too can have or be Madonna. Indeed, it was arguably Madonna's marketing strategy that enabled her to appeal first to white, urban and suburban working-class and middle-class girls who identified with her rebellion and flashy and trashy fashion statements, and then successfully to a wide range of different audiences, pulling in new fans with each successive career move, as I document below.

Already in her first music videos, Madonna is deploying fashion, sexuality, and the construction of image to present herself both as an alluring sex object and as a transgressor of established borderlines. On one hand, the video validates interracial sex and provides all-too-rare images of Hispanic barrio culture. Yet the two contrasting narrative sequences convey the message that while you might have a good time hanging out with Hispanics, it is the white photographer who will provide the ticket to wealth and success. But she ends up with the Hispanic youth and the narrative thus valorizes multi-relationships, for the Madonna character continues to see both guys during the narrative sequences, projecting the fantasy image that one can have it all, crossing borderlines from one culture to another, appropriating the pleasures of both cultures and multiple relationships.

The video also puts on display the contrasting fashion codes between upper-class culture and Hispanic culture, identifying Anglo culture with high fashion, high art, and luxury. By contrast, Hispanic culture is equated with urban ghettos, blue jeans, pool halls, and less expensive and stylish clothes and ornamentation. A later Madonna video, "La Isla Bonita," however, utilizes fantasy images of Hispanic fashion as an icon of beauty and romanticism. Such "multiculturalism" and her culturally transgressive moves (i.e. highly explicit sexuality and interracial sexuality) turned out to be highly successful marketing moves that endeared her to large and varied youth audiences.

Madonna became a major pop culture figure, however, with the beginning of her concert tours in 1985 and she began consciously marketing her own image and a wide range of fashion accoutrements, which she sold under the Boy Toy label. Already by 1985, the first "Madonna effect" was evident, displaying her powerful impact on her audience:

At concerts her per capita sales of T-shirts and memorabilia are among the highest in rock history. 'She sells more than Springsteen, the Rolling Stones or Duran Duran,' says Dell Furano, the concession merchandiser for her tour. At her San Francisco date, $20 T-shirts sold at the rate of one every six seconds. She began marketing "Madonna-wear," which she described as "sportswear for sexpots." The line included "a $25 lace tank top, a $30 sweatshirt, $20 pants and a medium-priced ($30) tube skirt that can be rolled down for public navel maneuvers."

(*People*, May 13, 1985)

While an up-scale version of Madonna-wear was also marketed, as were Madonna make-up kits, her image also encouraged thrift-shop down-scale fashion for the Madonna look: wearing underwear outside of skirts, loose t-shirts, cheap bracelets, earrings, chains, and crucifixes also provided appropriate decoration. Indeed, the Madonna look became known as "flash-trash," so that almost any teenage girl could afford to look like Madonna and share her attitudes and styles. Madonna fashion made it possible for teenage girls to produce their own identity, to make their own fashion statements, and to reject standard fashion codes.

During the Virgin Tour, Madonna wore a brightly colored jacket and tight micro-mini skirt, a sparkly lingerie harness and black lace stockings that stopped at the knee, and an array of ornaments, including crucifixes, a peace medallion, and bracelets. Prancing around in spiked boots, her belly button exposed, Madonna would take off the jacket to reveal a lacy purple shirt and black bra, accenting a lush and accessible sexuality. For the hit song, "Like a Virgin," Madonna appeared in a white wedding dress and screamed "Do you want to marry me" to which the girls and boys both answered, "Yesss!" Thrusting her hips as she sang, "You make me feel like a virgin," she unfolded a belly roll as she intoned, "touched for the very first time." This highly sexual rendition of the song mocks virginity, but also makes fun of sexuality by ironizing its codes and gestures. Her play with sexual codes reveals sexuality to be a construct, fabricated in part by the images and codes of popular culture, rather than a "natural" phenomenon. It also reveals sexuality to be a field of play, of self-creation and expression, and of desire and pleasure. From the beginning, Madonna would successfully exploit sexuality and would in turn present sexuality as natural, enjoyable, and fun – certainly a healthy attitude in a once puritanical culture.[4]

Madonna wannabees proliferated and she quickly became a model for identity, associating changes in identity with fashion and style changes. Lewis summarizes the early Madonna effect:

The shopping mall is a site around which female fan participation in female address videos coalesces. 'Madonna is everywhere,' writes one biographer, 'there is even a mall in California that people have nicknamed 'the Madonna mall' because so many girls who shop there try to look just like her.'. . . In response to the popularity of 'MadonnaStyle,' Macy's Department Store created a department called 'Madonnaland' devoted to selling the cropped sweaters

($30), cropped pants ($21) and a variety of jewellery accessories such as crucifix earrings and outsize 'pearl' necklaces ($4–59) resembling those worn by Madonna. The department became the location for the mobilization of Madonna fans in the summer of 1985 when Macy's sponsored a Madonna look-alike contest to coincide with the star's New York concert date.

(Lewis 1993: 144)

Madonna's deployment of fashion and sexuality during this early phase is more complex than it appears at first glance. While it is easy to dismiss the early Madonna's posturing as a shameless sex object, boy toy, and material girl who collapses identity into image and style, a closer reading of her music videos produces another picture. For instance, her music video "Material Girl" (1984) seems at first glance to be an anthem of Reaganism, which glorifies shallow materialism and celebrates greed and manipulation ("The boy with the cold hard cash/Is always Mr Right . . . cause I'm just a Material Girl"). On this reading, the song is a replay of Marilyn Monroe's "Diamonds Are a Girl's Best Friend" and is advocating the same calculating and shallow materialist attitudes.

Although Madonna has assumed a Monroe-like look in this video and does deploy some of the fashion and poses of Monroe's 1950s hymn to bourgeois materialism, a closer look at the music video provides some different perspectives. The musical numbers are enframed with a narrative in which a producer looks at the images of Madonna singing and begins courting her. He is casually dressed in a brown work shirt and appears to her as an employee of the studio, yet he asks her out and in the final scene they are seen kissing in an old truck which he had rented for the occasion.

There is thus a tension between the musical numbers which celebrate wealth and materialism, and the narrative which privileges "true love." On one reading, which Madonna herself asserted, the video shows the "material girl" rejecting her wealthy suitors in favor of a poor working boy. When confronted with the critique that she was celebrating crass greed, Madonna responded: "Look at my video that goes with the song. The guy who gets me in the end is the sensitive guy with no money" (*People*, March 11, 1985). On this account, Madonna turns down the guys courting her in the music and dance sequences for the poor but sincere guy shown in the "realism" sequences.

A closer reading raises questions, however, as to whether the "poor boy" in the video, played by Keith Carradine, is really "poor" and whether Madonna doesn't actually get a very rich and successful businessman in the video. The narrative images reveal the Carradine character to be a studio mogul who cleverly poses as a sincere poor dude who wins Madonna's heart. Thus, in "Material Girl" Madonna is all things to all people and has it every way: for conservatives of the Reagan years, she is a celebrant of material values, the material girl, who takes the guilt away from sex, greed, and materialism. For this audience, she is Marilyn Monroe reincarnated, the superpop superstar, the super-ideal male fantasy sex object and female fantasy boy toy icon. But for romantic idealist youth, she is the good girl seeking love, who chooses true love over material temptations. Yet in the music video narrative, she gets both love and a successful guy.

Thus, the music video of "Material Girl" arguably deploys modernist aesthetic strategies that put narrative and social codes in tension and that require an active viewer to produce meanings and interpretations from the polysemic text. The video also expresses elements of Madonna's own philosophy and, arguably, articulates some of her contradictions (i.e. trying to have it all ways). Thus, like modernist art, the music video creates an innovative structure, articulates the artiste's vision, and requires an active reader to decode the possible range of meanings.[5]

Moreover, the video "Material Girl" problematizes identity and decouples the link between expensive clothes, wealth, and position. Carradine wears a brown work shirt and pants and this is perfectly alright, the video suggests, indicating that fashion and identity are up to the individual and not societal codes. Madonna's images and music videos thus legitimate individual choice in appropriating fashion and producing one's image. Yet the most attractive images in the musical production numbers do celebrate high and expensive fashion, diamonds, and other costly ornaments as keys to a successful image and identity. And it could be that the powerful images of wealth and high fashion, reinforced by the musical lyrics, do privilege bourgeois materialism over romance and individual choice in the music video.

A high level of ambiguity, irony, and humor permeates Madonna's work and image. Her use of fashion is humorous and ironic, as are many of her videos and concert acts. The items marketed in her Boy Toy and Slutco lines are often humorous, as are the very titles of the lines themselves. Indeed, the much-maligned term Boy Toy itself is ironic and allows multiple readings. On one level, Madonna is a toy for boys, but on another level boys are toys for her, the Boy Toys are there for her toying around and the unchastity belt comes off at her whim and desire. Indeed, "Material Girl" shows the guys as Madonna's toys and her dance numbers with men during the Virgin Tour concerts present them as her underlings and accessories with whom she toys and dominates.

Crucially, the early Madonna projects in her videos and music an all-too-rare cultural image of a free woman, making her own choices and determining her own life. The early Madonna image of a free spirit floating through life on her own terms is perfectly captured in her role in Susan Seidelman's *Desperately Seeking Susan* (1985). The message here, consistent with Madonna's other early work, is that one can fundamentally change one's identity by changing one's fashion, appearance, and image. Madonna herself would dramatically exemplify this philosophy in her two succeeding stages in which she radically alters her image and identity.

Indeed, in 1986 alone Madonna metamorphized from the sluttish boy toy in some of her videos, concert performances, and *Desperately Seeking Susan* to the more sophisticated and serious young woman portrayed in the music video "Live to Tell," her new husband Sean Penn's favorite song and the theme of one of his movies. She then appeared as a short-haired young blonde teenager of "Papa Don't Preach," where the Madonna character decides against abortion when she becomes pregnant. This music video utilized a narrative and realist form to tell the story of a young woman with a problem whereas another music video from the year, "Open Your Heart," deployed a complex modernist deconstruction in which Madonna problematized the male gaze, appearing as a stripper in a "carousel" porn parlor and dancing off at the end with a young boy, in a Charlie Chaplin outfit, deconstructing oppositions between "sin" and "innocence", adults and youth. These music videos thus deployed different aesthetic strategies from the traditional narrative form of "Live to Tell" and the gritty realism of "Papa Don't Preach," in which images unproblematically illustrate the lyrics and the lyrics comment on the narrative action, to the deconstructive modernism of "Open Your Heart." Madonna was experimenting with different forms and styles, and in the process constructed a new set of images, and a new identity.

Madonna II: who's that girl?

Madonna had arrived. In 1985, her records had sold 16 million singles and albums. She had no. 1 pop hits with "Like a Virgin" and "Crazy for You," and by the time she was 26, Madonna had made seven Top-20 singles in seventeen months (it took Barbra Streisand seventeen years to do the same). Madonna made a successful film debut in *Desperately Seeking Susan* and her Virgin Tour established her as one of the hottest figures in pop music. She was featured on the cover of *Time* magazine and was profiled in *People*, *Newsweek*, *Rolling Stone*, and other popular magazines. Her first album, *Madonna,* eventually sold over three million copies and her album *Like A Virgin* racked up 4.5 million copies in domestic sales, with 2.5 million more worldwide by 1985. Moreover, Madonna *knew* that she was a superstar and plotted her moves accordingly.

Needless to say, Madonna deployed fashion and sexuality to produce the image that would mark her mid- to late 1980s stage, characterized by continued megasuccess as a recording star with best-selling albums and music videos, another successful concert tour ("Who's That Girl?"), a much-discussed and eventually failed marriage with movie actor Sean Penn, and two movies that flopped with critics and audiences (*Shanghai Surprise* and *Who's That Girl?*).

The first visible change in image had to do with her weight and body image. The early Madonna was soft and a bit chubby, but rigorous exercise and diet transformed her body. She also changed her hair and fashion styles, utilizing more glamorous haute couture fashion, while frequently changing her hair arrangements. In many photos and in the 1986 film *Shanghai Surprise* Madonna appeared more and more like Marilyn Monroe with glamorous, wavy, and fluffy blonde hair. She also emulated the look of other classic movie stars like Lana Turner and Marlene Dietrich. Yet in her rock videos "Cherish" and "Papa Don't Preach," Madonna sported short, cropped blondish hair (*à la* Jean Seberg in *Breathless*) and garish platinum blonde hair in the 1987 movie *Who's That Girl?*, which reprised the figure of the 1930s Hollywood screwball comedy heroine. The song "Like a Prayer" featured Madonna with her natural dark hair and she also appeared in red hair and various shades between light and dark in the videos, photos, and documentary footage of the period from 1986 to the end of the 1980s.

Madonna's 1987 "Who's That Girl?" tour, captured on the video-cassette *Ciao Italia!*, disclosed her to be twenty pounds lighter and highly athletic. For years, she had been dieting, exercising for hours each day, and even lifting weights to build up her body. The tour featured her energetic dancing, with break- dancer accompaniment, intricate lighting effects, seven or eight costume changes for the star, and dramatic shifts of image and mood throughout the show. Wearing a skimpy black corset at the start of the show, Madonna played to her sex-kitten image, but then shifted to the romantic sentimental mode of her album *True Blue*. But after wearing a 1950s prom dress to reflect the innocence of *True Blue*, she put a black leather jacket over the dress for "Papa Don't Preach," while the words "safe sex" were flashed on a huge screen at the back of the stage.

Mocking "Material Girl," Madonna wore a ridiculously tacky outfit and sang the lyrics with a high-pitched Betty Boop twang to ironize the lyrics. For "La Isla Bonita," she chose a Spanish-style cabaret dress and wore an international melange of clothes in "Holiday", which signalled the celebatory and wholesome attitude she was trying to promote. Eschewing the bawdy sexuality and sexual repartee which marked her earlier Virgin Tour, and that returned in even more extreme forms in the later Blonde Ambition and Girlie Show tours, Madonna is relatively restrained in her deployment of fashion and sexuality during this period, appearing to "mature" in appropriating more traditional images and fashion.

The stage of Madonna's *True Blue* deployment of more traditional images of women and sexuality, however, undercut her subversiveness as a fashion image and model for young women. Whereas the flash trash of the early Madonna legitimated creating your own fashion statements and mixed and matched cheap attire, Madonna II produced the traditional image of the slender, well-dressed beautiful women, forcing the "wannabees" to go to exercise salons, beauty parlors, and to buy expensive clothing, cosmetics, and jewelry.[6] Indeed, during this period, there was a marked turn to gyms, dieting, and the cultivation of slimness as the ideal for women. Madonna's image in the fashion magazines also sent out the message that high and tasteful fashion was back and that flash-trash and antifashion were out.

From 1987 to 1989, Madonna thus adopted more traditional fashion and attitudes, and tried to appear more respectful of traditional gender roles. Trying to make her doomed marriage with Sean Penn work, Madonna appeared in romantic love songs videos (*True Blue*), singing of the joys of devotion, commitment, and true love. Madonna decided to shed the trampy sex kitten look and boy toy image for a more conventional feminine appearance. As *Forbes* put it:

> She began singing in a deeper, more serious voice, and in a video from her third album wore honey-blonde hair and a demure flowered dress. In July 1987 she got herself on the cover of *Cosmopolitan* as a glamorous blonde, and in May 1988 she graced the cover of *Harper's Bazaar* as a prim brunette. Her 'True

Blue' album of that period sold nearly 17 million copies, and she sold more albums among the over-20 crowd than ever.

(October 1, 1990)

As noted, Madonna's marketing strategies successively targeted different audiences. While she appealed to young teenage girls in her early work, she quickly incorporated minority audiences with her use of Hispanic and black figures and culture in her videos and stage performances. The *True Blue* phase incorporated an older audience and perhaps a more conservative one, through her exploitation of more traditional images and types of song. Thus, rather than going for a "lowest common denominator" popularity, Madonna achieved her stardom through successively incorporating different audiences into her orbit.[7]

The effect of Madonna's second phase was thus to legitimate more traditional fashion and images of women. The period was an especially creative one in the field of music video. Her album *Like a Prayer* (1989) revealed her to have matured psychologically and musically. The songs deal with the pain of the breaking up of her marriage with Sean Penn, repressed guilt over her mother's death, conflicts with her father, and the pain and difficulties of growing up. The music video of the title song brings out religious motifs from Madonna's Catholic upbringing and incorporates a more complex modernist phase in her music video production, which would attract a large academic following. Although in her earlier videos and image construction, Madonna utilized crucifixes as part of her fashion attire, the music video of the track "Like A Prayer" is built primarily around religious images and themes. The video fuses religion and eroticism in a narrative celebrating love, both spiritual and carnal. The refrain, "In the midnight hour, I can feel your power, Just like a prayer, you know I'll take you there," could either refer to religious or sexual ecstasy.

Madonna brings out the latent eroticism in the Catholic religion and uses it for striking aesthetic and moral purposes. She also incorporates the joy and enthusiasm of black gospel music, thus fusing sacred and secular, Catholic and Protestant, themes and images. The video contrasts images of an inside and outside world, where the outside is the site of racial and sexual violence, bigotry, and injustice. The inside world of the church, however, is one of love, community, and goodness – powerful religious messages and images.[8]

The narrative of the "Like a Prayer" video depicts an innocent black man wrongly accused of a crime that the Madonna figure observes. She goes into a church, dreams of making love to the statue of a black saint, and then rescues the innocent black to flamboyant images of gospel singing, burning crosses (representing the evil of Klan bigotry), candles, and other religious iconography. For the dream/fantasy sequence of the video, Madonna wears a black slip which signifies sleep, the oneiric, and eroticism, exploiting the powerful symbolism and aesthetic effects of black. The imagery promotes integration and harmony between blacks and whites, with Madonna singing with a black choir in a black church, kissing one black man and saving another. The video thus projects a powerful image of goodness and morality, doing the right thing.[9]

Yet such are Madonna's contradictions that her use of images undercuts the religious message, as she appears dancing in church in a slip and her erotic behavior in the church probably goes beyond established boundaries of propriety – indeed Italian television banned the video under pressure from Catholic groups (Savan 1993: 88). But, as always, Madonna profits from her contradictions, appealing both to Catholics gratified to see some eroticism and life injected into its institutions and to see dramatization of its morality, as well as to lapsed or antiCatholics who are thrilled by subversive images, such as Madonna kissing a black man and dancing in her slip in a church.

In the music video of "Express Yourself" (1989), which is perhaps the culmi-nation of her second period, Madonna produces a highly complex modernist text that plays with issues of gender, sexuality, and class. Madonna's forest of symbols unfolds with images of a futuristic city in the air, supported by machinery below, drawing on the iconography of Fritz Lang's modernist film classic *Metropolis*. Madonna suddenly emerges standing up on a giant swan. Addressing herself to a female subject (a rather rare move), Madonna proclaims: "Come on girls, do you believe in love? Well, I've got something to say about it, and it goes like this." The lyrics of the song affirm self-expression, doing your best in all things ("Don't settle for second best, baby"), and overcoming obstacles to one's goals. The song employs the imperative mode and Madonna defiantly shouts "Express yourself!" at key junctures in the song. While a verse indicates that "What you need is a big strong hand to lift you to your higher ground," it is clear from the subtext, and the images that accompany the music video, that the "big strong hand" should be your own, and not the typical male helping hand.

Indeed, Madonna is constantly inverting relations of gender power and domina-tion in the video, putting on display the socially constructed images of women, and exhibiting the male fantasies that produce such images of women and sexuality. Utilizing as a frame for the video Lang's *Metropolis*, Madonna inverts the liberal humanist theme of the film, as Morton argues (in Schwichtenberg 1992). Lang's film represents conflicts between workers and capitalists in a futuristic city, as well as between fathers and sons, men and women. At the end, all conflicts are overcome in naive images of total reconciliation. Madonna's video, by contrast, presents stark and powerful images of the differences between capital and labor, and men and women. Images near the end of the video of two men fighting and of the quasi-violent encounter between Madonna and a male worker suggests the irreconcilability of the opposing interests of class and gender and continual struggle between the classes and sexes as the fate of the human species.

Or, one might read the images of the men fighting as a feminist critique of male violence and brutality – a reading supported by the text as a whole. The video presents a panoply of traditional patriarchal representations of women, beginning with Madonna standing on top of a swan and then representing her holding and becoming a cat, sliding across the floor and licking a plate of milk. In these images,

Madonna appropriates traditional feminine images, but then undercuts them by contrasting discordant images of women and assuming the male subject position, showing that all representations of gender are socially constructed and can be assumed and thrown off at will.

The most offensive image, from the standpoint of feminism, Madonna in bondage, can be read as the fantasy of the capitalist male who projects her onto a video screen, in bondage with an iron collar and chains. It is crucial to note that this image is presented as the fantasy of the patriarchal/capitalist of the video who puts on his monocle to feast his eyes upon Madonna in bondage shown on a video screen. The images here are obviously playing on the concept of cinema constructed by a male gaze, and its suggests that images which objectify women are the projection of males who fantasize women as sex objects. From this perspective, Madonna is putting on display the ways that male fantasy and power objectify women, fantasizing them as in bondage, as animals, as beautiful objects for male lust and domination.[10]

Within this display of male images, however, Madonna suddenly emerges in a suit, with a monocle, and grabs her crotch, signifying her assumption of the male position of power and control.[11] At one point, she rips open the jacket to reveal her breasts and to disclose that the male image is just another social construction, a subject-position that anyone can occupy. By implication, images of women are also subject positions, produced by male power, that women may choose to occupy, or may choose to vacate in favor of male subject positions – or something altogether different. This deconstructive reading suggests that "Express Yourself" puts on display the artificiality of images of gender and suggests that individuals can choose their own images and self-constructions. The lyrics of "Express Yourself" indeed order individuals to produce their own identity and to construct their own selves – a thoroughly modernist project that I will explicate further below.

And yet, once again, Madonna undercuts her own feminism by displaying herself in traditional fetishized images of women and as appearing as an object for the male gaze, as well as a subject in control of the narrative and the video itself. There are thus contradictions between Madonna's pop feminism, her deconstruction of dominant images of women, and her replication of precisely these images. Once again, however, Madonna profits from her contradictions, appealing both to feminists and to male viewers like the characters Beavis and Butt-Head who like to ogle female body parts. Thus, her anthem of liberation can be viewed either as a feminist text, or as just another objectification of women's bodies for male pleasure.

Madonna III: blonde ambition

Thus, the Madonna effects were increasingly contradictory. On one hand, she presents herself as a feminist in control of her life and career, and on the other hand, she presents herself as just another female body to titillate men and provide fashion models for women. During her third period, in the 1990s, she would continue to push the boundaries of sexual representation and to become an icon of sexual liberation. Moreover, she became even more eclectic in her use of fashion and in her image production, drawing on some of her earlier images, which she frequently quoted and sometimes parodied. Madonna also became political during this period, making statements on behalf of AIDS victims,[12] the homeless, saving the rain forests, women's rights, and in 1990 even made a "get out and vote" video, threatening to spank those who refused to vote. In 1992, she supported Bill Clinton for President.

After the break-up of her marriage with Sean Penn in 1989, Madonna continued to explore representations of sexuality and gender, entering upon the stage of her work where she would systematically challenge conventional representations of sexuality. This 1990s phase attracted legions of lesbians and gays, pro-sex feminists and sexual libertarians, and academics who would produce a cottage industry of Madonna readings that attempted to decipher her images and texts. It is quite remarkable the extremes to which Madonna has gone in crossing the boundaries of established norms of sexual representation. For Madonna has now deployed images of interracial sex, masturbation (in her concert tour), lesbianism, S. & M. sex, and orgies in her work, constantly trying to go beyond the boundaries of the sexually permissible.

During the 1990s, Madonna has thus exploited an especially flamboyant deployment of fashion and sexuality, producing a series of complex modernist music videos that expanded the boundaries of the art form and even led MTV to ban one of her productions, "Justify My Love," in 1990 and to rarely play "Erotica" in 1992. She also produced a book of erotic images, *Sex* (1992) and became herself, as an artifact of pop culture, regularly exhibited in magazines which intersperse interviews or stories with provocative images of Madonna in kiddy-porn poses, drag, or other provocative images. Madonna had obviously developed from young sex object on the move, to mature woman, prepared to control her own destiny and to move music video into new realms of image production.

In her most recent period, marked by a series of highly controversial rock videos, the Blond Ambition tour and the 1991 film of the tour (*Madonna: Truth or Dare*), the 1992 album *Erotica* and the book *Sex*, and her 1993 Girlie's Show, Madonna has been recognized as a top pop superstar and even "America's shrewdest businesswoman." Her publicity and marketing machine continued to pump out publicity at a furious rate and the public continued to be fascinated with every detail concerning Madonna's life.

But it was probably her rock videos of the late 1980s and 1990s in which Madonna most notably created wide cultural controversy that attracted the attention of academic critics and cultural theorists. Along with Michael Jackson, she is arguably one of the first rock video superstars and is perhaps the supreme master, or rather mistress, of the form. "Open Your Heart," "Like A Prayer," "Express Yourself," "Justify My Love," and "Vogue" are modernist masterpieces of video art. Breaking the rules of music videos which deploy expressive images to illustrate the lyrics, Madonna's best music videos contain a multilayered structure of images that require an active viewer to generate the sometimes complex meanings proliferating in the play of the music, lyrics, and images. Or, *à la* postmodernism, one can simply view her videos as a dazzling stream of images. For, as we shall see, Madonna employs both modernist and postmodernist aesthetic strategies, thus appealing to devotees of both.[13]

Densely crafted feasts of images, her music videos can be enjoyed on several levels by different audiences: teenage girls and boys can process the music and images in different ways according to their own fantasies; more sophisticated music and cultural critics can enjoy grappling with polysemic modernist texts and occasional uses of postmodern strategies; and students of popular culture can attempt to discover why and how Madonna is popular. Once again, we see how Madonna's "subversive" artistic practices also coalesce with a successful marketing strategy. Thus, Madonna should be interpreted in terms both of her aesthetic practices and her marketing strategies, and her works can thus be read either as works of art, or analyzed as commodities that shrewdly exploit markets. In fact, Madonna is interesting both as an aesthetic and a marketing phenomenon, and a multidimensional reading should interrogate both sides of the Madonna equation.

In the 1990s, Madonna has attempted to produce an identity as an artist. Her rock videos became increasingly complex, or attempted to expand the boundaries of the permissible in terms of male and female gender roles, overt sexuality, parody of religion, and modernist ambiguity. Fashionwise, she sometimes returned to the sexy and flamboyant attire of her early stage, but she mixed it with haute couture, futuristic technofashion, S. & M. chic, and a postmodern pastiche of various fashion styles, subverting oppositions between high and low fashion, much as postmodern art explodes established modernist cultural hierarchies between "high" and "low" culture. Yet, Madonna deployed the typically modernist strategy of shock in her outlandish use of fashion, sexuality, and religious imagery, especially in her rock videos, which are highly complex cultural texts that allow a multiplicity of readings.

If one conceives "postmodern art" to be a fragmented display of disconnected elements in a flat, superficial play of surface without any depth or meaning (as Jameson 1991 and others would have it), most of Madonna's work is emphatically not "postmodern" in this sense. Instead, both her more realist videos and modernist videos convey meanings and messages, though with her more modernist music videos like "Express Yourself," the meanings are often elusive and difficult to grasp. The modernist strategy of adopting shock techniques have been a constant in Madonna's work and although she deploys camp, irony, and humor, her subject matter and themes are often quite serious. So in a sense, Madonna is more modernist than postmodernist, though her work also embodies postmodern themes and aesthetic strategies as I indicate below.

Throughout the Blonde Ambition tour, Madonna played out a deconstructive drama of playing with gender roles, frequently wearing men's clothes, grabbing her crotch, and declaring she was the boss, thus occupying male gender positions. She also had her male dancers wear fake breasts, women's clothes, and submit to her power and control. The message was that "male" and "female" were social constructs that could be deconstructed and that women could occupy male positions, roles, and behavior and vice versa. Yet, as I shall argue in the conclusion, Madonna does not subvert relations of domination or offer egalitarian images of relations. Like conservative deconstruction, Madonna puts on display binary oppositions that constitute our culture and society, demonstrates their artificiality, and questions the prioritizing of one of the oppositions over the other, without putting anything new in its place. Thus, she tends to place women, primarily herself, in the position of power and authority which is rigorously exercised over men and women.

To deconstruct traditional gender oppositions and relations of power and domination, Madonna uses irony, humor, and parody to push the sensitive buttons of "masculine" and "feminine" and to provoke reaction to the overthrowing of traditional images and stereotypes and their exchange and mixture in the genders of the future, which would presumably be multiple rather than binary. There was indeed always a strong mixture of irony and satire in Madonna's work from the beginning and her concert performances became increasingly campy,[14] as was the dramatization of her life on the road in *Truth or Dare*. Her performance of "Material Girl" in the Blond Ambition tour, for instance, is pure camp, with Madonna and two female singers sitting on a raised platform in hair-curlers and bathrobes, singing the song with false accents, out of tune and in high-pitched voices. The image puts on display the labor and ridiculous activities that women go through to make themselves "beautiful" and mocks the ideal of the "material girl" (of course, on another level Madonna herself is the extreme example of almost superhuman labor and expense to make herself "beautiful," a contradiction that pervades her work and that I return to in the conclusion).

Her most striking music videos are highly aestheticized, using modernist techniques of the construction of compelling images. The orgy scenes in "Justify My Love" are highly abstract and theatrical and "Vogue" deploys posed images to celebrate pure camp ("Strike a pose! Vogue! Vogue!"). Indeed, "Vogue" parodies fashion conventions – modeling, posing, photography, and objectification – but reinforces them by identifying voguing with a gay dance phenomenon and then cultural celebrity. On the other hand, the video puts on display the conditions of production of the image by disclosing the poses of fashion and star images and the construction involved in the production of images.[15]

The video opens with parting feathers, signifying camp style and artificiality, and then presents a montage of posed images with her dance troupe assuming fashion poses. Two servants voguing while they clean the house suggests the desirability of image-creation throughout the spheres of everyday life. The frame centers on Madonna who orders "Strike a pose!" and a set of images shows her ensemble obeying. The lyrics sing of escape from everyday life through voguing, transforming oneself into a more desirable image, "You're a superstar, that's what you are!" Voguing, the lyrics suggest, is open to anyone ("It doesn't matter if you're black or white, if you're a boy or a girl") and produces aesthetic self-transcendence for all ("Beauty is where you find it"). But then the static images, derived from the fashion industry, are transposed into the gay dance style documented in *Paris is*

Burning and infused with erotic energy. And finally, Madonna's pantheon of privileged images ("Greta Garbo and Monroe . . . Bette Davis, Rita Hayworth gave good face") is illustrated by images of Madonna herself striking poses in the guise of the above mentioned celebrities.

Madonna has been attacked for "poaching" images and phenomena, like voguing, from gay culture and utilizing its images and style in her work, defused of its original context. She was also attacked by black critics for drawing heavily upon black music in her work and then leaving out references to blacks, or people of color, in her pantheon of images in "Vogue." In reference to the first criticism, one could argue that Madonna has done as much as anyone to "normalize" gay and lesbian sexuality in popular media culture, and is indeed idolized by many in the gay and lesbian communities. Likewise, she could respond to her black and other critics of color that she has done as much as anyone to promote black (and Hispanic) music, dancers, singers, and musicians, while attempting to break down color lines and barriers between the races. She could also answer that her pantheon in "Vogue" is arguably a gay male pantheon that includes precisely who she cites.

On the other hand, one could also argue that Madonna ultimately privileges whiteness and that the people of color around her simply highlight her distinctive whiteness. Moreover, her videos and concert performances replicate white superiority and power, showing Madonna totally in control of, overshadowing, and dominating everyone else. In any case, the complexity and sensitivity of issues of race, gender, sexual preference, and class that Madonna takes on demonstrates a courage to tackle controversial topics that few popular music figures engage with her consistency and provocativeness.

"Vogue" contains images of corsets and bras and the inside/outside fashion deconstruction that one observes in Madonna's videos and concert performances, in which bras, corsets, and panties are worn outside of blouses, skirts, or suits, suggesting that all fashion is artificial. Her images suggest that corset, bras, and other standard female attire are symbols of women's submission to cultural standards, which might as well be worn outside to make the bondage transparent. On the other hand, these icons of women's oppression to fashion standards are rendered erotic in Madonna's iconography, showing how one can transform signs of oppression into signs of mockery and libidinal enjoyment.

Madonna's modernist deconstruction was disseminated via an aesthetic of shock and excess defined by her fashion, attitude, and behavior. There were, of course, market reasons why one might adopt such strategies: they create an image, call attention to oneself, and sell. Intense narcissism is ever more visible as a key element in the Madonna phenomenon and one could read the 1990s Madonna as an image factory in which her own image is the meaning of her musical texts and other image productions. Madonna's continuing to go beyond herself and to push the boundaries of the permissible utilize modernist aesthetic strategies of excess, shock, spectacle, and theatricality. In the Blonde Ambition tour, Madonna produced a futuristic look, wearing far-out technofashion, suggesting new syntheses of technology and the human. Her blonde hair tied back severely, a microphone unit strapped to her head, and her body adorned with bustiers and futuristic clothes designed by Jean Paul Gaultier, Madonna appears as another species, a new technobody, designer-fashioned for the next century.

The Blonde Ambition show also features male dancers with fake breasts and women dancers with penises, suggesting the emergence of a new species in the technofuture, which subverts previous boundaries between men and women. Grabbing her crotch throughout the show, a defiant Madonna presents herself as an icon of power and sexuality. The dance numbers also exploit far-out fashion and explicit sexuality to constitute her identity as an iconoclastic figure of the transgressor against established conventions. She, like the successful modernist artist, thus establishes new norms by breaking the old ones.

However, her 1992 album *Erotica* and book *Sex* indicate that Madonna may be falling into a trap that could render her boring and predictable. The songs in her album and music video "Erotica" deploy some of the same images and blatant sexuality as "Justify My Love" and her earlier sexual provocations, and do not break any new ground. Her book *Sex* is something of an embarrassment with pictures on shabby paper with an aluminum cover and metal-binding that easily breaks (so I was told by a book store manager who showed me several broken books which had been returned). The pictures of S. & M. in particular are boring and predictable, and the text, supposedly recounting "Madonna's sexual fantasies," is also trite and unerotic.[16] Fashion is deployed in these works to shock and provide libidinal excitement, but by now such imagery is rather commonplace.

But in the best of her music videos, Madonna emerges as a modernist boundary-buster. Her concept of art privileges self-expression, experimentation, pushing the limits of taste, and crossing the borderline into new areas of experience and representation. Madonna has continued to push pop culture beyond previous boundaries and to subvert established rules, conventions, and limits. Her deployment of fashion and sexuality in particular shatters previous rules and conventions and established her identity as an iconoclastic modernist. On the other hand, so far her modernist moves have been extremely successful from a commercial point of view and Madonna emerges as much as clever businesswoman as artiste.

Thus, one must also grasp the "Madonna phenomenon" as a commercial enterprise. In April 1992, it was widely reported that Madonna had signed a $60 million deal with Time-Warner, which would market her albums, music videos, and films, providing her with large royalties, development money, and the opportunity to promote the work of young artists. Utilizing modernist terminology, Madonna said that she envisaged the contract as an opportunity to produce a group of collaborating artists, that constitute an "artistic think tank" which would be a cross between the Bauhaus, that revolutionized art, architecture, and design in Germany in the 1920s, and Andy Warhol's factory that brought together artists from film, music, painting, fashion, and other contemporary arts in the 1960s and beyond (*New York Times*, April 20, 1992, B1). *Forbes* reported that during the period 1991/2, Madonna earned $48,000,000, making her, once again, one of the most highly paid performers of the period (September 28, 1992). Madonna's art, fashion, and identity games have paid and call attention to the fact that media culture is commercial culture that sells cultural commodities to audiences.

MADONNA BETWEEN THE MODERN AND THE POSTMODERN

Concerning the deployment of fashion and sexuality, Madonna's cumulative message seems to be that you can do, say, and be anything that you want. The construction of one's own identity begins with fashion, with one's "look." Here the fashion message is that you can wear anything, that anything goes, that one can construct one's own look out of the materials of one's culture. Madonna's use of fashion as excess, of appearing in the most outlandish and *outré* costumes imaginable, suggests that fashion is not a rigid code, not a set of rules to which one must conform, but a field of imagination and creativity in which one can construct any image that one wants.

Of course, Madonna's linking of image, fashion, and identity also suggests that it is in one's look, in how one dresses and makes oneself up that identity is anchored – a debatable proposition. But, Madonna intimates, fashion is not enough: one must strike a pose, vogue, develop "attitude," behave in a certain way. Madonna's way is excess, shock, pushing beyond the limits, and always trying to develop something new. The Madonna way is to attract attention through going beyond the bounds of conventional attire and behavior. Such a position empowers people to dress, act, and be what they want at the same time that it enslaves people in the necessity of developing an image, striking a pose, constructing identity through style, forcing people to worry about how they dress and look and how other people will react to their image.

The Madonna phenomenon thus suggests that in a consumerist promotional culture identity is constructed through image and fashion, involving one's look, pose, and style. Identity is nothing deep as it was in much modern theory that assumed an essential self, or the project of developing an authentic selfhood. Whereas for Heidegger *Selbständigkeit* (standing-by-yourself, self-constancy) and *Wiederholung* (resolute repetition in the face of death of one's fundamental choice of selfhood) constituted authentic selfhood and identity (see Kellner 1973), for Madonna and postmodern identity-construction it is precisely change, constantly redeveloping one's look, and striking outrageous and constantly changing poses that constitutes one's image and identity. Of course, and curiously, Madonna is "authentic" in Heidegger's sense in that she has resolutely adhered to this project now in over a decade of shocking fashion, images, poses, and iconoclastic behavior, all of which have created and promoted "Madonna."

Moreover, fashion and identity for Madonna are inseparable from her aesthetic practices, from her cultivation of her image in her music videos, films, TV appearances, concerts, and other cultural interventions. Madonna's deployment of fashion and sexuality are structured by an aesthetic of creativity, of producing one's own look and identity. Her practice is linked to an aesthetic of excess and to this day, Madonna continues to go beyond the borders of the permissible, to subvert and transgress established boundaries in fashion and art. In this sense, the putatively postmodern Madonna is enacting a pop modernist aesthetic. Indeed, more considered and theoretically informed reflection on the Madonna phenomenon may deconstruct, or put in question, certain distinctions between modernism and postmodernism. Many academic discourses fail to adequately conceptualize modernism and describe as "postmodern" quite typical modernist aesthetic strategies, practices, and goals – or they inadequately theorize the "postmodern."

Madonna has been theorized as "postmodern" through her deployment of strategies of simulation, pastiche, her implosion of gender, racial, and sexual boundaries, and her use of irony and camp (see the articles in Schwichtenberg 1992). Yet boundary deconstruction, irony, and camp are arguably modernist strategies and in fact Madonna constantly deploys self-consciously modernist strategies, presenting her work as serious and transgressive art. In the 1990 *Nightline* interview and the 1991 film *Truth or Dare*, Madonna describes her work as "artistic," claiming that she refuses to compromise her artistic integrity. She also indicates that she wants to continue "pushing buttons," being "political," going beyond established boundaries, and creating new and innovative works of art – all self-consciously modernist aesthetic values and goals.[17] Thus, while one might interpret Madonna as "postmodernist" in the light of her uses of Baudrillardian categories of simulation and implosion, one should also be aware of the ways in which Madonna can be read as modernist.

For the most part, theorizing about the "postmodern" is as superficial and one-dimensional as the texts and practices described as postmodern in those terms. A complex and challenging phenomenon like Madonna puts in question and tests one's aesthetic categories and commitments. Yet Madonna does deploy a wide range of aesthetic strategies and so if one's definition of "postmodernism" is a set of cultural practices that combines traditional, modernist, and new postmodernist forms and themes, then Madonna can be interpreted as "postmodern." However, one should note the extent to which she draws upon classical modernist strategies, images, and forms in her most impressive music videos and concert performances of the past few years. She also has a large repertoire of "realist" music videos in which the images merely illustrate the lyrics of the song and produce realist narratives to accompany the words and music (i.e. "Papa Don't Preach," "Live to Tell," "Oh, Father," "This Used to be My Playground," and "Rain"). And in "Fever," she deploys explicitly postmodern image strategies in which the lyrics of the song, itself a pop song of the 1950s, are flatly intoned over abstract images of a bronzed and electronically contorted Madonna, presenting a flat surface of disconnected images without deeper meaning.

While some have attacked Madonna as being totally antifeminist and a disgrace to women, others have lauded her as the true feminist for our times and as a role model for young women. Camille Paglia, for instance, has celebrated Madonna as "Real Feminist" and an ideal of the strong, independent and successful woman, who successfully affirms her own power and sexuality and defies conventional stereotypes (*New York Times*, December 14, 1990, B1).[18] I too have stressed the extent to which Madonna reverses relations of power and domination and provides strong affirmative images of women. But one could argue that Madonna merely transposes relations of domination, reversing the roles of men and women, rather than dissolving relations of domination. In her concert performances, her dancers are mere appendages which she dominates and controls, overtly enacting rituals of domination on the stage. In the HBO Blond Ambition tour video of 1990, for example, she is constantly positioning herself in positions of power and control over the male (and female) dancers. In simulated sex scenes in the tour, Madonna was usually on top and in her infamous masturbation/simulated orgasm scene in "Like A Virgin," the male dancers first fondle Madonna and then disappear as she writhes in an exaggerated orgasm.

In response to this critique, one could argue that Madonna is constantly ironizing relations of domination, putting their mechanisms on display, and, as I argued in my reading of "Express Yourself," subverting them by disclosing the artificiality, constructedness, and reversibility of relations of power and domination. Yet in her "real" everyday relations with her cast, friends, and family in the documentary *Truth or Dare* (1991), she also positions herself as the mother of her troop and is constantly affirming her power over them, often admitting in interviews that she is a "bitch" and "control freak." Before each performance, Madonna says a "prayer," much like a football coach prepping his crew to go out and win the big one (in one sequence, she concludes by ordering her minions to go out and "kick ass"). In both work and leisure scenes in her concert film *Truth or Dare*, Madonna is clearly in charge and the opening song of the HBO documentary of the concert showed her with a whip in hand, proclaiming "I am the boss!"

One could, of course, argue that the film *Truth or Dare* is itself a put on that deconstructs the very genre of a film documentary by undermining the opposition between backstage and onstage (Pribram in Schwichtenberg 1992). In Madonna's entourage, backstage is onstage with the omnipresent camera catching every nuance and Madonna and many of her circle are obviously playing to the film being shot. Yet one could argue that the many images, scenes, and comments of her family, tour ensemble, friends, and fans capture aspects of the "truth" of Madonna and present perspectives on the "real" Madonna. For what is "Madonna" other than the effects she produces and generates, the public persona that she assiduously constructs? And the one thing that comes through repeatedly, reinforced by her many interviews and music performances, is that Madonna is in charge, that she totally dominates everyone around her.[19]

Madonna and Laurie

Madonna might be contrasted in this regard with avant-garde performance artist Laurie Anderson. While Madonna often presents herself as a sovereign subject who dominates her environment and controls those around her, Laurie Anderson presents more egalitarian images of social relations. In *Home of the Brave*, a 1986 documentary of her concert performances, Anderson slides in and out of interactions with members of her cast, which often privilege the other performers, or present ensemble singing or dancing, in which Anderson sometimes slides off to the side and other times merges with her ensemble. Madonna, by contrast, always dominates her entourage and is always the center of attention with the musical performance numbers highlighting *her* talents, importance, and, especially, stardom.

Madonna is thus the sovereign and centered modern subject, always in charge, always in control, while Laurie Anderson is more fragmented, dispersed, and decentered *à la* postmodern subjectivity. In her 1990 music video collection, Anderson presents a male "clone" of herself to help her with production and publicity and then clones a female, and both clones are rather grotesque. While Madonna grabs her crotch and prances in a male suit to symbolize her assumption of the prerogatives of male, phallic power, Anderson uses electronic devices to lower the octave of her voice, so that she sounds male – but an insecure, uncertain male voice signifying the frailty of personal and sexual identity. She dresses and sometimes looks androgenous, collapsing distinctions between "male" and "female" (themselves social constructs), while Madonna is invariably a "woman," even when she assumes male power (as when she bares her breasts after grabbing her crotch in the segment in "Express Yourself" in which she appears in a male suit, as if to say, "Look, I'm really a woman").

Madonna's texts are meaning-systems, which proliferate polysemic meanings and messages. Her performances on her music videos highlight the meanings of the words, or use images to undercut or subvert the meanings of the lyrics – as she chooses. Her music videos are often complex modernist systems of meaning, demanding interpretation and allowing multivalent readings. Madonna is a meaning machine and her performances articulate her ideology, vision, and messages. Indeed, one level of meaning perpetually conveyed in her music videos and performances is that Madonna herself is a superstar, that Madonna is cool, that Madonna rules. This narcissistic self-reference and self-promotion in her performances is perhaps the underlying meaning of all of her images which relentlessly signify "Madonna! Madonna! Madonna!"

Laurie Anderson's performance in *Home of the Brave*, by contrast, provides fragments of meaning which do not add up to any clear system of meanings. Her texts thus disrupt, in postmodern fashion, the signifying chain, her images and sounds do not connect, or add up to anything in particular. Rather, they present a collage of disconnected signifiers, of sounds and images that do not signify, or that merely point to themselves. Her performance is for the sake of performance, in the moment, and does not produce any particular statements, positions, messages or ideologies – unlike Madonna who is always in your face with her latest statement or message.[20] Laurie Anderson thus enacts a postmodern deconstruction of expression and identity, fragments and disperses her images and sounds, and resists developing systems of meaning. She follows David Byrne's injunction to "Stop Making Sense" and instead makes performances that are just that – performances.

Whereas Madonna is forever prancing around familiar everyday worlds (or exploring the utopian spaces of sexual fantasy), Anderson takes us to completely new and different worlds with different sights, sounds, and logic. One thus enters a new postmodern imagescape with Anderson where humans implode with technology, familiar instruments give out strange, electronically mediated sounds, and nothing is quite like it seems. Laurie Anderson herself often appears as an extraterrestrial and her Nietzschean *Ubermensch* (pointed to in her pop song "O Superman") is a curious synthesis of the human and technology, a new species of technohuman who produces new sounds, or as Sayre puts it, "a 'new noise' . . . in a new territory" (1989: 155).

In fact, Anderson deterritorializes her performance spaces that are themselves strange and yet familiar. She also focuses attention on the musical instruments played and in a highly implosive set of gestures merges the human and organic with inanimate instruments. Ties become pianos which emit electronic sounds, guitars become organic, bending and flapping, while humans merge with technology or become mere shadows and photographic images. Many of Anderson's performances are strongly compelling and emit intense and strange images and sounds that often take on a certain fascination and power. While Madonna's images signify and demand interpretation, Anderson's images resist interpretation. Her art is an erotics of surfaces and the play of light, sound, movement, word, and performance. Her texts are thus not polysemic, they resist reading, and revel in the their own play and deconstruction of meaning.

While Madonna tends to exploit the familiar genres of popular music, Anderson mixes pop, rock, jazz, blues, gospel, classical, and other idioms with new electronic sounds and computer-generated images to produce a new multi-media performance art – a postmodern implosion of "high" and "low" art and familiar music genres. At one point in *Home of the Brave*, she says "Welcome to difficult art," and then performs "Language is a Virus From Outer Space." The musical accompaniment mixes blues singers, with a jazz saxophone player, with rock percussion, guitar, and piano, mixed together in a hybrid pop sound. Words and images are flashed on the screen in the multi-media mode that Anderson uses, and she concludes by emitting electronic sounds by pounding on her head and gnashing her teeth.

In a sense, Anderson's work is not really difficult, it's just different: its fragments don't connect, it operates in a different space and time continuum, and its performances aim at otherness and strangeness rather than classical form, harmony and symmetry, or the proliferation of meaning *à la* modernism. By contrast, her gestures, sounds, images, and performance are simply strange and don't communicate anything at all – or what her signifiers communicate is simply themselves and no more. Yet, in a manner typical of avant-garde art, Anderson raises questions concerning what art – and in particular music and performance – really is. Like John Cage, Anderson seems to imply that sound itself is music and transgresses all musical boundaries mixing up familiar sounds with new electronically produced sounds. Likewise, performance in *Home of the Brave* combines musical numbers with storytelling, slices of everyday life, drama, comedy, and multi-media play.

Thus, in avant-garde fashion, Anderson uses some postmodernist techniques to interrogate what art is and expands its boundaries through her performances. Her performances do not add up to produce unifying meanings and her "text" is thus totally fragmented, with euphoric moments, but no deeper meaning. When she says "Language is a Virus From Outer Space," citing a phrase of author William Burroughs, who comes out on stage just before the performance to recite some typically Burroughsesque comments on eyes, images, and representations, followed by Anderson and company's performance of the song, there is no deep insight into language, and the performances and words that flash across the screen do not elucidate the phrase. Rather, the performance simply raises questions concerning what language is that forces thought and reflection (and discussion if the song is performed in a group situation).

Anderson is, of course, an avant-garde performance artist and Madonna is the reigning queen of pop, so this comparison is between two rather different species of culture. Yet such a comparison reveals the limits of Madonna's novelty and creativity and the differences between opposing aesthetic strategies. Yet, curiously, the difference is not between a robust and creative modernism and a flat and dull postmodernism, as some might have it. Instead, Madonna's aesthetic strategies are arguably modernist, while Laurie Anderson has been deploying arguably postmodernist strategies in some of her work, such as *Home of the Brave*. Madonna projects something of a individual style, vision, and voice, and attempts to produce innovative and complex texts within the form of music video. Some of her works do deconstruct familiar meanings, project a polysemic complexity of meaning that demands interpretation, and that provide texts in which sight, sound, and performance work together to generate a wealth of meanings. Likewise, Madonna always has a political agenda and is frequently promoting her version of feminism, sexual liberation, and self-creation.

Anderson, by contrast, deconstructs expression, fragments the signifying chain, implodes musical idioms, resists interpretation and produces a chain of signifiers that don't really signify, or that signify little beyond themselves – *à la* postmodernism. Yet such postmodern work doesn't "say anything," and evades the social commentary of Anderson's own earlier work in *United States*. Madonna by contrast is a commentary machine and constantly presents herself as a cultural revolutionary engaging in social critique, cultural innovation, and the promotion of social change. This brings us to some concluding reflections on Madonna's politics and effects.

The Madonna contradiction machine

Whatever the "truth" of Madonna (no doubt inaccessible in its multiplicity) it is clear that her music videos and concert performances constantly enact relations of power and domination and never portray egalitarian, reciprocal, or communitarian relations. As for Nietzsche, the will to power is at the center of Madonna's universe and Madonna represents herself as the subject of this will, as the center of power and all-powerful subject. Thus, whereas it is salutary that she presents images of powerful women overcoming male domination and while these images might help to empower women, they do not overcome the hierarchical structure of power and domination in our society. Nor do they present an alternative to the relations of domination and oppression that currently structure everyday life in contemporary societies.

Obviously, how one evaluates Madonna depends on one's specific politics and morality, and someone who cultivates an aesthetic of shock and excess, as does Madonna, is certain to offend and to become a target of criticism. Madonna, however, thrives on criticism, which, along with her deployment of fashion and sexuality, helps her produce an identity as a transgressor. Her breaking of rules has progressive elements in that it goes against dominant gender, sex, fashion, and racial hierarchies and her message that identity is something that everyone can and must construct for themselves is also appealing. Yet by constructing identity largely in terms of fashion and image, Madonna plays into precisely the imperatives of the fashion and consumer industries which offer a "new you" and a solution to all of your problems through purchasing products, services, and buying into regimes of fashion and beauty.[21] By privileging image, she plays into the dynamics of the contemporary promotional culture that reduces art, politics, and the fabric of everyday life to the play of image, downplaying the role of communication, commitment, solidarity, and concern for others in the constitution of one's identity and personality.

Madonna is thus emblematic of the narcissistic 1980s, a period still exerting a strong influence, in which the cultivation of the individual self and the obsessive pursuit of one's own interests was enshrined as cultural mythology. The imperative to "go for it!" echoes through the 1980s and Madonna went for it and got it. Yet in becoming the most popular woman entertainer of her era (and perhaps of all time), Madonna produced works that have multiple and contradictory effects and that in many ways helped subvert dominant conservative ideologies. As I have argued, Madonna's deployment of fashion and sexuality pushed buttons of race, sex, gender, class, and religion that provoked contradictory responses, that highlighted the social constructedness of these phenomena, and that indicated these artificial categories of everyday life could be changed, or at least one's attitude toward such things as race and sexual preference could be changed. In a sense, with the limitations that I have noted, Madonna helped bring marginal groups and concerns into the cultural mainstream and powerfully articulated the yearnings of young women for more independence and power.

And yet there have been strong criticisms from the marginal and oppressed groups whose images and style Madonna has deployed that she exploits people of color, gays and lesbians, and marginal sexual subcultures for her own purposes. bell hooks has argued that there is also a racist component in Madonna, who privileges herself and whiteness over people of color. Madonna is always in center frame and is always the dominant figure, appearing to hooks more as "plantation mistress" than as "soul sister" (hooks 1992: 157ff.). hooks notes that Madonna ultimately privileges the "blonde look" over her natural dark hair and so when the chips are down, the image Madonna most exploits is that of the quintessential 'white girl.' To maintain that image she must always position herself as an outsider in relation to black culture. It is that position of outsider that enables her to colonize and appropriate black experience for her own opportunistic ends even as she attempts to mask her acts of racist aggression as affirmation.

(ibid.: 159).

Yet one could also argue that Madonna's constant changes of style, including hair color, and her appropriation of black, Hispanic, gay and lesbian, and a vast array of other images circulate positive images of marginal subgroups through culture. In any case, Madonna is a site of genuine contradiction. On one hand, she promotes feminism, yet some of her images undercut feminist critiques of femininity, beauty, the objectification of women, and so on. On the other, Madonna sanctions revolt and individual construction of image and identity, yet the form in which she carries out her revolt is that of the models of the fashion and consumer industries. Madonna calls herself an artistic revolutionary and celebrates modernist subversion, yet her work is circulated in the commodity form of popular music and music videos, which are, after all, at bottom, advertisements for the songs.

While there is sufficient material both to celebrate and to criticize her, one should grasp the many-sidedness of the Madonna phenomenon and her multiple and contradictory effects. Indeed, Madonna is a provocative challenge to cultural studies. Unpacking the wealth of her artistic strategies, meanings, and effects requires deployment of a full array of textual criticism, audience research, and analysis of the political economy and production of pop culture in our contemporary media society. Her work has become increasingly complex and it is precisely this complexity, as well as her continued popularity, that has made Madonna a highly controversial object of academic analysis in recent years. Madonna allows many, even contradictory, readings which are grounded in her polysemic and modernist texts and her contradictory cultural effects. At dull gatherings, mention Madonna and you can be sure that there will be violent arguments, with some people passionately attacking and others defending her. Whether one loves or hates her, Madonna is a constant provocation who reveals the primacy of fashion and image in contemporary culture and the social constructedness of identity.

NOTES

1 The ideal type constructing a distinction between traditional and modern societies is in some ways an oversimplification, but I am using the distinction to attempt to highlight key features linking fashion, image, and identity in modern societies. For more on the discourses of modernity, their contributions and limitations, see Antonio and Kellner 1994 and forthcoming.

2 Much contemporary cultural studies focuses on textual analysis and/or audience reception alone, generally ignoring the political economy and production of culture. In his study of Madonna, for instance, John Fiske writes:

A cultural analysis, then, will reveal both the way the dominant ideology is structured into the text and into the reading subject, and those textual features that enable negotiated, resisting, or oppositional readings to be made. Cultural analysis reaches a satisfactory conclusion when the ethnographic studies of the historically and socially located meanings that *are* made are related to the semiotic analysis of the text.

(1989a: 98)

It is my argument, by contrast, that analysis of the political economy and production of culture is an important component which has been downplayed and even ignored in the recent boom in cultural studies, and that Madonna's marketing strategies have been essential to her success.

3 On the MTV channel, see Kaplan 1987 and the studies in Frith, Goodwin, and Grossberg 1993.

4 Madonna couldn't know at this time that the rise of AIDS would make sexuality an increasingly dangerous domain. Later, she would become an AIDS activist and insert "safe sex" messages into her concerts and albums. She would also, beginning around 1990, dramatize the dangerous aspects of sex itself.

5 Ann Kaplan (1987) interprets "Material Girl" and Madonna in general as symptomatic of postmodernism on the grounds that Madonna pastiches Marilyn Monroe and mixes genres and modes, such as realism and musical numbers in "Material Girl." But this is a partial reading of postmodernism and one could argue that for an artifact to be an example of "postmodernism," it should also deconstruct expression and meaning, rupture signifying chains, and project a flat play of signifiers, of euphoric images, that refuse meaning and interpretation, as in the concept of postmodernism, drawn from Jameson (1991), with which I am working. Contrasted to such a flat, postmodern text, most of Madonna's music videos demand interpretation and some contain complex aesthetic structures that express Madonna's own ideas and style, that require interpretive work and that produce multivalent readings, and are thus "modernist" in the sense that I am using the term. I return to this theme later in the chapter and contrast Laurie Anderson's use of postmodernist aesthetic strategies with Madonna's use of modernism.

6 See the study by Bordo in Schwichtenberg 1992, who relates this phase of Madonna's work to the production of "plastic bodies" in the entertainment and fashion industries, the proliferation of anorexia and other eating disorders, and obsession with dieting and weight loss.

7 To be sure, there was overlapping of her various stages and Madonna did not abandon her early audience and neglect their interests. One song on *True Blue*, "Where's the Party," continues the early emphasis on liberation from the cares of everyday life through partying with lyrical refrains "I want to free my soul" and "I want to lose control." Thus, there is always an emphasis in Madonna's work on partying and having a good time, legitimating hedonism and pleasure.

8 During the same week in which Madonna released her video of "Like A Prayer," her Pepsi commercial was broadcast which used the lyrics to the same song and a collage of images that transmitted the "drink Pepsi" message. A right-wing fundamentalist group, however, threatened Pepsi with a boycott if they did not pull the commercial and the craven corporation capitulated, proving once again that the religious right cannot appreciate aesthetic imagery which promotes the interests of religion and that capitalist corporations are both cowardly and antiaesthetic in their pursuit of profit. Her Pepsi commercial itself, attacked by some of her critics, is in fact a complex modernist musical video that deserves to be read in the pantheon of her music videos.

9 Just as Madonna is the vehicle of morality and liberal integrationism in "Like A Prayer," in the Pepsi commercial she "liberates" a group of Catholic schoolgirls who break into dance when Madonna appears, leading them to self-expression and drinking Pepsi, equated in the commercial with secular salvation and joy.

10 A similar deconstruction of the male gaze is present in the 1986 music video "Open Your Heart." The scenario showed Madonna working in a peep show, with sleazy men ogling her. She appeared somewhat distanced and cool, thus the video could be read as putting on display the modes of male voyeurism through which the objectification of women's bodies takes place. On this reading, Madonna refuses in the video to allow herself to be an object of male desire; the viewer who wishes to watch her in this mode is rendered uncomfortable by being put in the subject position of sleazy, voyeuristic males. Thus, although the video offers Madonna's body as a spectacle, as an object of voyeuristic pleasure, the framing of the images makes difficult fetishistic viewing by identifying voyeurism and the objectification of the female body as part of a social process that exploits women for the entertainment of pathetic voyeuristic males.

Susan Bordo (1992) counters that the video nonetheless reinforces the spectacle of women's objectification, that the viewer "is not *really* decentered and confused by this video," despite the "ambiguities" it formally contains, and that the narrative context is "virtually irrelevant" (1992). In fact, it is undecidable how different readers will process the video, and while the images of the video may reinforce voyeuristic viewing of objectified women's bodies, as Bordo suggests, the narrative context and juxtaposition of lyrics and images may disrupt, in modernist fashion, voyeuristic viewing. Like "Material Girl," the video of "Open Your Heart" may have contradictory effects and appeal both to cultural critics and feminists who love to see deconstruction and subversion, as well as to men who like to gaze upon women's bodies and women who gain pleasure in identifying with objectified females; lucky Madonna, whose polysemic texts attract a wide range of readings and audiences.

11 The monocle is used by the capitalist to gaze at Madonna in "Express Yourself," objectifying her into a sexual fetish. Yet, as we see in Greil Marcus' book *Lipstick Traces* (1989), the monocle was part of the repertoire of Dadaist Richard Huelsenbeck and can thus be read as a Dada symbol and a sign that all of these traditional images should just be mocked and rejected. Madonna's humor, irony, and camp would support just such a Dadaist reading.

12 Madonna started giving AIDS benefits in the late 1980s and her album "Like a Prayer" contained AIDS/HIV information and safe sex advice. In the 1990s, however, she became more overtly political for a variety of causes and began referring to herself as a "revolutionary."

13 I am using the term "modernism" in the traditional sense of cultural practices which break established rules, attempt to produce innovative forms, generate polysemic texts with multiple meanings, and that require an active audience/reader to produce meanings from the material of the text. A more recent "postmodern" take on modernism reduces the modernist tradition and practices to a high cultural elitism, enshrined in canonical texts in which modernist rebellions are transformed into new academic cultural norms. Against the modernist canons, postmodernist texts and practices subvert the modernist separation of high and low cultural forms, reject the attempt to produce monumental texts that break with tradition and that are expressive of an author's subjectivity, and often quote and pastiche previous works and forms. Many critics have interpreted Madonna as a "postmodern" artist (see Kaplan 1987, Fiske 1989a, Bordo 1992, and many of the other contributors to Schwichtenberg 1992), presumably because she works in the arena of media culture, but I prefer to read many of her signifying practices as a "pop modernism," that deploys modernist aesthetic strategies in the area of music video and concert performance. I have, however, suggested that she also deploys traditional realist and narrative strategies in her music videos, and have discovered one example of a clearly postmodernist strategy that I discuss below. I would therefore resist seeing a phenomenon like Madonna as intrinsically "postmodernist" and prefer interpreting modernism and postmodernism as aesthetic strategies and practices that performers like Madonna can deploy.

14 On camp, see Susan Sontag who defines it as an "unmistakably modern" (note: not "postmodern") sensibility, characterized by love of the unnatural, artifice, exaggeration, irony, involving play with cultural forms and images, involving a high level of theatricality and travesty (1969, 277ff.) – an excellent characterization of Madonna's aesthetic strategies.

15 Likewise, in the video of "Open Your Heart," Madonna displays the production of the objectification and fetishizing of women by displaying herself in a peep show. She deploys standard objectified and sexist images of women, but undercuts them by portraying the origins of fetishizing of bodies as sleazy dance parlors and voyeuristic male gazes of low-life or "perverted" men.

16 I suppose that this is just my opinion. One journalist describes how he was eventually brought to a masturbatory climax from the pictures, as did Carol A. Queen in Frank and Smith (1993: 139), a text devoted to discussion of the "event" of the book.

17 In the 1990 *Nightline* interview, Madonna defends "Justify My Love" as art, as "artistic expression," stating: "I think that's what art is all about, experimenting, but it is an expression, it is my artistic expression" (concerning sexual fantasy). She also admitted to "pushing the limits of what's permissible." In *Truth or Dare*, she talks about refusing to compromise the "artistic integrity" of her work when threatened by police in Toronto, who wanted her to tone down her concert masturbation scene. In a later discussion in the film, she indicated that she would continue "pushing buttons," exploring the limits of the permissible, and being political. Finally, in a 1992 *USA Today* interview, Madonna described herself as "revolutionary," the ultimate category of modernist theory and politics (October 9, 1992, p. D1).

18 Paglia's labelling of Madonna as "real Feminist" underscores the dogmatism and essentialism that characterizes Paglia's own work. For Paglia, there is a "real feminism" and Madonna is it, while other feminists are dismissed by Paglia. In fact, there are a multiplicity of models of feminism and to say one model is "real" while the rest are spurious is itself arrogant and dogmatic, for it is Paglia who denotes what "real feminism" is, enabling her to savage sundry versions of "false feminism." Likewise, Paglia theorizes the essentially and genuinely "feminine" and "masculine," binary opposites which she believes provide a metaphysical foundation for culture. In fact, as I have been arguing, "masculine" and "feminine" are social constructs. Moreover, there simply are many different models of feminism, which have their respective strengths and weaknesses (as opposed to there being one "true" feminism). Likewise, there are different models of masculinity and femininity circulating in contemporary society, rather than there being an essentially "masculine" and "feminine."

19 Madonna herself continually stresses the control element, as in the interview where she states:

> People have this idea that if you're sexual and beautiful and provocative, then there's nothing else you could possibly offer. People have *always* had that image about women. And while it might have seemed like I was behaving in a stereotypical way, at the same time, I was also masterminding it. I was in control of everything I was doing, and I think that when people realized that, it confused them.
>
> (Cited in McClary in Sexton 1993: 102)

20 Laurie Anderson's earlier five-hour synthesis of her performances *United States* contained more social commentary, reflections on culture, society, and technology, and arguably, a more discernible individual vision than the dispersed and decentered images of *Home of the Brave*. This disappointed some critics who wrote of the tour preceding the film:

> What was disappointing was the fragmentary nature of the evening. With her monumental, four-part, two-evening "United States," presented three years ago at the

Brooklyn Academy of Music, Miss Anderson pointed toward a statement larger than her individual songs. Now, perhaps ensnared by the ambiance and compromises of the rock world, she seems to have settled for songs, pure and simple. The tour program has a title, 'Natural History,' but it doesn't seem to mean much, and the songs don't point beyond their generalized Andersonian aura.

(John Rockwell, *New York Times*, March 4, 1986: C-13)

The critic obviously doesn't get the point that from the modernism and social critique of "United States," Anderson had moved toward the postmodernism of *Home of the Brave*. A reviewer of the film wrote:

I expected Anderson to follow up on the more serious aspects of 'United States' in her later work, deepening her comments on personal, social, and cultural foibles of our time. But she now seems less interested in criticizing our high-technology, low-introspection era than in reflecting it like a trend-conscious mirror. In her new film, Laurie Anderson the 'performance artist' has become Laurie Anderson the pop star - putting on quite a show, but focusing almost entirely on style rather than substance.

(David Sterritt, *The Christian Science Monitor*, May 2, 1986: 25)

This critic also just didn't get it; i.e. that Anderson had made a postmodern turn, deconstructing identity and the text, fragmenting and dispersing her images and sounds, resisting meaning, sense, and social commentary.

Yet it appeared that Laurie Anderson soon after returned to more political concerns in her next major stage show, "Empty Places," see "Laurie Anderson Gets Political," by David Sterritt, *The Christian Science Monitor* (October 25, 1989). Moreover, in her 1991 performance pieces, she spent much time describing her opposition to the Gulf War. Anderson continues her postmodernist experiments in her 1990 music video collection, but also returns to modernist social and critique. Thus, modernism and postmodernism are distinct aesthetic strategies that can be deployed for different ends, or combined, if one wishes.

21 *Entertainment* magazine in a special September 4, 1992, issue on fashion estimated that it could cost $377,012 to cultivate the Madonna look, if one adds up the expenses from a year's collection of clothes, jewelry, make-up, and services industries. The early Madonna, by contrast, legitimated mix-and-match fashion in which anything goes. Madonna's transformation of her fashion strategies and body images thus reflects increased immersion in consumer culture and a growing commodification of her image.

Chapter 9

Mapping the present from the future
From Baudrillard to cyberpunk

Jean Baudrillard was arguably the most important and provocative media culture theorist of the 1970s and early 1980s. His studies of simulation, implosion, hyperreality, and the effects of the new communication, information, and media technologies blazed new paths in contemporary social theory and challenged regnant orthodoxies. Baudrillard's claim of a radical break and rupture with modern societies won him acclaim as the prophet of postmodernity in avant-garde theoretical circles throughout the world. Baudrillard proclaimed the disappearance of the subject, political economy, meaning, truth, and the social in contemporary social formations. This process of dramatic change and mutation required entirely new theories and concepts to describe the rapidly evolving social processes and novelties of the present moment.[1]

Baudrillard described the emergence of a new postmodern society organized around simulation, in which models, codes, communication, information, and the media were the demiruges of a radical break with modern societies. In his delirious postmodern funhouse, subjectivities were fragmented and lost, while a new realm of experience appeared, rendering previous social theories and politics obsolete and irrelevant. Baudrillard's world was one of dramatic implosion, in which classes, genders, political differences, and once autonomous realms of society and culture imploded into each other, erasing boundaries and differences in a postmodern kaleidoscope. His style and writing strategies were also implosive, combining material from dramatically different fields, studded with examples from media culture in a new mode of postmodern theory that effaced all disciplinary boundaries. Baudrillard's postmodern universe was also one of hyperreality, in which models and codes determined thought and behavior, and in which media of entertainment, information, and communication provided experience more intense and involving than the scenes of banal everyday life. In this postmodern world, individuals abandoned the "desert of the real" for the ecstasies of hyperreality and a new realm of computer, media, and technological experience.

For some years, Baudrillard was a cutting-edge, high-tech social theorist, the most stimulating and provocative contemporary thinker. But by the early 1980s, Baudrillard ceased producing the stunning analyses of the new postmodern scene that won such attention in the previous decade. Burnt out and terminally cynical,

Baudrillard has instead churned out a number of mediocre replays of his previous ideas, seasoned by a banal metaphysical turn in his thought, resulting in a pataphysical scenario of the triumph of the Object over the Subject in the contemporary world.[2] Baudrillard's travelogues, notebooks, theoretical simulations, and occasional pieces fell dramatically below the level of his 1970s work, and it appeared to many that Baudrillard himself had become boring and irrelevant, the ultimate sin for a supposedly avant-garde postmodern theorist.[3]

While Baudrillard rambled and meandered during the later 1980s and into the present, cyberpunk fiction became the literary trend of the moment and for many the avant-garde of theoretical vision and insight. For its many enthusiasts, the work of William Gibson, Bruce Sterling, Rudy Rucker, John Shirley, Greg Bear, Lewis Shiner, and others provided the most compelling images and mapping of our contemporary high-tech and media culture. In particular, William Gibson's *Neuromancer* (1984) was received as one of the most important novels of recent years and a key text of the cyberpunk movement. Indeed, *Neuromancer* was a brilliant literary debut, winning every major prize for science fiction. For some, Gibson produced a whole new mythos and philosophical vision for the technological age. The always extravagantly enthusiastic Timothy Leary declared that Gibson

> has produced nothing less than the underlying myth, the core legend, of the next stage of human evolution. He is performing the philosophic function that Dante did for feudalism and that writers like Mann, Tolstoy [and] Melville. . . did for the industrial age.[4]

Gibson's other work is also compelling. His collection of short stories *Burning Chrome* (1986) provides powerful visions of a new type of technological society in which humans and machines are constantly imploding and the human itself is dramatically mutating. His subsequent novels *Count Zero* (1986) and *Mona Lisa Overdrive* (1988) continued the cyberpunk explorations of *Neuromancer*, utilizing some of the same characters and plots to further interrogate his themes of a rapidly mutating technological environment and its effects on human beings. Gibson's novel *The Difference Engine* (1991), co-authored with Bruce Sterling, presents an imaginative reconstruction of the world of the industrial revolution, set in nineteenth-century England. And *Virtual Reality* (1993) provides an early twenty-first-century vision of contemporary California as a dystopic technological nightmare in which vicious corporations struggle for dominance of new technologies.

Cumulatively, these texts produce one of the most impressive bodies of recent writing on the fate of hypertechnological society since Baudrillard's key texts of the 1970s. Like Baudrillard's best work, they illuminate the contemporary scene with a brilliant dance of concept, metaphor, image, and high energy prose. Both Baudrillard and the cyberpunks exploded boundaries between philosophy, social theory, literature, and media culture in providing texts that attempt to capture the dizzying vicissitudes and searing intensity of our new high-tech environments.

Crucially for this study, both illuminate the present through analysis of future trends that are already manifest.

Indeed, Gibson himself claimed that *Neuromancer* is "about the present. It's not really about an imagined future. It's a way of trying to come to terms with the awe and terror inspired in me by the world in which we live" (*Mondo 2000*, No. 7 [1990]: 59). Indeed, it is my contention that Gibson is mapping our present from the vantage point of his imagined future, demonstrating the possible consequences of present trends of development. In particular, he is charting the ways that new technologies are impacting on human life creating new individuals and new technological environments – precisely Baudrillard's themes in the 1970s.

Yet in a certain sense both Baudrillard and cyberpunk became phenomena of media culture who provided theoretical and fictional visions of a society increasingly dominated by media and information. Both portray a world in which new technologies and media are ubiquitous and in which human beings merge with technologies and lose control of these extensions of themselves and of their new techno-environments. In turn, both Gibson/cyberpunk and Baudrillard became popular phenomena of a media culture, pop celebrities hailed as gurus and prophets by audiences who may have no idea of the complexity of their thought and visions.

Hence, in this study, I wish to argue that while Baudrillard was one of the most advanced theorists of media culture and new technologies from the mid-1970s to the early 1980s, it is William Gibson and the cyberpunks who have carried out some of the most important mappings of our present moment and its future trends during the past decade. I shall suggest that Gibson's and the cyberpunk vision builds on Baudrillard's postmodern perspectives, but departs from the increasingly retro French theorist in significant ways. I read both Baudrillard and Gibson as providing mappings of the media and high-tech societies of the present and the uncertain trajectory toward a not-too-distant future that contribute important insights into the profound changes that we are now undergoing.

The present, in these mappings, is thus viewed from the perspective of a future that is visible from within the experiences and trends of the current moment. From this perspective, cyberpunk science fiction can be read as a sort of social theory, while Baudrillard's futuristic postmodern social theory can be read in turn as science fiction.[5] This optic also suggests a deconstruction of sharp oppositions between literature and social theory, showing that much social theory contains a narrative and vision of the present and future, and that certain types of literature provide cogent mappings of the contemporary environment and, in the case of cyberpunk, of future trends. I am therefore suggesting that Gibson can be read as a social theorist, while Baudrillard can be read as a science fiction writer, and both can be seen as providing cognitive mappings and poetic figurations to illuminate the constellations of our contemporary high-tech media culture.[6]

FROM BAUDRILLARD TO CYBERPUNK

Brian McHale has described the curious reciprocal influence between postmodern

fiction and science fiction (hereafter SF) during the past decade.[7] This interchange is symptomatic of the process of implosion that Baudrillard thinks characterizes a postmodern society in which different phenomena implode into each other. Cyberpunk fiction thus involves an implosion of the techniques of modernist and postmodernist fiction, the genre of SF, other popular generic codes, with the style and figures of the punk movement and other oppositional urban subcultures. In cyberpunk, the postmodern vision finds its paradigmatic literary expression and disseminates its insights back into the contemporary culture from which it derived its energy and edge.

The cyberpunk writers were first called things like the outlaw technologists, the neuromantics, and the mirrorshades groups – because mirrorshades are a prominent symbol of antiauthority in many of their works (Sterling 1986: ix-xii). Capitalizing on this image, Bruce Sterling published an anthology of cyberpunk fiction titled *Mirrorshades*, featuring a promotional blurb by author Michael Swanwick who wrote:

> These are all hot young verbal pilots who think nothing of taking forty-thousand tons of screaming heavy metal prose and throwing it straight at the ground in a forced power dive shedding sparks and literary chaos only to pull up at the last possible instant shy of total grammatical implosion just to see the horrified looks on the pale upturned faces of the civilians as the afterburners cut it.
>
> (inside back cover of book)

Such intense and hyperbolic prose is typical of the cyberpunks who strive to capture the rhythms, feelings, flux, images, and experiences of the present in their white-hot prose, on-the-edge characters, and fast-paced narratives that burn powerful images into their readers while projecting frightening and prescient visions of our often anxious present and even scarier future.

Eventually, the term "cyberpunk" stuck, though some have rebelled against the label. The term "cyber" is a Greek root signifying "control," and the term has been absorbed into the concept of "cybernetics," signifying a system of high-tech control systems, combining computers, new technologies, and artificial realities, with strategies of systems maintenance and control. The root "cyber" is also related to "cyborg," describing new syntheses of humans and machines and generally signifies cutting-edge high-tech artifacts and experience. The "punk" root derives from the punk rock movement, signifying the edge and attitude of tough urban life, sex, drugs, violence, and antiauthoritarian rebellion in lifestyles, pop culture, and fashion. Together, the terms refer to the marriage of high-tech subculture with low-life street cultures, or to technoconsciousness and culture which merges state-of-the-art technology with the alteration of the senses, mind, and lifestyles associated with bohemian subcultures.

As a subcultural phenomenon, cyberpunk in general thus signifies a hard-edged avant-gardist posture toward technology and culture, eager to embrace the new and ready to rebel against established structures and authorities in order to gain new experiences and to put new technologies to work. "The street has its uses," Gibson likes to say, and as a movement cyberpunk operates outside the law, rebelling against centralized state and corporate structures in favor of more decentralized subcultural use of science and technology to serve the needs of the individuals involved. Whereas much SF tends to focus on mainstream, conformist types of characters who operate within established institutions and law-and-order, cyberpunk literature and film tends to utilize more marginal and even low-life characters. And while hippie, punk, and previous oppositional subcultures tended to be antitechnology, cyberpunk culture embraces technology which is used for the individual's own purposes (although often against the purposes and interests of established institutions and usages).

As a genre, cyberpunk can be read as distant warning systems, cautionary morality tales, warning us about future developments in which there is no future that human beings can control and mold to fit their purposes. There is thus an important parallel between cyberpunk literature and Mary Shelley's nineteenth-century novel *Frankenstein*, which also provides warnings about new technologies running amok. Cyberpunk stands at the beginning of a new technological revolution, warning of its dangers, just as *Frankenstein* warned about an industrial and scientific revolution out of control.[8] But cyberpunk shows an entire universe already in a state of advanced disarray and moving rapidly toward a frightening future where everything is possible and survival becomes increasingly challenging.

Yet cyberpunks are not as negatively apocalyptic as some SF literature and film of the past few decades. Writers like Gibson stress both the negative and positive potentials of technology and a technological future and are neither techophobic nor technophilic. Much previous SF, by contrast, was technophilic, celebrating technology without critical reflection on its effects. Another strain of apocalyptic, dystopic literature, by contrast, was purely negative toward technology, seeing it leading simply to a catastrophic future. Cyberpunks, for the most part, are more dialectical, though there is a residue of dystopic pessimism in some of its writers.

As a literary phenomenon, the cyberpunk writers were anticipated by William Burroughs, Philip K. Dick, J.G. Ballard, and Thomas Pynchon, while rock music, drug culture, and computer culture are also important sources and influences on their writing and style. The cyberpunks come from widely different backgrounds, some from science, some from literature, others from rock music, and all seem familiar with oppositional countercultures. Despite differences in their visions, politics, style, and attitudes, the cyberpunk writers share a general sensibility and rootedness in the contemporary high-tech environment. Rather than fantasizing about the fate of empires in another galaxy and time, the cyberpunks confront the impending realities of our own world. Their writing style involves the piling-on of intense imagery and vivid description, byzantine plots, and bizarre and violent characters fighting for power and survival in the contemporary urban and corporate world. Speed and energy are features of cyberpunk narratives which are fast-paced, full of bizarre characters, twists of plot, and weird surprises – just like life in the high-tech society.

Unlike previous SF, often written by midwesterners, *Neuromancer* and other cyberpunk fiction is urban, dealing with new urban experiences of crime, drugs, sex, rock and roll, a high-tech and commercialized environment, and low-life and underground subcultures proliferating and fighting for wealth and survival. Cyberpunk fiction typically offers a dystopic view of an imminently arriving future where megacorporations control all aspects of life for nefarious purposes, where technology allows for more intense systems of control, but is always resisted by underground and countercultural forces, where everything has become commodified and life is dirt cheap (e.g., as in Gibson's novels where hired assassins are always active and various characters are always ready to kill for a price).

The cyberpunks are very much a product of the technological explosion of the 1980s with its proliferation of media, computers, and new technology. Their work is heavily influenced by the saturation of culture and everyday life through science, technology, and consumer culture and their writing presents an overlapping of the realms of high-tech and popular mass culture. As Bruce Sterling put it:

> Traditionally, there has been a yawning cultural gap between the sciences and the humanities: a gulf between literary culture, the formal world of art and politics, and the culture of science, the world of engineering and industry.
>
> But the gap is crumbling in unexpected fashion. Technical culture has gotten out of hand. The advances of the sciences are so deeply radical, so disturbing, upsetting, and revolutionary that they can no longer be contained. They are surging into culture at large; they are invasive; they are everywhere. The traditional power structure, the traditional institutions, have lost control of the pace of change.
>
> (Sterling 1986: xii)

Cyberpunk fiction provides a response to this situation, attempting to map contemporary technological, economic, social, political, and cultural realities, capturing the momentous changes, the intensity and dynamism, and the new possibilities and new threats to human beings. Thus, like postmodern theory and culture, cyberpunk fiction is a response to explosive proliferation of technology and mass culture which it embodies in its style and subject matter and in turn illuminates. Thus postmodern theory and culture and cyberpunk fiction are products of the same new high-tech environment and both serve to map and illuminate it.

From this perspective, postmodern theory is the first high-tech social theory and cyberpunk is a new high-tech literature for the jaded and hyped-up denizens of the computer and media age. Cyberpunk writing also responds to the predatory greed of unrestrained capitalism during the Reagan/Bush/Clinton era. The form of capitalism represented in cyberpunk film and novels is very much a global capitalism of mixed cultures and languages (e.g. *Blade Runner* and *Neuromancer*), of a homogenous mass culture and market-place stretching across the globe, constituting a global village and an everyday life permeated by products, cultural forms, and minutiae from all over the world. This form of capitalism is also a technocapitalism, an organization of society uniting technology with capital, in which technology (especially media, information, and communication) becomes capital and capital is increasingly mediated by technology. Indeed, in Gibson's universe, information is the privileged form of capital and the source of wealth and power.[9]

Likewise, the social world portrayed by cyberpunk fiction is a capitalism without restraint, reflecting the unleashing of giant corporations spurred by the conservative political regimes of the 1980s – Reagan/Bush, Thatcher/Major, Kohl, and others. In this social Darwinist world, capital is totally amoral, only the fittest survive and prosper (i.e. those fit for exploitation and corruption) and a vast underclass hustles and deals for survival in violent urban worlds. The vision of a totally amoral capitalist society is delineated in *Simulations* by Baudrillard who described capital as "immoral and unscrupulous"; its "primal (mise en) scene" involves "instantaneous cruelty, incomprehensible ferocity, fundamental immorality . . . it is a monstrous unprincipled undertaking, nothing more" (Baudrillard 1983a: 28–9).[10]

The vision of a world governed by mysterious corporate conspiracies is also that of Thomas Pychon who is one of the key influences on cyberpunk fiction.[11] In the world of cyberpunk, an unrestrained capitalism reduces society to shambles – the environment is wrecked, everything is increasingly artificial, and experience is technologically mediated. Another key Baudrillardian theme in cyberpunk is the implosion between biology and technology – human body parts are easily replaceable with technological prostheses, personalities are programmable, neurochemistry modifies intelligence and personalities, brains and computers interface and implode, and individuals enter strange new technological worlds. In addition, artificial intelligence strives for power, and individuals seek immortality through cryogenics, or externalization of their personalities in computer constructs. This is precisely the terrain mapped out by Baudrillard who explored in his 1970s and early 1980s texts the phenomena of simulation, implosion between humans and technology, cloning, genetic engineering, communication and media, and the proliferations and disseminations of the media and information society.

Baudrillard was thus a precursor and prophet of the brave new technological world being explored and mapped by cyberpunk, though as we shall see, cyberpunk fiction addresses themes that are ignored by Baudrillard.[12] In the following reading, I accordingly show the similarities between Baudrillard and Gibson's *Neuromancer*, suggesting that Gibson provides a concretizing and visualization of some of Baudrillard's abstract categories. There are also philosophical affinities between Baudrillard and cyberpunk: like Baudrillard, cyberpunk fiction problematizes the notion of the subject; concepts of reality and time and space are called into question with notions of cyberspace; implosion between individuals and technology subvert the concept of the human being; and the erosion of traditional values raises questions concerning which values deserve to survive and what new values and politics could help produce a better future. Indeed, both Baudrillard and cyberpunk call into question the very nature of contemporary society, culture, values, and politics, and thus force us to confront key theoretical and political issues.

NEUROMANCER AND THE BAUDRILLARDIAN VISION

Baudrillard's main categories of hyperreality, simulation, and implosion are all present in *Neuromancer* and there are interesting similarities and differences between their visions of the high-tech funhouse in which we play, suffer, and die. Both depict a high-tech information society where boundaries of all kinds have imploded – between cultures, between biology and technology, between reality and unreality (or simulation). In this world, simulations have displaced "reality," and the body and human subjectivity have been drastically altered by new technologies. In the following discussion, then, I would like to chart the similarities and differences between Baudrillard's postmodern and Gibson's cyberpunk vision.

While Baudrillard's vision is somewhat abstract, Gibson's maps a world where simulation and hyperreality are omnipresent, where processed and computer generated identities abound, where individuals are reconstructed and altered via genetic engineering, implants, and drugs, and where there is a confusing blurring of boundaries between physical and virtual reality, with attendant ontological confusion and indeterminacy – precisely the Baudrillardian vision in a compelling literary embodiment. Thus, both Gibson and Baudrillard describe a world where subjectivity, reality, and identity are called into question, but Gibson eschews the intense nihilism of Baudrillard and foregrounds a quest for value, identity, and expression of human qualities as a main structuring and motivating force of his future universe. But while the (anti) theorist Baudrillard tends to be abstract and detached, Gibson's texts exhibit a passion for objects, textures, and concrete particularity. As we shall see, Gibson holds onto certain categories that Baudrillard abandons, in particular the notion of a sovereign individual trying to control its environment and maintain its sovereignty in a dangerous and vertiginous world.

The style of *Neuromancer* is "postmodern" in the sense explicated by Jameson (1991), with Gibson combining traditional narrative and modernist literary techniques. Postmodern Gibson collapses distinctions between high and low culture and pastiches genres and conventions of popular fiction and film. *Neuromancer* is traditional in its attention to plot, character, and narrative (it is not metafictional), but is postmodern in the way it combines and implodes genres, mixing science fiction with the detective genre, noir crime stories, high-tech adventure stories, the western (the main character Case is described as a computer cowboy), corporate drama, myth, and fantasy. *Neuromancer* draws on Chandleresque visions of social corruption, with characters trying to preserve their humanity and integrity in an inhumane and corrupt world. Like pulp noir fiction, the plot includes elements of romance punctuated by deception, high-tech gangsters ranging from corporate criminals, to low-life street hustlers, gun molls and deceptive women, punk and oppositional subcultures, intricate corporate structures, an incestuous family drama, and science fiction fantasy characters such as Artificial Intelligence (AI) constructs trying to take over the world and computer constructs achieving "reality" in the cyberspace of computers.

The storyline concerns the adventures of Case, a computer data and information thief who has his nerve cells burned out by a biotoxin as punishment for stealing from his bosses. A mysterious individual named Armitrage, with a Special Forces background, hires him for a big job and provides an illegal black-market operation that enables Case again to access cyberspace through his mind and computer console. He is teamed with a professional criminal named Molly, who has many bio-implants, including razors which protrude from her fingernails. The narrative proceeds through traditional plot devices of assembling characters for the Big Heist. In Case and Molly's first adventure, they combine forces to steal a computer construct from a giant corporation, which they will use for their next job. The construct, "Dixie Flatline," is the reconstructed computer intelligence of the man who taught Case how to steal corporate data and who will help rob another, even bigger, corporation.

The second major adventure involves a trip to Freeland,[13] a planet owned completely by the Tessier-Ashpool family, whose mansion contains the AI (Artificial Intelligence) Neuromancer with whom Wintermute wishes to merge. This will involve penetration of the family mansion and a long section of the novel involves assembling the cast of characters: an evil man named Riveria who is able to project holographs and is hired to seduce the daughter of the Tessier-Ashpool family, 3Jane; a group of Rastafarians who provide muscle and assistance; and the AI Wintermute who appears in the form of various characters during the last part of the novel. The goal involves stealing the AI Neuromancer from the Tessier-Ashpool mansion, Straylight, using the key which 3Jane possesses to open the door to the room where Neuromancer is stored, a heist which requires Molly's expertise and Case's computer skills to disarm the computer security systems and to guide Molly in her quest to "free" Neuromancer so that it can merge with Wintermute.

The narrative and feel of the images is highly cinematic; in an interview Gibson conceded he relied heavily on film noir elements and was influenced by *Blade Runner*.[14] *Neuromancer* also has a traditional unraveling of the mysteries at the end, though the conclusion is bathed in mystery and ambiguity and is hard to decode *à la* high modernism. Like modernist texts, *Neuromancer* therefore requires an extremely active reader, though, as suggested, it is postmodern in terms of the form of the novel and its themes; indeed, the implosion of complex modernist fictional forms with pulp adventure motifs, conventions, and genres is itself "postmodern," combining modernist with traditional generic literary forms, style, and features.

The themes and vision of *Neuromancer* are highly Baudrillardian, featuring an implosion of national cultures in a totally imploded society, where the distinction between technology and nature is also eroded. The novel opens with technological imagery obliterating the very look of nature: "The sky above the port was the color of television, tuned to a dead channel" (Gibson 1984: 3).[15] The locale features a world in which races, cultures, nationalities are all imploded into one high-tech futuristic culture *à la Blade Runner*. National boundaries are no longer of much importance and, linguistically, discourses implode into each other, with bits and pieces of different languages – especially English, Japanese, French, and German terms – producing a new form of international polyglot. The novel also fuses computer and high-tech discourse, drug lingo, business and crime language, sub-culture language (most notably Rasta), media culture references, with esoteric allusions to music, painting, dance, and other forms.

As in the Baudrillardian vision (1993), aesthetics permeates everyday life with Case being described as an "artiste" early in the novel and all of the main characters are artists of one sort or another. Modernist art terminology and references also abound. Molly adopts the pseudonym "Rose Kolodny," referring to a work by Duchamps (Gibson 1984: 143; see also 207); and metaphors of dance, sculpture, and music are frequently used to describe the various characters' "moves," thus imploding art and professionalism. Indeed, even the commodity universe of *Neuromancer* is permeated with modernist art forms.[16] Seeking information concerning whether he is to be the victim of an assassination, Case visits the office of Julius Deane, who is one hundred and thirty-five years old and the recipient of yearly DNA resetting and genetic surgery. Entering his office:

> Neo-Aztec bookcases gathered dust against one wall of the room where Case waited. A pair of bulbous Disney-styled table lamps perched awkwardly on a low Kandinsky-look coffee tale in scarlet-lacquered steel. A Dali clock hung on the wall between the bookcases, its distorted face sagging to the bare concrete floor. Its hands were holograms that altered to match the convolutions of the face as they rotated, but it never told the correct time. The room was stacked with white fiberglass shipping modules that gave off the tang of preserved ginger.
>
> (12)

And so in Gibson, as with Baudrillard, aesthetic style permeates everyday life and high and low culture implode in a commodity universe. But above all *Neuromancer* projects a vision of implosion between humans and technology in a high-tech world of plastic surgery, implants, drugs, artificial organs, artificial brains, and genetic engineering. The bartender Ratz who serves Case in the opening scene has a prosthetic arm "jerking monotonously as he filled a tray of glasses with draft Kirin" (3). His teeth exhibit "a webwork of Eastern European steel and brown decay" (3). Molly's "glasses were surgically inset, sealing her sockets. The silver lenses seemed to grow from smooth pale skin above her cheekbones" (24). Her gun seems an intrinsic part of her and in the introductory scene, she "held out her hands, palms up, the white fingers slightly spread, and with a barely audible click, ten double-edged, four-centimeter scalpel blades slid from their housings beneath the burgundy nails" (25).

At the end of the electronic computer-disk version of his trilogy, Gibson claims that his novels were not merely about computers,

> but really they're about technology in some broader sense. Personally, I suspect they're actually about Industrial Culture; about what we do with machines, what

machines do with us, and how wholly unconscious (and usually unlegislated) this process has been, is, and will be.

(Gibson 1991: 564–5)

While some contemporary science fiction (e.g., Ballard's *Crash*) depicts a loss of the human and its transformation into an object in a Baudrillardian vision of total reification, or presents the disappearance of the human and the replacement of the human by technology, or new lifeforms, in Gibson's vision, the human lingers on. In particular, human emotions are the major motivation for the main characters, especially fear, hatred, loyalty, and perhaps love, though love is under question in the universe of Gibson's cyberpunk.

Gibson thus holds onto a romantic vision of individualism, of individuals controlling their destiny, fighting for sovereignty in a world of technology and giant corporations. Gibson's romantic individualism, however, is more like the German romanticism of Schiller which did not celebrate nature over culture as in Blake and some English Romantics, but rather deployed diversity, irony, and complexity to delineate the relations between humans, culture, and technology. Yet there is also some nostalgia evident in Gibson for things of the past and human feeling and sentiment.[17] Moreover, there are fears evident in Gibson's work concerning the consequences of technology getting out of control and supplanting human beings as master of the universe. In a sense, *Neuromancer* is a fantasy of computers, or artificial intelligence, taking over. It turns out that an AI named Wintermute is behind the machinations of the plot, desiring to merge with Neuromancer, to produce a new synthesis of ROM and RAM, of information and personality, thus, in effect becoming God – a new superbeing and intelligence capable of controlling the universe.

The episode in which Case and his associates stop off at the Rastafarian space colony of Zion, provides a theological flavor to the events. Zion represents a colony colonized by former Rasta travellers, who continue to live in space. The "elders of Zion" forecast the coming of the end of world and assign a ship, the *Marcus Garvey* (named after the leader of the back to Africa movement in the 1920s). They assign brother Maelcum as bodyguard and helper (perhaps an allusion to Malcolm X). The religious prophecy concerning the end of the world codes the triumph of technology as a religious thematic. Allegorically, their prophecy can be decoded to read: the end of world = the end of modernity, where human subjects ruled – or thought they ruled. Henceforth, computers and artificial intelligence programs will rule *à la* Baudrillard and their reign signifies that the end of the sovereignty of the human species is at hand.

Both Baudrillard and Gibson share a postmodern vision that is a reversal of the modern project for which technology is perceived as an extension of human beings, who use technology to control and dominate nature. This time, however, technology is taking over and is in control of humans who fight for their freedom, their power, their autonomy, their humanity. Indeed, at the end of *Neuromancer*, technology triumphs and the future of the human is uncertain. This theme is anticipated in the films *2001* (in which the computer Hal takes over the spaceship), in *Colossus: The Forbin Project* (in which Russian and U.S. supercomputers merge to attempt take over the world), and in *Demon Seed* (where a computer rapes Julie Christie and takes control of her house). In *Neuromancer*, however, Gibson portrays the struggle of an individual hero, who still has desires, hopes, fears, yearnings, hatreds, and memories struggling to retain control of his environment. He thus follows the tough-guy fiction tradition of Raymond Chandler who depicts individuals struggling for honor and sovereignty in a corrupt world. Like Chandler's detectives, Gibson's heroes have their own code of values and march to the beat of their own drum, despite all of the technological and corporate forces trying to control them.

Gibson's subjectivities are, to be sure, vulnerable and flawed, but they represent individual selves trying to survive, maintain control, and even to preserve honor and dignity in a threatening world. This preservation of individual subjectivity represents a major departure from Baudrillard, for whom the subject is a term in a terminal, lost in the ecstasy of communication (1983c: 128). For Baudrillard, the subject lives "no longer as an actor or dramaturge but as a terminal of multiple networks" (ibid.). Gibson's characters by contrast have standard human emotions and live out adventures of romance, intrigue, deals, and quests for identity, power, and meaning, yet the body is diminishing in importance and the characters are most alive in the realm of "cyberspace."

The term "cyberspace" was first used by Gibson in his 1982 short story, "Burning Chrome" to refer to a computer generated virtual reality (Gibson 1986). It is now a common term that designates various kinds of computer generated spaces – e.g. various information services and communication systems, virtual reality systems (computer generated audio/visual/tactile experiences, tele-presence, and so on). The concept was embodied in the 1982 movie *Tron*, in which the characters entered into computers for adventures in computerland. The TV series *Max Headroom* drew on the concept, as did Hollywood films like *The Lawn Mower Man* and *The Ghost in the Machine*.

"Cyberspace" is defined by Gibson in *Neuromancer* as:

> A consensual hallucination experienced daily by billions of legitimate operators in every nation . . . a graphic representation of data abstracted from the banks of every computer in the human system. Unthinkable complexity. Lines of light ranged in the nonspace of the mind, clusters and constellations of data. Like city lights receding. . .
>
> (51)

This definition of cyberspace as a "consensual hallucination" is, however, somewhat misleading for the phenomena now being described by the term are the current and real phenomena of the present moment, such as computer data-base systems, e-mail and on-line computer communication, satellite television, and virtual reality games and machines. These phenomena are neither hallucinatory, nor subjective, but are simply the spaces and networks of a high-tech and media society.[18]

In Gibson's universe, money, data, software, patents, government records, military secrets, individual's profiles and other important data are stored in cyberspace, which is accessible to computer cowboys who access it through their consoles and with electric wires on their head called "trodes" (presumably short for electrodes), enabling individual minds to interface with the computer world. Cyberspace for Gibson has a colorful architecture and form; as he imagines it, it is three-dimensional and navigable. Such is the speed of technological change, and the way that "reality" imitates the most fantastic fiction, that corporations are indeed storing data in graphic configurations, employing security systems to prevent theft, unwanted accessing, and computer viruses.[19] In any case, the world of information in cyberspace for Gibson has a shape and structure, it is a universe and reality unto itself.

The hyperreal realm of cyberspace, accessed through computers, is more real and involving in Gibson's universe than the world of everyday experience. Case refers to his body contemptuously as "meat" and a "prison of flesh" (6; see also 9, passim). Bodily experience, including sex, is relatively uninteresting and unimportant for him; his orgasm is described as a "flaring blue in a timeless space, a vastness like the [Computer] matrix" (33). Only when Case enters cyberspace, it seems, does he become truly alive and his craving to enter the realm of computer-space replicates strivings for religious transcendence (or the frenzied need of drug addicts).

Although Gibson does not indulge in a Nietzschean pathos of life and celebration of the body, he replicates familiar Nietzschean motifs of the will to power and the will to identity as major drives of human beings. Gibson's universe, like Nietzsche's, is one of struggle and the motif of self-overcoming, of constant transcendence, is also a major (Nietzschean) motif in Gibson. And although interpersonal relationships and love are relatively unimportant for Case, yet a residue of romanticism runs through Gibson's work. In its very absence, Gibson's texts promote a yearning for romantic love. Trust, betrayal, and male–female relationships are a major theme for Gibson, as they were in the noir detective fiction to which his work is deeply akin.

Gibson's characters move back and forth from cyberspace to "the real" (i.e. as depicted in the novel's narrative space), and like Baudrillard's disappearing subjects live in a world in which it is impossible to distinguish between simulation and reality in a universe in which the body inhabits what Baudrillard called "the desert of the real" (1983a: 2). Throughout the novel, it is not clear if the characters are in "real" space, in computer space, in implanted memory, in simstim space (a computer simulation of reality), or in other realms of cyberspace. Thus the very concept of reality disappears à la Baudrillard and the implosion between "reality" and other dimensions of experience create a new multi-dimensional and disorienting realm of experience.

Although Gibson makes use of the Baudrillardian themes of simulation and hyperreality, the cyberspace of *Neuromancer* is complex, deadly, full of mysteries, multidimensional, and a scene of adventure, whereas Baudrillard's ecstasy of communication by contrast is flat, one-dimensional, explicit and without depth or mystery, being fully visible and "obscene" (1983c: 130–1). Whereas Baudrillard's postmodern world is cool, operational, rationalized and functionalized, and without secrets and surprises, Gibson's universe is hot, violent, opaque, mysterious, and full of secrets, surprises, and threats.

For Gibson, technology is anthropomorphized with a car that talks and drives itself (87f.),[20] and computer constructs that have personalities. Humans, however, are technologized with implants, surgery, drugs, and genetic engineering altering the very substance of the individual and producing new syntheses of the human and technological. Indeed, *Neuromancer*'s allegory of technology taking over concretizes Baudrillard's vision (1990) of the triumph of the object. Moreover, Gibson, like Baudrillard, does not simply replicate techno-phobic impulses, but describes a new state of affairs in which technology takes on more power and sovereignty than human beings. At one point, some French police arrest Case, accusing him of betraying his species by working for an artificial intelligence. Evoking the Faust legend, a French agent says to him:

You have no care for your species. For thousands of years men dreamed of pacts with demons. Only now, are such things possible. And what would you be paid with? What would your price be, for aiding this thing to free itself and grow.

(163)

Yet Gibson betrays no sympathy for this position and the reader is positioned to applaud Case's escape from these police.

The novel is also about power and the sort of immortality that corporations and, presumably, computers, and individuals who interface with technology may attain. "Power," in Case's world, means corporate power and corporate control of information and technology. The zaibatsus, the multinationals that shaped the course of human history, in Gibson's world had transcended old barriers. Viewed as organisms, they had attained a kind of immortality. "You couldn't kill a zaibatsu by assassinating a dozen key executives; there were others waiting to step up the ladder, assume the vacated position, access the vast banks of corporate memory" (203). In this world, the corporate family Tessier-Ashpool "was an atavism, a clan" (203), who wanted to keep possession of their wealth and power within their family unit. The Tessier-Ashpool clan thus represents an earlier form of capitalism, family capitalism, now obsolete in the global, transnational context.

From this perspective, the artificial intelligence (AI) Wintermute represents a new form of technocapitalism, in which computers and an impersonal corporate structure control information and power, and individuals gain power according to one's ties to the corporation and field of corporate data. 3Jane's mother, Marie-France, had a different vision of future corporate structures than her old-fashioned, patriarchal father (whose death she in effect engineers) and that vision is programmed into the AI Neuromancer. Her mother imagined "us in a symbiotic relationship with the AI's, our corporate decisions made for us. Tessier-Ashpool would be immortal, a hive, each of us units of a larger entity" (229). Although old

Ashpool killed his daughter Marie-France, her vision presumably triumphed at the end as this strategy had been programmed into Neuromancer, who is to merge at the end with Wintermute.

In this sense, *Neuromancer* is an allegory about the demise of family capitalism and the triumph of a new form of corporate capitalism in which technology assumes the dominant position. But it is also an allegory about the triumph of technology over the human and the quest for immortality. The AI Wintermute wants to become part of something bigger, ultimately to merge with Neuromancer, to become a new higher intelligence, to merge intelligence and personality to produce a higher life-force, God – but not God the Father. Moreover, in this form of computer omnipotence, technology becoming God, there is no resurrection of the body, *à la* Christianity and Buddhism.[21] Wintermute may get a personality but there is no hint that he will have a body, nor is there a hint at what sort of deity he will be.

Thus, the future in which technology takes over is presented as an open question. Gibson does not indulge in technophobic and apocalyptic fright, but simply depicts a situation in which computers appear to have taken over.[22] Perhaps the computer construct Dixie Flatline provides a hint as to the future and fate of Wintermute/ Neuromancer. Dixie, who only becomes alive when he is plugged into a computer and his program is turned on and used, can talk, interact, and move through the field of cyberspace, but the construct is bored with its virtual life and begs Case to erase him, as if this form of immortality (i.e. with no body resurrected) is unsatisfactory and even intolerable (Wintermute eventually grants Dixie its wish, erasing him). This scene seems to imply that computer immortality is no immortality at all, that without the resurrection of the body there can be no eternal happiness. Or is this simply a limitation of the ways that humans are wired, and that computers can very happily live forever without a body, this peculiar frame and density of human beings? On the other hand, we know, and Gibson knows, that all technology is quickly obsolete and will soon be museum pieces – see Gibson's introduction to the electronic publishing of his trilogy which makes this point (1991).

Furthermore, the old Tessier-Ashpool patriarch was also dissatisfied with his cryogenic immortality, although in his case it may have been the manipulations of 3Jane that caused his discomfort. Case, too, seems to have gained some computer immortality at the end of the novel, which closes with a passage:

> He spent the bulk of his Swiss account on a new pancreas and liver, the rest on a new Ono-Sendai [computer console] and a ticket back to the Sprawl.
> He found work.
> He found a girl who called herself Michael.
> And one October night, punching himself past the scarlet tiers of the Eastern Seaboard Fission Authority, he saw three figures, tiny, impossible, who stood at the very edge of one of the vast steps of data. Small as they were, he could make out the boy's grin, his pink gums, the glitter of the long gray eyes that had

been Riveria's. Linda still wore his jacket; she waved, as he passed. But the third figure, close behind her, arm across her shoulders, was himself.

(270–1)

And so Case too seems to have achieved a form of immortality as a computer construct, living forever in cyberspace. This is simply presented as a mystery at the end of the novel and is neither celebrated, nor even probed in any way. It allegorizes a condition in which implosions of the humans and technology may produce new species which live in new arenas of space and time, and thus point to a postmodernity beyond the current point where technology and humans coexist in contradictory and unstable relations.

Perhaps the main limitation of Gibson's *Neuromancer* is the sketchy and inadequate presentation of the synthesis between Wintermute and Neuromancer, which is presented quite abstractly and with little detail. On the way to the final showdown, Neuromancer makes Case brain-dead and he is thrown into a cyberspace world where he has a confrontation with Neuromancer who takes the form of a Brazilian boy (243–4). In abstract, poetic diction, Neuromancer tells Case its name and tells how "Marie-France, my lady, she prepared this road" (i.e. programmed it), "but her lord choked her off before I could read the book of her days" (i.e. she was killed by her father before you could realize her plans to restructure the corporation under the control of technology). The AI then explains: "Neuro from nerves, the silver paths. Romancer. I call up the dead . . . I *am* the dead and their land . . . . Stay. If your woman is a ghost, she doesn't know it. Neither will you."

Neuromancer then tells Case that "the choice is yours," as if Case could decide whether he wanted a sort of (dead) immortality in cyberspace (which Case encounters again in the last page), or to return to his bodily (meat) existence. Case returns to consciousness and his body, but it is not made clear why, nor is it clear exactly what Neuromancer is offering Case. As noted, it is also not clear what the significance is of the merger between Wintermute and Neuromancer, or the significance of the fusion between ROM and RAM, intelligence and personality. The Neuromancer character is inadequately undeveloped and it is uncertain what is in store for humans controlled by technology and the fate of the human in a technological world.[23]

Yet Gibson neither glorifies nor condemns the artificial intelligence attempting to augment itself. "Wintermute" is a sign for dead technology; "Winter" signifies cold and lifeless and "mute" signifies silent; the term thus sets up an antinomy between dead technology vs. live people – but without any Nietzschean pathos of the superiority of life, of human life, over all dead things. Case, after all, contemptuously describes his body as "meat" and there are no celebrations of the body or nature; indeed, the scene of cyberpunk seems to be a postholocaust environment where nature has shrivelled and died: animals are rare and some species, like horses in *Neuromancer*, have even disappeared. "Human nature" for Gibson is merely memories and emotions like fear, anger, and hatred, and a mutable body, capable of assuming new forms in its implosions with technology.

Thus, although Gibson, unlike Baudrillard, holds to a romantic individualism, he is no "humanist" in any sentimental way, nor is he a technophobe. As in Baudrillard's vision, technology has won, that's that, and let the adventure continue. Yet the novel also suggests a new sort of immortality: if one's brain, one's intelligence, could be cloned, one could live for ever. *Neuromancer* depicts the creation of an artificial intelligence that lives and the duplication of humans (Dixie Flatline and Case) in cyberspace worlds who gain a sort of cybernetic immortality. Now this truly would be a rupture in history if objects controlled human subjects and produced the space of another lived reality – a fantasy of the later Baudrillard also suggested in Gibson. And with the overcoming of finitude in the transcendence of death, the human would surely disappear because the deepest human emotions have to do with fear of death and hatred of those who threaten one's life. Moreover, in both Baudrillard's and Gibson's universe technology can remake and drastically change humans, both externally and internally. With humans becoming more technological and technology becoming more human, a new implosion of humans and technology ushers in a new historical epoch in the world of cyberpunk with a new historical subject (or disappearance thereof in a world of objects). Such a universe would deserve being described in terms of a postmodern rupture and would constitute a genuine break in history.

Yet perhaps *Neuromancer* suggests that without resurrection of the body, eternal life is not satisfying, or perhaps the AI will be perfectly happy without a body and human form. Who knows? In any case, Gibson's universe is an open one. What will happen next is uncertain and the technological future is unknown. But if we know that significant changes have occurred we have a better chance of surviving and thriving than if we continue to live with the illusions of the past.

MAPPING THE FUTURE; ILLUMINATING THE PRESENT

Gibson's *Neuromancer* and other cyberpunk fiction offer a valuable mapping of a possible trajectory from the present to the future, pointing to key developments in technology that will produce a different future. Cyberpunk fiction offers an unflinching and realistic look at the powers that structure our world and raises important issues about how technology structures our experience and the status of the human being as the infrastructure of society shifts from industry and production to a media and information culture, in the new era of technocapitalism. There is thus an interesting difference in cyberpunk fiction from the traditional historical novels described by Lukàcs and Jameson, which attempted to illuminate the present by providing critical visions of the past (a strategy also employed by writers of "magic realist" fiction like Marquez and Carpenter). But cyberpunk, by contrast, illuminates the present by projecting visions of the future that highlight key phenomena of the current moment and their possible effects.[24]

Gibson and Baudrillard thus provide an archaeology of the future in order to delineate the structures, tendencies, and dynamics, of the present. These "distant warning systems" provide cautionary morality tales that suggest the future consequences of certain trends and phenomena of the present. Like *Brave New World*, *1984*, and other prescient projections of the future, Baudrillard and cyberpunk provide both useful mapping and therapeutical functions. Extrapolating from present technological, cultural, and social trends to possible future results both helps individuals map their present social constellations and develop abilities to cope with future-shock as the future inevitably hits us in the face with the speed of electronic information and the force of a nuclear explosion.

Gibson and the cyberpunks are therefore not as dystopic as Baudrillard or such prognosticians of the present/future as Huxley and Orwell. Cyberpunks are much more positive toward technology than their predecessors and while they are not naively techno-philic, they are not techno-phobic either, tending rather to balance their appraisals of the effects of technology, seeing both positive and negative aspects to the technological explosion and implosion of technology, culture, and the human in the contemporary era. The products themselves of technological consumer cultures, including personal computers, VCRs, walkmen and CB radios, cable and satellite television, designer drugs, and the other paraphernalia of a high-tech consumer society, the cyberpunks see technology as omnipresent, but as presenting new possibilities for individual pleasure and freedom, as well as destruction and enslavement.

Neuromancer and other works of cyberpunk fiction also pose deep philosophical questions concerning the nature of reality, subjectivity, and the human in a high-tech world: what is authentically human as the lines are being blurred between humans and technology? What is human identity if it is programmable? What is left of notions of authenticity and identity in a programmed implosion between technology and the human? What is "reality" if it is capable of such vast simulation? How is "reality" under erosion today and what are the consequences? Obviously, Gibson does not answer these questions, but at least his works pose them and force us to think them through.

As with Baudrillard, it is ultimately the politics of Gibson's work that are most problematical.[25] Gibson's cyberpunk heroes are not really models of political or cultural resistance. If anything, they fit in all too well, involving themselves totally in interactions with new technologies. To be sure, they are often marginal characters, or beyond the law, and his books often portray groups of resistant countercultures, but his main characters are never political rebels, and political rebellion in Gibson's novels is often portrayed negatively.[26] Although subcultural resistance is positively portrayed in Gibson's sketches of the "Panther Moderns" (which combine iconography of the 1960s Black Panthers with the British Mod subcultural groups), there are rarely political revolutionaries in Gibson's basically postpolitical cultural and technological world.

Gibson's nostalgia for romantic individualism, artifacts of the past, and lack of politics are countered, however, by a sense of the ambiguous effects of technology and he, like most cyberpunk writers, is much more affirmative of technology and possibilities for humans to use new technologies for their own ends than Baudrillard. In a sense, Gibson is simply very American–affirming the importance of individual sovereignty against social and economic forces. He is very American in his vision of the redemptive powers of science and technology. For Gibson, beyond the frontier lies new opportunity and in his stories, novels, and voyages always have a destination and goal. As Csicsery-Ronay points out,

> Gibson and his protagonists embark in story after story on quests to restore value and meaning. They have an advantage over the earlier inhabitants of modern fiction, in that the cyberspace promises that it may be possible artificially to construct transcendence. Because the cyberspace has already absorbed the affects and objects in the past that were associated with sacredness and value, Gibson's protagonists have no choice but to try out artificial transcendence.
>
> (1992: 226)

Baudrillard vs. cyberpunk

Baudrillard, by contrast, dissolves meaning and the subject in the ecstasy of communication and is scornful of efficacious individual action, denying even the possibility of individual sovereignty in a world ruled by objects. He sees technology triumphant in a posthuman world and evidences little nostalgia for the erased humanity in a technological universe. Baudrillard seeks no transcendence and seems content to document the foibles and follies of the contemporary era. There is nothing new under the sun for the jaded Frenchman who has seen it all, or who thinks that everything has already been said, shown, and done and that all one can do is to play with the pieces.[27]

In his post-1980s works, Baudrillard presents the spectacle of an alienated European intellectual surveying the collapse of modernity which he coolly and ironically chronicles in his texts. His nihilistic and cynical vision of the present age is fully visible in his travelogue *America* (1988) where Baudrillard travels[28] through the United States and sees the future in the American present. Or, put differently, Baudrillard sees contemporary America as science fiction, as a futuristic signscape that is the fate of the West, a present that will be Europe's and everywhere's future.

Baudrillard constantly remarks on the science fiction hyperreality of the USA today. Salt Lake City "has the transparency and supernatural, otherworldly cleanness of a thing from outer space" (2). In the research institutes in Torrey Canyon, "all the future biological commandments are being devised;" they are "sublime, transpolitical sites of extraterritoriality, combining as they do the earth's undamaged geological grandeur with a sophisticated, nuclear, orbital, computer technology" (4). The New York marathon is an "end-of-the-world show . . . bringing the message of a catastrophe for the human race" (pp. 19–20). And the great Western desert appears to Baudrillard as a "fragment of another planet (at least predating any form of human life), where another, deeper temporality reigns, on whose surface you float as you would on salt-laden waters" (68).

Baudrillard's short essays on *America* illustrate his continuing fascination with semiology, with signs, reading the U.S. as a constellation of signs, as an "astral America."[29] Baudrillard's sign fetishism reduces the complexity and contradictions of the United States to a play of signs. The early Baudrillard was very immersed in semiotics, the study of signs and signifying systems. While he rejected the formalism and objectivism of much semiology, he held onto its mode of seeing, reducing the world to signs. This vulgar semiological vision informs America where Baudrillard claims that America is a "giant hologram" in which "information concerning the whole is contained in each of its elements" (29). Following this principle, Baudrillard does not hesitate to make massive generalizations about his theoretical object. America is the "*only remaining primitive society*" (7); it is a "realized utopia" (75ff.); and it is a cultural desert and wasteland. He uses the desert as the key metaphor for interpreting America and describes "the American miracle" as "that of the obscene" (8), in which everything is revealed, visible, present, and unhidden. This shallow, superficial society is characterized by "deserts of meaninglessness" and his trip through America produces "a barely perceptible evaporation of meaning" (8, 9).

"America" is thus an allegory for a country that is for him a play of pure signs, devoid of meaning, purpose, or value. Baudrillard's semiological reduction of America to a desert, to an empty space, to meaninglessness, to pure structure and event, is partially a result of his methodological choice to privilege speed and driving as his mode of access to his object, as well as privileging deserts over cities. Speeding through America, with his car stereo blasting and a trusty bottle of whiskey as a companion, evacuates meaning and presents the spectacle of pure speed, pure travelling, pure signs floating by in an empty indifference, absent of meaning.

Yet unable to adhere to this ascetic methodological principle, Baudrillard frequently slows down, especially in the cities, and then everything he sees signifies something, everything is a sign of something else. Break-dancers signify to him, as they spiral around on the ground, an attempt to dig a hole for themselves, radiating "the ironic, indolent pose of the dead" (19); California jogging is "like . . . so many other things . . . a sign of voluntary servitude" (38); the "smiling eyes" of squirrels at Irvine betray "a cold, ferocious beast fearfully stalking us" (48); television sets left on in empty rooms in the Porterville hotel reveal TV "for what it really is: a video of another world, ultimately addressed to no one at all, delivering its images indifferently, indifferent to its own messages" (50); and an exit sign on a freeway is "a sign of destiny" (53). Most memorably, Americans smiling at Baudrillard signify:

> The smile of immunity, the smile of advertising: 'This country is good. I am good. We are the best'. It is also Reagan's smile – the culmination of the self-satisfaction of the entire American nation. . . . Smile and others will smile back. Smile to show how transparent, how candid you are. Smile if you have nothing to say. Most of all, do not hide the fact you have nothing to say nor your

total indifference to others. Let this emptiness, this profound indifference shine out spontaneously in your smile. *Give* your emptiness and indifference to others, light up your face with the zero degree of joy and pleasure, smile, smile smile. . . Americans may have no identity, but they do have wonderful teeth.

(34)

Mixing science fiction apocalypse with his obsessive semiology, many things signify for Baudrillard "the end of the world," including the New York marathon (19f.) and California with its appliances, joggers, intellectuals working on word-processors, political sects, overweight and anorexic individuals, and mentally-ill people walking the streets (31ff.). Yet, Baudrillard also feels that although America "is a world completely rotten with wealth, power, senility, indifference, puritanism and mental hygiene, poverty and waste, technological futility and aimless vi-olence," it "has about it something of the dawning of the universe" (23). Moreover, America, he constantly says, is the center of the world (14, 23, 28, 77f.), the model toward which the rest of the world is moving.

Although Baudrillard rarely uses the category of the postmodern in this text, he constantly equates America with modernity, as the prototypical modern society, that was always free of feudalism and the limitations of traditional society, that represented modernity in its purest forms (75ff.). Thus the "end of the world" which he constantly experienced in America could be read as the end of modernity and the dawning of a new world could be read as the advent of a new postmodernity. Baudrillard, however, does not put this in these terms and so his reflections are merely off the cuff remarks which betray a latently apocalyptic imagination that is never fully unleashed.

In a sense, Baudrillard's *America* represents his semiological imaginary running amok. The French tourist reduces everything to signs and fails to see their material underpinnings and effects, the social structure in which signs are embedded, or the history that produces sign and structure. His semiological reductions are especially evident in the study of "Utopia Achieved" in which he contrasts the U.S. with Europe and other parts of the world. For Baudrillard, the U.S. is the "original version of modernity," it has no past traditions or history, "it lives in a perpetual simulation, in a perpetual present of signs" (p. 76). Europe, by contrast, has a history, has political and cultural traditions (and thus has politics and culture), and depth. America, however, exhibits

what might be called the zero degree of culture, the power of unculture. It is no good our trying more or less to adapt, their vision of the world will always be beyond our grasp, just as the transcendental, historical *Weltanschauung* of Europe will always be beyond the Americans. Just as the countries of the Third World will never internalize the values of democracy and technological pro-gress. There are some gaps that are definitive and cannot be bridged.

(78)

Note here how Baudrillard employs ideal types of America, Europe, and the Third

World, which he maintains in their purity, claiming that there are some gaps and differences that cannot be transcended. Such essentialist ideal-type thinking is of course characteristic of the worst of modern theory that postmodern theorists reject, yet Baudrillard falls prey to a mode of thinking based on cultural stereotypes and bordering on racism.[30] This is curious for Baudrillard's own earlier analyses of implosion included citing the implosion of racial differences in contemporary societies.

The cyberpunk vision

As I noted, the vision of a radical implosion between races, cultures, and parts of the world is central to Gibson's cyberpunk vision and surely this vision describes the actual breaking down of boundaries between America, Europe, and the Third World, which is a trend of the present. Yet there are contradictory trends toward more assimilation, breaking of racial boundaries and cultures, and homogenization of society and culture confronted with growing racism, emphasis on cultural and national differences, and fragmentation. But Gibson and Baudrillard tend toward an implosive view of race and culture and thus do not properly grasp the explosion of difference and conflict in the present moment.

In other respects, however, Gibson and the cyberpunks have a more accurate and illuminating vision than that of Baudrillard, which remains stuck in an obsolete and pernicious model of ideal types (i.e. of races and gender) and which is devoid of political economy, class, and analysis of capitalism.[31] The world of cyberpunk by contrast is constituted by the new forms of technocapitalism, including transnational corporations, especially US and Japanese firms, and the proliferation of new technologies. The world of cyberpunk is a high-tech world where information is the most desired commodity, where computers and cyberspace provide access to new realms of experience, where drugs, cloning, and implants produce new implosions of humans and technology. This is precisely Baudrillard's 1970s theoretical world, which he abandoned in favor of exploring "the desert of the real" in America and other contemporary sites of the disappearance of meaning, the subject, history, politics, and the real.

As opposed to the reductionism of the semiological imaginary, one needs a more multiperspectival social theory that combines political economy, sociology, culture, philosophy, and radical politics – precisely the mix of cyberpunk and the postmodern theory at its best of Foucault, Deleuze and Guattari, Jameson, and others. Baudrillard, by contrast, has turned to a one-dimensional semiological reductionism, to sign fetishism, that reduces the complexity of America and the contemporary world to a few choice signs, which generally signify to Baudrillard the end of the world and the reign of emptiness and meaninglessness. Desert hereafter and forever.

Yet, the meaninglessness, indifference, and emptiness that Baudrillard finds in America is precisely his own emptiness and alienation. By contrast, the most advanced American forms of culture, like cyberpunk, express the energies of the new technological society, the joy and power of utilizing new technologies, the ecstasy of interfacing, the potency of accessing new information and engaging in new forms of communication, the transcendence of seeing images and artifacts from all over the world, including the best of film and television, all there at one's fingertips. Yet cyberpunk also depicts the downside of the new technological society, the fact of growing discrepancies of wealth and power between rich and poor, the mushrooming underclass, exploding into crime and violence, the growing power of criminal and drug cultures.

The section on "Utopia Achieved" in *America* asserts constantly that America lacks culture, by which he means European high culture. Baudrillard never really engages American culture, such as jazz, blues, rap, or any form of popular music; he seems to think that American art is completely below the level of European art; and although he constantly refers to the important effects of Hollywood cinema, he sees cinema, television, and other American cultural forms as mere space, form, speed, and part of the American "way of life" and thus not as genuine culture in the European sense. Such binary thinking (high vs. low, European vs. American culture) is extremely dubious and has been rejected by most postmodern theory and practice, showing Baudrillard regressing to elitist European modernist prejudices. Cyberpunk, by contrast, revels in the forms of popular art, as well as modernism.

For the most part, Baudrillard travels through middle-class and luxury America which he describes as a "utopia achieved" (pp. 75ff.). He rarely sees the poor, the underclass, or the virulent racism and sexism of U.S. society. He failed to see the deteriorating social conditions for the middle class, for whom life is no utopia and whose decline in standard of living cost George Bush the 1992 election. Although Baudrillard recognizes the mentally ill wandering about in the streets, he does not recognize the prevalent problem of homelessness, and the origins of this problem in the specific conservative policies of Reagan and Bush. At one point, however, he does taken cognizance of the problem of the poor. He recognizes that the easy Californian/American life of the achieved utopia

> knows no pity. Its logic is a pitiless one. If utopia has already been achieved, then unhappiness does not exist, the poor are no longer credible. If America is resuscitated, then the massacre of the Indians did not happen, Vietnam did not happen. While frequenting the rich ranchers or manufacturers of the West, Reagan has never had the faintest inkling of the poor and their existence, nor the slightest contact with them. He knows only the self-evidence of wealth, the tautology of power, which he magnifies to the dimensions of the nation, or indeed of the whole world. The have-nots will be condemned to oblivion, to abandonment, to disappearance pure and simple. This is 'must exit' logic: 'poor people must exit.'
>
> (111)

Baudrillard then discusses the disenfranchisement of the poor, their falling into a "Fourth World desert zone," as if "the Last Judgment had already happened" (112). These passages accurately depict the logic and mentality of Reaganism, but in fact this mentality fell victim to history, rather than eternalizing itself in a transpolitical and transhistorical ideal type, as Baudrillard's analysis would have it. Instead, during 1992 this Fourth World became all too visible in the Los Angeles and other urban insurrections in the United States and has found its cultural voice in rap (see Chapter 5), a form ignored by Baudrillard. Moreover, the problems of the poor, homeless, and other victims of the conservative policies were the products of the failed economic policies of Reagan, Bush, and the Republicans, the analysis of which Baudrillard also ignores (it remains to be seen whether Clinton and the Democrats will do any better in addressing these problems).

Moreover, the passage just cited constitutes Baudrillard's one reflection on the poor and underclass in his entire book. In most of the travelogue, he speeds through the deserts and cities, either alone or hanging out with the academics who invite him for lectures. Cyberpunk, by contrast, explores the lower depths, the refused and rejected of capitalist affluence. It also depicts the higher powers, the corporate entities and forces that monopolize wealth and power, as well as the information and technologies that are becoming the new arbitrators of wealth and power. Cyberpunk explores the intensities, possibilities, and effects of new modes of technologically mediated experience, while Baudrillard speeds through the ancient landscapes of the West, and engages in hackneyed reflections on the desert, the emptiness of cities, and the end of the world.

On the whole, Baudrillard reveals himself in his U.S. travelogue to be reductive, hopelessly reactionary, obsolete, and very European. Baudrillard, the old fart, makes fun of intellectuals on their word processors (34ff.), not knowing that they are plugging into cyberspace, accessing incredible amounts of data at unforeseen speed, engaging in new types of communication through bulletin-boards, e-mail, computer data-bases and on-line discussion, and writing at new speeds and with new intensities. Baudrillard by contrast exhibits a rather regressive mentality in the book, gaining satisfaction from speed, from travel in his automobile, an experience that he had already declared obsolete.[32] His private mythologies of speed, cars, and desert, even give rise to archaic fantasies, leavened by whiskey, as when he writes:

> Death Valley is as big and mysterious as ever. Fire, heat, light: all the elements of sacrifice are here. You always have to bring something into the desert to sacrifice, and offer it to the desert as a victim. A woman. If something has to disappear, something matching the desert for beauty, why not a woman?

(66)

One might object to my reading of Baudrillard's *America* as proto-social theory that his text is just literature, that it is merely a travelogue, that irony is his dominant trope, and that I am taking it too seriously.[33] Yet I would insist that both Baudrillard and cyberpunk provide illuminating visions of contemporary society, that they are describing key trends and phenomena of the present, that they are mapping in important ways the social world in which we live and die, and that they therefore contribute to social theory, even though they do not follow the protocols or methodologies of established schools of thought. In recent years, there have been many calls to reject the models of modern social theory in favor of experimenting with new modes of theoretical discourse and analysis, and I am suggesting that Baudrillard and cyberpunk be read in this light. My argument is that even Baudrillard's philosophical travelogues and diaries like *Cool Memories* are a form of social theory that can be appraised according to how they contribute to theorizing and illuminating present social trends, phenomena, and experiences, or criticized to the extent that they mystify, ignore, or distort contemporary social realities.

Thus, in a sense, even Baudrillard's antitheory is a form of theoretical vision and mapping. On one hand, Baudrillard is offering a new kind of discourse that combines the discourse of social theory with storytelling, narrative asides, cultural observation and criticism, and aphorisms. Yet he often claims that he is providing insight into the present situation, charting its novelties and breaks from the past, proclaiming the death of modern phenomena and the need for new theoretical strategies and responses to the disappearance of the modern.

Although Baudrillard provides some essential tools to analyze our media culture, there is a complete lack of analysis of the apparatus that produces hyperreality, implosion, simulations, and the proliferation of images, information, and the ecstasy of communication which produce his postmodern rupture. Baudrillard's erasure of political economy and production disables serious attempts to theorize contemporary culture and communications. critical theory today should thus reject Baudrillard's "overcoming" of political economy and create new syntheses of political economy, semiotics, and social theory in order to map the novelties and conflicts of the present age.

The mappings of cyberpunk and much postmodern theory thus need critical social theory to trace the vicissitudes of our media culture, to contextualize its artifacts and to trace their effects. Baudrillard, by contrast, theorizes a flat, depthless, superficial ecstasy of communication in which images and discourses circulate in a hyperreal space, losing all contact with the real. Curiously, this is precisely the fate of his own theory, which he admits is a simulation and which floats and mutates in a hypertheoretical space more and more cut off from the realities and sufferings of everyday life. His theoretical fictions explode theory into fragments and pieces which he believes capture the reality of today's highly fragmented and disintegrating society. There is, however, something left of the belief that theory, in whatever form, can capture the real.

Baudrillard's wager: pieces of theory, theory fragments and simulations, can do what the old, more coherent and rational social theories could do: provide a mapping of our present condition, produce orientation for thought and action, help us cope with the changes and conflicts of social life. Yet Baudrillard's own theory arguably fails to capture the realities of the time and disables critical theory and democratic politics. And so cyberpunk moved up to the front-lines of avant-garde attempts to map contemporary social reality, summoning social theory and cultural studies to theorize its insights, mappings, and blindspots.

Thus, in a sense Baudrillard does what modern social theory has done since the nineteenth century, to chart out the vicissitudes of a new (then modern) era (see

Antonio and Kellner, forthcoming), but he does so in novel ways. I have argued that in this sense Gibson's writings and cyberpunk also contain a form of social theory and that this work has been more useful in recent years for developing analyses and understanding of our contemporary society than Baudrillard, an issue which I will take up in the concluding sections.

LITERATURE, SOCIAL THEORY, AND POLITICS

Building on Jameson's theory of cognitive mapping, I have suggested that both the theoretical productions of Baudrillard and the (science) fictive texts of Gibson project mappings of the trajectory from the present to the future. From this perspective, theories, like Baudrillard's, map out present social conditions, trends, and possible futures based on extrapolation from the present to the future – as do some modes of literature, especially SF and cyberpunk. Moreover, I suggest that it is their analyses of the future that map the present, pointing to what is novel and significant in our present and potential future effects. It is my claim that especially the 1970s texts of Baudrillard and Gibson and cyberpunk both chart salient aspects of our high-tech media society, using the means of theoretical discourse, metaphor, narrative, allegory, and other techniques to illuminate distinctive features of our present and rapidly approaching future worlds.

The present moment is undeniably a tense one with new technologies careening out of control and the socio-political establishment and its institutions collapsing (the communist world), or seemingly incapable of coping with the challenges of the contemporary era (the capitalist world). It is accordingly a moment for bleak and pessimistic visions and Baudrillard and Gibson provide appropriate articulations of present moods of panic and anxiety concerning the present and future (attitudes anticipated in the prophetic world of Pynchon and Burroughs), as well as mappings of those forces causing the dis-ease of the present moment.

Cyberpunk activism

Baudrillard is more gloomy and despairing than Gibson, though Gibson thinks his book is optimistic and that the future will be far less hospitable than what he depicts as the present in *Neuromancer*.[34] Other critics also think that Gibson's book is optimistic and presents hope for the future in new interactions between humans and technology (Leary 1990: 53f.). In general, cyberpunks eschew attacking technology *per se* and focus on the social forces that employ it for destructive and evil purposes. In Gibson's work and other cyberpunk fiction, technology and communication systems are represented as a fundamental means of power and hence as something important for democratic control. There is thus a kind of populism in the cyberpunk movement which advocates individuals using technology for their own purposes and engaging in media and technological activism.

Indeed, a whole new "hackers" ethic has emerged which espouses information for the people, fighting corporate control and monopoly of information. New computer data-bases and bulletin boards have emerged which present new sources of information and communication. The intense interaction between people on computer bulletin boards, ranging from discussions of classical music to soap operas and politics, has now become visible to the mainstream (*New York Times*, December 1, 1992: B1). These boards are a new source of interaction, making accessible diverse types of information and communication, allowing people to express their opinions in a public forum that is participatory and interactive (as opposed to the one-way communication system of broadcasting).

Other subversive potential for democracy of technological inventions such as home computers and other technologies are present in cyberpunk fiction and in the movements which are using technology to promote human change. Camcorders enable individuals to film police violence, as in the famous Rodney King affair when an amateur filmed the police brutally beating a black man arrested for speeding. Public access television, community and CB radio, and bulletin board and interactive computer systems enable individuals to air their views, to debate issues of concern, to participate in social and cultural dialogue. Such technologies thus facilitate individual participation and make possible two-way social communication. Not, to be sure, the sort of face-to-face interaction valorized by liberal political theories of the public sphere, but new modes of communication in a new computerized and mediatized public sphere, one as important for the future of contemporary politics as the previous public sphere of liberal democracy.

Cyberspace democracy: the new spaces of computer and media communication make possible more participation in public debate, more outlets for political and cultural expression, and more different voices and visions than in the precomputer society. The realm of the public sphere has thus been expanded, allowing for a vitalization of democracy, which has been decaying and in crisis for decades (see Kellner 1990a and the conclusion to this book).

By contrast to cyberpunk activism, Baudrillard is technophobic and apolitical, showing a future in which technology rules and the subject disappears, without exploring ways in which new technologies can promote the growth of subjectivity and produce new modes of experience, information, and democratic participation and interaction. Baudrillard scorns alternative media, speaking contemptuously of "the negative ecstasy of radio," in which alternative voices are articulating their views and positions (1983c: 131–2). He has no cultural politics in his post-1980s writings, whereas earlier he promoted various forms of oppositional culture.[35]

Moreover, Gibson and cyberpunk offer a critical mapping of the corporate forces that control technology and this work raises issues about ownership and control of technology, about its uses and abuses. Gibson depicts the continued power of capitalism, showing the desire for profit and power as basic motivations of human beings in a competitive capitalist world. Thus for Gibson the imperatives of capitalist accumulation and the competitive struggle for limited amounts of goods continue to be the organizing principle of society. Gibson's mappings thus raise the question of who should have access to information and who should control it, in a world in which information and knowledge are power. Further: what are the potential uses and abuses of cyberspace, artificial intelligence, and genetic engineering? Gibson presents these developments as inevitable, as happening before our eyes and into tomorrow, forcing us to confront the implications of the information and technology explosion that we are currently experiencing.

Baudrillard, by contrast, obliterates the problematic of power and subjectivity describing high-tech cybernetic systems, but never the forces, groups, nor individuals that control them. By erasing political economy from the conceptual framework of his theory, Baudrillard ultimately falls prey to technological determinism. There are few references to capitalism or political economy in Baudrillard's later works and he seems to be describing a new technological order in which technology alone rules, mercilessly imposing its imperatives and demands on human who are henceforth powerless to control the products of human creativity.

Gibson's texts, by contrast, induce us to reflect about how technology can both enhance human life and be a destructive force. This indeed is *the challenge* of our technological future: how can we use technology to enhance human life, promote democracy, and produce a better future? While Gibson's novels do not answer these questions, they help us think through the nature of our present society and what challenges and dangers we face in the future. And yet many are claiming that the moment of cyberpunk is over, that it is now obsolete, and that we should move onto to new concerns.

Forget cyberpunk?

It is has been argued that cyberpunk fiction has perhaps already had its positive effects within SF literature and is now out of fashion and *passé*.[36] It has been mapped, charted, dissected, and anthologized, laid out in a useful academic anthology by Larry McCaffery in *Storming the Reality Studio* (1991).[37] The essays tell you everything you want to know about cyberpunk – its literary and cinematic antecedents, its origins and trajectory, its themes and obsessions, its sociological moorings, and relationship to SF and postmodern literature. The fiction selections gave the reader a good sense of the style, feel, intensity, and hipness of cyberpunk writing and its affinities for cinema, MTV, the drug culture, and the cyberspace of computer universes. Reading through the texts of cyberpunk fiction one gets the sense that the key moves have already been made, that the initial founding documents have already charted out the iconography, lingo, themes, and style of cyberpunk writing and that everything henceforth is derivative. Indeed, as Csicsery-Ronay notes:

> how many formulaic tales can one wade through in which a self-destructive but sensitive young protagonist with an (implant/prosthesis/telechtronic talent) that makes the evil (megacorporations/police states/criminal underworlds) pursue him through (wasted urban landscapes/elite luxury enclaves/eccentric space stations) full of grotesque (haircuts/clothes/self-mutilations/rock music/sexual hobbies/designer drugs/telechtronic gadgets/nasty new weapons/exteriorized

hallucinations) representing the (mores/fashions) of modern civilization in terminal decline, ultimately hooks up with rebellious and tough-talking (youth/artificial intelligence/rock cults) who offer the alternative, not of (community/socialism/traditional values/transcendental vision), but of supreme, life-affirming *hippness*, going with the flow which now flows in the machine, against the specter of a world-subverting (artificial intelligence/multinational corporate web/evil genius)? Yet judging from even the best of writers in Sterling's anthology, for cyberpunks, 'hippness is all.'[38]

(1991: 184)

In fact, the creation/dissemination/assimilation of cyberpunk fiction has been so rapid that the process of parody and pastiche has already become a standard narrative device. For instance, Kathy Acker in *Empire of the Senseless* has already produced a parody (or pastiche, it is undecidable) of *Neuromancer*. Cyberpunk fiction had its moments, like Baudrillard, its brilliant breakthroughs, and then its boring repetitions. Both of these avant-gardist writings/theories have had their highs and lows, their hits and misses, and so now perhaps it is time to move on to something new and different: beyond Baudrillard, beyond cyberpunk. The Something New is perhaps more ecological, more womanly, more communal, and more innovative, envisaging as yet unforeseen modes of writing, living, and relating. As Lewis Shiner noted in his farewell to cyberpunk, the cyberpunks do not really address the current national need for spiritual values and do not deal with the problems of disintegrating families, addictions to alcohol and drugs and tobacco and sex. Instead of answering contemporary questions of values and meaning, cyberpunk offers instead "power fantasies, the same dead-end thrills we get from video games and blockbuster movies like '*Rambo*' and '*Aliens*.' Its gives Nature up for dead, accepts violence and greed as inevitable and promotes the cult of the loner."[39]

Perhaps Shiner (and we) should be more generous to his ex-comrades however. For it has been the merit of cyberpunk to be on the cutting edge of radical writing and mapping of the present as we head toward a frightening, but exhilarating, new technological future. To be sure, cyberpunk literature began repeating and parodying itself almost immediately, it is a boy's club of high-tech power fantasies and low-life subcultural highs, and is an expression of and response to a period of unparalleled social reaction – the Reagan/Bush years – which are now history. But it is among the merits of cyberpunk to have caught the Weltgeist of its epoch on the run and articulated prescient mappings and visions of the future with deadly accuracy. Some of Gibson's most far-out fantasies are already high-tech realities and no doubt tomorrow will surpass today in technological speed, surprises, and nightmares.[40]

Further, although cyberpunk fiction may have had its moment and exhausted its creative energies, it appears that cyberpunk as a mood, as an attitude, and even as a cultural movement of alternative technology and lifestyles may continue to thrive and be with us for some time. Books and articles on cyberpunk fiction, culture, and uses of technology are proliferating and computer data-bases and bulletin boards are rife with debates and discussions about cyberpunk. Taken as a broad cultural phenomenon, then, cyberpunk continues to have creative energies and effects, appearing as cutting-edge and radical. And yet we are still seeking the philosophies that will help orient our lives, the theories that will chart the trajectory of contemporary history, and the politics that will fight against the worst and produce the best that it is possible for us to imagine. Baudrillard and cyberpunk will no doubt be part of that mapping and vision, but only a part, however indispensable. And so we should probably not forget cyberpunk as we create new theories and politics, for the future may yet have some new surprises and revelations and postmodern theory and cyberpunk are only part of the story that remains to be told and made as we rapidly approach the next century.

NOTES

1 On Baudrillard, see Kellner 1989b, Best and Kellner 1991, and Kellner 1994a. I draw in this chapter on my previous work on Baudrillard, but present some new perspectives and juxtapose Baudrillard with cyberpunk fiction in order to indicate his contributions and expose his limitations.
2 See, especially, Baudrillard 1990 [1983], and the discussion in Kellner 1989b, Chapter 6. The "pataphysics" is that of Alfred Jarry and his "school"; see the discussion in Kellner 1989b.
3 One could argue, of course, that Baudrillard was never a "postmodern" theorist, that he was always rooted within a certain current of oppositional French thought rooted in nineteenth-century romantic and bohemian currents, in Jarry and pataphysics, and in thinkers like Nietzsche, Bataille, and Debord and the Situationists (something like this is argued in Gane 1991a and 1991b). But against such readings, I would insist that Baudrillard's interest derived from his claims to be theorizing radically new phenomena, trends, and experiences of the present moment and that he derived his cultural power and influence precisely from his novel descriptions of new technologies, cultural and social forms, and experiences for which the label "postmodern" has been a generally accepted description (see Kellner 1994a). Curiously, at the very moment when Baudrillard dropped the theoretical ball, losing his initiative, Gibson and cyberpunk picked it up, beginning their explorations of the new future world which Baudrillard had been exploring.
4 *Mondo 2000*, No. 7 (1990): 56. Science fiction fans and devotees of postmodern literature were no less effusive. See the articles in McCaffery 1991. In addition, literary and cultural journals, magazines, and computer bulletin boards have had countless laudatory analyses and discussions of Gibson and cyberpunk in recent years.
5 This is indeed how I recommended that one read Baudrillard in Kellner 1989b: 203f.
6 The term "cognitive mapping" derives from Jameson 1984 and 1991; see the discussions in Kellner 1989c and Best and Kellner 1991 of the difficulties of mapping the contemporary moment.
7 See McHale in McCaffery 1991 and McHale 1992.
8 Interestingly, William Gibson and Bruce Sterling joined talents to produce a novel about a different path for the industrial revolution titled *The Difference Engine* (1991). This novel imagines that the computer appeared earlier, that technocratic radicals under Lord Byron governed England during the explosion of the Industrial Revolution, and that working-class revolution in England was narrowly averted – though the novel postulates that in the United States, the South won the Civil War which broke out some decades

earlier, that the South was the dominant power in the U.S., that Texas was an independent state, and that Manhattan was a socialist commune governed by Karl Marx and his followers.

9 On the concept of technocapitalism, see Kellner 1989a, Chapter 7 and 8.

10 This surprisingly accurate characterization of capital is undercut by an earlier analysis by Baudrillard which proclaims "the end of political economy" in the society of simulations (see Baudrillard 1976: 20ff. and the discussion in Kellner 1989b: 61ff.). Such passages point to the Marxist origins of Baudrillard's thought which are not entirely suppressed even in his most violent polemics against the great bearded one.

11 On Pynchon's influence on cyberpunk, see McHale 1991: 315ff. Gibson frequently cites Pynchon as a major literary influence; see the discussion in the interview with Timothy Leary, op. cit.: 62f. and with McCaffery 1991: 267. On Pynchon's mapping of contemporary capitalism, see Best 1992.

12 Baudrillard (1981) was also impressed by one of the precursors of cyberpunk fiction, J.G. Ballard, writing an enthusiastic study of his novel *Crash*.

13 This reference is a perhaps an homage to Burrough's *Naked Lunch* which invents a "Freeland Republic, a place given over to free love and continual bathing" (Burroughs 1959: 21).

14 See Gibson's interview in McCaffrey 1991. On *Blade Runner* and dystopic science fiction films, see the discussion in Kellner and Ryan 1988.

15 Henceforth, page references to *Neuromancer* will be put in the text without citations. If the reader has not yet read *Neuromancer*, I would recommend that she or he do so before proceeding with my reading.

16 Art and technology continue to implode in Gibson's later novels. *Count Zero* involves a quest for a mysterious object, reminiscent of the works of Joseph Cornell collected in the Chicago Art Institute. In *Mona Lisa Overdrive*, one of the characters, Slick Henry, uses his robotic sculptures as weapons during an attack on his house. And all of Gibson's work features implosion of human beings and technology.

17 Gibson once sold antiques and his work evidences a love for special old artifacts. He is likewise nostalgic concerning old forms of individuality and humanity, forms that are disappearing in the technological societies of the present. Like Orwell in *1984*, Gibson marshals sentiments for antique objects that signified a happier and simpler time to present critique of the present debased form of social life.

18 Initially, there was nothing quite like Gibson's cyberspace, but some crude approximations of it, such as simulation devices or virtual reality glasses, but studies are now proliferating on cyberspace and virtual reality which present Gibson as the prophet of this new space and experience (see the articles on cyberspace in Benedict 1991). I have found hundreds of newspaper and journal articles in various data-bases which describe contemporary forms of cyberspace and which attribute the origin of the term to Gibson. This is clearly an example of someone coining a term and idea and inventors following by creating the actual embodiments of it.

19 On the new worlds of information theft, see Hafner and Markoff 1991 and Sterling 1992.

20 Baudrillard (1983c: 127) imagines a new communicative interaction with cars that replace the pleasure of the intoxication and power of speed and Gibson provides the next stage of development and concrete image of this fantasy. Interestingly, in a *Rolling Stone* interview, Gibson notes that he was listening to Bruce Springsteen's *Darkness on the Edge of Town* when he was writing *Neuromancer* and: "I was wondering if there couldn't be a mythology of computers that had something in common with Springsteen's mythology of cars" (*Rolling Stone*, December 4, 1986: 107).

21 The theme of the resurrection of the body is an esoteric one in Christianity, found in the Gospels, but not always promoted as dogma. Certain sects of Buddhism, however, represented paradise or Nirvana in very concrete terms with resurrected bodies enjoying

the pleasures of the flesh (see the painting of "Paradise" in the Japanese national museum in Tokyo).

22 Gibson's subsequent cyberpunk novels deal with the later adventures of many of the same characters, but do not focus on the latter trajectory of Wintermute/Neuromancer, whether its reign was benign or oppressive, suggesting that the mega-program broke up into a plurality of decentralized programs. Gibson's later fictions, however, imply that humans continue to have a certain amount of sovereignty, though it is always threatened by corporations and technology.

23 In a subsequent novel, *Count Zero*, which takes place seven years after the action of *Neuromancer*, it appears that the unitary AI intelligence-sentience has fragmented into a multiplicity of warring gods, presented as a pantheon of voodoo deities. It is as if the center could not hold and the future was condemned to relive wars of conflicting deities: precisely Max Weber's vision of modernity.

24 Modern theory also attempts to understand the present from the standpoint of the past; consider Condorcet's essay on historical stages, Comte's three stages of history, Marx's historical periodizations, Nietzsche's genealogies and comparative histories, and Weber's massive historical treatises, discussed in Antonio and Kellner, forthcoming. In this sense, Foucault is a modern theorist, as was the early Baudrillard in his sketch of stages of history in *Simulations*. Understanding the present from the standpoint of the future, then, is part of an arguably postmodern stance, or at least that of cyberpunk.

25 See my critical appraisal of Baudrillard's politics in Kellner 1989b.

26 See the extremely negative portrayal of working-class revolution in Gibson and Sterling 1991.

27 In a 1984 interview, Baudrillard describes the postmodern as

> the characteristic of a universe where there are no more definitions possible. . . . . One is no longer in a history of art or a history of forms. They have been deconstructed, destroyed. In reality, there is no more reference to forms. It has all been done. The extreme limit of these possibilities has been reached. It has destroyed itself. It has deconstructed its entire universe. So all that are left are pieces. All that remains to be done is to play with the pieces. Playing with the pieces – that is postmodern.
>
> (1984: 24)

One could describe cyberpunk fiction, which was appearing just as Baudrillard was pontificating, either as something new and unexpected, or as precisely a playing with the pieces of contemporary culture, and thus as a "game of vestiges," to use Baudrillard's term.

28 In the following section page references to *America* will appear in the text without citations.

29 In a polemic against my reading of Baudrillard's *America*, Mike Gane attacks my "symptomatic" reading, and then claims that I do not really undertake such a reading (see Gane 1991a: 178ff.). But in fact I read *America* as symptomatic of Baudrillard's sign fetishism, as the projection of his semiological imaginary on the object "America." Gane is thus the poor reader, totally misinterpreting my reading, distorting completely my critique, and then offering his own hopelessly muddled "reading," as "a mirror of Baudrillard's own form of writing, that is fatally or poetically" (p. 182). The ever elusive Gane forces the reader to go to a footnote, however, to discover what he means by an "appropriate superficial" form of "fatal reading": "This is only one moment of a reading: that which follows an (apparently) regressive epistemology into the fatal and the *pars totalis*. It follows the ascent to poetic ecstasy. Yet this becomes perverse, in Baudrillard's own thought: a pure collection" (p. 228). Gane's own book is a similarly perverse "pure collection" of fragments swirling about Baudrillard and his critics that have no continuous arguments, coherent organization, sustained interpretive theses, or criticisms.

To my mind, his muddled and confused prose and inability to mount a coherent argument or interpretation contributes to the collapse of meaning that Baudrillard himself so well describes.

30 Indeed, Baudrillard's later writings abound with sexist and racist remarks, based on his surprising turn to a metaphysical imaginary grounded in the sort of binary thinking that he had earlier rejected. See my critique in Kellner 1989b, Chapter 7. He also fails entirely to see the endemic racism in the United States (see the analysis of racial mixing, pp. 82ff.) and engages in racist asides such as: "As is well known, the Americans are fascinated by the yellow-skinned peoples in whom they sense a superior form of cunning, a higher form of that absence of truth which frightens them" (85). Here Baudrillard passes off his own prejudices and fears as that which "is well known" in America.

31 Baudrillard does mention that America is "an advanced bastion of capitalism" (90), but nowhere analyses American capitalism, perhaps excusing himself from doing so with the specious claim that "capital can never actually be grasped in its present reality," that it is always outrunning and eluding theory (p. 80). He thus affirms the classical Marxist position of "the absolute initiative capital enjoys as historical event" (80), but disinge-nuously proclaims the impossibility of theorizing it.

32 In the "Ecstasy of Communication," Baudrillard (1983c) compares the mythologies of modernity, such as speed and driving an automobile, with the experiences of postmod-ernity, exemplified in the "ecstasy of communication," especially through interaction with media, computers, and new technologies. He declared "obsolete" a mode of experience which he soon after immersed himself in.

33 Baudrillard does recognize that he is plunging into "the fiction of America," entering into "America as fiction" (p. 29). In a later article, he insisted that his reflections on America are "basically a *fiction*" (Baudrillard 1993: 243f.). Yet I would argue that his text provides a model of American society, a theoretical vision of America, and that his fictive enterprise actually deconstructs dichotomies between fiction and social theory, as does cyberpunk fiction. But while cyberpunk provides crucial insights into new trends, processes, experiences, and problems, Baudrillard's post-1980s work tends to tell us more about Baudrillard himself than the objects of his writing and he is missing what is original about contemporary American society and the proliferation of new technologies and new modes of technological experience, topics that he once followed and charted with interest and acuity.

34 Gibson thinks the terror of the future will be boredom and conformity induced by the likes of Jerry Falwell and the radical right (*Mondo 2000*, Nr 7: 59).

35 See Baudrillard's earlier emphasis on the importance of cultural politics in *The Mirror of Production* (1975) and the section on New York graffiti in *L'échange symbolique et la mort* (1993 [1976]): 118ff.), a section curiously omitted in the English translation of *Simulations* (Baudrillard 1983a). Beginning in the later 1970s, however, he became increasingly contemptuous of all cultural and media activism.

36 This is claimed by Csicsery-Ronay (1991) and by Fitting (1991).

37 See also the articles in *Mississippi Review* Nos. 47–8 and *Critique* (Spring 1992).

38 McCaffery's reader (1991) also illustrates the claim of the increasing repetitiveness of cyberpunk through its selection of primary texts, many of which are derivative of Gibson's work, or imitate writers like Burroughs or Pynchon.

39 Lewis Shiner, "Confessions of an Ex-Cyberpunk," *New York Times*, XX, 1991, op-ed page.

40 In interviews, Gibson has noted how computer hacking and the computer virus scare confirmed his fantasies which he insists were projections of his imagination rather than inductions from technical knowledge.

Conclusion
From the future back to the present

The contemporary capitalist societies and cultures that have been the topic of these studies are in a situation of seemingly permanent crisis with deteriorating social conditions increasing human suffering. In the United States, more than 34 million people live below the poverty level; over 3 million are homeless; over 10 million are out of work; and millions lack basic health insurance and guaranteed medical care (Hoffman 1987). During the 1980s, the distribution of wealth took billions from the poorest 20 percent, while the wealthiest grew vastly richer. At this time, "the gap between the richest and poorest families became wider than at any time since the 1940s: the take-home income of the poorest fifth of the nation fell 5.2 percent, while that of the wealthiest fifth grew 32.5 percent and the middle fifth's grew only 2.7 percent. The inflation-adjusted, after-tax income of the richest 1 percent grew 87 percent and nearly equals the total income of the poorest 40 percent. In 1990, according to a report by the Center on Budget and Policy Priorities, the top fifth's after-tax income will equal that of the rest of the population combined" (Grossberg 1992: 313).

Data released by the Congressional Budget Office in March 1992 showed that "between 1977 and 1989, income expanded for all Americans by a total of $740 billion, and an astonishing $550 billion of this – 74 percent – went to the top 1 percent of U.S. families. The incomes of this tiny elite of 600,000 families grew from an average of $315,000 to $560,000 over the twelve-year period (in inflation-adjusted US dollars)" (McQuaig 1993: 62). Moreover, these statistics show that people on the low end of the income-scale actually saw their incomes decline.

The proportion of low-income earners in the U.S. labor force continued to rise and their condition continued to decline, while high-income workers' wages continued to rise, creating a two-tier wage structure and growing class divisions, according to a 1994 report issued jointly by the Labor and Commerce Departments of the Clinton Administration (*Associated Press*, June 3, 1994). The report noted that the "real" hourly compensation of American workers stagnated in the last two decades and actually fell for male workers, a development "unprecedented in the past 75 years in this country" (ibid.). In Britain as well the richest 10 percent is reportedly "almost twice as well off as it was in the late 1960s, while living standards of the poorest sixth are worse than at the beginning of the 1980s," according to two major reports published in England during 1994 (*The Daily Telegraph*, June 3, 1994).

Furthermore, in 1988, "the nations of the world spent over $110 for each man, woman, and child on military expenses – overwhelmingly more than on food, water, shelter, health, education, or protecting the ecosystem" (French 1992: 37). Moreover:

> From 1980 to 1984, world military spending grew from $564 billion to $649 billion (in 1980 prices), a growth rate of over 3.5 percent. Over 5 percent of the production of the world, 27 times more than was spent on overseas development, was spent on the military in 1983, most by industrialized countries. Global military expenditures in 1985 were $900 billion, more than the income of half the human race. Military expenditures surpassed the combined GDP of China, India, and all of sub-Shararan Africa – a sum comparable to the combined GNP of all of Africa and Latin America.
>
> (French 1992: 37)

Meanwhile, the conditions of everyday life, even in the metropoles of the United States, are deteriorating dramatically. Numbers of homeless and unemployed continue to grow; epidemics of cancer, AIDS, and other deadly diseases proliferate with no cure in sight; crime and violence are on the rise; tobacco, drugs, and alcohol take millions of casualties yearly; drinking water continues to be contaminated by toxic chemicals and basic foods are adulterated with chemicals, additives, and pesticides, many of which contribute to deadly diseases. Accidents and deaths in the workplace grow, while people are subject to increased surveillance, insecurity, and cutbacks on social benefits.

As compensation for decaying social conditions, those who can afford it are offered an always increasing dose of media culture and consumption. Numbers of channels on cable television continue to multiply, with current estimates of more than 500 channels on the horizon. There are also predictions of the imminent arrival of supplementary programs available on demand via computer. The hours of television watching continue to grow, the amount of advertising continues to increase, and the colonization of leisure and society by media culture continues apace.

But those who are most exploited and oppressed by the social order can afford little more than the "free" entertainment provided by media culture, especially television. As an escape from social misery, or distraction from the cares and woes of everyday existence, people turn to media culture to produce some meaning and value in their lives. Sports offer identification with glamour, power, and success, empowering those who identify with winning teams and stars. Soap operas and situation comedies provide education for coping in the contemporary social order, while action entertainment demonstrates who has power and who doesn't, who can and cannot exercise violence, and who does and does not get awarded with the benefits of the "good life" in the media and consumer society. Advertising demonstrates how to solve problems and how to be happy, successful, and popular –

through proper commodity behavior. Films glamorize the "American way of life" and provide unreal models of identification, while images of violence constantly increase.

Many individuals practicing cultural studies celebrate this culture and way of life and thus contribute to the perpetuation of an unjust and oppressive social order. I have attempted to develop critical perspectives on contemporary society and culture in this book and believe that surrender of criticism and oppositional resistance is nothing more than capitulation to a way of life that produces incredible misery and suffering for people throughout the world.

People in the future may will look back at this era of political and media culture with disbelief. Perhaps denizens of an age of interactive technologies will look back at the passive couch potatoes of this era in wonder. Perhaps those able to access information from a wealth of sources from computer data-bases will be astonished that in this era the vast majority of people depended on television for their prime source of information. Perhaps later generations who have accessible a vast array of significantly different and better cultural texts at their fingertips will be amazed that people actually watched the programs of commercial television, radio, and film during the present era. Perhaps individuals in a future age will be astonished that people watched so much television, saw so many poor films, listened to so much mediocre music, and read such trashy magazines and books, hour after hour, day after day, year after year.

It is conceivable that the society of the future will look back at our age of media culture as an astonishing age of cultural barbarism, in which commercially driven culture industries pandered to the lowest common denominator, pouring out films, TV shows, novels, and other artifacts that depicted violence as the way to solve problems, that debased women and people of color, and that repeated the same old tired genre formulas over and over. The endless sequels of popular film and eternal recurrence of the same in the fields of television, popular music, and other forms of media culture might strike a future age as highly primitive and barbaric. A future age might look at an era that idolized Sylvestor Stallone, Madonna, Michael Jackson, Beavis and Butt-Head, fashion models, and other celebrities as highly peculiar, very weird indeed. Future generations may look at our advertising-satu- rated culture as the crudest and crassest commercialism, as the one of the most amazing wastes of time and resources in the history of civilization.

Perhaps future historians will be astonished that during the 1980s and 1990s, the period of these studies, mediocrities like Ronald Reagan, George Bush, and Bill Clinton were Presidents of the United States; that reactionary Margaret Thatcher and nullity John Major ruled England; that Helmut Kohl and his pedestrian conservative party ruled Germany; that Italy was ruled by Christian and Social Democrats who were revealed to be highly corrupt, followed by the election of a media baron who rode to power on the electorate's disgust with the existing political system; that lackluster conservatives Brian Mulrooney and Kim Campbell gov- erned Canada; that undistinguished Boris Yeltsin ruled Russia after the collapse of the Soviet Union; and that similar mediocre, greedy, corrupt, and vicious individuals ruled much of the world.

Future ages might look back on the incredible concentration of wealth and striking class differences, the phenomenal amount of world hunger and poverty, the deadly diseases, the violence and social disorder, and lack of humane and egalitarian social institutions and perceive this society as truly astonishing. Our time might one day be looked upon as a dark age of incredible ignorance and backwardness where life is much more nasty, brutish, and short than it needs to be.

Perhaps our time will be looked at as an especially backward period when individuals had not yet adjusted to new technologies, when they were overwhelmed by new media, and not yet well enough educated to govern themselves and control the technologies and media. Perhaps future generations will laugh at our pretensions to "enlightenment" and "modernity". Perhaps a future generation will come to terms with the new media and technologies and use them to enhance their individual lives. Perhaps the growing choice of media artifacts will empower individuals to increase their realm of choice and control over their culture and thus to increase their autonomy and sovereignty. Perhaps in the future there will be media study groups, like the book study groups of our era, in which individuals gather together to critically dissect media artifacts and media education is a standard part of schooling from grade school on up to the universities and beyond. Perhaps individuals will learn to use the new technologies to communicate with each other, to produce their own media artifacts which are circulated and distributed throughout society, so that previously marginalized voices are able to speak, so that the full range and diversity of cultures find expression, so that individuals and groups can speak to others, be creative, and participate in the production of society and culture.

Perhaps future individuals and governments will discern the importance of culture and subsidize a wide range of cultural artifacts, freeing cultural expression from the tyranny of the market and the iron yoke of advertising. Perhaps the works of the monstrous media conglomerates – Time/Warner, SONY/Columbia, Paramount/Viacom/Blockbuster, Disney/America – will be shunned and abhorred by audiences who find their products intrinsically debased, insulting, and boring, and these conglomerates will wither away, to be replaced by a vibrant spectrum of media cultural expression and a wide range of visions and voices.

Perhaps, but perhaps not. Perhaps the future will spend more time watching more and ever stupider products and the lowest common denominator will sink ever lower, to an era of cultural barbarism impossible to envisage in the present. Perhaps the present will appear as a golden age of individualism, freedom, and democracy to future inhabitants of dystopic societies, much as the postholocaust, apocalyptic science fiction films represent our late twentieth century present as utopian compared to the dismal future depicted in the films.

Cultural studies can play some role, however modest, in the struggle for a better future. Cyberpunk, science fiction, and a future-oriented cultural studies can articulate imagined and possible futures and help to guide our present and future choices and action. Reflection on possible media futures calls attention to the urgency of impending tasks for cultural studies that have been neglected or suppressed in the tumult and confusion of the present.

On the positive side, we are living in exciting times in which new media and technologies are producing new possibilities for communication, cultural expression, and ways of living everyday life – at least for privileged individuals. We should not forget, however, the misery of the vast majority and should struggle so that they can attain the same opportunities as those more fortunate. Moreover, we need to consciously come to terms with our new technologies and culture and devise ways to use them to enhance our lives and to make them available to all. This requires reflection on media and technology and the challenges and problems of living in a new media/technological society. With these concerns in mind, I would suggest that cultural studies needs to address several topics that have been pointed to in recent years, but not really incorporated into its projects and problematics.

CRITICAL MEDIA PEDAGOGY

Cultural studies has often underplayed the importance of developing pedagogies for promoting critical media literacy. While the Frankfurt School believed that the culture industries were overwhelmingly manipulative and overwhelmingly ideological, some versions of cultural studies argue that the media merely provide resources for audience use and pleasure. Avoidance of its images and messages seems to be the upshot of the Frankfurt School critique, while some cultural studies simply celebrate sports, Elvis, fandom, and other media phenomena.

The Frankfurt School's total rejection of mass culture seems inappropriate, as media culture is here to stay and, if anything, its products are becoming increasingly popular and powerful. Yet mindless celebration of media culture, without cultivation of methods to promote critical media literacy, is equally pernicious. Thus, it is important to pursue a project of developing a critical media pedagogy and to teach ourselves and others how to critically decode media messages and to trace their complex range of effects. It is important to be able to perceive the various ideological voices and codes in the artifacts of our common culture and to distinguish between hegemonic ideologies and those images, discourses, and texts that subvert the dominant ideologies.

It is also important to learn to discriminate between the best and worst of media culture and to cultivate oppositional subcultures and alternatives to media culture. You are what you see and hear every bit as much as what you eat, and it is therefore important to impress upon individuals the need to avoid media culture junk food and to choose healthier and more nourishing products. This requires learning discrimination and cultivating tastes for the better products of media culture, as well as alternative forms of culture ranging from poetry, literature, painting, to alternative music, film, and television.

McLuhan to the contrary, today's media-saturated younger generations are not naturally media-critical or truly media-literate. Thus, developing critical media literacy requires developing explicit strategies of cultural pedagogy and many dominant schools of contemporary theory – such as the Frankfurt School, cultural studies, and most postmodern theory – have failed to develop a critical media pedagogy.[1]

Within educational circles, there is a debate over what constitutes the field of media pedagogy with different agendas and programs. A traditionalist "protectionist" approach would attempt to "innoculate" young people against the effects of media addiction and manipulation by cultivating a taste for book literacy, high culture, and the values of truth, beauty, and justice. Neil Postman in his books *Amusing Ourselves to Death* (1985) and *Technopolis* (1992) exemplifies this approach, attacking media culture and championing print media. A "media literacy" movement, by contrast, attempts to teach students to read, analyze, and decode media texts, in a fashion parallel to the cultivation of print literacy. Media arts education in turn teaches students to appreciate the aesthetic qualities of media and to use various media technologies as tools of self-expression and creation. Critical media literacy, finally, builds on these approaches, teaching students to be critical of media representations and discourses, but also stressing the importance of learning to use the media as modes of self-expression and social activism.[2]

I would personally endorse this latter comprehensive approach that would teach critical skills and how to use media as instruments of social change. The technologies of communication are becoming more and more accessible to young people and average citizens and they should be used to promote democratic self-expression and social change. Thus, technologies that could help produce the end of participatory democracy, by transforming politics into media spectacles and the battle of images, could help in invigorating democratic debate and participation.

MEDIA AND CULTURAL ACTIVISM

Cultural studies has been especially negligent of developing strategies and practices for media intervention and the production of alternative media. There has been little discussion within cultural studies circles concerning how radio, television, film, computers, and other media technologies could be transformed and used as instruments of social enlightenment and progress. Likewise, the Frankfurt School seemed inherently skeptical of media technologies and viewed them as totally controlled by capitalist corporations.[3] Indeed, when the classical theories of the culture industries were being formed, this was more or less the case. The failure of cultural studies today to engage the issue of alternative media is more puzzling and less excusable since there are today a variety of venues for alternative film and video production, community radio, computer bulletin boards and discussion forums, and other forms of communications in which citizens and activists can readily intervene.[4]

Thus, cultural studies today should discuss *how* the media and culture can be transformed into instruments of social change. This requires more focus on alternative media than has previously been evident in cultural studies and reflections on how media technology can be reconfigured and used to empower individuals. It requires developing activist strategies to intervene in public access television, community radio, computer bulletin-boards, and other domains currently emerging. To genuinely empower individuals requires giving them knowledge of media production and allowing them to produce artifacts that are then disseminated to the public. Increasing media activism could significantly enhance democracy, making possible the proliferation of voices and allowing those voices that have been silenced or marginalized to speak.

Critical media pedagogy and activism require new roles and functions for intellectuals. Media and computer culture is producing new cyberspaces to explore and map, and new terrains of political struggle and intervention. The new cyber-intellectuals of the present may not be the organic intellectuals of a class, but we can become technointellectuals of new technologies, cultural experiences, and spaces, charting and navigating through the brave new worlds of media culture and technoculture. These technologies can be used as instruments of domination or liberation, of manipulation or social enlightenment, and it is up to the cultural producers and activist intellectuals of the present and future to determine which way the new technologies will be used and developed and whose interests they serve.

A democratic media politics will accordingly be concerned that the new media and computer technologies will be used to serve the interests of the people and not corporate elites. A democratic media politics will strive to see that media are used to inform and enlighten individuals rather than to manipulate them. A democratic media politics will teach individuals how to use the new technologies, to articulate their own experiences and interests, and to promote democratic debate and diversity, allowing a full range of voices and ideas to become part of the cyberdemocracy of the future.

MEDIA AND CULTURAL POLITICS

There has also been a failure in cultural studies to discern the importance of media and cultural politics. The question of *who* will control the media of the future and debates over the public's access to media, media accountability and responsibility, media funding and regulation, and what kind of cultures are best for cultivating individual freedom, democracy, and human happiness and well-being will become increasingly important in the future. The proliferation of media culture and technologies focuses attention on the importance of media politics and the need for public intervention in debates over the future of media culture and communications in the information highways and entertainment byways of the future.

One of the key issues of the future will concern whether communications and culture are increasingly commodified or are decommodified. Defenders of commercial television in the United States are always praising "free television," a dubious product, however, only made possible at the expense of allowing advertising to clutter the airwaves and giving advertisers and commercial interests significant power over programming, while making advertised commodities more expensive to consumers. In the future, however, even individual TV programs may be commodified, owned by corporations which will charge for everything. Likewise, today computer bulletin boards and routes of communication on the Internet are free to those who have university, or government, accounts, whereas all computer communication may be commodified in the future, as is telephone communication. The struggle here is therefore to decommodify computer communication and information, to make the Internet and other information highways of the future open to everyone, free of charge, to expand public access television and community radio, and to develop alternative cultural institutions and practices that are funded by the community or state and made available to the people.

In France, the government carried out an experiment, providing free Minitel computers to all telephone customers. These computers were initially to be used for getting information, like time, weather, train and airplane schedules, and the like. But they were soon used for public computer communications, with discussion groups, bulletin boards, and other uses quickly developing. The point is that computers will be part of the standard package of every household of the future, much like television today, and efforts must be made so that everyone who does not currently own a computer can get one and become part of the new culture and society that they will make possible, rather than restricting use of the new technologies to those privileged groups able to purchase them.

Indeed, the very concept of "information *super*highways" contains a democratic core that could provide a terrain and discourse of struggle. While the notion that information superhighways will automatically guarantee a free flow of useful and abundant information to all is obviously ideological, a flim-flam promotional discourse to sell the agenda of powerful corporations, the superhighway metaphor has some significance for democratic struggles. For our national highway space is that of a public domain, part of a public space open and accessible to all, free of charge. The danger of the corporate information and entertainment scenarios of the future is that megacorporations will own and control these resources, charging fees for entry and use, transforming freeways into tollways.

Thus, while Internet and other computer networks are currently free, there are plans to take them over and privatize them, charging for use and access. Against such plans, one should utilize the discourse of the public sphere and public domain and struggle to keep these highways open and accessible to all, free of charge and free from corporate control. Likewise, a democratic media politics will struggle for community television and radio, providing public access for all citizens so that the entire community can take part in democratic discussion and debate (See Kellner 1990a).

The free flow of information and communications is essential to a democratic society and thus democracy requires that powerful instruments of information and communication be accessible to all. Keeping the information superhighways open to all, protecting current highways like the Internet, and struggling to open it to more people is thus a key element of a contemporary democratic media politics. Without a *free* flow of information, citizens cannot be adequately informed and without access to forums of public discussion and debate, citizens are excluded from the dialogue that constitutes the very heart of participatory democracy.

In fact, there are currently powerful struggles going on within and between government, business, and the public concerning who will control the new technologies of the so-called information superhighway, who will profit from them, and what role the public will play in determining the future of our new technologies and media culture. Individuals need to get involved in these debates and informed concerning the importance of the issues involved. For instance, there are recent attempts to censor communication on the Internet, to commodify communication on it, charging for what is now free, to allow commercial uses of it, and to open it to corporate domination. Other groups are struggling to preserve free communication, to guarantee democratic access and participation, and to make the resources of the new technologies open and accessible to everyone, thus promoting, rather than restricting, democracy. These struggles will determine the future of our culture and society and are therefore of prime importance to those concerned with the future of democracy.

It is possible that failures to address political economy and to adequately develop a media politics within cultural studies is a main source of the avoidance of public policy concerns within cultural studies that Tony Bennett has been criticizing (1992, in Grossberg et al.). Without a sense of how the larger social forces (i.e. the nature of the broadcasting industry, state policy towards communications, etc.) impinge on everyday life, it is impossible to grasp the relevance of public policy and media politics on the nature of the system of communications and culture in a given society. Yet in a context in which new technologies of communications are creating dramatic changes in culture, leisure activity, and everyday life, one should perceive the importance of media politics and the ways that the system and framework of communications in a given society help determine what sort of programming and effects are produced.

But without situating discussions of public policy within the context of social theory and political economy that analyzes existing configurations of power and domination, discussions of public policy are hopelessly abstract and beside the point. In the United States, during the reign of Reagan and Bush (1980–92), there really weren't any openings for progressive public policy interventions, on the national level. Instead, the political urgency at the time was defending liberal gains of the past against conservative onslaughts (I would imagine that something like this was also the case in England during the regimes of Thatcher and Major, and in other countries ruled by conservative governments).

On the other hand, the era of conservative rule saw many exciting local interventions, with lively alternative cultures proliferating and intense political struggles, often cultural in focus, taking part on the local level. This experience perhaps influenced the postmodern politics which emphasized local, rather than global, struggles, but it is important to see that both local and national struggles and issues are important. On the local level, one can often more visibly make a difference, though even rearguard defensive operations on the national level are important, as are public policy interventions that advocate genuine reform on any level. The neglect of cultural politics by critical cultural and communications studies is distressing and is a sign of the depoliticalization of intellectual life in the present moment.

Thus cultural studies can be of importance for the radical democratic project. A critical media pedagogy can cultivate citizenship by helping form individuals free from media manipulation, capable of criticizing media culture and of obtaining information from diverse sources, allowing an informed citizenry to make intelligent political judgements. Critical media pedagogy can thus serve as part of a process of social enlightenment, producing new roles for critical and public intellectuals. Media culture itself is producing new public spheres and the need for intervention in new arenas of public debate – community radio, public access television, computer bulletin boards, and so on. Media culture is producing new texts and the need to cultivate a media literacy able to read and decode images, scenes, narratives and spectacles of the sort central to media culture.

Yet media culture also presents the challenge to cultivate new spaces for political discussion and interaction, to produce alternative forms of media and culture, to use the media to promote social enlightenment and to think how media culture can be used for democratization. The challenge of media culture thus produces new vocations for the intellectual: its ubiquity and complexity requires critical intellectuals to subvert disciplinary boundaries and to draw on a range of disciplines to understand media culture. It challenges public intellectuals to use media culture to promote democratization and to produce new spaces and alternatives alongside media culture. In other words, it is both a mistake to turn one's back on and to ignore media culture as it is and to totally uncritically embrace it. Media culture must be thoroughly analyzed, and possibilities should be explored to intervene within mainstream culture as well as to provide alternative modes of culture and discourse outside of its conventional forms and genres. Media culture is perhaps our fate and cultural ambience as we rush toward the future and we must therefore chart this new terrain and see how we can make it work for the goals of increasing freedom, happiness, democracy, and other values that we wish to preserve and enhance.

Thus, cultural studies has some important tasks for the future and can become part of a process of empowerment and enlightenment. On the other hand, it can easily degenerate into just another academic niche, with its canonized texts, stars, and comfortable institutional homes. It is up to us and to the next generation to determine the future of our media and technological society and it is to be hoped that they will use cultural studies as a weapon of social critique, enlightenment, and change, rather than just as another source of cultural capital.

NOTES

1 On critical media pedagogy, see Giroux 1992 and 1994; Scholle and Denski 1994; McLaren *et al.*, forthcoming.
2 On media and communications politics, see Kellner 1990a and Schiller 1989.

3 The exception here was Walter Benjamin (1969).
4 For more on alternative media, see Kellner 1990a and forthcoming.

References

In the following reference list, I cite books referenced in the text, or that were useful in developing some of my positions and interpretations. Newspaper articles cited in notes are not reproduced here.

Abercrombie, N. *et al.* (1980) *The Dominant Ideology Thesis*. London: Routledge & Kegan Paul.
Adorno, T.W. (1974) *Minima Moralia*. London: New Left Books.
Agger, Ben (1991) *Cultural Studies*. London: Falmer Press.
Alterman, Eric (1992) *Sound and Fury*. New York: HarperCollins.
Althusser, Louis (1971) *Lenin and Philosophy*. London: New Left Books.
Anderson, Benedict (1983) *Imaginary Communities*. London: Verso
Anderson, Perry (1980) *Arguments Within English Marxism*. London: New Left Books.
—— (1969) "Components of the National Culture," in Alexander Cockburn and Robin Blackburn, eds. *Student Power*. Harmondsworth: Penguin.
Ang, Ien (1985) *Watching Dallas*. New York: Methuen.
Antonio, Robert and Douglas Kellner (1994) "Modern Social Theory and the Postmodern Critique," in David Dickens and Andy Fontana, eds. *Postmodernism and Social Inquiry*. New York: Guilford Press.
———— (forthcoming) *Modernity and Its Theorists*. London: Sage Books.
Aronowitz, Stanley (1993) *Roll Over Beethoven*. Hanover, New Hampshire: University Press of New England.
Baker, Houston A. (1993a) "Spike Lee and the Commerce of Culture," in Manthia Diawara, ed. *Black Cinema: History, Authorship, Spectatorship*. New York: Routledge.
—— (1993b) *Black Studies, Rap and the Academy*. Chicago: University of Chicago Press.
Baraka, Amiri (1993) "Spike Lee at the Movies," in Manthia Diawara, ed. *Black Cinema: History, Authorship, Spectatorship*. New York: Routledge.
Barrett, Michele (1980) *Women's Oppression Today*. London: Verso.
Barthes, Roland (1957 [1972]) *Mythologies*. New York: Hill and Wang.
Barthes, Roland (1977 [1975]) *Pleasures of the Text*. New York: Oxford University Press.
Baudrillard, Jean (1981 [1975]) *Toward a Critique of the Political Economy of the Sign*. St. Louis: Telos Press.
—— (1976) *L'échange symbolique et la mort*. Paris: Gallimard. Translation: *Symbolic Exchange and Death*. London: Sage, 1993.
—— (1983a) *Simulations*. New York: Semiotext(e).
—— (1983b) *In the Shadow of the Silent Majorities*. New York: Semiotext(e).
—— (1983c) "The Ecstasy of Communication," in Hal Foster, ed. *Anti-Aesthetic*. Seattle: Bay Press.
—— (1984) "Interview: Game with Vestiges," *On the Beach*, 5 (Winter): 19–25.

—— (1988) *America*. London: Verso.

—— (1990) *Fatal Strategies*. New York: Semiotext(e).

—— (1993) *The Transparence of Evil*. London: Verso.

Beauvoir, Simone de (1952) *The Second Sex*. New York: Knopf.

Beck, Ulrich (1992) *Risk Society*. London: Sage Publications.

Bell, Daniel (1960) *The End of Ideology*. New York: The Free Press.

—— (1973) *The Coming of Post-Industrial Society*. New York: Basic Books.

—— (1976) *The Cultural Contradictions of Capitalism*. New York: Harper and Row.

Benedict, Michael (1991) *Cyberspace: First Steps*. Cambridge, Ma.: MIT Press.

Benjamin, Walter (1969) *Illuminations*. New York: Harcourt, Brace & World.

Bennett, Tony (1990) *Outside Literature*. London: Routledge.

—— (1992) "Putting Policy into Cultural Studies," in Lawrence Grossberg *et al. Cultural Studies*. New York: Routledge.

Berland, Jody (1992) "Angels Dancing: Cultural Technologies and the Production of Space," in Lawrence Grossberg *et al. Cultural Studies*. New York: Routledge.

Berman, Marshall (1982) *All That is Solid Melts Into Air*. New York: Simon & Schuster.

Berman, Russell (1984) "Modern Art and Desublimation," *Telos* 62:31–58.

Best, Steven (1992) "The Apocalyptic Imagination: Pynchon's *Gravity's Rainbow*," *Centennial Review*, Vol. XXVI, No. 1 (Winter): 59–88.

Best, Steven and Douglas Kellner (1987) "(Re)Watching Television: Notes Toward a Political Criticism," *Diacritics*, Summer: 97–113.

———— (1991) *Postmodern Theory: Critical Interrogations*. London and New York: Macmillan and Guilford.

Bloch, Ernst (1986) *The Principle of Hope*. Cambridge, Ma: MIT Press.

—— (1991 [1935]) *Heritage of Our Time*. Berkeley: University of California Press.

Blundell, *et al.* (1993) *Relocating Cultural Studies*. New York: Routledge.

Boggs, Carl (1984) *The Two Revolutions: Gramsci and the Dilemmas of Western Marxism*. Boston: South End Press.

—— (1991) "Social Movements and Political Strategy in the Aftermath of the Gulf War" (unpublished MS).

Bono, Paola and Sandra Hemp, eds. (1991) *Italian Feminist Thought*. Oxford: Basil Blackwell.

Bordo, Susan (1992) "'Material Girl': The Effacements of Postmodern Culture," in Cathy Schwichtenberg *The Madonna Connection*. Boulder: Westview.

Brantlinger, Patrick (1990) *Crusoe's Footprints*. London and New York: Routledge.

Brenner, Johanna (1993) "The Best of Times, The Worst of Times: US Feminism Today," *New Left Review*, 200: 101–60.

Britton, Andrew (1986) "Blissing Out: The Politics of Reaganite Entertainment," *Movie* 31/32: 1–42.

Britton, Andrew, Richard Lippe, Tony Williams, and Robin Wood (1979) *American Nightmare: Essays on the Horror Film*. Toronto: Festival of Festivals.

Bronner, Stephen and Douglas Kellner (1989) *Critical Theory and Society: A Reader*. New York: Routledge.

Bürger, Peter (1984 [1974]) *Theory of the Avant-Garde*. Minneapolis: University of Minnesota Press.

Burroughs, William (1959) *Naked Lunch*. New York: Grove Press.

Butler, Jeremy G. (1985) "*Miami Vice* and the Legacy of Film Noir," *Journal of Popular Film and Television*, Vol. 13, No. 3: 132–43.

Cahoone, Lawrence E. (1988) *The Dilemma of Modernity*. Albany, N.Y.: State University of New York Press.

Canadian Journal of Political and Social Theory, Special Issue on Ideology, Vol. 7, Nos. 1–2. (Winter–Spring 1983).

Carey, James (1989) *Communication as Culture*. Boston, Unwin Hyman.

Centre for Contemporary Cultural Studies (1979) *On Ideology*. London: Hutchinson.
—— (1980) *Culture, Media, Language*. London: Hutchinson.
—— (1981) *Unpopular Education: Schooling and Social Democracy in England since 1944*. London: Hutchinson.
—— (1982) *The Empire Strikes Back: Race and Racism in 70s Britain*. London: Hutchinson.
Chodorow, Nancy (1978) *The Reproduction of Mothering*. Berkeley: University of California Press.
Chomsky, Noam (1989) *Necessary Illusions*. Boston: South End Press.
Clark, Ramsey (1992) *The Fire This Time*. New York: Thunder Mouth Press.
Clover, Carol (1992) *Men, Women, and Chain Saws: Gender in the Modern Horror Film*. Princeton: Princeton University Press.
Collins, Jim, Hilary Radner, and Ava Preacher Collins, eds. (1993) *Film Theory Goes to the Movies*. New York and London: Routledge.
Connor, Steven (1989) *Postmodernist Culture*. London and New York: Blackwell.
Coward, Rosalind and John Ellis (1977) *Language and Materialism*. London: Routledge & Kegan Paul.
Cox, Oliver (1948) *Caste, Class and Race*. New York: Doubleday; Reprinted 1970, Monthly Review paperback.
Crawford, Alan (1980) *Thunder on the Right*. New York: Pantheon.
Cross, Brian (1993) *It's not about a Salary: Rap, Race, and Resistance in Los Angeles*. London: Verso.
Csicery-Ronay, Istvan (1991) "Cyberpunk and Neuromanticism," in Larry McCaffery, ed. *Storming the Reality Studio*. Durham: Duke University Press.
—— (1992) "The Sentimental Futurist: Cybernetics and Art in William Gibson's *Neuromancer*," *Critique* (Spring 1992): 221–40.
David, Erik (1994) "It's a MUD, MUD, MUD, MUD World," *Village Voice* (February 22, 1994): 42–4.
Davies, Ioan (forthcoming) *Cultural Studies, and After*. London and New York: Routledge.
Davis, Mike (1986) *Prisoners of the American Dream*. New York: Verso.
Decker, Jeffrey Louis (1993) "The State of Rap: Time and Place in Hip Hop Nationalism," *Social Text* 34: 53–84.
Deleuze, Gilles and Felix Guattari (1977) *Anti-Oedipus*. New York: Viking.
Denton, Robert E., ed. (1993) *The Media and the Persian Gulf War*. Westport, Connecticut: Praeger.
Denzin, Norman (1991) *Images of Postmodern Society*. Newbury Park and London: Sage Press.
Derrida, Jacques (1976) *Of Grammatology*. Baltimore: Johns Hopkins University Press.
—— (1978) *Writing and Difference*. Chicago: University of Chicago Press.
Dyson, Michael (1993a) *Reflecting Black*. Minneapolis: University of Minnesota Press.
—— (1993b) "Between Apocalpyse and Redemption: John Singleton's *Boyz 'N' the Hood*," in Jim Collins, *et al. Film Theory Goes to the Movies*. New York and London: Routledge.
Eisenstein, Zillah (1979) *Capitalist Patriarchy and the Case for Socialist Feminism*. New York: Monthly Review Press.
Emery, Michael (1991). "How Mr Bush Got His War: Deceptions, Double-Standards & Disinformation." Westfield, N.J.: Open Magazine Pamphlet Series; originally published in the *Village Voice*, March 5, 1991: 22–7.
Eveland, McLeod, and Signorielli (forthcoming) "Behind the Lines: An Analysis of Actual and Perceived Public Support For the Persian Gulf War."
Ewen, Stuart (1988) *All Consuming Images*. New York: Basic Books.
Ewen, Stuart and Elizabeth Ewen (1982) *Channels of Desire*. New York: McGraw-Hill.
Exoo, Fred (1987), editor, *Democracy Upside Down*. New York: Praeger.
Faludi, Susan (1991) *Backlash*. New York: Crown Publishers.
Fanon, Frantz (1965) *The Wretched of the Earth*. New York: Grove Press.

Featherstone, Mike (1991) *Consumer Culture and Postmodernism*. London: Sage.
Ferguson, Tom and Joel Rogers (1986) *Right Turn*. New York: Hill and Wang.
Fiske, John (1986a), "Television: Polysemy and Popularity," *Critical Studies in Mass Communication*, Vol. 3, No. 4: 391–408.
—— (1986b) "British Cultural Studies and Television," in R.C. Allen, ed. *Channels of Discourse*. Chapel Hill: University of North Carolina Press: 254–89.
—— (1987a) *Television Culture*. New York and London: Routledge.
—— (1987b) "Miami Vice, Miami Pleasure," *Cultural Studies* Vol. 1, No. 1: 113–19.
—— (1989a) *Reading the Popular*. Boston: Unwin Hyman.
—— (1989b) *Understanding Popular Culture*. Boston: Unwin Hyman.
—— (1993) *Power Plays. Power Works*. New York and London: Verso.
Fitting, Peter (1991) "The Lessons of Cyberpunk," in Constance Penley and Andrew Ross, eds. *Technoculture*. Minneapolis: University of Minnesota Press.
Foster, Hal, ed. (1983) *The Anti-Aesthetic*. Seattle: Bay Press.
Foucault, Michel (1970) *The Order of Things*. New York: Pantheon.
—— (1977) *Language, Counter-Memory, Practice*. Ithaca, New York: Cornell University Press.
—— (1979) *Discipline and Punish*. New York: Vintage Books.
Frank, Lisa and Paul Smith (1993) *Madonnarama*. Pittsburgh: Cleis Press.
Fraser, Nancy (1989) *Unruly Practices*. Minneapolis: University of Minnesota Press.
Freire, Paolo (1972) *The Pedagogy of the Oppressed*. New York: Herder & Herder.
French, Marilyn (1992) *The War Against Women*. New York: Ballantine Books.
Friedman, Alan (1993) *Spider's Web*. New York: Bantam Books.
Frisby, David (1985) *Fragments of Modernity*. Cambridge: Polity Press.
Frith, Simon, Andrew Goodwin, and Lawrence Grossberg (1993) *Sound and Vision: The Music Video Reader*. London and New York: Routledge.
Fromm, Erich (1941) *Escape From Freedom*. New York: Holt, Rinehart and Winston.
Gane, Mike (1991a) *Baudrillard: Critical and Fatal Theory*. London: Routledge.
—— (1991b) *Baudrillard's Bestiary*. London: Routledge.
George, Nelson (1988) *The Death of Rhythm and Blues*. New York: Pantheon.
Gerbner, George (1992) "Persian Gulf War: The Movie," in Mowlana *et al.* eds. *Triumph of the Image*. Boulder, Colorado: Westview.
Gerbner, George and Larry Gross (1976) "Living with Television: The Violence Profile," *Journal of Communication* (Spring): 173–99.
Gibson, J. William (1986) *The Perfect War. Technowar in Vietnam*. Boston and New York: The Atlantic Monthly Press.
Gibson, William (1984) *Neuromancer*. New York: Dell Books.
—— (1986) *Burning Chrome*. New York: Arbor Books.
—— (1991) Computer text version of Gibson's Cyberpunk trilogy.
Gibson, William and Bruce Sterling (1991) *The Difference Engine*. New York: Bantam.
Gilroy, Paul (1991) *"There Ain't No Black in the Union Jack"*. Chicago: University of Chicago Press.
Giroux, Henry (1992) *Border Crossing*. New York: Routledge.
—— (1993) "The Era of Insurgent Multiculturalism in the Era of the Los Angeles Uprising," *The Journal of the Midwest Modern Language Association*, Vol. 26, No. 1 (Spring): 12–30.
—— (1994) *Disturbing Pleasures*. New York: Routledge.
Gitlin, Todd (1978) "Media Sociology: The Dominant Paradigm," *Theory and Society*, Vol. 6: 205–53.
—— (1987) ed. *Watching Television*. New York: Pantheon.
Goldman, Robert (1992) *Reading Ads Socially*. London and New York: Routledge.
Goldman, Robert and Stephen Papson (forthcoming) *Sign Wars*. New York: Guilford Press.
Gorz, Andre (1982) *Farewell to the Working Class*. Boston: South End Press.

—— (1985) *Paths to Paradise*. Boston: South End Press.

Gouldner, Alvin W. (1976) *The Dialectic of Ideology and Technology*. New York: Seabury.

Gramsci, Antonio (1971) *Selections from the Prison Notebooks* New York: International Publishers.

—— (1992) *Prison Notebooks. Volume 1*. New York: Columbia University Press.

Grossberg, Lawrence (1982) "Ideology of Communication: Post-Structuralism and the Limits of Communication," *Man and World*, 15: 83–101.

—— (1987), "The In-Difference of Television," *Journal of Communication Inquiry*, Vol. 10, No. 2: 28–46.

—— (1989) "The Formations of Cultural Studies: An American in Birmingham," *Strategies*, 22: 114–49.

—— (1992) *We Gotta Get Out of this Place*. New York and London: Routledge.

Grossberg, Lawrence, Cary Nelson and Paula Treichler (1992) *Cultural Studies*. New York: Routledge.

Guerrero, Ed (1993a) "Spike Lee and the Fever in the Racial Jungle," in Collins *et al. Film Theory Goes to the Movies*. New York and London: Routledge.

—— (1993b) *Framing Blackness: The African American Image in Film*. Philadelphia: Temple University Press.

Habermas, Jurgen (1975) *Legitimation Crisis*. Boston: Beacon Press.

—— (1987) *The Philosophical Discourse of Modernity*. Cambridge, Ma.: MIT Press.

Hafner, Katie and John Markoff (1991) *Cyberpunk: Outlaws and Hackers on the Computer Frontier*. New York: Simon and Schuster.

Haley, Alex and Malcolm X (1965) *The Autobiography of Malcolm X*. Baltimore and London: Penguin.

Hall, Stuart (1980a) "Cultural Studies and the Centre: Some Problematics and Problems," in Hall *et al. Culture, Media, Language*. London: Hutchinson.

—— (1980b) "Encoding/Decoding," in Hall *et al. Culture, Media, Language*. London: Hutchinson.

—— (1981) "Notes on Deconstructing 'the Popular'," in R. Samuel, ed., *People's History and Socialist Theory*. London: Routledge.

—— (1986a) "The Problem of Ideology – Marxism without Guarantees," *Journal of Communication Inquiry*, Vol. 10, No. 2 (summer): 28–44.

—— (1986b) "On postmodernism and articulation: An interview," *Journal of Communication Inquiry*, Vol. 10, No. 2: 45–60.

—— (1990) *The Road to Renewal*. London: Verso.

—— (1992) "What is this 'Black' in Black Popular Culture?" in Gina Dent, ed. *Black Popular Culture*. Seattle: Bay Press.

Hall, Stuart and Martin Jacques, eds. (1983) *The Politics of Thatcherism*. London: Lawrence & Wishart.

Hall, Stuart and Paddy Whannel (1964) *The Popular Arts*. London: Hutchinson.

Hall, Stuart, *et al.* (1980) *Culture, Media, Language*. London: Hutchinson.

Harms, John and Douglas Kellner (1991) "Towards a Critical Theory of Advertising," *Critical Perspectives in Social Theory*, 11: 41–67.

Hartmann, Heidi (1981) "The Unhappy Marriage of Marxism and Feminism," in Lydia Sargent, *Women and Revolution*. Boston: South End Press.

Harvey, David (1989) *The Condition of Postmodernity*. Oxford: Blackwell.

Hebdige, Dick (1979) *Subculture*. London: Methuen.

—— (1988) *Hiding in the Light*. London and New York: Routledge.

Herman, Edward and Noam Chomsky (1988) *Manufacturing Consent*. New York: Pantheon.

Hoffman, Abie (1987) *Steal This Urine Test*. New York: Viking/Penguin.

Hoggart, Richard (1958) *The Uses of Literacy*. New York: Oxford University Press.

hooks, bell (1984) *Feminist Theory: From Margin to Center*. Boston: South End Press.

—— (1990) *Yearning: Race, Gender, and Cultural Politics*. Boston: South End Press.

—— (1992) *Black Looks: Race and Representation*. Toronto: Between the Lines.

—— (1993) "Malcolm X: Consumed by Images," *Z Magazine*, (March): 36–9.

Horkheimer, Max and T.W. Adorno (1972) *Dialectic of Enlightenment*. New York: Seabury.

Howard, Dick and Karl E. Klare (1972) *The Unknown Dimension*. New York: Basic Books.

Hunter, James Davison (1991) *Culture Wars*. New York: Basic Books.

Hutcheon, Linda (1989) *The Politics of Postmodernism*. New York: Routledge.

Jameson, Fredric (1979) "Reification and Utopia in Mass Culture," *Social Text*, 1 (Winter): 130–48.

—— (1981) *The Political Unconscious*. Ithaca: Cornell University Press.

—— (1983) "Postmodernism and the Consumer Society," in Hal Foster, ed. *The Anti-Aesthetic*. Seattle: Bay Press.

—— (1984) "Postmodernism, or the Cultural Logic of Late Capitalism," *New Left Review*, 146: 53–93.

—— (1990) *Signatures of the Visible*. New York and London: Routledge.

—— (1991) *Postmodernism, or the Cultural Logic of Late Capitalism*. Durham: Duke University Press.

—— (1993) "On 'Cultural Studies'." *Social Text*, 34: 17–52.

Jeffords, Susan (1989) *The Remasculinization of America*. Bloomington: Indiana University Press.

—— (1994) *Hard Bodies*. New Brunswick, N.Y.: Rutgers University Press.

Jeffords, Susan and Lauren Rabinovitz (1994) *Seeing Through the Media: The Persian Gulf War*. New Brunswick, New Jersey: Rutgers University Press.

Jewett, Robert and John Lawrence (1988) *The American Monomyth*. Lanham, MD: University Press of America; second edition.

Johnson, Richard (1985/6) "What is Cultural Studies Anyway?" *Social Text*, 16: 38–80.

Johnson, Sam and Chris Marcil (1993) *Beavis and Butt-Head. This Book Sucks*. New York: Pocket Books.

Kaplan, Ann (1987) *Rocking Around the Clock: Music Television, Postmodernism, and Consumer Culture*. London and New York: Methuen.

Katz, Elihu and Paul F. Lazarsfeld (1955) *Personal Influence*. New York: The Free Press.

Kellner, Douglas (1973) *Heidegger's Concept of Authenticity*. Columbia University, University Reprint Service.

—— (1978) "Ideology, Marxism, and Advanced Capitalism," *Socialist Review*, 42 (Nov–Dec): 37–65.

—— (1979) "TV, Ideology, and Emancipatory Popular Culture," *Socialist Review*, 45 (May–June): 13–53.

—— (1980) "Television Images, Codes, and Messages", *Televisions*, Vol. 7, No. 4: 2–19.

—— (1981) "Brecht's Marxist Aesthetic: The Korsch Connection," in Betty Weber and Herbert Heinin, eds. *Bertolt Brecht: Political Theory and Literary Practice*. Athens, Ga.: University of Georgia Press.

—— (1982) "Television Myth and Ritual," *Praxis*, 6: 133–55.

—— (1984) *Herbert Marcuse and the Crisis of Marxism*. London and Berkeley: Macmillan and University of California Press.

—— (1985) "Public Access Television: Alternative Views," *Radical Science Journal*, 16 *Making Waves:* 79–92.

—— (1987) "Baudrillard, Semiurgy and Death," *Theory, Culture & Society* Vol. 4, No. 1: 125–46.

—— (1988) "Postmodernism as Social Theory: Some Challenges and Problems," *Theory, Culture & Society*, Vol. 5, Nos. 2–3: 239–70.

—— (1989a) *Critical Theory, Marxism, and Modernity*. Cambridge and Baltimore: Polity and Johns Hopkins University Press.

—— (1989b) *From Marxism to Postmodernism and Beyond: Critical Studies of Jean Baudrillard*. Cambridge and Palo Alto: Polity Press and Stanford University Press.

—— ed. (1989c) *Jameson/Postmodernism/Critique*. Washington, D.C.: Maisonneuve.

—— (1989d) "Reading Images Critically: Toward a Postmodern Pedagogy," *Journal of Education*, Vol. 170, No. 3: 31–52.

—— (1990a), *Television and the Crisis of Democracy*. Boulder, Colorado: Westview.

—— (1990b), "Fashion, Advertising, and the Consumer Society," in *Questioning the Media*. Beverley Hills and London: Sage.

—— (1991) "Reading Film Politically: Reflections on Hollywood Film in the Age of Reagan," *The Velvet Light Trap* No. 27 (Spring): 9–24.

—— (1992a) "Toward a Multiperspectival Cultural Studies," *Centennial Review*, Vol. 26, No. 1: 5–41.

—— (1992b) *The Persian Gulf TV War*. Boulder, Colorado: Westview.

—— ed. (1994a), *A Baudrillard Reader*. Oxford: Blackwell.

—— (1994b) "Ideology, Culture and Utopia in Ernst Bloch," in Tom Moylan and Jamie Owen Daniel, eds. *Ernst Bloch Revisited*. London: Verso.

—— (forthcoming) "Overcoming the Divide, " *Communication Theory*, Vol. 5, No. 1 (1995).

Kellner, Douglas and Michael Ryan (1988) *Camera Politica: The Politics and Ideology of Contemporary Hollywood Film*. Bloomington, Ind.: Indiana University Press.

King, Stephen (1981) *Danse Macabre*. New York: Everett.

Kolb, David (1986) *The Critique of Pure Modernity*. Chicago: University of Chicago Press.

Kolko, Gabriel (1991) "Obsessed with Military 'Credibility'," *Progressive*, (March): 24–6.

Kroker, Arthur, and Cook, David (1986) *The Postmodern Scene*. New York: Saint Martin's Press.

LaMay, Craig, *et al.* (1991) *The Media at War*. New York: Gannett Foundation Media Center.

Lash, Scott (1988) "Discourse or Figure? Postmodernism as a 'Regime of Signification'," *Theory, Culture & Society*, Vol. 5, Nos. 2–3 (June): 311–36.

Lash, Scott and Jonathan Friedman (1992) *Postmodernism and Identity*. London: Blackwell.

Lash, Scott and John Urry (1987) *The End of Organized Capitalism*. Cambridge: Polity Press.

Lazarsfeld, Paul (1941) "Remarks on Administrative and Critical Communications Research," *Studies in Philosophy and Social Science*, 9: 2–16.

Leary, Timothy (1990) "Quark of the Decade," *Mondo 2000*, 7: 53–6.

Lee, Spike (with Lisa Jones) (1988) *Uplift the Race: The Construction of School Daze*. New York: Simon & Schuster.

—— (1989) *Do the Right Thing*. New York: Simon & Schuster.

Lee, Spike (with Ralph Wiley) (1992) *By Any Means Necessary: The Trials and Tribulations of the Making of Malcolm X*. New York: Hyperion.

Lepenies, Wolf (1988) *Between Literature and Science: The Rise of Sociology*. Cambridge: Cambridge University Press.

Lewis, Lisa (1993) "Emergence of Female Address on MTV," in Frith *et al. The Music Video Reader*. London and New York: Routledge.

Lohmann, Georg (1980) "Gesellschaftskritik und normativer Massstab," in A. Honneth and U. Jaeggi, eds. *Arbeit, Handlung, Normatativitat*. Frankfurt: Suhrkamp.

Lorde, Audre (1984) *Sister Outsider*. California: The Crossing Press.

Lyotard, Jean-François (1984) *The Postmodern Condition*. Minneapolis: University of Minnesota Press.

McAllister, Matthew P. (1993) "'What Did you Advertise with the War, Daddy?': Using the Persian Gulf War as a Referent in Advertising," in Robert E. Denton *The Media and the Persian Gulf War*. Westport, Connecticut: Praeger.

McCaffery, Larry, ed. (1991) *Storming the Reality Studio*. Durham: Duke University Press.

Macdonald, Dwight (1944) "A Theory of Popular Culture," *Politics*, Vol. 1, No. 1: 23–6.
—— (1957) "A Theory of Mass Culture," in Rosenberg and White, eds. *Mass Culture*. Glencoe, Ill.: The Free Press.
—— (1962) *Against the American Grain*. New York: Random House.
McGuigan, Jim (1992) *Cultural Populism*. London: Routledge.
McHale, Brian (1991) "POSTcyberMODERNpunkISM," in Larry McCaffery, *Storming the Reality Studio*. Durham: Duke University Press.
—— (1992) "Elements of a Poetics of Cyberpunk," *Critique*, Vol. 33, No. 3 (Spring): 149–76.
Macherey, Pierre (1978) *A Theory of Literary Production*. London: Routledge & Kegan Paul.
McLaren, Peter (1993) "White Terror and Oppositional Agency," *Strategies* 7: 1–37.
McLaren, Peter, Rhonda Hammer, David Sholle and Susan Reilly (forthcoming) *Popular Culture and Self-Production*. New York: Peter Lang.
McQuaig, Linda (1993) *The Wealthy Banker's Wife*. London and Toronto: Penguin.
Marable, Manning (1982) *How Capitalism Underdeveloped Black America*. Boston: South End Press.
Marcus, Greil (1989) *Lipstick Traces*. Cambridge, Mass.: Harvard University Press.
Marcuse, Herbert (1964) *One-Dimensional Man*. Boston: Beacon Press.
—— (1955) *Eros and Civilization*. Boston: Beacon Press.
—— (1968) *Negations*. Boston: Beacon Press.
Marx, Karl (1906) *Capital*. New York: The Modern Library.
—— (1973) *Grundrisse*. London: Penguin Books.
Marx, Karl and Friedrich Engels (1975) *Collected Works*. New York: International Publishers.
—— (1978) *The Marx–Engels Reader*, ed. Robert C. Tucker. New York: Norton; second edition.
Mead, David (1991) "Technological Transfiguration in William Gibson's Sprawl Novels," *Extrapolation*, Vol. 32, No. 4: 350–60.
Mitchell, Juliet (1974) *Psychoanalysis and Feminism*. New York: Pantheon.
Morton, Melanie (1992) "Don't Go for Second Sex Baby!," in Cathy Schwichtenberg *The Madonna Connection*. Boulder, Colorado: Westview.
Mowlana, Hamid, George Gerbner, and Herbert Schiller (1992) *Triumph of the Image*. Boulder, Colorado: Westview.
Nicholson, Linda (1985) *Gender and History*. New York: Columbia University Press.
Nietzsche, Friedrich (1968) *The Will to Power*. New York: Random House.
—— (1969) *The Genealogy of Morals*. New York: Random House.
Nimmo, Dan and Mark Hovind (1993) "Vox Populi: Talk Radio and TV Cover the Gulf War," in Robert E. Denton *The Media and the Persian Gulf War*. Westport, Connecticut: Praeger.
O'Connor, Alan (1989) "The Problem of American Cultural Studies," *Critical Studies in Mass Communication* (December): 405–13.
Offe, Claus (1985) *Disorganized Capitalism*. Cambridge: Polity.
Ollman, Bertell and Edward Vernoff, eds. (1982) *The Left Academy*. New York: McGraw Hill.
Patterson, Alex (1992) *Spike Lee: A Biography*. London: Abacus.
Pecheux, Michel (1982) *Language, Semantics, and Ideology*. New York: Saint Martin.
Poster, Mark (1991) *Mode of Information*. Cambridge: Polity Press.
Postman, Neil (1985) *Amusing Ourselves to Death*. New York: Viking-Penguin.
—— (1992) *Technopolis: The Surrender of Culture to Technology*. New York: Random House.
Pribram, E. Deidre (1992) "Seduction, Control, and the Search for Authenticity: Madonna's

Truth or Dare," in Cathy Schwichtenberg, ed. *The Madonna Connection*. Boulder, Colorado: Westview.

Prince, Stephen (1993) "Celluloid Heroes and Smart Bombs: Hollywood at War in the Middle East," in Robert E. Denton, ed. *The Media and the Persian Gulf War*.

Radaway, Janice A. (1984) *Reading the Romance*. Chapel Hill: University of North Carolina Press.

Reed, Adolph (1993) "The Trouble with X," *The Progressive* (February): 18–19.

Reid, Mark A. (1993) *Redefining Black Film*. Berkeley: University of California Press.

—— (forthcoming (a)) "The Brand X and PostNegritude Frontiers."

—— (forthcoming (b)) "African-American Cultural Studies: Towards a Politics of the PostNegritude."

Ricoeur, Paul (1970) *Freud and Philosophy*. New Haven: Yale University Press.

—— (1984) *Time and Narrative*. Chicago: University of Chicago Press.

Riesman, David, *et al*. (1950) *The Lonely Crowd*. Garden City, N.Y.: Anchor Books.

Rifas, Leonard (1994) "Supermarket Tabloids and Persian Gulf War Dissent," in Susan Jeffords and Lauren Rabinowitz *Seeing Through the Media: The Persian Gulf War*. New Brunswick, New Jersey: Rutgers University Press.

Ritzer, George, ed. (1990) *Frontiers of Social Theory*. New York: Columbia University Press.

Robinson, Lillian (1978) *Sex, Class, and Culture*. Bloomington: Indiana University Press.

Rosenberg, Bernard and David White, eds. (1957) *Mass Culture*. Glencoe, Ill.: The Free Press.

Rosenthal, Michael (1992) "What was Postmodernism?" *Socialist Review*, Vol. 92, No. 3: 83–106.

Ross, Andrew (1988) *Universal Abandon?*. Minneapolis: University of Minnesota Press.

Rowbotham, Shelia (1972) *Women, Resistance, and Revolution*. New York: Vintage.

Ryan, Michael (1982) *Marxism and Deconstruction*. Baltimore: Johns Hopkins University Press.

—— (1989) *Culture and Politics*. London: Macmillan and Johns Hopkins University Press.

Said, Edward (1978) *Orientalism*. New York: Random House.

Salinger, Pierre, and Eric Laurent (1991). *Secret Dossier: The Hidden Agenda Behind the Gulf War*. New York: Penguin Books.

Sargent, Lydia (1981) *Women and Revolution*. Boston: South End Press.

Savan, Leslie (1993) "Commercials Go Rock," in Simon Frith *et al*., eds. *Sound and Vision: The Music Video Reader*. London and New York: Routledge.

Sayre, Henry M. (1989) *The Object of Performance*. Chicago: University of Chicago Press.

Scatamburlo, Valerie (1994) "Critical Pedagogy, Multiculturalism, and Political Correctness," Masters Dissertation, Department of Communication, Windsor University, Canada.

Schiller, Herbert (1989) *Culture, Inc*. New York: Oxford.

Schorr, Juliet (1992) *The Overworked American*. New York: Basic Books.

Schudson, Michael (1984) *Advertising: the Uneasy Persuasion*. New York: Basic Books.

Schwichtenberg, Cathy, ed. (1992) *The Madonna Connection*. Boulder, Colorado: Westview.

Segal, Lynne (1991) "Feminism and the Future," *New Left Review* 185: 81–91.

Sexton, Adam (1993) *Desperately Seeking Madonna*. New York. Delta Books.

Shaheen, Jack (1984) *The TV Arab*. Bowling Green, Ohio: The Popular Press.

Shaw, Martin and Roy Carr-Hill, (1991) "Mass Media and Attitudes to the Gulf War in Britain," *The Electronic Journal of Communication*, Vol. 2, No 2 (Fall). (pp?)

Shiner, Lewis (1991) "Confessions of an Ex-Cyberpunk," *New York Times*, January 7: A19.

Sholle, David and Stan Denski (1994) *Media Education and the (Re)Production of Culture* Westport, Conn.: Bergin & Garvey.

Showalter, Elaine (1985) *The New Feminist Criticism*. New York: Pantheon.

Shusterman, Richard (1992) *Pragmatist Aesthetics, Living Beauty, Rethinking Art.* Cambridge, Mass.: Blackwell.

Simons, H.W. ed. (1990) *The Rhetorical Turn: Invention and Persuasion in the Conduct of Inquiry.* Chicago: University of Chicago Press.

Solop, F.I. and N.A. Wonders (1991) "Reaction to the Persian Gulf Crisis: Gender, Race, and Generational Differences," paper presented at American Association of Public Opinion Research.

Sontag, Susan (1969) *Against Interpretation.* New York: Dell.

Spivak, Gayatri (1988) *In Other Worlds.* New York and London: Methuen.

Sterling, Bruce ed. (1986) *Mirrorshades.* New York: Ace.

—— (1992) *The Hacker Crackdown.* New York: Bantam Books.

Theweleit, Klaus (1987) *Male Fantasies.* Minneapolis: University of Minnesota Press.

Thompson, E.P. (1963) *The Making of the English Working Class.* New York: Vintage.

Thompson, John (1984) *Studies in the Theory of Ideology.* Cambridge: Polity Press.

—— (1990) *Ideology and Modern Culture.* Cambridge and Stanford, Cal.: Polity Press and Stanford University Press.

Toop, David (1984) *The Rap Attack: African Jive to New York Hip-Hop.* Boston: South End Press.

Turner, Graeme (1990) *British Cultural Studies: An Introduction.* New York: Unwin Hyman.

Venturi, Robert (1972) *Learning from Las Vegas.* Cambridge, Mass.: MIT Press.

Wallace, Michelle (1992) "*Boyz 'N' the Hood* and *Jungle Fever*," in Gina Dent, ed. *Black Popular Culture.* Seattle: Bay Press.

Warner, William (1992) "Spectator Aesthetics," in Grossberg *et al. Cultural Studies.* New York: Routledge.

Warshow, Robert (1962). *The Immediate Experience.* New York: Garden City.

Waxman, Chaim (1968) *The End of Ideology Debate.* New York: Simon & Schuster.

West, Cornell (1992a) "A Matter of Life and Death," *October* 61 (Summer): 20–7.

—— (1992b) "Nihilism in Black America," in Gina Dent, ed., *Black Popular Culture.* Seattle: Bay Press: 37–47.

Wexler, Philip (1992) *Becoming Somebody.* London and Washington, D.C.: The Falmer Press.

Williams, Raymond (1958) *Culture and Society.* New York: Harper and Row.

—— (1962) *The Long Revolution.* London: Penguin.

—— (1976) *Keywords: A Vocabulary of Culture and Society.* London: Fontana.

—— (1977) *Marxism and Literature.* New York: Oxford University Press.

—— (1981) *Culture.* London: Fontana.

Williamson, Judith (1978) *Decoding Advertisements.* London: Marion Boyers.

Willis, Ellen (1984) "Radical Feminism," in Sohnya Sayres, ed. *The Sixties Without Apology.* Minneapolis: University of Minnesota Press.

Wilson, Elizabeth (1985) *Adorned in Dreams: Fashion and Modernity.* London: Virago.

Winter, James (1992) *Common Cents.* Montreal/New York: Black Rose Books.

Wolin, Richard (1984) "Modernism versus Postmodernism," *Telos* 62: 9–30.

Wood, Robin (1986) *Hollywood from Vietnam to Reagan.* New York: Columbia University Press.

Woodward, Bob (1991) *The Commanders.* New York: Simon & Schuster.

Wuthnow, Robert (1989) *Communities of Discourse.* Cambridge, Mass.: Harvard University Press.

X, Malcolm (1992) *The Final Speeches.* New York: Pathfinder Press.

Zavarzadeh, Mas'ud (1991) *Seeing Films Politically.* State University of New York Press.

Index